HONG KONG

&

MACAU GUIDE

YOUR PASSPORT TO GREAT TRAVEL!

CRITICAL ACCLAIM FOR
RUTH LOR MALLOY'S <u>CHINA GUIDE</u>!
– Now in its 8th Edition for 1994-1995 –

"The most comprehensive and practical of the many recent books I've seen. An up-to-date, informative, guide to China travel."
Loren Fessler, author of *China* and *Chinese in America*

"This hefty book is packed with facts, maps, and terrific tips on everything from accidents to earthquakes, toilets to tipping. (A) first-rate history of the awakening giant, Malloy answers most questions a novice traveler might have."
Paul King, *The Toronto Star*

"This guide may be the best once-over-lightly look at China ... it not only covers destinations, restaurants, hotels and shopping, but also gives you a passing acquaintance with useful aspects of Chinese culture."
Keith Graham, *The Atlanta Journal/The Atlanta Constitution*

"For my money, this is the best book on the market. Malloy has put together a comprehensive book which calls it like it is, but at the same time explains why it is like it is! You won't be able to put this book down, so loaded is it with ancedotes, tips, and down-to-earth common sense. If it sounds like I'm raving, it's because this book definitely deserves it!"
Lorraine Williams, *The Budget Traveler*

ABOUT THE AUTHORS

Ruth Lor Malloy is a Canadian of Chinese ancestry. She is a veteran travel writer, freelance photographer, wife, and author of guidebooks to China for more than 20 years, including the long-selling China Guide, now in its 8th edition published by Open Road Publishing. She is co-author of *On Leaving Bai Di Cheng*; *The Culture of the Yangtze Gorges*; *Post Guide Hong Kong*; and *Hong Kong Gems and Jewelry*. Ruth is currently editor o f the *Travel China Newsletter* and a collector for museums. She travels frequently to China and Hong Kong and currently lives in Kazakhstan and Toronto, Canada.

Linda Malloy, Ruth's daughter, is a gardener for the City of Toronto in the summers and travels the world in the winters. She started in the publishing business at age 16, working for the Associated Press in Hong Kong. When she's not gardening or traveling, Linda is a freelance writer.

HIT THE OPEN ROAD WITH OPEN ROAD PUBLISHING!

Open Road Publishing now has guide books to exciting, fun destinations on four continents, but, oddly enough, some people out there still don't know who we are! We're old college pals and veteran travelers who decided to join forces to bring you the best travel guides available anywhere!

No small task, but here's what we offer:

• All Open Road publications are written by authors, authors with a distinct, opinionated point of view – not some sterile committee or team of writers. Our authors are experts in the areas covered and are polished writers.

• Our guides are geared to people who want great vacations, great value, and great tips for both standard tourist sites *and* fun, unique alternatives.

• We're strong on the basics, but we also provide terrific choices for those looking to get off the beaten path and *experience* the country or city – not just *see* it or pass through it.

• We give you the best, but we also tell you about the worst and what to avoid. Nobody should waste their time and money on their hard-earned vacation because of bad or inadequate travel advice.

• Our guides assume nothing. We tell you everything you need to know to have the trip of a lifetime – presented in a fun, literate, no-nonsense style.

• And, above all, we welcome your input, ideas, suggestions to help us put out the best travel guides possible.

HONG KONG

&

MACAU GUIDE

YOUR PASSPORT TO GREAT TRAVEL!

RUTH LOR MALLOY & LINDA MALLOY

OPEN ROAD PUBLISHING

Front and back cover photos courtesy of Hong Kong Tourist Association (HKTA), New York. Inside photos courtesy of Hong Kong Economic & Trade Office, Washington, DC; and Macau Tourist Information Bureau, Los Angeles. Maps by Sally Geier. Hong Kong maps based on maps provided by HKTA.

TABLE OF CONTENTS

MAPS & SIDEBARS

MAPS

SIDEBARS

ACKNOWLEDGMENTS

Many people are responsible for this book: travelers who took the time to share their experiences and impressions with us, and hotel officials who talked not just of business but of the problems and joys of living and working in Hong Kong and Macau. There were also the innumerable residents, business travelers in airport waiting rooms and tourists in hotel elevators.

We are especially grateful to David Barrett, Susan and Keith Bentz, Constance Ching, S.J.Chan, Nida Cranbourne, Gerald Chen, Julie S. Fernandes, Loren Fessler, Joyce Fu, Dana Goetz, Alison Hardie, Barbara Heeney, Steven Jones and Mary Bruns, Amy Liu Mei Heung, Allison and Saul Lockhart, Sheila Purves, Mark Roberti, John Thompson, Yvonne Wain, Mary Willes, Nelson Young and Hannah, Ronen and Iris Zion.

We would not have been able to research this book without the help of Bob White and the late Tim Baxter of Baxter Communications (Canada), Canadian Airlines International Ltd., China Travel Service (Canada), China National Tourism Administration (Beijing), Kim Chui and Associates, Goway Travel (Toronto), Hong Kong Convention and Exhibition Centre, Hong Kong Tourist Association (Suzanna P.L.Leung, Ian R. Cook, Karisa Yuen-Ha Lui, Stanley Chan, and Stephen Wong), Link Asia Tours (Toronto), Morningside Tours (HK) and Trinity Travel (Toronto).

We wish to thank the following Hong Kong hotels and their knowledgeable staffs for their help: Holiday Inn Crowne Plaza, Holiday Inn Golden Mile, Hong Kong Renaissance, Furama Kempinski, Island Shangri-La, Mandarin Oriental Hong Kong, New World, New World Harbour View, Newton Hong Kong, Nikko, Omni Hong Kong, Regal Airport, Regal Hong Kong, The Excelsior, The Park Lane, The Peninsula, The Ritz-Carlton, Island Shangri-La, Sheraton Hong Kong and Victoria.

For Macau, we were assisted by the Macau Government Tourist Office (Paula Paz and Manuel Pires Jr.), the Macau Tourist Information Bureau (Karen Fawcett and Brian Cuthbertson), Hyatt Regency, Holiday Inn Macau, Hotel Lisboa, Mandarin Oriental Macao, the Pousada Ritz and Juan Michael Swing of the Lisboa Casino. In Shenzhen, we have to thank the Shangri-La Shenzhen Hotel, Shenzhen Tourist Association and Shenzhen Tourism Bureau. In Guangzhou, we were helped by the Holiday Inn City Centre, Michael Sun of the Guangzhou Tourist Corporation, Gitic Riverside Hotel, Guangzhou Tourism Bureau and Guangdong Provincial Tourism Bureau.

Our gratitude also goes to our editors and publishers, Jonathan Stein and Avery Cardoza, to Tom Gunderson for his support and company, to Stewart, Pat and Jim for their patience, and especially to Michael Malloy, husband and father, who was home alone while the authors had a glorious time working in Hong Kong. Andrew, Judy and Michael Wark deserve a special mention. Not only did they share their vast knowledge of the area with us but they were always there to help. To them we dedicate this book, in honor of their generosity and love.

1. INTRODUCTION

Hong Kong is one of the most exciting and exotic cities in the world. It is an ultramodern, fast-paced place of the future blended with the traditional, Chinese culture of the past. As soon as you land you feel the excitement. Everywhere in this futuristic land of monolithic skyscrapers and neon lights, people are making lots of money. In this book, we will also show you the small temples, large country parks, bustling markets and quiet monasteries, as well as the world's fourth and fifth tallest buildings.

Hong Kong has some of the world's best hotels, an incredible variety of food and there's so much to do! Come with us shopping to clothing markets, factory outlets and air-conditioned malls with hundreds of stores. We'll show you a reproduction of an exquisite ancient Chinese village and the fishing boat homes of Aberdeen. We'll guide you to intriguing old temples, lovely Victorian buildings from Hong Kong's 150-year British history and to beautiful outlying islands and mountains. We'll direct you to the giant tropical fish tank and penguins of Ocean Park.

We'll tell you where to take the best photo of the harbor and how to get to the world's largest bronze Buddha. We'll show you the best places to eat, drink, dance, shop and walk in Hong Kong, day or night. We offer plenty of choices so you can find the attractions that interest you most. Then we'll guide you to nearby Macau with its touches of old Europe and ancient China.

Hong Kong is also the easiest place in the world to experience Chinese culture. Hong Kong is small and a snap to get around. Most menus and signs are in English, which is spoken by many local Chinese and its streets are safer than North America's. We'll introduce you to the mysteries of *fung shui, tai chi chuan,* and Chinese opera.

Hong Kong is a fascinating mix of British and Chinese and yet it is neither. In mid-1997, however, after its British administrators leave and the Chinese take it back, there are bound to be changes. As interesting as those changes will be, the time to see Hong Kong in all its unfettered glory is *now*!

REGIONAL MAP

2. OVERVIEW - EXCITING HONG KONG & MACAU!

We lived in Hong Kong for four years and never tired of it. It has a lot to offer and doesn't have to be expensive. Over half of Hong Kong's attractions are free. We will even tell you about our favorite places that most tourists don't know about. We'll steer you to where you can make friends and show you how to avoid the crowds and traffic jams. When is the best time to visit? Do you want to stay longer? Get a job? Most visitors stay less than a week, but for us, four years was not long enough.

Hong Kong is skyscrapers, crowded streets, great shopping, delicious food, Chinese culture, beautiful parks, terrific temples and a thriving economy. It is also 1997, the year it returns to China and a whole lot more. Let us introduce you to the Hong Kong we know. Check-off what you want to do and figure out the number of days it will take.

HONG KONG ISLAND

The historical and commercial heart of Hong Kong is called **Central**. This is where you'll find the contrasts of today and yesterday, the oldest British buildings from the 1800s alongside tall, modern architectural wonders. Explore **Hong Kong Park**, the lush **Botanical and Zoological Gardens**, the popular **Li Yuen alley markets** and the world's longest system of covered escalators. Central is also the home of **Lan Kwai Fong**, the most popular eating and drinking neighborhood that's packed almost 24 hours a day. From Central, you can take the famous tram to the Peak, for the most beautiful city view in the world.

Western is west of Central and is a traditional Chinese area, full of tiny antique shops and the island's most famous temple, **Man-Mo**, dedicated to the God of War and the God of Literature – both under the same roof.

Wanchai is east of Central. Here you can take a trip up sixty floors in an outdoor glass elevator. There's also the **Hong Kong Arts Centre** and the **Hong Kong Convention and Exhibition Centre**. Wanchai has been the Suzie Wong red light district since World War II and you can still find traditional British pubs, girlie bars and tattoo parlors here.

Next is **Causeway Bay** and the weird and colorful **Tiger Balm Gardens** with its gaudily-painted statues. There are also two temples, street markets and Japanese department stores. In **Victoria Park**, people still practice *tai chi chuan*, race model boats, go lawn bowling and walk their birds. Nearby is the **Happy Valley race track**, a spectacular setting for galloping horses especially at night.

In **Aberdeen**, cruise through the harbor, where families live on boats with dogs and potted plants. Thousands of lights and gold dragons decorate the famous floating restaurants. You can also go to **Ocean Park** and visit its shark tunnel, free-flying butterfly house and more. Take the cable car to watch a show in its spectacular theater. The backdrop is the sea and misty islands. Explore the **Middle Kingdom**, which recreates an ancient Chinese village, or cool off in the wave pool at **Water World**.

The **south side** of the island is completely different; green, tropical and sparsely inhabited. Take an exciting bus ride to **Repulse Bay** for the most popular beach or continue on to famous **Stanley Market** with its temples, and nearby beach with windsurfing all year round. Hike along the water catchment that follows the road. It carries rain water into the huge, fish-filled **Tai Tam reservoir** and gives you great views of the **South China Sea**.

KOWLOON

Kowloon is where you'll find **Tsim Sha Tsui** – shopping heaven. It's almost impossible not to shop here! There is a mall with 600 shops. We're convinced it has more camera shops per square mile than anywhere else in the world. But there's a lot more than shopping. Visit the **Space Museum**, the **Cultural Centre**, theaters, and the art museum.   At **Kowloon Park**, you'll find flamingos and the largest mosque in Hong Kong. The **Museum of History** has reproduced an old Hong Kong street. Kowloon is the start of Hong Kong's best ferry ride which takes only seven minutes to Central.

Nearby is **Tsim Sha Tsui East**. The least crowded downtown district has an incredible **Science Museum** with hundreds of interactive exhibits. A few minutes by MTR (subway) from Tsim Sha Tsui are **Yau Ma Tei** and **Mong Kok**, which are full of street markets. There are individual markets for birds, clothing, and jade. You can buy just about anything and see Cantonese opera at the **Temple Street Night Market**.

A little farther north is **New Kowloon** where the beautifully carved wooden shops and houses of **Sung Dynasty Village** will take you back a thousand years. Don't miss our favorite temple, **Wong Tai Sin**, where you can get tips on horseracing from fortune tellers, visit a herbal medicine clinic and explore a traditional Chinese garden.

NEW TERRITORIES

This area of Hong Kong is full of old Chinese buildings and country parks. On the MTR line in **Tsuen Wan**, see a monastery, an incredible temple and a fascinating, restored, walled village. On the KCR train line, head for **Sha Tin**, climb up to **10,000 Buddhas Monastery** and view the mummified body of its founder, covered in gold leaf. Visit the **Shatin racetrack** or the park inside it. On the LRT line, check out **Ching Choon temple** with its hundreds of Chinese bonsais and the **Ping Shan Heritage Trail**. This one-hour walk takes you to nine of Hong Kong's oldest Chinese buildings including temples, ancestral worship halls and its only surviving ancient pagoda.

THE ISLANDS

Relax on Hong Kong's islands with their tiny fishing villages, gold sand beaches, and sea goddess temples. Breathe the clean air and get some exercise. On the ferry to the islands, see the ever-changing scenes in the harbor. If you're lucky, you'll glimpse a sailing junk with crimson sails, or a luxurious ocean liner gliding through the water. Soak up the soft green magnificence that is **Lantau Island** and hike its paved paths down from Asia's largest bronze Buddha to **Tai O** fishing village. Stroll on tiny **Cheung Chau Island** and end a peaceful afternoon gorging on sweet fresh, steamed prawns in its waterside food restaurants.

HONG KONG SKYLINE

CHINESE CULTURE

Everywhere in Hong Kong, look for tiny shrines with burning incense, mirrors above doorways reflecting away evil spirits, herbal medicine shops with deer antler aphrodisiacs and red wedding dresses. Chinese culture permeates Hong Kong in less obvious ways too. *Fung shui* affects real estate prices and lucky number license plates sell for over $1 million US dollars each. Hong Kong is a great place to experience Chinese culture. It's easy to get around in English and you don't need a visa. There was no Chairman Mao interrupting culture here for thirty–plus years.

You can experience Chinese culture all over Hong Kong. Visit the many ornate temples and monasteries and have your fortune told the Chinese way. Join a *tai chi chuan* class or go to the New Territories and look for the ladies with the fluttering donut hats. Eat your way through innumerable dishes and many different kinds of Chinese cooking. Go to the museums of history, art, police and tea ware. Read books on Chinese culture. Hong Kong book stores and libraries have a lot in English. Try to time your visit to include traditional festivals. Our section on Deities, Festivals, and Temples in our "Land and People" chapter will tell you everything you need to know.

BRITISH CULTURE

One hundred and fifty years of British influence has left its mark. Hong Kong is still the home of the British armed forces and some lovely Victorian buildings. Start counting Rolls Royces, and chalk up two points if you spot the pink one or the Governor's license plate (number 1). You get four points if you see barristers wearing white, powdered wigs and long black gowns. Eat and drink at one of the many British pubs. Or take high tea in the **Peninsula's** elegant lobby.

HOTELS

Hong Kong has some of the best hotels in the world. The **Regent** with its great view of the harbor, the historic old **Peninsula** and the **Mandarin Oriental** with its antiques, are consistently included in international lists of the world's top hotels. The **Island Shangri-La** has the biggest landscape painting in the world. The modern, 1920s-inspired **Grand Hyatt**, with its black marble lobby and curving staircases has redefined the word "elegant". We'll also tell you about the many moderate hotels and budget guest houses, where you can get a room for under HK$200.

CHINESE CUISINE

You can eat almost anything anywhere in Hong Kong. People ask what kind do you feel like eating, rather than where do you want to eat.

There's about ten different kinds of Chinese cuisines. Our favorites are Cantonese *dim sum* and Mongolian barbeque. The adventurous might want to sample duck's tongues, camel's hump, *geo* (gooey) duck clams or chicken feet, Chinese style. Try Korean barbeque, Burmese, or Lebanese food. In the mood for French, Italian, or Tex Mex? It's all here!

There are a lot of unique places to eat in Hong Kong. Dine in a revolving restaurant with an everchanging view of the glittering harbor and majestic **Peak**. Take your pick of succulent, tasty *dim sum* pastries from carts wheeled to your table. Choose live seafood from fish tanks and have it cooked to your specifications.

NIGHTLIFE

Hong Kong never sleeps. You can shop until midnight in **Tsim Sha Tsui** and till 2am in the night market, where you'll also find fortune tellers and street performers. Some bars and clubs never close.

There's so much to do. Take a cocktail cruise on a junk and admire the lights, check out the breathtaking view from the **Peak** or go bar hopping in **Lan Kwai Fong**, **Wanchai** or **Tsim Sha Tsui**. Hong Kong has something for everyone: pubs and ballet, hi-tech discos and theater, topless bars and a symphony orchestra.

SHOPPING

Hong Kong is like one gigantic shopping plaza and except for perfume, alcohol, and tobacco, it's all tax free! There's an amazing number of malls, fascinating markets, alleys, factory outlets and shops.

You can get great deals on jewelry, clothes, Chinese antiques, quality silk and pretty well anything made in China. You can buy 40-carat diamonds, plastic toys, Chanel dresses, T-shirts for as little as US$1.30, and an incredible variety of photographic, stereo, and electronic equipment. Shopping is Hong Kong's favorite pastime.

MACAU

An hour by ferry, but a world away, is beautiful, little **Macau**, the oldest European settlement on the China coast. It is dotted with pastel-colored, Portuguese colonial buildings and houses that could have been transplanted from 1920s Shanghai. Macau's **casinos** have inspired many to call it the Las Vegas of the East.

Try to spend at least two days here. It's a lot cheaper than Hong Kong. Portuguese and Macanese food is fantastic. Stay or just eat in a gorgeous one-hundred-year-old hotel or a fort from the 1600s.

Macau has some wonderful temples, peaceful islands, the best classical Chinese garden, **Maritime** and **Grand Prix museums**, great restaurants (did we mention the food?!), antique stores, markets, 24-hour casinos and a lot more.

THE GATEWAY TO CHINA

It's easy to go to China from Macau and even easier from Hong Kong. You can hop over the border to **Shenzhen** for a one-day trip, to see detailed, hand-crafted miniatures of Chinese tourist attractions or meet China's ethnic minorities in their tribal costumes. You can go south to resorts in **Zhuhai**, or **Sun Yat-sen's home** in **Zhongshan**.

If you have two or three days, visit nearby **Guangzhou**, ancestral home of many overseas Chinese and the fastest developing area in the world. There's also **Guilin** with its ethereal mountains straight out of a Chinese painting, and the capital, **Beijing**. Take a boat to **Shekou**, **Guangzhou**, **Toishan**, **Hainan**, **Xiamen** or incredible **Shanghai**. Take a bus to **Shenzhen**, **Shantou**, and **Fuzhou**, or express train to **Guangzhou** and **Foshan**. There are direct flights to over 25 cities in China.

For more detailed information on China, please consult the latest edition of *China Guide* by Ruth Lor Malloy, also published by Open Road Publishing.

THE BEST OF HONG KONG!

Send us your vote!

Best Amusement Park: *Ocean Park, Aberdeen, Hong Kong Island*
Best Bus Ride: *Central to Repulse Bay, Hong Kong Island*
Best City Park: *Hong Kong Park, Central, Hong Kong Island*
Best Ferry Ride: *Star Ferry, Tsim Sha Tsui, Kowloon*
Best Garden: *Botanical Gardens, Central*
Best Hotels: *Peninsula & Regent, Tsim Sha Tsui*
Best Museum: *Hong Kong Museum of History, Tsim Sha Tsui*
Best KidsMuseum: *Science Museum, Tsim Sha Tsui East, Kowloon*
Best Pub: *Ned Kelly's Last Stand, Tsim Sha Tsui*
Best Romantic Spot: *The Peak, Central, Hong Kong Island*
Best Shopping Mall: *Pacific Place, Central, Hong Kong Island*
Best Night Market: *Temple Street, Yau Ma Tei, Kowloon*
Best Day Market: *Stanley Market, Hong Kong Island*
Best Temple: *Wong Tai Sin, New Kowloon*
Best Tram Ride: *Peak Tram, Central, Hong Kong Island*

MACAU

If you are in Hong Kong, don't miss Macau! It's only a comfortable one hour away by jetfoil and is famous for its beautiful old buildings, great food, cheaper prices, slower pace and gambling. Very few westerners go to Macau and during the week there are almost no tourists.

We urge you to go because we like it. Ruth spent her honeymoon there; Macau is for lovers. It is also for explorers, adventurers, gamblers, and those interested in history, culture, and food. It is the oldest European settlement in China, pre-dating Hong Kong by 300 years. It is developing rapidly, so go now before the old Macau disappears!

THE BEST OF MACAU!

Best Beach: *Cheoc Van, Coloane Island*
Best Casino: *Lisboa Hotel, downtown*
Best Church: *Sao Domingo, downtown*
Best Garden: *Lou Lim Ieoc, east*
Most Romantic Hotel: *Pousada de Sao Tiago, south*
Best Museum: *The Maritime Museum, south*
Best Resort: *The Westin, Coloane Island*
Best Restaurant: *Bela Vista, south*
Best Romantic Spot: *Taipa Village, Taipa Island*
Best View: *Guia Fort, east*
Best Dim Sum: *Holiday Inn*

MACAU'S HOTELS

You can stay in a Portuguese fort from the 1600s or a beautiful 100-year-old colonial hotel, overlooking the harbor. If you like sports, the **Westin Resort** is linked to Macau's only golf course. It has a swimming pool and lots of other facilities, all overlooking Macau's largest beach. The less expensive **Hyatt Hotel** has a health club, swimming pool, tennis, squash, etc. Gamblers should try the **Lisboa Hotel**, which houses Macau's largest casino and most famous cabaret show. The **Mandarin Oriental**, **Hyatt Regency**, and **Holiday Inn** also have casinos.

MACAU'S FOOD

Oh the food! Not only is it fantastic, it's also cheap! People go to Macau for the excellent Portuguese and Macanese cuisine. It is a unique type of Portuguese food with spicy Indian, Malay, African and South American influences. Of course, there's delightful Portuguese wines to go with it. You have to eat at the **Bela Vista** and/or the **Pousada de Sao Tiago**. Then there are so many other wonderful restaurants, you'll wish you could stay for a month!

MACAU'S GAMBLING

Macau is for gamblers. You can bet on the horses and then visit the casinos! They are open 24 hours a day. The biggest, the **Lisboa**, has never closed since it opened in 1972. There is also a **Chinese floating casino**.

Most gambling places have unique, traditional Chinese games that probably exist in no other casinos in the world. The stakes are among the highest and the minimum bet at one of the Lisboa's VIP rooms is HK$20,000! But, don't worry, most minimums are $20-50. Although there are official maximums, they are usually negotiable.

MACAU'S ATTRACTIONS

There is much to see and do in Macau! Downtown, you'll find the heart of Macau, **Leal Senado Square**, surrounded by a market, Macau's most beautiful church and other historic buildings. The **Lisboa** and **Floating Casinos** are nearby.

In the south, there's **Penha Church** with Macau's most pleasant view, the fabulous **Maritime Museum** across from the **A-Ma Temple** and Macau's two historic hotels.

In the western part, Macau's most famous attraction, the fascinating facade of **Sao Paulo Church** is below historic **Monte Fort**. And you can't miss the **Old Protestant Cementary** and the nearby **Camoes Museum and Gardens**, named after the famous poet.

Head east for **Guia Fortress**, Macau's highest point. There's also the **Grand Prix Museum** for racing fans, the best traditional **Chinese Garden**, **Lou Lim Ieoc** and the intriguing **Kun Iam Temple**. North of it, you will find the **Barrier Gate** with China.

The islands are another world. In **Taipa Village**, the **Taipa House Museum** is on the most beautiful street in Macau. Go to the **Chapel of St. Francis Xavier**, **Coloane Park**, the beaches, the golf course and horseback riding.

HOW TO USE THIS BOOK

Hong Kong (and this book) uses the British system of numbering floors. There's the ground floor and then the first floor. The first floor is the American second floor. The Chinese system is the same as the American, but you won't even notice, unless you can read Chinese.

The travel agencies, hotels, restaurants, and other enterprises listed here free of charge should be able to help you. As far as we can see, they are reliable, but a mention in this book is not necessarily a recommendation. They are listed to show your options.

Hong Kong changes rapidly. Prices go up, buildings are torn down, and new ones appear. If you find anything new or different, please write to us via our publisher, so we can make changes in future editions.

> *Price quotes in this book are in Hong Kong dollars. One US dollar is worth about HK$7.70at press time. They are bound to go up.*

The first part (and the bulk) of this book, Chapters 3–15, is devoted to Hong Kong. The second part, Chapters 16–25, is devoted to Macau. Chapters 26 and 27 feature reference and bibliography information for both Hong Kong and Macau.

Quick Reference: Where is everything?
We have arranged Hong Kong's districts in the following order:
Hong Kong Island – Central, Western/Sheung Wan, Wanchai, Causeway Bay, Aberdeen, Repulse Bay, Stanley.
Kowloon Peninsula – Tsim Sha Tsui, Tsim Sha Tsui East, Yau Ma Tei, Mong Kok, New Kowloon.
New Territories – *Along the MTR line*: Tsuen Wan, Sai Kung, Clearwater Bay; *Along the KCR line*: Sha Tin, Tai Po, Fanling, Sheung Shui; *Along the LRT line*: Tuen Mun, Ching Chung, Ping Shan Heritage Trail, Yuen Long.
Outlying Islands – Lantau, Lamma, Cheung Chau.

GUIDE TO ABBREVIATIONS

aka – *also known as*
ext. – *extension*
/F – *floor (i.e. 3/F - 3rd floor)*
HKTA – *Hong Kong Tourist Association*
KCR – *Kowloon-Canton Railway*
LRT – *Light Rail Transit*
MTR – *Mass Transit Railway (HK's subway).*

ENJOYING THE DAY AT ONE OF HONG KONG'S BEAUTIFUL PARKS

3. A SHORT HISTORY

BEGINNINGS

Hong Kong's modern history began in the 1800s, when the British and Chinese empires clashed over a flower called the poppy and out of a barren rock blossomed one of the most exciting cities in the world.

Hong Kong had a few visitors as early as 4000 BC who left behind neolithic pottery and tools. Rock carvings on Hong Kong, Lantau, and Cheung Chau Islands may be 3000 years old. The first group of people were boat people, the ocean-dwelling Yue, who appeared during the **Bronze Age** (1500-221 BC). Archaeologists found bronze coins from the **Qin** (Ts'in) dynasty (221-207 BC). They excavated an intact **Eastern Han Dynasty** (25-220AD) tomb which was discovered in 1955.

There was a bit of excitement in 1277, when the last emperor of the Song dynasty, a child of ten and his court fled the invading Mongols, to Kowloon. He was the only emperor ever to step foot on Hong Kong soil and he later drowned in the Pearl River near Canton (Guangzhou). One version is that a loyal official jumped into the river with the emperor, just before circling Mongol ships moved in for the kill. This official may have been Hau Wong Yeung. Not much else happened in Hong Kong, a remote and sparsely populated outpost of the Chinese empire until the mid-1800s.

At that time, China considered herself the center of the universe, the Middle Kingdom, the most powerful nation on earth. It was blissfully unaware that Britain was militarily superior. She considered Britain and all other nations inferior, barbarian tributaries. China's initial contacts with Europeans did not improve this view. They were adventurers, explorers and pirates, loud, extremely rude and smelly. The Chinese established trade anyway, but to protect the Chinese people from evil influences severely restricted the foreigners.

They confined the British, along with American, French, Dutch, and Parsee (Indian) traders to a luxurious island and forbade them from entering nearby Canton. The foreigners were only allowed to trade with a tiny group of merchants called the *co-hong*. However, the British wanted to trade with all of massive China.

The British had become addicted to Chinese tea in the 1600s and had nothing to trade but cold, hard silver. China was self-sufficient. Then the British started to smuggle in Indian opium. This relieved their trade deficit, but China's leaders did not want opium in their country. Britain felt that the opium trade was morally repugnant, but economically essential.

And so our story begins with two of the most powerful nations on earth and their two addictions. The British wanted free trade; the Chinese didn't. There were bound to be problems.

MILESTONES IN HONG KONG'S HISTORY

1834 – Britain sent **Lord Napier** as the Superintendent of Trade to try and expand legitimate commerce. Unfortunately, he followed orders and went to Canton without permission and then tried to approach the viceroy (governor) as an equal! This, in the Chinese view, was insulting behavior, against regulations and got him nowhere. China retaliated by cutting off supplies to the British merchants, stopping trade and demanding that Napier leave Canton. Napier, whose name the Chinese translated into the characters for *Laboriously Vile*, brought in two gunboats which the Chinese stopped. Sick and defeated, he retreated to Macau and died the same year. This was the beginning of the **gunboat diplomacy** that characterized Chinese-British relations for the next twenty years. In 1835, opium smuggling into China reached 40,000 chests from 4-5,000 chests (each about 130 pounds) in the 1820s.

1839 – China sent **Commissioner Lin Tse-hsu (Lin Ze-Xu)** to stop the trade. He surrounded the factories, cut off supplies and demanded all the foreign mud (opium) on foreign ships. **Charles Elliot**, the new Superintendent of Trade, handed over 20,000 chests and promised their British owners that the crown would reimburse them. Lin destroyed the opium and then allowed the merchants to leave for Macau, their off-trading-season home.

Then a British shore party got into a brawl in Hong Kong and a Chinese man was killed. Lin demanded that the murderer be handed over for execution. Elliot refused.

Lin and imperial troops advanced on Macau. The British merchants and their families were forced to flee to Hong Kong harbor where they lived on ships. There were a few minor skirmishes and then in 1840, British reinforcements arrived and the **First Opium War** began. The British blockaded rivers and attacked towns. Eventually, **Commissioner Keshen (Qishan)** agreed to negotiate.

1841 – The resulting **Convention of Chuenpi** (aka **Chuanbi**) ceded Hong Kong Island to the British. A week later, the Union Jack was raised in Hong Kong.

Many mainland Chinese arrived to work and/or escape Chinese justice. The British were continually surprised at the large number willing to live under their rule. The island's population rose and the efficient British began urban planning.

Captain Belcher of the *HMS Sulphur*, surveyed the island and may have named its peaks. The British held land auctions and built Queen's Rd. **Jardine** and **Matheson**, the founders of the one of the largest opium-trading companies and the only company from that era that still exists, built the first house on the site of what is now Flagstaff House in Central.

This was all a little premature. **Lord Palmerston**, the Foreign Secretary, called Elliot back to England and gave him a good tongue lashing. Lord Palmerston had wanted access to all of China, not just "a barren island with hardly a house upon it." He exiled Elliot to Texas. Keshen's fate was worse. He had given up a piece of the celestial empire. This had never been done. He was yanked back to Peking (Beijing) in chains and disgrace. The Convention was never signed and the war resumed under the new Superintendent of Trade, **Sir Henry Pottinger**.

1842 – Pottinger blockaded rivers, captured a few cities and was about to take Nanking (Nanjing), when the Chinese agreed to negotiate. This ended the first opium war in which tens of thousands of Chinese and hundreds of British died. Pottinger and Keshen's replacement, **Keying** signed the **Treaty of Nanking**. It opened up four port cities including Shanghai, reimbursed the British for the destroyed opium of 1839 and officially ceded Hong Kong Island to the British. This was the first of the unequal treaties imposed on the Chinese by the British.

1843– **Queen Victoria** officially declared Hong Kong Island a colony and made Pottinger the first governor. The colony had grown rapidly during the war with more roads, houses, barracks, and a prison.

1851-64 – Chinese refugees flooded into Hong Kong because of the **Taiping Rebellion** against the **Manchus**, who had ruled China since 1644. The population grew from under 10,000 in 1841 to over 100,000 in the 1860s.

1856 – Chinese officials boarded the *Arrow*, a ship flying a British flag and arrested some of her crew, accusing them of piracy. When the Chinese refused to return them to the British, the **Second Opium War** (aka **Anglo-Chinese War**) began and continued on and off until 1860.

1857 – The chief Chinese baker in Hong Kong tried to poison British residents with arsenic, but he used too much and his victims vomited the poison before it could harm them. The American Captain **"Bully" Hayes** captured the handsome American pirate, **Eli Boggs**, commander of two dozen armed junks, for a reward.

1858 – The British, with the help of the French, seized Canton and headed toward Tientsin (Tianjin). The British and Chinese signed the

1859 **Treaty of Tientsin**, whereby the Chinese agreed to open more trading ports and to recognize British diplomats. A year later, the first British ambassador on his way to Peking, tried to force his way through a Chinese blockade on the Pei Ho River. The Chinese won this battle and war resumed. The British marched all the way to Peking this time and burned and looted the summer palace. The emperor fled, the Chinese surrendered and signed the **Treaty of Peking**. The British acquired Kowloon Peninsula (up to Boundary Street) and Stonecutter's Island. Armed hostilities between China and Britain came to an end, but the opium trade continued into the 1900s.

1869 – Hong Kong was a wild frontier town, full of pirates, brothels, liquor stores, opium dens and crime. The Suez Canal opened and European butchers, bakers, tailors and wives took this shorter, safer route to Hong Kong which slowly became a little more civilized. The 1860s and 70s was a slow time in Hong Kong's history as it faced a recession and competition as a port from Shanghai.

1880s–1890s – Hong Kong prospered and received its share of important visitors. In 1880, the governor appointed the first Chinese member of the Legislative Council. In 1881, the King of Hawaii visited and so did the future King George V and his brother, Prince Edward. In 1889, **Rudyard Kipling** stopped by and was appalled at the number of drunken sailors, liquor stores and brothels, and the colorful language of the European prostitutes. In the 1890s more than three guide books to Hong Kong were published. Bubonic plague struck in 1894; 2,500 mainly Chinese died and half the population fled the colony.

1898 – The British leased the New Territories for 99 years, adding 32 square miles. When this lease runs out in 1997, all of Hong Kong, will return to China.

1900-1919 – In 1900, the **Boxer Rebellion** against foreign domination in China occurred, resulting in a wave of refugees. In 1906, a typhoon took thousands of boats and 10,000 lives. In 1911, Dr Sun Yat-sen's revolutionaries, overthrew the Manchus, the Ching (Qing) dynasty. This resulted in more refugees. In 1912, the **University of Hong Kong** and the **Kowloon-Canton Railway** opened.

1920s – Hong Kong's population had swelled from 250,000 in 1900 to 600,000 in 1920. Piracy was rampant. Pirates often boarded ships as passengers, stealing from and holding fellow travelers for ransom. In 1922, the seaman's strike closed the harbor and spread to domestic servants. In 1925, a general strike paralyzed Hong Kong.

1937-41 – During the **Japan-China war**, more refugees arrived. The population almost doubled to 1.5 million. In the early 1940s, many European women and children evacuated to Manila as the Japanese moved closer.

AGAINST ALL ODDS!

Hong Kong's survival through the years has been astounding. It was notorious for disease; in 1841, one quarter of the British military died of fever. Malaria, cholera, dysentary, typhoid, and bubonic plague were common. Devastating typhoons (hurricanes) hit its coast again and again, breaking ships like match sticks and flattening villages. Pirates preyed on ships and some estimate that as much as 20% of the Chinese were opium addicts, until World War II. Thousands died when fires broke out in shanty villages, quickly erected by the waves of refugees.

Despite everything, Hong Kong grew and prospered. The hard working Chinese thrived in the stable, less corrupt, capitalist climate that the British maintained. Chinese, Europeans, and Americans came to Hong Kong to make money as quickly as possible and return home wealthy.

1941-World War II – On Sept 10, **Sir Mark Young** became Governor. On Nov 16, two battalions of barely trained Canadian troops arrived. On Dec 7/8, Japan attacked Hong Kong at almost the same time as Pearl Harbor and the Philippines. Hong Kong defended itself as best it could. There were many heroes including a voluntary group called the **Hugheseliers** made up of about 60 men over age 55 with some well into their seventies. It had some of the wealthiest and most powerful men in the colony. They valiantly defended the North Point Power Station for 18 hours until they ran out of ammunition. A few managed to escape.

Although the British had given up on Hong Kong before the war even started, **Prime Minister Winston Churchill** sent a message on Dec 21: *There must be no thought of surrender ... Every day that you are able to maintain your resistance you and your men can win the lasting honour...* With only about 10,000 Chinese, British and Canadian troops and virtually no air or sea support, Hong Kong heroicly held out for two and a half bloody weeks and surrendered on Christmas day.

The Japanese occupied Hong Kong for four long, ugly years. They imprisoned 2,500 British men, women and children in Stanley and kept British and Canadian soldiers in camps in Kowloon. There were many unsung heroes; the ones that survived, the few that managed to escape and the fewer that made it 1,200 miles to Chungking (Chongqing) and freedom. While many Chinese fled Hong Kong, some stayed and a few helped sneak food into the prison camps and spied on the Japanese, who made their headquarters at Government House.

1945 – World War II ended. Hong Kong's 1941 population of 1,600,000 people had shrunk to 600,000. However, in 1949, the Communists defeated the Chinese Nationalists. China closed itself to the outside world and many more refugees came. By 1950, Hong Kong's population of over two million, surpassed its pre-war high.

1951 – After China supported North Korea against South Korea and the United Nations, the world body ordered an embargo against China. Hong Kong lost about one-third of its foreign exchange, but bounced back by greatly expanding its textile industry. It was so successful that in 1959, Britian limited the import of Hong Kong textiles.

1953 – A huge fire in a squatter village left over 50,000 homeless. Hong Kong began a public housing program that now houses half the population.

1965–75 – American military men flocked to Hong Kong for rest and recreation during the Vietnamese war. In 1967, Hong Kong experienced pro-communist riots and terrorist acts, inspired by the Chinese **Cultural Revolution** and the **Red Guards**. It outlawed firecrackers. In an unrelated move, it also outlawed concubines. However, if you already had concubines, you were allowed to keep them.

1970s – This was a time of development in Hong Kong. In 1972, it built the cross-harbor tunnel and a year later the first new town development in the New Territories began. In 1979 it opened the **MTR** (subway). Other notable events were the fiery destruction of the new Jumbo Floating Restaurant in Aberdeen in 1971 and the collapse of the stock market in 1973. In 1974, Hong Kong established the **Independent Commission Against Corruption** (**ICAC**) because of police corruption, and a year later, Queen Elizabeth II became the first reigning monarch to visit Hong Kong. In 1972, China reopened itself to visitors. Vietnamese refugees began to arrive in Hong Kong after 1975.

1980 – In thirty years Hong Kong's population had grown from two million to five million. Hong Kong previously had a **touch-base** policy for Chinese refugees who managed to get to an urban area. They could become Hong Kong citizens. This lenient policy now ended. Hong Kong now repatriates almost all illegal immigrants back to China.

1984 – The British and the Chinese signed the **Joint Declaration**, agreeing that Hong Kong would return to China in 1997. People panicked. A lot of money left Hong Kong and many locals moved to other countries.

1985 – The people elected the first non-governor-appointed **Legislative Council** members.

1989 – Thousands flooded the streets to protest and to grieve for the victims of the **Tiananmen Square** tragedy in Beijing. Many Hong Kong people talked of leaving. Then **Deng Xiao Ping** made his southern journey encouraging investment and development and openness to the outside world in terms of trade. The Chinese economy took a turn for the better and people stayed. The impending death of Deng will certainly affect Hong Kong. What happens in China will always be felt in Hong Kong.

1992 – Police arrested almost 100 illegal immigrants daily, up from 70 the year before. They sent them back to China.

1993-1994 – **Governor Chris Patten** clashed with China over the democratization of Hong Kong, the building of the new airport on Lantau, and the use of government surplus funds. Fear about the takeover has abated and Hong Kong is growing like there is no tomorrow. In the past three years, the colony's two tallest buildings were built. Many people who left in the 1980s returned as jobs were not so readily available in North America and Australia. About 10% of the population have foreign passports and can leave when they want to. Most have a wait-and-see attitude.

THE FUTURE

On **July 1, 1997**, Hong Kong will return to Chinese administration. Hong Kong is a historical phenomenon, balancing precariously on the brink of destiny. It has always been a ping-pong ball between the Chinese and British. You can tell your grandchildren you were there before the British withdrawal, that you knew it when it was booming, the greatest city in Asia, a classic example of pure capitalism at its best.

The Joint Declaration provides for the **Hong Kong Special Adminis- tration Region** (**HKSAR**) to have a lot of autonomy. The **Basic Law** says that laws previously in force will continue with a few exceptions for 50 years. The Chinese are not stupid; they will not make changes to a proven, successful formula. Or will they?

Most people feel that everything is going to be fine, as long as they can keep making money. But, there are two major changes that will probably occur: increased corruption and censorship. Already, China is influenc- ing the Hong Kong media. In 1994, the Chinese government pulled out all of its official entries in the **Hong Kong Arts Festival**, to protest the screening of two independent features from mainland China. Journalists have been toning down anti-Chinese rhetoric in a kind of self-censorship. They are afraid of upsetting China and affecting their jobs after 1997. Ruth met a local, 20ish, Chinese journalist who says she will stay after 1997 because "someone has to keep press freedom alive".

Another major worry is corruption, which is bad for business. There is a lot in China and whether it will spill over, remains to be seen.

The details of the Basic Law are being laboriously worked out now. In response to some conflicts, China has threatened an earlier-than-1997 takeover and to change some laws, such as Governor's Chris Patten's controversial, democratization attempts in 1997. Many business interests oppose his policy. Many people feel discussions with Beijing now are a waste of time. China's policy will ultimately depend on who's in power there.

The **new airport** has been a source of conflict. Hong Kong decided to build it without consulting China. Was Britain trying to use up foreign exchange reserves, leaving nothing for China and giving out contracts to its own companies? The Chinese want the surplus funds to build Asia's biggest naval station on Stone Cutter's Island. That is another quarrel.

Many Hong Kong people feel that everything will be fine. China, especially Shenzhen and Hong Kong have been economic partners for a long time. China has made considerable investments in hotels, manufacturing, real estate and financial services in Hong Kong and vice versa.

Said one foreign-educated Chinese local who is not planning to leave, "If the Chinese are fighting inside the family, they won't show it outside. They will try to show unity. The Chinese want to show the world they can do a better job than the British. They won't let Hong Kong collapse."

Join the guessing game. What do you think will happen in 1997? At press time the Hong Kong government was planning no special celebrations for July 1, 1997. For many, the change of administration will not be a time for rejoicing.

BUSTLING HONG KONG HARBOR

4. LAND & PEOPLE

THE LAND

Hong Kong is tiny, a pimple as they say, on the belly-button of China's rounded southeast coast. It is surrounded on almost four sides by water and islands. Its coastline zig-zags in and out of former pirate coves and harbors, and is ringed by fishing villages, skyscrapers, container terminals and rugged rocky cliffs. Mountains and hills cap most of it.

You may be surprised that 40% of Hong Kong is protected park land, one of the highest ratios in the world. There are 21 country parks and 14 special areas. The tallest peak, **Tai Mo Shan** in the New Territories, towers to 957 meters. **Lantau Peak** on Lantau Island is second at 933 meters.

Hong Kong means *Fragrant Harbor* and is a total of 1,070 square kilometers (400 square miles) of land. It is slightly smaller than Los Angeles, with almost double the population. Roughly 38 kilometers long and 50 kilometers wide, most of its land is in the northern New Territories which borders China. Hong Kong Island covers 77.5 square kilometers and Kowloon 12 square kilometers. There are also 235 outlying islands. Two-thirds of the territory is water.

Hong Kong is located 320 kilometers south of the Tropic of Cancer in the sub-tropics, on the fringe of the Indo-Pacific Reef Complex. You can actually find coral in Double Haven and Mirs Bay. Three thousand years ago, it was part of a tropical forest with wild elephants and crocodiles.

Fauna

Hong Kong has an amazing abundance of animals and birds. The small Chinese leopard cat, several species of civet cat, wild boars, porcupines, bats and numerous reptiles including large pythons, make their home here. You can find macaque monkeys in **Kam Shan Country Park** in the New Territories and hear barking deer on Hong Kong Island. The last tigers (yes, tigers) were killed in the New Territories in 1915 and near Stanley on Hong Kong Island, during the Japanese occupation in the 1940s.

Many species of birds live in Hong Kong and 200 species of butterflies flutter in its breezes. Birds include ducks, hawks, eagles, herons, bright blue kingfishers and even cockatoos. The latter are probably the descendents of those released before the Japanese invasion. **Mai Po Marshes** is a 380-hectare bird sanctuary with more than 250 species observed. An egretry in **Yim Tso Ha** has five species. The nesting season is April to September.

WATCH OUT FOR SNAKES!

There are some dangerous snakes: the bamboo, cobras, sea snakes, kraits, coral and vipers. The green bamboo snake is the only aggressive one. However, in the four years we hiked in the hills here, only one member of our family saw a poisonous snake. A cobra got in the way of Mike Malloy above Stanley and he dropped a rock on its head!

Flora

The abundance of rain and humidity has blessed Hong Kong with lush foliage and colorful flowers. The official floral emblem is the deep pink flower of the bauhinia blakeana or Hong Kong orchid tree. It is recognized by its double-lobed leaves which resemble a camel's footprints and blossoms from early November to the end of March. This flower is beginning to replace the Queen on the new coins, in preparation for the Chinese takeover. Ironically, the tree was named after a British governor, Sir Henry Blake, who ruled from 1898 to 1903.

Being in the sub-tropics, both temperate as well as tropical plants thrive here. Don't be surprised by coconut palms, bread fruit, rubber trees, cotton trees, banyans, frangipani, hibiscus and mangosteens. Look for the bright red flame trees and what we call firecracker trees with bright orange, elongated blossoms resembling a string of firecrackers. Hong Kong has Norfolk pine, guava, figs and many species of bamboo. June is lichee season.

Agriculture and Fishing

Only about 8% of the land is suitable for farming; Hong Kong, however, still manages to produce 20% of its own fresh vegetables, almost 40% of its chickens and about 50% of its fresh flowers! In at least one of the flat arable patches in Shatin, high-quality rice for export to Beijing used to grow. The local fishing fleet has 4,500 vessels, employs 21,000 fishermen, and supplies 55% of local consumption. 150 commercially-important fish swim in Hong Kong waters.

THE PEOPLE

The **population** is 5,919,000, with a people/land ratio of 5,590 per square kilometer, one of the most densely populated in the world. 22% of the population live on Hong Kong Island, 34% in Kowloon and New Kowloon and about 44% in the New Territories. About 60% of the population was born in Hong Kong and 34% in China. Half the population live in government-assisted housing, one of the only forms of social welfare.

Almost 98% of the population is Chinese. The rest are Americans, British, Filipinos (890,000), and a few other nationalities. Most of these are female *amahs* (domestic helpers or maids) who send their extra money back to their families. Most musicians in hotels and bars are Filipinos. In 1994, the population also included 29,000 Vietnamese refugees. Hong Kong has been trying to repatriate most of them. Even though they live in squalid, detention camps, many do not want to go back home and have been protesting with violence and hunger strikes.

For many years, Hong Kong has accepted 35 mainland Chinese citizens a day as legal immigrants. Since January, 1994, this number has increased to 105 a day, making the development of trade unions and better working conditions difficult. One can also expect a change in the fundamental character of the Hong Kong people as these migrants fill the void left by departing citizens.

Hong Kong receives about nine million visitors a year. 15% are North Americans and the rest are from Taiwan, Japan, and Southeast Asia. There are 1.7 million visitors from China. The people you see on the streets are not all locals.

LANGUAGES

The official languages are Chinese and English, taught in all schools. The Chinese population is primarily Cantonese-speaking, but Mandarin or *pu tong hua*, the official language on the mainland, is becoming common. Children learn three spoken languages in school. Luckily, the writing for Cantonese and Mandarin is similiar.

HOW TO SAY IT IN BRITISH

There have been a few bar fights because some overly sensitive Americans did not understand that the British word for cigarette is **fag**. *Other useful words include* **lift** *(elevator),* **nakered** *(exhausted),* **tram** *(street car),* **flat** *(apartment), and* **bird** *(woman).*

ETHNIC GROUPS

There are smaller Chinese groups who still practise their unique customs and speak their own mutually unintelligible dialects. They live in isolated areas of the New Territories and on some islands.

The **Hakka** or *guest people* originated in Shandong and northern Hunan and first arrived from Fujian and Jiangxi in the late 17th century. They have their own unique cuisine, unrelated to Cantonese cooking, and their language may be the original Mandarin, before it was modified. The most famous Hakkas are the author Han Suyin and Hong Xiuquan, leader of the 19th century Taiping Rebellion.

Traditional Hakka women are very visible. On their heads, they wear a flat brim with no crown, trimmed by a short black curtain (to keep away the flies). They dress in a black apron, decorated on festive occasions with an embroidered triangle on the chest. You can sometimes see them working on the roads, in parks or raking Sha Tin racetrack. They pose for a fee in the walled village of **Kam Tin**, on the LRT line, in the New Territories.

The **Hoklo** are a tiny minority who were traditionally farmers and boat people. They probably arrived in the late Ming dynasty (1368-1644) from Fujian, and speak a Fujianese (Fukienese) dialect. Their center is the **Mirs Bay** area in the New Territories. Unlike the Tanka, their traditional boat is open and long and they wear a flat-brimmed hat with crown.

HONG KONG'S FUTURE ARTISTS

The **Punti** (**Penti**) or *original inhabitants* were the first settlers. They took all the best land. Many came, fleeing the Mongol threat in the 11th and early 12th centuries. Most arrived during the Ming.

The **Tanka** or *boat people* call themselves *shui jen* (water people). The 200,000 in Hong Kong are believed to be descendants of the aboriginal inhabitants (the **Yue** of Malay-Oceanic stock). Until the 1700s, Chinese law forbade Tankas from living on shore. The reason is obscure, but was probably punitive.

Many Tankas have a shrine to **Tin Hau**, goddess of heaven and fisherfolk, on the bows of their boats. On her birthday, they head to the temple in **Joss House Bay**. The traditional hat is high brimmed, mushroom-shaped and small, so that a gust of wind is less likely to dislodge it.

The Tanka provide water transport, fish, and operate lighters which are small boats with cranes for loading and unloading. The lighters look like baby chicks nestled against the giant ocean-going ships in the harbor. Although cargo vessels sail into docks for loading in most of the world's large ports, this traditional method remains in Hong Kong. In an effort to get their children to schools, the government has been moving the boat people into apartments.

Boat people, when eating fish, will not turn it over when the top half is consumed. They take off the bone and continue. If they turn the fish over, it means their boat will turn over. Some people think that the popular Chinese game of mahjong was invented by boat people as tiles do not blow away in gusts of wind as easily as cards.

The British

Somehow, colonialism brings out the best and worst in British people. As rulers, many Brits looked down on the Chinese people, who for a long time were subject to prejudicial laws. Chinese could not own land on the Peak or travel at night without a pass. On the other hand, some Brits have opened schools and hospitals and many volunteer with Vietnamese boat people, Chinese orphans, and more.

The British allowed Chinese culture to flourish. In the beginning, Chinese law governed local Chinese except for forms of torture. Concubines were not outlawed until the 1960s and mui-tsai, bought-female servants, were common in the 1920s. In 1994, villagers protested outside the Legislative Council, when it suggested changing ancient laws that prohibited daughters from inheriting land in the New Territories.

The British in Hong Kong run the range from the Governor to business people and missionaries. British and Gurkha troops are still stationed here. Three armed Scottish guards got very drunk one night in the 1980s and took over the airport for several hours, until they sobered up.

The Indians

Britain ruled India when Hong Kong was born. Indian **Parsee** traders played an active role in the development of the colony and Sikhs came as members of the British Army. Many **Sikhs** later joined the Hong Kong police force and you will still see them guarding banks with shot guns or working as doormen. The **Sikh Temple** at 371 Queen's Road East in Wanchai was founded in 1901, and like Sikh temples elsewhere provides free temporary bedspaces for visitors. Services are Sunday mornings.

The **Hindu Temple** in Happy Valley serves the 12,000 Hindus in the city. It offers yoga classes and wedding ceremonies. Hindus here celebrate festivals such as the throwing of colored water during the Holi festival, the Birthday of Lord Krishna, and Diwali, the festival of lights.

The Jews

They have lived in Hong Kong since the 1800s and contributed mightily to its prosperity. The earliest were Sephardic Jews from Baghdad and Bombay. The **Sassoons** and **Kadoories** are the most famous. Before World War II, many European Jews fled from Hitler to Shanghai, the only place they could go without a passport. After the war some, including the Kadoories, moved to Hong Kong. Recent diplomatic relations between China and Israel has encouraged a new wave of business migrants from Israel.

There are now four different congregations. **Chabad** have their own school. **Sephardic** have their own restaurant with Middle Eastern food on Macdonnell Rd. There are also **Reform** and **Traditional** Jews. The **King David Club** has 260-member families, a Jewish day school, Sunday School, great food and some books on Jewish history for sale. It is in Melbourne Plaza on Queen's Rd. Central, but might move soon beside the synagogue on Robinson Road. There is a Jewish cemetery in Happy Valley with graves marked in English and Hebrew, established in the 1850s.

The **Ohel Leah synagogue** was built in 1901 by Lord Kadoorie for his mother and is the oldest synagogue in southern China. There is an *Asia Pacific Survival Guide for Jewish Travellers* published by the A.P. Jewish Association, GPO Box 5402 CC, Melbourne, Victoria 30001, Australia, (03) 602-1622; (03) 676- 7467. It lists Jewish sites.

The Muslims

Fifty thousand Muslims live in Hong Kong. Half are Chinese, and the rest are Indian, Indonesian, Malay, Pakistani, African and Middle Eastern. They worship in five mosques, the oldest built in the 19th century. The most convenient and the largest is the one in Kowloon Park, Tsim Sha Tsui. The **Osman Ramju Sadick Islamic Centre** in Wanchai has a mosque, community hall, library and medical clinic. There is also a Muslim cemetery in Happy Valley and in Cape Collinson in Chai Wan.

Hong Kong Chinese

Overall, they are a curious blend of the Chinese traditionalist and the consumeristic capitalist. Some businessmen in their three-piece suits won't close a deal until they've consulted their favorite fortune tellers. Children in formal school uniforms study computers at school and burn incense in a temple. Wizened, old Chinese ladies dressed all in black, play the stock market. Some huge, multinational companies hire fung shui masters, whenever they build anything.

Hong Kong has the most television sets, cellular phones and Rolls Royces per capita and its people drink the most cognac. It held the record for the longest parade of Rolls Royces (114), until Hollywood beat it. There is no guilt associated with being wealthy and people admire and are inspired by the rich. They think "Hey, good for him; the hard work paid off. One day I'll be there too". Few if any think "I wonder whose lives he ruined to get to the top?" People are as likely to talk about the cost of things as the weather. Shopping is the number one sport.

In the last few years, Hong Kong people have developed a growing pride in being Chinese. Foreign colonial control is dwindling and China is a growing economic power. More British people are working in traditional Chinese jobs, such as waiters and hotel clerks. This year is the first time that we saw white people handing out leaflets on the street and begging.

In spite of the years of British influence, Chinese people are still Chinese and conservative. To get married in Hong Kong if you're under 21, you need permission from your guardian. No decent Chinese girl goes to a bar alone. When a foreign women goes alone, people wonder about her morals. Newspapers recently reported on charges of sexual discrimination again a supermarket chain that gave free medical benefits to families of male employees but not to families of female employees.

RELIGION

Most people are **Buddhist** and/or **Taoist** and practice ancestor worship. They do not necessarily "belong" to any organized temple. Chinese people tend to be very pragmatic, worshipping the most appropriate god for each problem or all gods for a very serious one. They try to cover all the bases. When a friend prays successfully to one god for a baby boy, then other women try it too. It is not unusual for one person to baptize his children as Christians, hang *fung shui* mirrors outside his apartment, burn incense to a deceased grandfather, and then retire to contemplate in a Taoist or Buddhist monastery.

The keepers of various religions here are equally flexible. Statues of Buddhist saints can be found in Taoist temples and vice versa. You can tell which god is most successful by the prosperity of the temple. There are about 360 temples registered with the government.

Buddhism

Buddhism was founded in India by Prince Gautama, who was born in the 6th century BC. Brought up in the confines of a palace, he decided at the age of 29 to search for life's meaning. Giving up all his wealth and power, he wandered the world for six years, and then having found answers that satisfied his soul, he preached his ideas for 45 years: the **Four Noble Truths** and the **Noble Eightfold Path to Nirvana**.

As the Buddha or enlightened one, the former prince taught that the source of all suffering is selfish desire, and one must stop all craving for it. Some sects believe in living spiritually without worldly goods. The Chinese follow the **Mahayana** school of faith and good works, which believes Buddha is divine and can answer prayers. You will see people worshipping, holding smoking incense in both hands, bowing to the statues or kowtowing, head to the ground.

The Buddha or **Sakyamuni** is known as **Sik Ka Fat** in Hong Kong. **Maitreya** or **Mei Lak Fat**, the fat Laughing Buddha, is still to come to earth. **Kwan Yin** is the Buddhist goddess of mercy.

ANCESTOR WORSHIP

This common belief explains why sons are important. Only males can perform rituals for the ancestors and carry on the family name. Deceased ancestors influence the fortunes of the living, so it is important to keep them happy. If there are no male heirs, a male from another family can be adopted for this purpose.

*Traditionally, one clan lived in one village and worshipped their shared ancestors in an ancestral hall. The name of each important ancestor was carved on a small tablet. Ancestors who were really special, like those who had passed their exams and become civil servants, might have their own shrine. This way, the ancestors were kept within the community. Halls can be two or three attached buildings. Some are still used in the New Territories. The best is that of the Tang clan on the **Ping Shan Heritage Trail** (LRT). A modern ancestral hall is in the **Ching Chung Temple** in the same area.*

You can worship any dead relative. We once saw a poignant scene on a traffic island in Repulse Bay. A bicycle lock and a spark plug sat on a make-shift altar with burning incense to keep the spirit of the accident victim happy. One Chinese-Canadian we know, after consulting a geomancer and moving his brother's grave to a better fung shui site, now consults his brother in business decisions and is doing well.

Taoism

A sage named **Lao Tzu** founded this religion 1800 years ago. His message was conveyed to the world by a disciple named **Mencius**. Taoism teaches that everything exists through the interplay of two opposite forces: male-female, positive-negative, hot-cold, light-dark, heaven-earth, yin-yang, etc. Taoists try to achieve harmony out of these conflicts through the **Tao** or the **Way**.

Taoism is closer to nature than other religions, its saints finding enlightenment after spending years meditating in caves and on mountain tops. Taoism has been diluted by superstition. Its adherents believe in charms and spells, ghosts and nature spirits. If ghosts are believed to be haunting a building, Taoist priests will perform ceremonies to exorcise them. **Tin Hau** and **Pak Tai** are Taoist deities.

Christianity

There are 500,000 Christians. Half are Protestant and half are Roman Catholic. Many of the churches originally had refugee congregations with roots in China. The **Hong Kong Chinese Christian Church Union** and the **Hong Kong Christian Council** help to co-ordinate the work of most of the churches. Today there are many seminaries, colleges, secondary and elementary schools, hospitals and other services like homes for the elderly. Most religious services are in Chinese.

The largest group of Protestants are the Baptists and then the Lutherans. The first Roman Catholic Church was established in 1841 and in 1969, **Francis Chen-peng Hsu** became the first Chinese bishop of Hong Kong. In 1988, the bishop was made a cardinal. There are 275 Catholic schools with almost 300,000 pupils.

In 1849, local citizens and the British military built St. John's Cathedral in Central, the first Anglican church in the Far East. The first woman Anglican priest was ordained in Hong Kong in 1944.

DEITIES & TEMPLES

There are gods or patron saints for just about everything from barbers to bean curd makers. Temples tend to be very smoky as long incense spirals can smolder for two or three weeks. Be careful of falling ash. Contemplating and exploring a quiet temple is a wonderful experience, but so are festivals, when worshippers arrive to pay homage with lots of burning incense, food and kowtows of deepest reverence. Festivals are also great for photographers.

Tin Hau

The **Goddess of Heaven and fisherfolk** is worshipped only on the south China coast and is the most popular deity here. She usually wears an ornate gold crown with hanging strands of pearls. She is believed by many to be originally named **Lin Ma-tzu**, a woman who lived in Fujian province over a thousand years ago. In an out-of-body state, she saved members of her own family from a shipwreck. Two Fujian fishermen brothers, saved by the goddess, built the first temple in the Hong Kong area in 1012.

In 1278, Kublai Khan proclaimed her Queen of Heaven. She is often flanked by the fierce statues of **Thousand-Li Eye** and **Favorable-Wind Ear.** You will find Tin Hau temples in Causeway Bay, Stanley, Yau Ma Tei (our favorite) and Lantau, Lamma, Cheung Chau and Peng Chau Islands.

Ask the Hong Kong Tourist Association (HKTA) about special ferries going to her birthday party at the temple in Joss House Bay (Clearwater Bay, New Territories). It is worthwhile seeing the colorful boats with shrines, flags, and lion dancers.

Kwan Yin

(aka **Kwun Yum, Guan Yin, Kun Iam**) is the Buddhist **Goddess of Mercy**. A favorite especially of women, Kwan Yin can have several heads and arms and might be carrying a vase or a child. The most common image of her is dressed all in white with a shawl draped partially over her head. Her hair is drawn up into a bun on top. She came to China as the male Hindu god **Avalokita** or **Avalokitsvara**.

Around the 12th century, his statues started becoming feminine to attract more worshippers. She is referred to as a *pusa, bodhissattva,* or saint, a human who achieved enlightenment but opted to return to earth to help others. She has temples in Stanley and Cheung Chau and her statues are found also in Buddhist and Taoist temples everywhere.

Hau Wong

The Marquis was a real person named **Yang** or **Yeung Liang Chieh**. Scholars do not agree on his identity but local people believe he was the loyal minister, bodyguard or general who saved the young Song emperor from capture by the Mongols. His small temples are called **Hau Wong** or **Yeung Hau** and are unique to Hong Kong. You can find them in Tai O and Tung Chung on Lantau Island, and in Yuen Long and the Ping Shan Heritage Trail, New Territories.

Wong Tai Sin

He was born around 328 AD in China, a shepherd who turned boulders into sheep and cinnabar into a drug that helped him become immortal. He has a reputation for healing the sick, answering prayers and predicting the future. His temple attracts the largest number of fortune tellers in the city and over 2,000 worshippers a day. It is packed at New

Year's. Although you will not find a Wong Tai Sin temple in China, you will find one in new Kowloon and in Toronto.

Kwan Kung

(aka **Kuan Yu, Guan Yu**, or **Kuan Tai**) is the **God of War**. Soldiers, pawn shop owners, and curio dealers worship him. You can find his shrines in police stations and ironically, also in triad dens. He carries a sword and usually has a red face. He was a general who lived from 160 to 219 AD. China's oldest extant novel, *The Romance of the Three Kingdoms*, relates his story. He is also the subject of many operas as he heroically chose death over revealing secrets. His temples are on Cheung Chau and Lantau islands. He is also honored at the **Man Mo Temple** in Western and in Tai Po in the New Territories.

The **God of Literature and Civil Servants** lives with the God of War at Man Mo Temple in Western and Tai O. They are an odd couple.

Another uniquely local God is the child **Tam Kung** who cures illnesses and controls the weather. He is a god of boat people. Dragons and lions dance and brightly decorated boats arrive for his birthday at his temple in Shaukeiwan. He is credited with protecting his followers from cholera in the 1960s.

Other popular deities include the **Earth God** who has altars in many temples and near villages, and **Shing Wong**, the **City God**.

FESTIVALS
Bun Festival

The **Bun Festival** on **Cheung Chau Island** is a unique phenomenom with three 20-meter-high towers of lucky buns stacked around the **Temple to the god Pak Tai**. These are dismantled on the third night by people who want their supposedly curative powers. They take them home to eat when ill.

This festival is also to placate the ghosts of the victims of pirates (who are also supposed to eat the buns) and is an affirmation of vegetarianism. It is a good place to see Chinese folk opera as it was originally performed in make-shift theatres, Taoist priests, lion dancers, and the parade of beautiful children floating over the heads of the crowd.

Believers built this temple to Pak Tai, the Taoist Sea God in 1783 to protect the island from an outbreak of plague. A few years later, local fishermen found a statue of Pak Tai floating in the sea and this statue helped protect them from another epidemic of plague in the late 19th century. The festival started as a thank-you to the god for saving them. The statue found in the sea now wears a crown hung with pearls given on the occasion of Britain's Princess Margaret's visit to the temple in 1966.

DRAGON BOAT FESTIVAL

*Festivals worth making a special trip for are Ching Ming (see below for more information) and the **Dragon Boat Festival**, especially if you are participating. The dragon boat races were inspired by the poet-statesman **Chu Yuan** (Quyuan, 338-278 BC) who tried unsuccessfully to warn the King of Chu about the rival who would become China's first emperor. Chu Yuan drowned himself in despair because he was proved right.*

Corporations, banks, airlines, clubs and villages sponsor teams. Foreigners, locals, men and women race the long slender dragon boats. So can you. In memory of Chu Yuan's loyalty, his persistence and his brilliant poetry, dragon boats race in other parts of the world as well. Many teams go to Hong Kong to compete. Check venues with the HKTA and for a place on a junk to see the races from the water. If races are still in Stanley, you can just go and watch from the shore. Be sure to eat rice dumplings wrapped in bamboo leaves, a traditional part of this festival.

Ching Ming Festival

Ching Ming sounds like a sad occasion, but it's more like a picnic. It is the spring cleaning of the graves, repainting and repairing, and the annual worship of the ancestors. Thousands of people converge on Hong Kong's many cemeteries, bearing barbecued baby pigs, fruit, rice, buns and liquor. They burn incense, pour the liquor, and leave paper money (hell notes) and a bowl of rice and meat beside the gravestones.

But Chinese people are very practical and sit around eating most of the food themselves. It is the essence of the food that is shared with the deceased. *When do your ancestors eat the food?* says the foreigner in the old joke. The Chinese replies: *The same time your ancestors smell the flowers.* Cheung Chau Island is a good place to see this. More convenient are the cemeteries in Happy Valley.

Moon Festival

The **Mid-Autumn** or **Moon Festival** is a time to enjoy the most beautiful full moon of the year. It has been a holiday for the last 1400 years. You go to parks or waterfronts with colorful lighted lanterns in many shapes, like rabbits, airplanes and cars. Moon cakes, an important part of the festival, originated in the Yuan dynasty when the enemies of the ruling Mongols passed messages to each other, baked in the cakes. As a result, the Ming dynasty overthrew the Mongols. Moon cakes are small, rich, light brown square pastries and the best have many egg yolks to symbolize the moon. You will see stores and restaurants full of these cakes.

Festival of the Hungry Ghosts

The **Festival of the Hungry Ghosts** is for spirits with no one to worship them and thus condemned to a homeless, peaceless existence. The living burn joss or incense sticks outside buildings and beside curbs, hoping to end their misery and keeping them from doing mischief.

Chinese New Year

The most important festival is **Chinese New Year**. It is the only time everything is closed for three or four days for family reunions and celebrations. It is not really a time to visit Hong Kong except to be with family. New Year's is an occasion for paying off debts, wearing new clothes and starting over with a clean slate. On the first few days, people give lucky money called lai see in red envelopes (obtained free from the banks). Married people give to unmarried ones, employers give to staff, superiors to inferiors, and everyone gives to children. Lai see is usually paper money (so they can't tell the amount). If you want, you can join in the fun by giving to the children of friends and to hotel staff serving you.

Traditions have developed. On Day 1, everyone is nice and pleasant, a day for family reunions; on Day 2, everybody goes visiting; on Day 3, people are so tired of being nice that they tend to quarrel. Day 7 is everybody's birthday and all Chinese babies are one year older than they would be elsewhere. Day 15, like Day 1, is supposed to be meatless. It marks the end of the New Year celebrations with the lantern festival, a festival for lovers.

Chinese New Year's is the time to spend money on presents and parties. Almost everywhere, local people put up red signs with calligraphy wishing all kinds of good luck and even "travel safe and sound." They buy trees with tiny gold oranges as a wish for wealth. Colorful lights and displays decorate large buildings throughout the city. People usually visit temples to pray for success and health in the New Year. They tie a wish onto a tree and consult fortune sticks. Most people avoid cleaning their homes on New Year's day, so they won't sweep away the good luck. A few traditions that are disappearing are the annual report on the family's activities to the Kitchen God and children kow towing to their elders.

During the New Year holiday, people eat a lot, especially food with wishful names. There's a cake with a name that sounds like "high" and eating it is a wish that you will go higher and be successful. Dried oysters *ho si*, sounds like "good business." *Fat choy*, the black hair-like moss, is another favorite because the words sound like prosperity in business. People usually wish each other *Kung Hai Fat Choy*. A classier new year wish is *Ho Sun Hay*. *Sun Nien Fai Lok* is a wish for new year's happiness.

Firecrackers are a traditional part of the new year's celebrations, because the word *nien* means year and also sounds like "wild beast" which frightens away the good luck. Firecrackers scare away the beasts. They are banned however. People might explode firecrackers in isolated places of the New Territories and islands where the policemen are deaf. They are legal in Macau.

Corporations organize spectacular communal fireworks on the second night. These blossom noisily in the harbor from three barges as the water becomes a stage and the buildings and mountains above it a huge outdoor amphitheatre. Fireworks start promptly at the announced time. In past years, it's been 8pm. Find a good spot on the waterfront early. People book restaurants with good views a year in advance.

BELIEFS

Hong Kong's Chinese customs came of course from China, and some of these have developed differently from the motherland. Religion, ancestor worship and other beliefs were squashed when China became communist in 1949. Hong Kong developed in other directions. Along with Singapore, its obsession with *fung shui* is almost unique, and it's now exporting the practice back to China, and to other parts of the world where Hong Kongers have migrated.

You won't find the same obsession with **magic numbers** in China. It's only recent that the lucky number "8" has been showing up in vast quantities in telephone books there. Hong Kong has wish plates instead of vanity plates for its cars. In 1994, businessman Albert Yeung broke a world record for the most expensive. He paid $13 million for a "9" because in Cantonese it sounds like "longevity," "happiness" and "dog." 1994 was the year of the dog. Kung fu actor Jackie Chan bid $10 million. The money goes to charity. In 1993, someone bought the second most expensive plate a number "2" for $9.5 million. "2" sounds like the word for easy.

Fung Shui

This is **geomancy**, the placing of graves, dwellings, doors and furniture in harmony with natural forces and is related to Taoism. *Fung Shui* is more an art or a pseudo-science than a religion and in some cases makes practical sense. It is so pervasive in Hong Kong that many resident foreigners also consult geomancers to better their lot in life. *Fung* means wind and *shui* means water. *Fung shui* symbolizes the elements of nature.

Good luck comes from dragons who live in mountains, and it is best to site a structure or village with its back to mountains. If you don't have mountains, you plant trees for the dragons to live in.

It is also preferable for a structure to face south, but this is not always necessary if there are other factors. As spirits only travel in straight lines, windows and doors should not be in line with each other as the good luck will go in one side of a building and out the other. Buildings must not interfere with the flow of chi, the cosmic breath which brings harmony.

It is also preferable for a structure to be surrounded on three sides by running water, and if it isn't, the geomancer may suggest a fountain in front. He might tell you that a door should be hinged in another direction or to get a tank of gold fish with a black one to absorb the bad luck.

There are a lot of *fung shui* rules and believers spend millions of dollars readjusting buildings and offices. Bad is the building at the end of a cul de sac, the end of a funnel receiving all the bad spirits. Pacific Place has the most expensively-preserved tree in the world; it was built around a sacred tree. The new Bank of China is believed to be unlucky because it has sharp angles like a razor, a no-no. One of the angles points threateningly at government house. Symbolic, no? The two radio antennae on the bank's roof look to local people like joss sticks over a grave stone. Banks especially have spent millions of dollars to avoid bad fung shui. But the communists don't believe in such things, and stand defiantly.

Undesirable also is an entrance directly into a building. We heard a story recently of a very well-known banker who died 20 years ago. He ignored advice while renovating his house and built the staircase directly into his bedroom. He was 39 years old and robust. Six months after the remodelling, he died.

Fortune Telling

The Chinese have several methods of fortune telling. One is by studying the shape of the head and face, or face reading. There is also palm reading and astrology. Sometimes a live bird will pick out a piece of paper with your future on it. All of these are in places like Temple Street Night Market (Yau Ma Tei), Wong Tai Sin Temple (New Kowloon) and Middle Kingdom in Aberdeen.

You will find fortune sticks in temples. Take the cylinder of sticks called the chim, and shake it gently up and down. One stick will edge its way higher than the others and might even fall out. This is your fortune. Take the stick to a monk or priest who will give you a piece of paper which corresponds with the number on the stick. You will need someone to translate it.

Medicine

Don't worry. Hong Kong has both western hospitals and traditional Chinese medical practices. A herbal medicine "doctor" can tell you what is wrong just by feeling your pulse. He prescribes combinations of herbs which you might have to boil for six or seven hours, a difficult job if you're in a hotel. Dr. F.K. Lau, who speaks some English has been helpful to an American friend of ours where western medicine has failed her. He's at

88 Commercial Bldg., 28-34 Wing Lok St.C., 544-1872. 10am-12:30pm and 1:30-7pm. Mon-Sat. $60.

There is an incredible variety of Chinese aphrodisiacs which tend to resemble penises. If a man wants to improve his love life, he should try crushed deer antler, narwhal tusks, dried sea horses, geo duck clams and snakes.

Zodiac

The Chinese believe in a 60-year cycle with 12 animal years and five elements (wood, fire, earth, metal and water). Anyone who has lived 60 years has experienced everything in life and is therefore "venerable" or wise. Each year has 365 or 366 days, and is characterized by an animal and an element.

For example, 1994 is the **Year of the Dog**, a bad time for attacking the enemy because resistance will be strong and well guarded by the dog (of course). You should review your own defense system and avoid risky ventures. The dog symbolizes inner strength and fortitude, so it's a good year for health and marriages.

You might want to buy a symbol of the year as a souvenir for a friend.

WHAT KIND OF ANIMAL ARE YOU?	
Rat:	1912, 1924, 1936, 1948, 1960, 1972, 1984
Ox:	1913, 1925, 1937, 1949, 1961, 1973, 1985
Tiger:	1914, 1926, 1938, 1950, 1962, 1974, 1986
Rabbit:	1915, 1927, 1939, 1951, 1963, 1975, 1987
Dragon:	1916, 1928, 1940, 1952, 1964, 1976, 1988
Snake:	1917, 1929, 1941, 1953, 1965, 1977, 1989
Horse:	1918, 1930, 1942, 1954, 1966, 1978, 1990
Sheep:	1919, 1931, 1943, 1955, 1967, 1979, 1991
Monkey:	1920, 1932, 1944, 1956, 1968, 1980, 1992
Rooster:	1921, 1933, 1945, 1957, 1969, 1981, 1993
Dog:	1922, 1934, 1946, 1958, 1970, 1982, 1994
Boar:	1923, 1935, 1947, 1959, 1971, 1983, 1995

Weddings and Funerals

You are lucky to be invited to a wedding, especially if the family is trying to show off its wealth and laying on a great banquet. One should take a gift of money to the couple, at least the price of the meal. If you are single, give a minimum of $300. A couple could give $500. Never give $400, as 4 is an unlucky number.

The host family usually invites guests for 5pm but don't go until 8pm, unless you want to play mahjong, cards, or karaoke (the electronic singsong). First dishes probably won't appear until 9:15pm or so. Drink what's at the table and don't order anything else. You don't need to propose toasts unless you know the couple well. Wedding banquets frequently have 12 courses and dessert so don't gorge on the first few.

White is the color of mourning, red the color of happiness. You must certainly not wear red to a funeral. Traditional brides still wear red, but many now wear white, western wedding gowns. You might see a genuine traditional funeral with lots of rituals on Cheung Chau Island near the ferry in the late afternoon or in temples in the New Territories. Survivors burn hell bank notes of humongous denominations, and paper houses, cars, servants, etc. to help the dead in the afterlife.

TRIADS

The Chinese **mafia**, *or* **triads**, *is a group of several, different, independent and usually competitive organizations. Some are more like street gangs, while larger ones have branches all over the world. They started out as secret societies at least 2000 years ago and have been involved with political rebellion throughout China's history. They operated underground against the Japanese occupation. Today, they are organized crime. Each group has its unique initiation ceremonies, tattoos, blood-letting rituals and laws.*

In some areas, triad loan sharks prey on gamblers and collect "protection" money from businesses. They control some of the prostitution and illegal immigration and are usually behind jewelry-store robberies, contract murders and other crimes. The only possible danger to you is being caught in the cross-fire of the rare armed robbery of a gold store. However, we haven't heard of a tourist getting hurt that way. It is illegal to be a triad member. Look for the Triad Gallery in the Police Museum.

GOVERNMENT

Hong Kong is a colony of Britain. It is administered locally by the Hong Kong Government, under a governor, representing the queen. It has a **Legislative Council** (**LEGCO**) with 30% elected membership, an Urban Council with 38%, and a Regional Council with 33% elected membership. All other policy-makers are appointed. Britain is responsible for Hong Kong's foreign affairs and security. Although Hong Kong people have never really had much say in the government, this has never bothered most of them. They feel that the government's job is to keep things running smoothly, so that the populace can make money.

The government is the biggest land owner and makes most of its income from land leases. It also benefits from taxes on income, profit, rents, hotels and restaurants, the lottery and horseracing.

THE ECONOMY

Hong Kong is the most purely capitalistic place in the world and one of the most successful. The government rarely interferes with business or the economy, there are few import duties and no sales tax, and the maximum income tax is only 15%. In 1992, Hong Kong boasted an unemployment rate of 2-3% and a HK$2 billion surplus!

It thrives because of the incredibly, hard-working Chinese people. Many work six days a week or more on one or several jobs. Other contributing factors are the stability and the efficiency of the British administration, and as from the beginning, the China trade. Hong Kong and China are each other's biggest trading partners and Hong Kong ships about 70% of China's exports.

Hong Kong is among the world's largest exporters of clothing, watches, radios and toys. It is also strong in manufacturing textiles, jewelry, plastics, electronics, electrical appliances and clocks. It has a large movie industry and is a printing and publishing center. Linda once received a postcard from the Grand Canyon that was printed in Hong Kong! Tourism is its second biggest foreign exchange earner.

To service its business in trade, Hong Kong is a world center of banking, communications, storage, insurance, shipping and transportation. It has the busiest container port in the world. Office rents in Central are the highest in the world. One of its most lucrative crops is skyscrapers, which thrive on rock and hillsides. They are built with the aid of bamboo scaffolding, tied together with plastic string! Hong Kong's high land values are the result of real estate speculators and a shortage of commercial land in a booming economy.

The race continues between Shanghai and Hong Kong to be China's main port. Shanghai expects to beat Hong Kong in the next century. Shall we take bets now?

5. PLANNING YOUR TRIP

CLIMATE

Hong Kong is subtropical. It never gets below freezing and you can swim in the ocean until November – if you're adventurous. The best time is cool, sunny October and November, with an average temperature of 22.6°C (73°F) and low humidity. December-January is cooler but sunny with an average temperature of 16°C (61°F). January is the coldest, driest month.

February to May isn't bad if you don't mind clouds and warm rain. March to May has 80% humidity. Avoid June to September, especially July and August, when the heat and humidity are oppressive. If you have to go, it's not all that bad, because most places have air-conditioning. The tourist season is October-January.

GETTING TO HONG KONG

Almost everyone goes by air. Book as early as possible. Hong Kong is the hub of Asia's airline network. Its airport facilities are currently pushed to overcapacity and the congestion will not be relieved until its new airport is open after mid-1997. However, with the opening of the Macau airport in mid-1995, you will be able to fly to Macau, which is otherwise one hour by ferry from Hong Kong.

By Air

You should choose your airlines according to their safety record, routing, price, smoking and service. There are lots of choices. Ruth liked Canadian Airlines because of the direct flight (with a change in Vancouver) and baggage checking between Toronto and Hong Kong. It had three movies, no smoking, clean bathrooms and quick, cheerful service.

Linda liked Korean Airlines because it was the cheapest and she could smoke. She did have to spend the night in Seoul because of bad weather in Chicago, but at KAL's expense. Ruth has also flown Korean. Her total travel time was 22 hours westward from Toronto and 24 hours eastward from Hong Kong including stops. Ugh!

You should feel confident with Cathay Pacific because it's Hong Kong's airline and the pilots are the most experienced with the narrow Hong Kong runway. Service is good and its frequent flier points can be combined with other airlines and some hotels. Its subsidiary Dragonair flies from other parts of Asia. Britain's Virgin Atlantic Airways has a beautician in its top class giving facials and aromatherapy on its London-Hong Kong flights, a great way to pass the time.

Get a window seat away from the wing to see the view because landing in Hong Kong is an amazing experience. Get an aisle seat if you have to get up frequently or want to see the movies better. Flights from Europe and North America are long. Ask for a seat with more leg room if necessary. In the air, do get up to stretch and exercise from time to time. Drink lots of non-alcoholic beverages and go easy on the food to minimize jet lag.

By Cruise Ship

Stops are usually less than two days, which will give you a taste of Hong Kong. Passenger ships dock at **Ocean Terminal** in Tsim Sha Tsui, a huge shopping mall where the first store you'll see is Toys R Us! This is close to two top hotels (Peninsula and Regent) with upmarket shopping malls and great restaurants. You can easily take tours and hop across the harbor on the Star Ferry to Central. Cruise lines that stop in Hong Kong include **Crystal Cruises, Cunard, Holland American Lines, Pearl Cruises, Princess Cruises** and **Royal Cruise Lines**.

By Land or Water From China

See China in Chapter 15, "Excursions and Day Trips."

Flying to Other Countries from Hong Kong

You can get slightly cheaper airfares to other Asian countries like Thailand and the Philippines in Hong Kong. It is probably cheaper to book a China tour before you leave North America. See Chapter 15.

TRAVEL AGENTS & OTHER ARRANGEMENTS

If you are planning on staying in moderate to expensive hotels, travel agents can sometimes get bookings for you more cheaply. They make their money from commissions and get discounts for frequent bookings. They don't charge you for their services.

To save time and money, we suggest a mini-package of flights, transfers, hotels, some tours and a few meals. Ask your agent about hotel quality and taxes. Is this a group or individual tour? Will you have an escort? Hong Kong is easy to get around and you can join a city tour once there.

Travel agents can also help you with insurances, arrangements to other places and changes in flight schedules. They might also link you up with a fellow traveler to share hotel costs.

Most travel agents can get you a passport and if needed, visas. On the other hand, Linda booked her own flight through an agent and stayed mainly in rooms with private baths in Chung King Mansions which she booked herself. This is the cheapest possible arrangement except for staying with friends. Travel agents cannot book most budget hotels and guest houses.

Travel Agents Who Have Hong Kong Packages

Abercrombie and Kent books packages with the Mandarin Oriental Hotel. *1520 Kensington Rd., Oak Brook, Ill., 60521-2141. (800)323-7308, (708)954-2944. Fax (708)954-3324.*

Avia Travel can book packages and hotel rooms for a minimum of two nights and is usually the cheapest around. *Contact Sue Lai, Manager, Avia Travel, 5429 Geary Blvd., San Francisco, CA 94121. (415)668-0964 or (800)950-2842. Fax (415)386-8519.*

China Travel Service has a Hong Kong-Beijing package from Vancouver. *556 West Broadway, Vancouver, B.C. V5Z 1E9, Canada. (604)872-8787 or (800)663-1126. Fax (604)873-2823.*

Goway Travel in Toronto has a five-night package that includes rooms, some meals, sightseeing and transfers and uses the Wharney and the New World Hotels. *2300 Yonge St., Toronto, Ont., M4P 1E4, Canada. (416)322-1032. Fax (416)322-1109.*

IPI InterPacific Tours International has a Hong Kong CitiPak for four days and three nights for only hotels (no tours) like Regent, Mandarin, the Omnis, Prudential and Majestic. It combines its Hong Kong tours with cities in China. *111 East 15th St. at Park Avenue South, New York, NY 10003. (212)953-6010, (800)221-3594. Fax (212)953-0350.*

Japan and Orient Tours, Inc. uses the New World Hotel and the New World Harbour View. *3131 Camino del Rio North, Suite 1080, San Diego, CA 92108-5789. (619)282-3131; fax (619)283-3131.*

Orient Flexi-Pak Tours has Hong Kong packages or tours combining Hong Kong with China, southeast Asia or Korea. It uses the Omni Hong Kong and New World Hotel but can book you into a long list of hotels usually for less than the published rate here. It depends on the season. *630 Third Avenue, New York, NY 10017. (800)545-5540 or (212)692-9550. Fax (212)661-1618.*

Pacific Delight Tours Inc. uses United Airlines and the JW Marriott, Nikko, Hyatt Regency and New World Hotels. *132 Madison Avenue, New York, N.Y. 10016. (212)684-7707 or (800)221-7179 (except N.Y. state). Fax (212)532-3406.*

Swan Travel in Vancouver flies to Hong Kong via Taipei and uses the Newton Kowloon Hotel. *Park Square, 107-5701 Granville St., Vancouver, B.C., V6M 4J7. (604)266-3300 or (800)663-2111. Fax (604)266-8867).*

Tour East flies clients twice a week by Korean Airlines from Toronto on a 7-day, 6-night Hong Kong land package with the Kimberley Hotel (or equivalent). It also has Beijing-Hong Kong and Singapore-Hong Kong packages. *ContactTour East Holidays, 1033 Bay Street, Suite 302, Toronto, M5S 3A5. (416)292-8855 or (800)263-2808. Fax (416)292-9877.*

HEALTH INSURANCE

This is your choice. See Health Concerns in Chapter 6, "Basic Information," for the price of doctors and hospitals in Hong Kong. Health-care quality is good and except in unlikely emergencies, we don't see any need for evacuation insurance.

FORMALITIES AND VISAS

Citizens of the United States and 20 other countries can enter Hong Kong without a visa and stay for one month. Citizens of Canada, Australia and other Commonwealth countries don't need a visa and can stay three months. British passport holders can stay 12 months. Extensions are only granted in special cases such as employment or injury. If you haven't got a passport valid for your trip, get one. You need one to enter Hong Kong. Give yourself plenty of time to get a copy of your birth certificate, photos, etc. Passports might take three or four weeks to obtain.

You don't need any shots or malaria pills but the British consulate recommends polio and typhoid shots. And you should have your tetanus up to date.

HONG KONG CUSTOMS

You can take in free of duty 200 cigarettes, 50 cigars or 250 grams of tobacco, one liter of wine or liquor, and 60 milliliters of perfume. Prohibited are firearms (which Hong Kong Customs can store for you until you depart) and parts of, or whole specimens of, endangered species (which will be seized). By the way, cigarettes cost about US$3 a pack in Hong Kong. Liquor is also more expensive than in North America.

CUSTOMS IN YOUR OWN COUNTRY

Get a booklet with customs regulations. Phone the U.S. Customs Service or Canada Customs. It will tell you what you cannot bring back into your own country. If you are taking expensive jewelry or a new-looking camera, register it with customs before you go. You don't want to pay duty on it when you bring it back. Products made from endangered species such as leopard, tiger, crocodile, alligator or elephant ivory are not allowed into Canada or the U.S. and will be seized.

It is easier to get information before you leave. You could save a lot of money knowing different customs rates. Diplomatic missions abroad do not always have the latest information.

US Customs

US citizens are allowed a duty-free exemption of $400 on accompanied baggage every 30 days if you are out of the country for over 48 hours. You must pay 10% on the next $1000 worth of goods, even though items like uncut gems are normally dutiable at 2.3%. The allowance includes a maximum of 200 cigarettes (one carton) and one liter (33.8 fl.oz.) of alcoholic beverage. You can mail gifts worth US$50 or less, but the receiver cannot accept more than one duty-free parcel in one day.

Canadian Customs

Canada has a duty-free personal exemption on CDN$100 worth of goods after 48 or more hours absence, and a duty-free exemption once a year, after seven days' absence of CDN$300. On the next $300, you pay approximately 15%. The $100 and $300 exemptions must be claimed on separate trips. The allowances are supposed to include all goods acquired while away including gifts. You may send duty-free gifts from abroad to friends or relatives in Canada, each gift valued at no more than CDN$60. Each should have a gift card or be gift wrapped, said Revenue Canada. These must not be alcoholic beverages, tobacco, or advertising matter.

If you exceed your import limits, try to group the items according to the rate of duty. For example, Canada only charges 7% tax on books, and no tax on signed one-of-a-kind works of art and antiques over 100 years. Use your exemption for the other things, and declare the books, art objects and antiques.

Enforcement of all regulations is at the whim of customs officers. However, if you do not declare your acquisitions honestly, you risk a fine and confiscation.

RESERVING A ROOM IN ADVANCE

We highly recommend that you reserve a room ahead of time. Hotel occupancy rates average about 90% and you don't want to be looking for a hotel room after a 20-hour plane ride! Most of the chain hotels in our listings have toll-free 1-800-numbers. You can also call or fax them directly.

Ask about clubs you can join for discounts and upgrades. Chains like the Holiday Inn have them.

HOTEL CHAINS, RESERVATION AGENCIES, & 1-800 NUMBERS

Holiday Inns: 1-800-HOLIDAY
Hyatt International Corp: 1-800-233-1234
Leading Hotels of the World: 1-800-223-6800
New World Hotels International: 1-800-227-5663 or
    1-800-44UTELL
Nikko: 1-800-645-5687
Omni: 1-800-THE OMNI
Orient Hotel Reservations: Sino-American Tours, 1-800-221-7982
Preferred Hotels: 1-800-323-7500
Ramada Worldwide Reservations: 1-800-854-7854, 1-800-228-9898
Regal: 1-800-222-8888; 1-800-233-9188
Shangri-La International: 1-800-942-5050
Sheraton International: 1-800-325-3535
Steigenberger: 1-800-223-5652
Utell: 1-800-44UTELL.

SAVING MONEY

This takes time and price comparisons. Three months before you go, search the advertisements in travel sections of newspapers, ask your travel agent, airlines like Cathay Pacific and Canadian Airlines, the American Automobile Association or the agents above for the cheapest flights and tour packages. Check with your state or provincial tourist offices to determine the legitimacy of obscure agents. Phone hotels with 1-800-toll-free numbers in North America about special rates and packages.

Some hotels have packages with the fourth night free or include breakfast and perks from December to the end of February. In trying to keep prices down, tour packages from travel agents may use lesser-known hotels that may be just adequate. Look up our assessment, and if it's not what you want, ask your agent for something better. Travel agents specializing in the Far East should be able to book cheaper group-fare prices on flights and maybe cheaper hotel packages. Look for them in Chinatowns and Korean communities.

Keep your eyes and ears open for news about Hong Kong and China. Prices will go down if there is another disaster (heaven forbid) like Tiananmen Square. Go to Hong Kong as soon as possible because the inflation rate is about 10% a year and hotel prices have been known to double.

Get an AT&T, Bell Canada or any telephone calling card if you plan to make many long long-distance calls. For **AT&T**, *call 1-800-327-9012.* For **MCI**, *call 1-800-476-SAVE.* For Canada, call your local telephone company. These should make calls cheaper than from your hotel but are more expensive than going to the Telecom office.

If you're staying longer than four days, ask the Hong Kong tourist office in North America if *Hong Kong a la Carte* is still available. This free booklet has coupons for mainly 10% discounts at some stores and restaurants.

WHAT TO PACK

Check first with your airline about your suitcases: the number, dimensions and weight of your free baggage allowance. Trans-Pacific for economy class, it is usually two bags with a maximum 30 kg. (66.6 lbs.) each bag, but airlines differ. A carry-on bag also has limits. Consider other flights. From Hong Kong to China, the limit is sometimes 20 kg. total.

For leisure visitors, take what you feel comfortable in, preferably natural or mixed fabrics, because of the humidity. If you're going in hot weather, bring a light sweater for the cold air-conditioning. If you're going on business, take a suit. Business people dress up all year round, even in the hot, sticky summer. Take good walking shoes. Take your bathing suit if your hotel has a pool or you want to brave the beaches. The nice thing about Hong Kong is its abundance of relatively cheap clothing for sale.

For fancy restaurants and expensive discos, there are dress codes ranging from jackets and ties to "smart casual." Most will reject flip flops, sleeveless or collarless shirts, shorts on men, or ripped clothing. In a few places, jeans and sneakers are forbidden.

Take credit cards: **Visa**, **American Express**, and **MasterCard** are accepted most places, **Diners** in some. You can use your Visa bank card to get cash in a money machine in Hong Kong. This can be cheaper than sending money through Western Union. Ask your bank about the fee for use. See Money in Chapter 6.

Most hotels have reliable wake-up calls, can lend you hairdryers and give out free shampoo. Hong Kong has lots of cheap umbrellas for rain and they make good souvenirs. Take what you need like sun screen, cosmetics, toiletries and prescription medicines. Hong Kong has just about everything for sale but prices can be higher than at home. And why waste time looking, when you should be out having fun?

Make sure you label your suitcase with your name and telephone number inside and out. And if you expect to do a lot of shopping, take an extra suitcase or buy one there. For addressing postcards, you can print your address list on labels so you can just stick them on. Take the fax or telephone numbers of people you want to contact. If you expect to be entertained by friends, take gifts from home: maple candy, perfume, baseball caps, the spices for fried, green tomatoes, or a Mexican taco kit. This assumes that you will cook it too.

QUICK CHECKLIST

- *passport*
- *plane ticket (or other transportation tickets)*
- *hotel room reserved in Hong Kong at least for the first night*
- **Hong Kong and Macau Guide**
- *money*
- *packed suitcase*
- *health insurance if you want*
- *If you're on business: business cards*
- *If you're a shopper: list of North American prices of what you want to buy, to compare.*

ARRIVING IN HONG KONG

This is one of the most spectacular landings in the world. The plane skims between apartment blocks and alights on a narrow runway that sticks out into the water. If a plane overshoots, it lands in the harbor, but few do. Exciting, no? Flights land or take off every two minutes in this, the world's fourth busiest airport, open only from 6am to midnight.

A bus may take you from your plane to the airport. Your flight crew should have passed out arrival forms on the plane. If not, look for them before you line up for immigration. The immigration officer will give you back a copy for your **Departure Card**. Keep this. You'll need it when you leave but don't worry if you lose it. Your next stop is baggage retrieval. Lots of free luggage carts are available and you can make free local telephone calls.

After customs, go to the **Buffer Hall** where the Hong Kong and Macau tourist associations have information desks with free useful publications and advice. If you need a hotel room, talk with the hotel representatives in the Buffer Hall and compare prices. Change only enough money to get you to your hotel. The airport rates are terrible. If your reservation includes an airport transfer, leave the Buffer Hall through the Hotel Transport exit. Another door leads outside to the waiting crowds and to a taxi and bus stand. The airport is 20 minutes from Tsim Sha Tsui and 40 minutes from Hong Kong Island, depending on traffic.

If you don't want to go downtown, the Regal Airport Hotel is connected by a ramp with the airport. Staff are usually available on the airport side to help put baggage on a moving conveyor belt. There is very expensive baggage storage in the airport departure hall. You can stay in the airport, but not overnight. It has some gift shops, restaurants, fast food places, and postal and telecommunications services.

GETTING TO TOWN

Taxi prices are listed on a board and all taxis have meters. Air-conditioned "Airbuses" are the cheapest way to leave the airport. They run every 15-20 minutes from 7am-11:30pm. You'll need exact Hong Kong change.

There are four airbuses: **A1**-Tsim Tsa Tsui, $9, stops at 23 major hotels; **A2**-Central and Wanchai, $14, 17 major hotels ending at the Macau Ferry Pier; **A3**-circular route to Causeway Bay $14, 3 hotels; **A5**-circular route to Tai Koo Shing $14, 4 hotels. *For more information call the hotline, 745-4466.*

LEAVING HONG KONG

If you are flying out on Cathay Pacific, you can use its downtown check-in service on Level 4 of Pacific Place. If you're leaving early in the morning, you might want to stay overnight at the Airport Regal Hotel, which has airport information in its rooms and monitors in its lobby.

Some airlines start check-in three hours ahead. It is a good idea to ask for the check-in time and get there early. Many airlines overbook their seats in high season and there might not be room for you until a later flight. There are lots of free luggage carts. You pay a $50 airport tax to your airline on checking in.

After check-in, you are almost forced to go to a restaurant or directly into the transit lounge. The airport has a few stores but no other place to sit and wait. You have to complete a departure card. If you've lost yours, you can get another after Security. There are no restrictions on the export of products and currency.

The **Transit Lounge** has a snack bar, duty-free stores, money exchange, toilets and telephones. In the pre-boarding areas, there are toilets, but no food, no telephones and theoretically no smoking. You may go by bus to your plane.

Warning: Check-in counters are closed 40 minutes before takeoff. Gates are closed 10 minutes before boarding time.

You should **reconfirm** your return flight at least 72 hours ahead of time and give your contact telephone number to the airline. It could cancel your reservation if you don't.

AVOIDING PROBLEMS

Inform people at home how you can be reached. If you don't know your hotel, you can tell them to write you at **Post Restante**, *GPO, Hong Kong*. This is the equivalent of General Delivery. In Hong Kong, pick up your mail at the General Post Office beside the Star Ferry in Central. You can also have mail delivered at American Express. Check with its offices in the U.S. for the exact Hong Kong address.

In case of extreme emergency, they can try to reach you through your consulate in Hong Kong. See "Basic Information".

In case of loss, leave one copy at home with friends and take a photocopy of the front pages of your passport (the pages with your photo and passport number), your travelers checks receipts, a birth certificate or other proof of citizenship, and credit cards. You will need these in case you lose your passport, travelers checks and credit cards. Get the toll-free telephone number of your credit card bank in case of loss. Take extra passport photos.

If you need more money after you leave home and don't have a credit card, it takes five working days for your bank to get money to you. Your bank will need your passport number.

When traveling, keep your valuables in separate places like one credit card and part of your travelers checks in your money belt and one credit card and the rest of your travelers checks in your neck safe. If you lose one, you can pay with the other.

TRY THE LOCAL LANGUAGE: CANTONESE

Learn some Cantonese as a goodwill gesture. It might save you some money and make you some friends. However, you can get around in English. You might want to learn Mahjong too. It is a good way to make friends.

BACKGROUND BOOKS

You can get more out of a place when you read about it before you go or while you're there. Here is a list of some good books on Hong Kong. See also our bibliography.

*means currently available in Hong Kong.

Nonfiction

Our favorite is the fun and fascinating *Myself a Mandarin** by Austin Coates, an all-powerful judge in the New Territories in the 1950s, with no knowledge of law! *I Sailed With Chinese Pirates** by Aleko E. Lilius is a journalist's first-hand account of time spent in a Hong Kong jail and adventures with both male and female pirates in Macau and Canton in the 1920s.

Jackie Pullinger, an incredible woman who successfully heals drug addicts through prayer, writes about her experiences in the notorious and now vanished walled city in *Chasing the Dragon** and *A Crack in the Wall**. *The Rise of the Refugee God** by Graeme Lang and Lars Ragvald is about the Hong Kong deity and temple Wong Tai Sin.

The book on Hong Kong history is the dry *A History of Hong Kong* by G.B. Endacott, which gets bogged down in statistics. Jan Morris' *Hong*

Kong: An Epilogue to An Empire* is better. Other interesting histories are *The Private Life of Old Hong Kong: Western Women in the British Colony 1841-1941** by Susanna Hoe and *The Taipans: Hong Kong's Merchant Princes** by Colin Crisswell, a good book on the history of Hong Kong through the lives of the wealthy traders that shaped its development. *City on the Rocks: Hong Kong's Uncertain Future* by Kevin Rafferty is also good.

Fiction

Unfortunately, there is not much good modern fiction around. *The World of Suzie Wong* (1957) by Richard Mason is the most famous, about a Chinese prostitute with a heart of gold and the man who loved her. This is also a 1960 movie.

Tai Pan by James Clavell is a favorite. It is a romantic epic of a trader, his mistress, his sons and his rivals during the birth of Hong Kong in the early 1800s. Clavell also wrote *Noble House*, which we don't like. It is a cruder story of big business and spies (FBI, CIA, KGB, SI, etc.) set in the 1960s. Both are easy reading.

Dynasty by Robert Elegant is half fiction and half the history of Hong Kong, China and World War II. *The Honorable School Boy* by John Le Carre is an excellent spy novel set in Hong Kong and Britain. *Love is a Many-Splendoured Thing** by Han Suyin is still a classic, set in the 1950s. You can still hear the title song from the movie in Hong Kong.

THE BUSINESS TRAVELER
The Hong Kong Businessman

Hong Kong was built on the sweat of people who arrived to better themselves and to escape wars and political upheavals. Many lost everything with the takeover of China by the Communists. They don't want to lose a second time.

How are they different from business people elsewhere? They are tough but ethical, financially driven, straight forward, very astute and refreshing. They are more relationship-oriented; you need to build friendship and trust before you can proceed very far and contacts are important. For this reason, it is best to have an introduction, to accept invitations to banquets and to host banquets yourself. Much business is still done with a handshake.

Foreign business people in Hong Kong are also saying: "In China, the rules keep changing. In Hong Kong, decisions are fast and efficient." "Hong Kong people are out to make as much money as possible; North Americans are out to cheat their governments." "Decisions are made at the top. They are quick. Families own companies." "They don't give you all the information you need. There's lots of secrecy."

Preparation for Your Trip

You must take **business cards**, if possible in English and Chinese. Most big North American Chinatowns have print shops or you can have them printed in Hong Kong. Business cards are given and received with both hands, thumbs up. When you receive one, read it carefully and respectfully.

Forget your cards? Contact **Business Cards and Photocopies Lofty Virtue Publication Centre** *(46 Queen's Rd. E., Wanchai, Hong Kong Island. 527-7877/527-7577).* They cost $240 for the first 300 and $40 per 100 after that. It takes one week. They also do photocopies for $.50. Letter-size photocopies are slightly longer and thinner than those in North America.

Hong Kong has many opportunities for hard-working people with initiative and ideas. Most people work five and a half days a week or more.

Learn as much as you can about the person you're trying to impress and take a gift of something personal and novel, like the new kind of golf ball. Other corporate gifts: a new book about your company or a picture book about your country, a fancy briefcase or an unusual pen. Be aware that some Hong Kong business people are very rich and probably have the latest in electronic gadgets already. They don't have much leisure time. The most prestigeous bottled gift you can give is Remy Martin's Louis 13. Second is Remy Martin XO Special, and third is Hennessy Cognac.

Helpful Sources of Information

The **American Chamber of Commerce** has recently published or updated their books: *Establishing an Office in Hong Kong, Doing Business in Today's Hong Kong,* and *Living in Hong Kong.* The chamber is located at: *10/F, 1030 Swire House, 7 Chater Rd. Central. Mail: GPO Box 355, Hong Kong. 526-0165; fax 810-1289.*

The **Hong Kong Trade Development Council** promotes Hong Kong products overseas through its 43 offices around the world, a trade enquiry service. It has a computerized database of more than 60,000 Hong Kong companies and 100,000 mainland China contacts. It is a quasi-government organization. *Address: 38-39\F, Convention Plaza, 1 Harbour Rd, Wanchai. 833-4333; fax 824-0249.*

The **Hong Kong Exporters' Association**, *Rm. 825, Star House, 3 Salisbury Rd, Tsim Sha Tsui. 730-9851; fax 730-1869.*

Canadian Chamber of Commerce, *13/F, One Exchange Square, Connaught Place, Central. 526-3207; fax 845-1654.*

MAKING FRIENDS

We feel a few days in Hong Kong isn't enough. We love the place and part of loving it is knowing the people. So how do you meet the locals? By showing an interest, asking lots of questions and requesting introductions to other people. Find people who share your interests, be they English-speaking or Cantonese or Filipino. Go to church, or join the group of **Morris Dancers** for an evening if that's your thing. *(For the Morris Dancers, contact Judith Hassey Squire, A130 Cape Rd., Chung Hom Kok. Home telephone and fax 813-9614. Work 574-8240.)*

The **Hong Kong Convention and Incentive Travel Bureau** has a list of Associations & Societies in Hong Kong with addresses and telephone numbers. It is available from the Hong Kong Tourist Association (HKTA). It includes the Society for the Prevention of Cruelty to Animals, amateur astronomers, backgammon freaks, hot air balloonists, bird-watchers, Robbie Burns fans, classic cars, Chinese chess and the Confucian Academy. And we've only skimmed from A to C.

Offer to volunteer at a church, synagogue, temple or mosque, or with a service club like Rotary or Lions. Most agencies prefer to train volunteers who stay for longer terms than one or two days. But a few agencies can use a hand for a day or so.

Mavis Barrett of **Treats** would like volunteers to visit sick children or take underprivileged children or Vietnamese detainees on excursions. Write to her before you arrive at: *fax 898-3385 or Flat 19A, Block F, Senior Staff Quarters, Pamela Youde Nethersole Eastern Hospital, 3/F, Lok Man Rd., Chai Wan, Hong Kong. Upon arrival telephone her at 889-1332.*

Oxfam works in 11 different countries in Africa and Asia in development work. It has two tiny stores with factory bargains and second hand goods and clothes. It needs volunteers to do just about anything alongside Hong Kong volunteers. *Telephone John Torgrimson, Director, and ask if you can help. 391-6305 or fax 789-9545.* You could also write before you arrive to *Oxfam, G/F, 3B June Garden, 28 Tung Chau St., Tai Kok Tsui, Kowloon, Hong Kong. E-mail igc:oxfamhk geo2:oxfamhk.*

Phone the **American Women's Club**, *527-2961 and 527-2962 or write ahead: Monticello C-7, 48 Kennedy Rd., Hong Kong. Fax 865-7737.* Sometimes they need volunteers.

STAYING LONGER AND MORE CHEAPLY

Yes, it is possible. All you have to do is leave Hong Kong at the end of your month or whatever, spend a day or so in China or Macau, and enter again for another one or three months, depending on your passport. Legal extensions are hard to get. Call the **Immigration Department Inquiry Hotline**, *824-6111.*

Expatriate residents do look for flat-sitters when they are away, but have to know you well enough to trust you. You can stay at some hostels and hotels at cheaper monthly rates. Universities, schools, and hospitals have hostels too, which might be available during vacation periods. Your religious connection might be able to help. Network!

LIVING & WORKING IN HONG KONG

In 1994 the **South China Morning Post** published 135 pages of help-wanted advertisements on Sundays. There are lots of jobs available. It is better to get a job before coming. People hired abroad tend to get the best perks, such as housing. Companies advertise openings in newspapers and magazines around the world. Hong Kong has professional headhunters who recruit executives for multinational corporations. Hong Kong is short of people for financial, insurance, real estate and business services jobs. They are looking for management and commercial skills. In Hong Kong, look at the want ads and the free newspaper Recruit that appears in MTR stations about 5pm on Fridays and Mondays. There are more opportunities for hard working, go-getters than in North America. Linda met a 26-year-old man, who worked with a novelty company and made US$100,000 a year. He said he could never go back to North America, because he would never make as much. But the basic salary for a waiter has been $7000 a month plus tips with no tax on the first $30,000 per year.

You improve your chance of getting a job if you speak Cantonese or Mandarin, and write Chinese as well as English. However, we met a number of hotel public relations people who couldn't speak a word of Chinese. It is easy for United Kingdom passport holders to get a work permit. Others should get a three-month permit to stay while you hunt.

Accommodations are expensive. A three-bedroom apartment in comfortable Discovery Bay on Lantau Island can be over $18,000 a month and rising. Flats closer to Central and on the Peak are much more. Many foreigners live in Chai Wan, Sha Tin and islands, like Lamma, because it's cheaper. Some people commute from Shekou or Shenzhen, China to the New Territories, because living in China is cheaper.

The only American school in Hong Kong is the **International School**. It is very expensive and has long waiting lists.

6. BASIC INFORMATION

BARBERS AND HAIRDRESSERS

Barbers and Hairdressers are in many hotels. We recommend Fathima Jowarsha, 2/F of the **Mandarin Oriental Hotel** *825-4850*. Cheaper and good are **Ocean Barbers**, *2/F*, **Omni The Hong Kong Hotel**, *Ocean Terminal 730-2669*, and the **Salisbury YMCA** *369-2211*.

BOOKSTORES

Two of the biggest: the **Hong Kong Book Centre Ltd.** *(basement, On Lok Yuen Bldg, 25 Des Voeux Rd, Central. 522-7064)* and **Swindon Books** *(13-15 Lock Rd, Tsim Sha Tsui. 366-8001)*, which has an office supply store next door. The Hong Kong Book Centre also has stores in the *basement of the Landmark and in Shop 303, Exchange Square, both in Central.* There are three Swindon Books *in Harbour City and one at the Star Ferry in Tsim Sha Tsui.*

The **Government Publications Office**, *in the General Post Office building, next to Star Ferry, Central,* has the most books on Hong Kong. The most convenient store is **The South China Morning Post Book Shop** (aka **The Family Bookshop**), *Star Ferry Pier in Central (open 8am-8:30pm, Sun 10am-7pm)*.

There's a large **South China Morning Post Book Shop** *in Times Square, at Causeway Bay MTR.* The long-established **Kelly and Walsh** *is located in Pacific Place at Admiralty MTR.*

CANTONESE PHRASES

Ask someone to say these for you. Listen carefully. Cantonese has nine different tones.

• Good Morning	*Jo sun*
• Hello/how are you?	*Nay ho ma?*
• Good-bye	*Joy geen*
• Thank You	*Doh jieh* (for a gift)
• Thank You	*Um goy* (for a service)
• How much?	*Gay doh cheen?*
• Good grief!	*Aye yah*
• MTR	*Day ha dee*
• Numbers:	*(1) Yat, (2) Yee, (3) Sam, (4) Say, (5) Mm, (6) Lok, (7) Chut, (8) Bat, (9) Gow, (10) Sup, (11) Sup yat, (12) Sup yee, (20) Yee sup, (30) Sam Sup,* etc.

Many Chinese words are commonly used by westerners and English newspapers in Hong Kong such as *taipan* (big boss, usually a head of a big corporation), *tai tai* (first, head wife) and *gwailo* (foreigner or literally foreign devil).

CHILDREN

Hong Kong is a great place for kids. Chinese people love them and are fascinated with foreign ones. **Ocean Park's Water World** and the **Middle Kingdom**, both in Aberdeen, are the best amusement parks. Then there's the **Science Museum** in Tsim Sha Tsui East with over 500 hands-on exhibits. The **History Museum**, the **Space Museum**, and **Kowloon Park** are all in Tsim Sha Tsui. The **Botanical and Zoological Gardens**, **Hong Kong Park**, and the **Peak** are reached from Central and country parks are close by. They can ice or roller skate and play electronic games at **Taikoo Shing Plaza** or bicycle or horseback ride on Lantau Island. They can ride the ferries or walk along the waterfront from Tsim Sha Tsui to Tsim Sha Tsui East.

Children get all kinds of discounts on public transportation, admissions and accommodations. Those under 12 can usually stay with you free in most hotels. HKTA has a free **Hong Kong Adventureland package** for kids, with postcards and stickers.

The hotels with the most outdoor space are the Grand Hyatt and the New World Harbour View in Wanchai. However, The New World Harbour View would prefer that older children stay in a separate room, because the rooms are small. The Park Lane (Causeway Bay) is across from Victoria Park and near Toys R Us and a whole floor of electronic games in Windsor House. The Excelsior Hotel is also closeby. The Island Shangri-La, Conrad, and Marriott are near Hong Kong Park in Central. The Mandarin Oriental has a special program for children. The Grill on Sundays has a children's buffet table. The Grand Plaza Hotel is above the Taikoo Shing mall.

The YMCA and YWCA hotels and all Chinese restaurants are used to families with children. And of course, so is McDonald's. However, the Mandarin's Pierrot Restaurant is only for 12 years and up.

COMPLAINTS

Regarding shopping, restaurants and hotels, consult the **Hong Kong Tourist Association** (**HKTA**). They can only act if guilty businesses are members. You can also call the **Consumer Council Complaints and Advice Hotline**, 304-1234.

CONSULATES AND TRADE COMMISSIONS
- **Australia** *585-4133*
- **Austria** *523-7555*
- **Bangladesh** *827-4278*
- **Belgium** *524-3111*
- **Brazil** *525-7002*
- **Britain** *523-0176*
- **Canada** *810-4321*
- **Colombia** *545-8547*
- **Denmark** *827-8101*
- **Finland** *525-5385*
- **France** *529-4316*
- **Germany** *526-5481*
- **Greece** *774-1682*
- **India** *528-4475*
- **Indonesia** *890-4421*
- **Israel** *529-6091*
- **Italy** *846-6500*
- **Jamaica** *823-8216*
- **Japan** *522-1184*
- **Korea** *545-9500*
- **Malaysia** *527-0921*
- **Mexico** *521-4365*
- **New Zealand** *526-7898*
- **Philippines** *810-0183*
- **South Africa** *577-3279*

- **Spain** *521-7433*
- **Sweden** *521-1215*
- **Thailand** *521-6481*
- **US** *521-1467*

ELECTRICITY

It is 220 volts. Most hotels have adapters for shavers.

EMERGENCIES

Phone 999 for ambulance, police and fire in extreme emergencies. The police crime hotline is *527-7177*, enquiries *866-6166*. St. John's Ambulance (free), Hong Kong Island *576-6555*; Kowloon *713-5555* (For Hospitals see "Health Concerns" below). If you lose your travelers' checks, take your receipts to American Express or whatever bank, to get a refund. If you lose cash, you're out of luck. If you have no money, contact your bank at home to send you more. Western Union is quicker. If you lose your credit cards, call your bank collect immediately so it will not charge you for any purchases incurred after the loss. If you lose your passport, contact your consulate. The telephone numbers are above.

GARDENS

The **Zoological and Botanical Gardens** in Central are the best. A small, modern Chinese garden is at **Wong Tai Sin Temple**. The **Ching Choon Temple** on the LRT line in the New Territories has a tiny garden and hundreds of Chinese bonsai plants. The only time that the public is allowed into the **Governor's garden** is around the first Sunday in March, to view the blooming azaleas. The best example of a traditional Chinese garden is in Macau.

GAMBLING

Only two forms of legalized gambling exist: the horse races and the lottery. Mahjong games at weddings are illegal if for money but everybody does it. Recently some mahjong players were arrested for playing in an illegal gambling hall. They were fined $500 and $1000.

HANDICAPPED

HKTA publishes a free booklet, *Access Guide for Disabled Visitors*, an extensive list of buildings, shops, parks, hotels, restaurants and places of worship with facilities for people in wheelchairs. Best are the newer buildings. Some hotels such as the Island Shangri-La, The Ritz-Carlton, The Peninsula, Hong Kong Renaissance and Newton Kowloon have rooms designed for people in wheelchairs.

HEALTH & MEDICAL CONCERNS

Many hotels have doctors on call, but may charge $850 or more. Add $200 for middle-of-the-night calls. **Anderson & Partners** are reliable doctors with offices around the city, who charge $295 for a consultation *(523-7036/523-8166)*. Some hotels like the Omni Hong Kong have a duty nurse.

The privately-run **Hong Kong Adventist Hospital**, *40 Stubbs Rd, Hong Kong, 574-6211* is a first-class, western-style hospital. It costs about $2,100 for a private room, or $1,200 each for a shared, which includes food and general nursing. **Matilda Hospital** *849-6301, 849-0100* is also private.

Hong Kong has many cheap, public hospitals with excellent doctors, but you may be in a ward with 20 or more people. **Queen Elizabeth Hospital**, *Kowloon 710-2111*; **Queen Mary Hospital**, *Hong Kong Island 819-2111 or 855-4111*. Private rooms are expensive and cost $2,590 including food and general nursing for non-residents. You might have to line up for emergencies at the Adventist Hospital. Hong Kong residents don't pay in public hospitals. All have to wait in line with the most critical treated first.

The **Health Department** *(Room 905, 393 Canton Rd, 368-3361) is open 9am-1pm and 2-4pm*. It charges $55 for a cholera injection. You can get some drugs (such as Larium for malaria at pharmacies) without a prescription. The heat and humidity in the summer can be overpowering. Drink lots of fluids, avoid the sun and if you just can't take it any more, head for an air-conditioned mall or movie.

HISTORIC BUILDINGS

Most surviving Victorian buildings are in Central on Hong Kong Island. The best way to see old Chinese buildings is take the HKTA **Heritage tour** or follow the **Ping Shan Heritage Trail**, on the LRT line in the New Territories. The **Antiquities Office** has a display and brochures on historic landmarks. See "Tsim Sha Tsui" in Chapter 14.

HOLIDAYS, FAIRS, AND FESTIVALS

Dates for most Chinese festivals are based on the Chinese calendar and change every year. We've provided dates for you through December 1995. For details on festivals, see Chapter 4, "Land and People."

Warning: Chinese New Year's is the worst time of the year to visit Hong Kong for shopping, business, and travel to China. Most things are closed for three days. Hotels and transportation with China are also difficult to book during Trade Fair time in Canton (Guangzhou) and long Hong Kong holidays like Easter and Christmas.

An asterisk (*) means public holiday with schools, offices and banks closed.

A pound sign (#) means date to be confirmed, so check with HKTA.

1994: October – 2 Birthday of Confucius; 13* Chung Yeung Festival; 21-Nov.12 Asian Arts Festival; October 15-25 Guangzhou Trade Fair in China; 23 Remembrance of Kwan Yin; **November** – 25-27 International Kart Grand Prix; **December** – 22 Winter Solstice; 25*Christmas Day; 26* and 27* first and second weekdays after Christmas; Super Star Wushu (Martial Arts) Exhibition#; International Invitation Lion Dance Championships#.

1995: January – 1* New Year's Day; 2* the first weekday; 24 Kitchen God Reports to Heaven; Jan 31-February 2*Chinese New Year's (Year of the Pig), 3-day holiday; **February** – 2 Birthday of Che Kung; 14 Spring Lantern (Yuen Siu) Festival; **March** – 19 Birthday of Kwan Yin; **April** – 2 Birthday of Pak Tai; 5*Ching Ming Festival; 14* Good Friday, 15* and 16* Easter Monday; 15-25 Guangzhou Trade Fair in China; 22 Birthday of Tin Hau; **May** – 7 Birthdays of Buddha and Tam Kung, and #Cheung Chau Bun Festival; **June** – 2*Tuen Ng Festival (Dragon Boat Festival); 10# Queen's Birthday; 10-11 International Dragon Boat Races; 12# Monday following Queen's Birthday; **July** – 10 Birthday of Lu Pan; 16 Enlightenment of Kwan Yin; **August** – 2 Seven Sisters' Festival; 10 Hungry Ghosts' Festival; **September** – 9 Mid-Autumn Festival; 10 Monkey God Festival; 21 Birthday of Confucius; **November** – 1 Chung Yeung Festival; 11 Remembrance of Kwan Yin; **December** – 23 Winter Solstice.

See also Macau dates and contact HKTA to verify dates after May 1995.

HOURS

Business: *9am-5:30 or 6pm, lunch 1pm-2pm. Saturdays 9am-1pm. Closed Sundays.*

Banks: *9am-4:30pm, Saturday 9am-12:30pm, closed Sundays.*

Stores: *in Central 9, 9:30 or 10am-6 or 7pm. In Causeway Bay and Tsim Sha Tsui. 10am-9 or 10pm. Some open past midnight.*

INFORMATION

Call **HKTA information service** *at 801-7177, 8am-6pm, Saturdays and Sundays 9am-5pm.*

For upcoming events pick up the weekly *Hong Kong Diary* at a HKTA Centre, which gives a bare-bones listing of theater, concerts, cultural shows, festivals, etc. *Hong Kong This Week* is a more descriptive weekly.

City News is a monthly with extensive sports listings and is also available free at HKTA and City Hall. *Hong Kong* magazine is a free weekly, found at some book and record shops. *TV and Entertainment Times* comes with *The Sunday Morning Post. TV & Entertainment* is $12 weekly, and is available at newsstands and bookshops.

LANGUAGE

English is an official language and is taught in the schools. **Cantonese** is more widely spoken. All government signs, like street and transportation signs are bilingual and most well-dressed people in urban areas speak English. If you have problems communicating, telephone an HKTA office and the staff should help you.

LAUNDRY

One of the cheapest places to do laundry is **A1 Company**, *Chung King Mansions, 40 Nathan Rd, Tsim Sha Tsui.* Go in straight and make the second left. Wash costs $20 for five pounds or less. Dryclean costs $20 for pants. More expensive but conveniently-located cleaners are in the Central MTR station near the Mandarin Hotel, in the Forum building between the two Exchange Towers, and on the G/F, with entrance on the east side of the New World Hotel in Tsim Sha Tsui. These are cheaper than hotels but take longer. It might be less expensive to buy a cheap tee-shirt than to pay your hotel to wash one.

LIFE IN HONG KONG

Like any large city, Hong Kong isn't perfect. You will encounter crowds, heavy traffic, garbage, air pollution, noisy jack hammers, a few incredibly-rude shopkeepers in tourist areas, and waiting in lines for public phones, taxis, public toilets, etc.

People generally have a very small living area. Some families share a room the size of your bathroom, taking turns sleeping in the beds. Most don't need as much personal space as Westerners. If you get tired of the crowds, you can escape to the islands, Macau, or the New Territories. There's also the south side of Hong Kong Island, any nice hotel or restaurant, or one of Hong Kong's many wonderful country parks.

MAIL

The **general post office** is next to the Star Ferry in Central and is open weekdays 8am-6pm, Saturdays 8am-2pm, and closed Sundays. You can pick up your mail at the Post Restante here. There is also one at 10 Middle Road in Tsim Sha Tsui. You can buy stamps and mail letters at any first class hotel or ask your hotel for the closest post office branch.

MANNERS

People pass things to each other with two hands, thumbs on top and perhaps a nod of the head as a token bow of respect. You hand your calling card so the recipient can read the writing without turning it. When you receive a card, read it with interest and perhaps make a relevant comment. When using an interpreter, look at the person you are actually speaking with, not the interpreter.

Be aware that Chinese people smile when happy or embarrassed, and when they don't know what to say. They will nod "yes, yes" even though they don't understand a word you're saying. When in doubt, ask questions that require full sentence answers. Try not to lose your temper or they will think you're uncivilized. Chinese frequently react to anger by ignoring you and trying to disappear.

If you are invited to dinner in a home, take a gift. It can be something from your country to eat and share like chocolates, nuts, liquor or special wine from your country. If trying to impress, give a bottle of Hennessey XO or any XO cognac. Novelties are great too, unless they're made in Hong Kong. You can always give lucky money to the children.

Typically Chinese is the seating arrangement at the dinner table. The guest of honor sits beside the host and always faces the door. Let your host tell you where to sit. Basic courtesies in North America apply to Hong Kong. But uniquely Hong Kong is the practice of tapping your right index finger when tea is poured into your cup. It means thank you and symbolizes a *kow tow*, a head to the ground in reverence.

Foreigners are usually disgusted by the Chinese spitting on the street. However, the Chinese probably feel the same about the way we keep our phlegm in a handkerchief and carry it around like a treasure in our pockets. Burping shows that you are not embarrassed about letting your bodily functions interrupt your enjoyment of a meal. Slurping helps you avoid burning your lips with hot tea or soup. These are not signs of appreciation as many foreigners believe.

MARRIAGE

This takes some planning and will take about two to five weeks. Write for a form from **The Hong Kong Marriage Registration**, *3/F, Low Block, Queensway Government Offices, 66 Queensway, Hong Kong.* You must have two witnesses over 18 years of age and pay a fee ranging from $210 to $570.

MONEY MATTERS

The US dollar was about $7.7 Hong Kong at press time. Money changers, hotels, and the airport are the worst places to change money.

Banks are the best, but some like the Hongkong Bank, Chartered Bank, and Hang Seng Bank charge a hefty $50 service fee per transaction.

Exchanging money is best at smaller local banks like the **Liu Chong Hing Bank** *at 24 Des Voeux Rd. Central, 841-7419*. **Wing Lung** has many branches, the most convenient on *Connaught Rd. Central 841-7419 and the New World Harbour View Hotel arcade in Wanchai*. Slightly less again with no service charge is **American Express** *on Queen's Road Central across from the Landmark, 811-1200*. **Sogo** department store in Causeway Bay has changed travelers checks at better than the hotel rate and never asked us to shop there. Avoid other money changers. Generally, you get a slightly better rate for cash than for travelers checks.

There are also lots of North American banks such as Chase Manhattan, Citibank, Toronto-Dominion and Bank of Nova Scotia. Check with your own bank about fees for money machines. **Hongkong Bank money machines** spew out cash for Global Access, ETC, Electron, Visa and Plus System cards.

Many shops, restaurants, and most hotels accept credit cards (Visa, American Express, MasterCard, and less so Diners) but ask first. Some stores do not like credit cards because of counterfeits and the 2-3% service charge they have to pay. A few charge 3-4% extra for credit card payment.

Again, unless otherwise noted, all prices in this book are given in Hong Kong dollars.

MTR

Mass Transit Railway, Hong Kong's subway. See "Getting Around Town."

MUSEUMS

The best museums are the **Hong Kong Museum of History** and the **Museum of Art** in Tsim Sha Tsui. Other interesting museums include the **Police Museum** (see Chapter 14, "Central") and the **Sam Tung Uk Museum** (a restored walled village) in Tsuen Wan, the New Territories.

The **Space Museum** in Tsim Sha Tsui and the **Science Museum** in Tsim Sha Tsui East are also good. For ceramics, try the **Tsui Museum of Art** in the old Bank of China building next to the Hongkong Bank in Central. The entrance is on the west side.

NEWS MEDIA

The most popular **newspaper** is the 90-year-old *South China Morning Post*. Others are *The Hong Kong Standard, Eastern Express* (1994), and *The Asian Wall Street Journal. The Far Eastern Economic Review* and *Asiaweek* are weekly news magazines.

The monthly **magazine** *Windows* and the newspaper *China Daily* are owned by Chinese government interests. American magazines and newspapers are available in big hotels and from vendors. *The Tatler* is a glossy gossip magazine about Hong Kong's rich and famous.

Hotels have a variety of **television** channels. All offer two English channels, one of which gives you the *CBS Evening News with Dan Rather* in the morning. Some hotels have the 24-hour *Asian Business News* from the Asian Wall Street Journal, *CNN* and *NBC* as well. Many hotels offer the Hong Kong Channel, an hour's helpful program of history, sightseeing and hotel description.

PARKS

Hong Kong has some wonderful city parks, such as **Kowloon Park** in Tsim Sha Tsui, **Hong Kong Park**, and the **Botanical Gardens** in Central. There are many country parks as well. *For more information, write or call the Country Parks Division, Agriculture and Fisheries Dept., 12/F, 393 Canton Rd., Kowloon (733-2132).*

They have free brochures on a number of parks: Country Parks Tree Walks, the Hong Kong Trail, the Lantau Trail and the 100-kilometer Maclehose Trail. The Government Publications Centre next to the Post Office in Central sells books and maps. See also Walks later in this chapter.

PHOTOGRAPHY

You should have no problems taking photos anywhere except at the Chinese border and of quaintly-dressed village women who demand money. To be polite, always ask first, especially in temples. For good lighting, go from October to January. Ruth likes shooting photos at dusk with its magical moisture-filtered light, or dawn for an hour or so before the light gets too harsh. Shooting photos from the front of the top story of a tram at dusk with 400 ASA film is great fun.

Hong Kong has high quality processing which costs about the same as in North America. You pay only for prints that turn out, even if it's your fault. You can buy most popular films, but not Kodachrome. Most places charge between $1.40-$2.00 a print plus a $15 processing fee. The cheapest place is **A-1 Laundry** (Chung King Mansions, 40 Nathan Road, Tsim Sha Tsui) which charges $.70 per print, but the quality is not the best. For camera shops, see "Shopping".

PLACES OF WORSHIP

Notices of Christian services are in Saturday's *South China Morning Post*. Hotel concierges should have a list.

- **Catholic Cathedral**, *Central, Hong Kong Island, 524-0681*
- **English Methodist Church**, *Wanchai, 575-7817*
- **Kowloon Mosque**, *Kowloon Park, Tsim Sha Tsui, Kowloon, 724-0095*
- **-St. John's Cathedral** (Anglican), *Central, 523-4157*
- **Synagogue Ohel Leah**, *70 Robinson Rd, Midlevels, Hong Kong Island, 801-5440*
- **The Church of Jesus Christ of Latter Day Saints**, *#7 Castle Rd, Midlevels, 559-3325*
- **Society of Friends** (Quakers), *849-6532/527-6821/563-3395*

PRECAUTIONS

Compared to cities in North America, Hong Kong is very safe. Only policemen and bank guards are allowed to carry guns. However, you should take normal precautions. Personal violence like muggings is rare, but there are pickpockets and purse snatchers especially in crowded places. Do not leave your purse unwatched on the counter of a store, even for a minute.

Always use the peep hole in your hotel door before opening it to strangers. If in doubt about unexpected repair people, phone the reception desk to check first, before letting them in. Always double lock your door to avoid embarrassing the chambermaid.

When you travel, carry your money, credit cards and other documents in a necksafe or money belt under your clothing. If possible, use hotel safes in your room. Use hotel safe deposit boxes but do not leave credit cards there as the cards could be used and returned. Keep your credit card receipts and corresponding bills. Counterfeiting of cards and credit card fraud are common.

Avoid dark, deserted places and be careful walking across streets. Don't hike in isolated places alone. A slip on a slippery, moss-covered rock in a stream-bed might mean being attacked by mosquitos all night or until some help happens along.

SAFETY FOR WOMEN

Hong Kong is safer than most big cities. There are almost always people around. Most of the western women we know will walk anywhere at any time of day.

Chinese men are a little less aggressive than Westerners, but that can change when they're drunk. Linda once had a drunk grab her in an elevator and try for a kiss. A hard slap stopped him cold. Be very wary of flattering modelling offers, which might actually end up being prostitution offers. Generally avoid dark, empty areas at night, drunk men, Wanchai when a naval ship is in, and bars with British soldiers.

SAVING MONEY

Check out our budget hotel section, or spend some nights in Macau, Shenzhen, or on the overnight ferry to Guangzhou. Buy food at grocery stores and have a picnic. Eat at fast food outlets like McDonald's or markets like Temple St. Always check prices from the menu outside before you enter any restaurant. Make a note of what you have ordered with prices and check it against your bill. Waiters can make "mistakes".

Eat one big meal a day and snack on store or deli-bought goodies and granola bars the rest of the time. Good bake shops are **Deli France** *(1/F Worldwide House at Pedder St. and Des Voeux Rd.)* and **Lucullus Gourmet Shops** *(Shop 249, Ocean Centre. 730-0332;* **Basement 2**, *Sogo Department store, Causeway Bay 574-1318;* **10C**, *Ice House St. Central, 868-9449).* For your big meal of the day, eat lunch (not dinner) from buffets even in fancy hotels. The **Sheraton** has an all-you-can-eat Salad Bar 11-3pm for $55 plus 10%. The **Park Hotel** has a tea buffet for $58.30 weekdays including tax. The **Hong Kong Renaissance** has a tea buffet for $55-58 from 3pm-5:30pm with won ton, noodles and dessert. The **Oasis Bar** in the **New World Harbour View Hotel** has a weekday $58 Hungry Hour from 5-7:30pm with a good variety all-you-can-eat buffet.

Take public transport as much as possible. Do not be intimidated by taxi drivers who are reluctant to give you change. Ask for it firmly. If they don't hand over, threaten to call the police or make a note of the license number and report them. Avoid tours. You can do many things without one but you need a good guide book. Take ours. You can supplement it with free pamphlets from HKTA.

Do not touch the mini-bar in your hotel room. Avoid laundry services in hotels. Do your own or use local laundries. See "Laundry" above. Comparison shop for everything including hotels and restaurants. Don't be afraid to ask for discounts in hotels. Avoid buying expensive things at tourist attractions and hotels. See Chapter 12, "Shopping."

Banks, some stores, apartment blocks, restaurants and hotels have free telephones. While hotels might charge $3 to $5 per local call from guest rooms, there is always a public phone in the lobby which only costs $1. The time of long distance calls makes no difference to the U.S., but if you're calling Canada, calls are cheaper from 1pm to 7pm Hong Kong time. It's cheaper to call from Hong Kong than from China. But if you are also going to China, wait until you get there to get a haircut or shop for China-made goods. Don't rent a cellular phone. They are very expensive here. Rent a pager instead. See also "Money Matters" above.

SENIORS

"Silver Travelers" over 65 ride free on the **Star Ferry**. You also pay less for public transportation, museums, arts center and some tours, but so far no discounts in hotels except for the Sheraton and Holiday Inn, and a handful of hotel coffee shops. The Excelsior Hotel gives 10%.

STORAGE OF LUGGAGE

Most hotels will store your luggage free, particularly if they know you will be back to stay. The airport Left Luggage Booth is now expensive at $30 per piece for the first day or part thereof, $40 per piece for the second day, and $80 for the third. If you leave luggage for 14 days, it's $1030 per piece! Stow it at your hotel.

STREET ADDRESSES

One street might have different names on various stretches. Odd numbers are usually on one side and even on the other. Numbers tends to go upwards from east to west on the Hong Kong side, and from the harbor on both sides. In Tsim Sha Tsui, numbering progresses from west to east. With many buildings being torn down and rebuilt, street signs and numbers have not always kept up with the changes.

STUDENTS

There are not many student discounts available. The **Hong Kong Student Travel Bureau** *(1021, 10/F, Star House, Tsim Sha Tsui, 730-3269)* can get you discounts on tours and airfare, if you have an **International Student Card**. These are available at most student travel agencies in your own country (i.e., **Travel Cuts Toronto**, *416-798-2887*).

TELECOMMUNICATIONS

Telephone News

All Hong Kong telephone numbers will have a 2 added in front on January 1, 1995. The number 123-4567 will become 2123-4567 then. Radio pagers will start with 7 and mobile phones 9.

Local telephone calls are free. Plentiful public phones cost $1 for each call and are in most hotel lobbies, MTR and KCR stations, on the street and around the Star Ferry. You can also use $2 coins and even Chinese one yuan coins.

Calling Hong Kong

852 is the international telephone code for Hong Kong. If you are direct dialing from North America dial 011-852-number.

Calling from Hong Kong

Here are the country codes for:
• **Australia** – *61*

- **Canada** – *1*
- **China** – *86*
- **India** – *91*
- **Japan** – *81*
- **Macau** – *853*
- **Malaysia** – *60*
- **The Philippines** – *63*
- **Singapore** – *65*
- **Thailand** – *66*
- **UK** – *44*
- **USA** – *1*

Important Numbers

- *1081* – free directory assistance for Hong Kong and Macau
- *010* – for collect and operator-assisted calls. More expensive.
- *011*– for calls to be charged to a calling card via an operator.
- *013* – overseas calls, conference calls and interpreters.
- *888-2888* – Hong Kong Telecom Enquiries

Home Direct access numbers will put you in touch with a home operator, for collect or calling card calls:

- **Australia** *800-0061*
- **Canada** *800-1100*
- **China-Shanghai** *800-0186*
- **Hawaii** *800-1188*
- **Macau** *800-0853*
- **Singapore** *800-0065*
- **Thailand** *800-0066*
- **USA**: **AT&T** *800-1111*, **MCI** *800-1121*, Sprint 800-1877, **TRT/FTC** *800-1115*

International Direct Dial (IDD)

Dial 001-country code-area code-number. Dial 003-country code-etc. if you want the operator to call you afterwards with the charges. This is handy if you're staying with friends and need to know how much to reimburse them.

Long distance calls can be made from most hotels but they charge a service charge and/or a percentage even if you dial direct. It is cheaper to call the above access number on a public rather than hotel telephone and then dial direct. You have to give your calling card number and you are charged for a minimum of three minutes. If you are calling from a hotel, the hotel charges you for a local call only.

If you don't have a calling card, you can use a public pay phone (and a pound of $1, $2 and $5 coins), or buy a stored value **Phone Card** at an

HKTA Information and Gift Centre, Telecom offices, and some 7-11 stores. They come in denominations of $50, $100 and $250. There are also about 100 Creditcard phones that take major credit cards.

24-hour Telecom offices are at Shop B, LG Basement, Century Square, 1-13 D'Aguilar St. Central and at 10 Middle Road, Tsim Sha Tsui, behind the Sheraton Hotel. There is also one in the Passenger Terminal Building, Hong Kong Airport, 8am-11pm daily.

The cheapest way to communicate with North America is to have your friends telephone you.

Faxing could be cheaper if you have a lot to say and can do it in one page. Make sure your writing is clear in black ink. At a Telecom office a local fax costs $10. To most Southeast Asian countries it's $30; to UK, North America, and Australia it's $35. To save on faxes, try to find a Hong Kong friend with a fax machine. Transmission should cost about a quarter of the price of the Telecom office and local faxes are free.

TEMPLES

Of Hong Kong's hundreds of temples, the best is **Wong Tai Sin** in New Kowloon, the most spectacular is **Po Lin Monastery** on Lantau with the world's largest bronze Buddha statue, and the most bizarre is the **Temple of the Ten Thousand Buddhas** in Sha Tin, the New Territories. You will find some wonderful, less touristy temples and monasteries on the LRT, and at the end of the MTR line at Tsuen Wan, both in the New Territories.

TIME

New York and Toronto are 11 or 12 hours behind depending on Daylight Savings or Standard Time. Thus, 12 noon in Hong Kong can be 11pm or midnight in New York the previous day.

TIPPING

Hong Kong people rarely tip and you don't have to unless the service has been exceptional. Restaurants add 10% service charge, so an additional 5% is appropriate. If there is no service charge, then 10%. Give taxi drivers the small change or more, washroom attendants $1, bellmen $5-$10 per load and a tour guide $10-$20 per day.

TOURIST ASSOCIATION (HKTA)

Your friend. If you have any questions call the **HKTA hotline** at 801-7177, 9am-5pm everyday. This must be one of the most helpful tourist associations around. They are generous with free booklets, brochures, maps, guides and information. These include guides for shopping, dining and nightlife, sightseeing and culture, and much more. You can also buy walking tour booklets for $25, and souvenirs. If you have language problems in a store, telephone the HKTA. Overseas offices are listed under addresses in the back.

If a complaint regards an HKTA member, call the **Membership Department** (801-7278), weekdays, 9am-5pm; Saturdays 9am-12:45pm, closed Sundays. HKTA member stores prominently display its red sailing junk symbol. Members pay a $2,200 fee and HKTA mediates disputes.

Visit one of its **Information and Gift Centres**, listed below:

- Star Ferry Concourse, Tsim Sha Tsui, Kowloon. Open weekdays 8am-6pm, Saturday and Sunday 9am-5pm.
- Shop 8, Basement, Jardine House, 1 Connaught Place, Central, Hong Kong Island. Open weekdays 9am-6pm. Saturday 9am-1pm. Closed Sundays.

TYPHOONS

A direct hit by a typhoon (tropical cyclone) only happens every ten years. If a typhoon is coming, turn on a radio or television or telephone 187-8066 for information. If you need help with unexpected problems, ask your hotel, airline or consulate. Try the Hong Kong Tourist Association.

Signal 1: The center of the storm is within 800 kilometers.

Signal 3: A strong wind is expected or blowing in Victoria harbor at a sustained 41-62 kilometers per hour with gusts over 110 kilometers per hour. Winds are expected to increase within 12 hours of the announcement of this signal. It is a good idea to get a flashlight, a battery-operated radio in case of power outages, and food and water for two or three days. Get lots of reading material and towels and some friends. Plan a party.

Signal 8: Winds are expected or blowing in Victoria harbor at a sustained 63-117 kilometers per hour with gusts over 180 kilometers per hour, about 12 hours after the announcement of this signal. All offices close and employees are sent home. Many converge on grocery and video stores for provisions. A direct hit is not imminent, but stay inside strong buildings. The danger is falling flower pots and debris from roofs and balconies. Don't worry. Almost all Hong Kong buildings have survived years of typhoons.

Signal 9: Winds increase significantly. Stay away from exposed windows and doors. Air-conditioners have been sucked out of buildings. Do not go outdoors until the "all-clear" is given. Use the towels if leaks develop.

Signal 10: Hurricane force winds are expected or blowing with sustained speeds 188 kilometers per hour or more and gusts over 220 kilometers per hour. Hang in there! Enjoy an exciting experience, one of nature's wonders. The eye of the storm is calm. There's more to come. Wait for the "all-clear". Don't expect roads to be clear for a day.

WATER

Tap water in urban Hong Kong is safe to drink.

GREAT DAY FOR A BIKE RIDE!

7. GETTING AROUND TOWN

Hong Kong has one of the best public transportation systems in the world. In some cases there are over 20 different ways (buses, ferries, trains, taxis, feet, etc.) to get from point A to B. Don't worry, we only list the fastest and most convenient.

Avoid traveling during rush hours, 8-10am and 4-7pm, especially through the Cross-Harbour Tunnel. The Eastern-Harbour Tunnel between Quarry Bay and Kwuntong usually has less traffic. If you do go through the tunnels, try to do so in air-conditioned vehicles because of the poor air.

Don't be shy about asking for directions. Filipinas have the best English and are very helpful. Most business people speak English well.

PUBLIC TRANSPORTATION

Generally, people over 65 and children under 11 pay a discounted rate. Children under two are usually free. There is no smoking in any of the vehicles and in some cases no eating.

SEEING HONG KONG -
ON YOUR OWN OR BY TOUR?

If you have more time and enjoy challenges, do try it on your own. Many people do. This way, you get a deeper experience of Hong Kong. Taking public transportation or taxis, following maps and asking for directions and the best places to eat, gets you closer to Hong Kong people. Who knows, you might get invited to a wedding!

Hong Kong and Kowloon are relatively easy. They are small and the MTR is great, well marked and many people speak English. If you keep your eye on the Peak, the tram line and the harbor, you should know where you are most of the time.

Getting around the New Territories is a little harder as fewer people speak English, there are many peaks and shorelines, and the distances are greater. Linda tried it by public transport and even though her destination was written in Chinese, the bus driver left her off 10 minutes away from Kam Tin, which is in the middle of nowhere. Still, she had a happy time and saw a war-game exercise she would have otherwised missed. Aside from that, she had no problems.

BY BUS

Hong Kong has single and double-decker public buses most of which run from 6am-midnight. Exact change is required and you usually pay when you get on. Major bus stops are at Exchange Square in Central and the Star Ferry in Tsim Sha Tsui.

Buses are usually a little cheaper than the MTR (about $3-9), but much more confusing. Hong Kong has hundreds of bus routes. If you want to travel by bus a lot, pick up the free sheets on bus routes at HKTA. If that's not enough, the Government Publications Office has a 500-page listing of all public transportation routes. To stop a bus, go to a bus stop with the number of the bus you want, and wave when you see it approach.

The main bus companies are:
- **CMB** (**China Motor Bus Company**) *on Hong Kong Island, 565-8556*
- **Citybus**, a new company, *873-0818*
- **KMB** (**Kowloon Motor Bus Company**) *in Kowloon and the New Territories, 745-4466.*

For information on buses to the Peak, Repulse Bay, Stanley (the best bus ride), Aberdeen, the New Territories and Lantau, see individual listing.

Mini-Buses

Public Light Buses are yellow and red buses and stop anywhere except in front of yellow curbs. They cost $2-6 and you pay when you get off. Destinations are written in English in microscopic print. **Maxi-cabs** are larger yellow and green mini-buses. They cost $1-8 and you pay when you get on. You also wave them down. Neither stop for you when full. No half-fares for children who take up seats.

BY CAR

It is not a good idea to drive yourself. There's left-hand drive, gridlock traffic, many one-way streets and almost no parking downtown. Hong Kong drivers are usually orderly, but it's less stressful, a lot cheaper and often faster to use convenient public transport. There is a theory that if all the cars were on the road at the same time, no one would be able to move.

If you insist on renting, you're better off hiring a car with a driver who speaks English. If you find a taxi driver you can communicate with, ask him how much for a day or half day. Some hotels have chauffeured

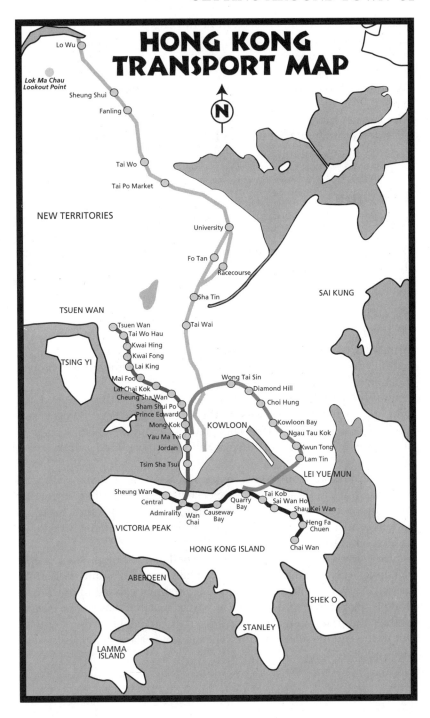

Mercedes, Daimlers, and Rolls Royces with English-speaking drivers. The Mandarin Oriental Hotel charges about $730 per hour for a Rolls for a minimum of two hours.

The only time we might suggest driving yourself is to explore the New Territories. Avoid rush hours when leaving and returning. Roads are well marked. You can drive for one year on your own driver's licence. You must carry it and photo ID when you do.

Intercontinental Hire Cars Ltd. *(338-3689)* rents cars with driver for $220 per hour for a minimum of three hours. **Avis** *(890-6988)* charges $620 per day.

BY FERRY

If you are going to the outlying islands, always check ferry schedules to make sure you can get back and when. For Star Ferry, see Chapter 14, "Tsim Sha Tsui;" for hoverferries, see Chapter 14, "Islands" and "Tsim Sha Tsui East;" for Jetfoils, Hydrofoils, and Jumbo-cats, see Chapter 17, "Macau."

BY FOOT

Hong Kong is a great place to walk. There's much to see: little red shrines in shops, vendors with bright orange octopus legs, traditional red wedding dresses, Rolls Royces and people talking on mobile telephones. We walk more in Hong Kong than anywhere else.

But there's a technique to it. Watch locals. Go with the flow. Look right and then left when crossing the street. At corners, be especially careful of cars making turns. They have the right of way and know it. Believe it or not jaywalking is illegal and you can be fined, but the law is rarely enforced.

If you find the going slow, look up to see if there are any elevated sidewalks you can escape to. We especially love the ones in Central that go in and out of air-conditioned buildings. Or look around for MTR stations which frequently have exits on both sides of the street. Go underground where you can walk without fear of cars.

Downtown Hong Kong is very crowded and although most people walk quickly, some shuffle along at a snail's pace. For some mysterious reason, everyone stops on escalators. Sometimes walking in downtown Hong Kong is more dodging and weaving. Imagine that you're playing football and trying to make a touchdown. It isn't all like this, of course. Out in the countryside, you can walk and not see anyone. See Walks in Chapter 6.

BY HELICOPTER

Call 802-0200. These fly from the Macau Ferry Pier and are good for sightseeing and transportation.

BY RICKSHAW

An American Baptist missionary invented rickshaws in Japan in the late 19th century. They were quickly adopted in Hong Kong. They and their ancient drivers hang out near the Star Ferry in Central. They will pose for pictures for $10-$20. Be sure to settle on a price before you do this or go for a ride.

BY TAXI

Taxis are available when the meter's little red flag is raised or the roof light is on. They cannot stop at yellow curbs. Some taxi drivers do not speak English but they can call on their radios for a translator. The charge at flagfall is $11.50 plus $1 for every 200 meters thereafter. Tip small change. If you use the Cross-Harbour Tunnel, you must pay double the $10 toll. Other tunnels are cheaper and you only pay one way. Taxis operate 24 hours a day. If you book by telephone or have a piece of luggage add $5. *You can telephone for a taxi on the Hong Kong side at 574-7311 or 861-1008. On the Kowloon side it's 760-0411.*

Taxis on Hong Kong Island and Kowloon are red, in the New Territories green, and on Lantau Island blue. It is hard to catch taxis during the shift change between 4-5pm and like everywhere else, it is almost impossible during rain or rush hour. Where do they all go? To find them, look for places where they would go like hospitals, hotels and restaurant areas. It is easy to get a taxi during the day at the Star Ferries until about 4pm.

Sometimes a taxi from one side of the harbor will refuse to go to the other side or will turn you over to a taxi from the other side. This is because most drivers, like many residents, only know one side. When you see the traffic in the Cross-Harbour tunnel, you'll understand the other reason. Drivers don't want to spend their time in traffic jams. We suggest you take the Star Ferry or the MTR to cross the harbor. It is much more pleasant.

If you see a taxi with the red flag up and maybe a towel and arm on top of it, it means the driver wants to go to the other side of the harbor and will take you for half the usual tunnel fee. If you want such taxis, they hang around Causeway Bay, the Excelsior Hotel and Convention Centre in Hong Kong. You can look for them around Chatham Rd. in Tsim Sha Tsui. Ask hotel door men.

Taxi drivers prefer to use the faster highways even if it means going a long way out of the way (at your expense). Sometimes it's a legitimate route because of one-way streets, but usually it makes taking a taxi very expensive. *If you have any complaints, get the taxi's number and call the 24-hour Police Hotline 527-7177.*

Always ask your hotel about shuttle buses. These are usually free and should get you downtown. The Grand Hyatt uses a quaint London taxi.

BY TRAIN

This is the way to go. Hong Kong has three clean, fast, safe, convenient, air-conditioned, user-friendly train systems. Best of all there's no traffic or stop lights. Pick up a free MTR/KCR Tourist Guide from any MTR or KCR ticket office or Hong Kong Tourist Association (HKTA). It has pictures, descriptions of attractions and maps of all three systems.

MTR

MTR stands for **Mass Transit Railway**, but no one calls it that. (Enquiry Hotline 750-0170.) Hong Kong's subway is quick and pleasant, unless you're claustrophobic and try it at rush hour. Trains run every five minutes from 6:10am-12:45am. Fares range from $3.50-$9.00. Change is available from machines, ticket offices and Hang Seng Bank booths in each station.

USING THE MTR

Buy a credit-card-like ticket from a vending machine or a stored-value ticket in the station. The price depends on the length of the trip. Put the card through the slot in the turnstile and retrieve it after you pass through. Keep Your Ticket. At the end of the trip, feed it again to a turnstile to get out of the subway. If you still have credit on the stored-value ticket, you get the ticket back. The amount will show up on the turnstile. If you have a tourist ticket, you get it back in the end as a souvenir.

Getting out of stations can be confusing, because they can have from one to nine exits, emerging in different areas. All stations have neighborhood maps showing the exits, streets, main buildings, and where you are.

If you plan on using the MTR a lot, buy a stored-value ticket at any ticket office. You're charged less for each ride and you don't have to wait in line. Stored-value tickets come in $25 (tourist souvenir ticket), $70, $100 and $200 denominations. The higher the price, the more you save. You can travel as far as you want on your last ride, even if you only have $1 left on the ticket.

The small, free, 100-page *MTR Guide Book* is available at MTR ticket offices. The Lost Property Centre is at Admiralty Station. The MTR started in 1979 and just keeps growing. Its three lines run over 43 kilometers and reach 38 stations. It carries over two million passengers daily and achieves speeds up to 80 kilometers an hour.

KCR

The MTR connects with the **Kowloon-Canton Railway (KCR)** at Kowloon Tong MTR station, exit B. The KCR is almost the same as the MTR, except that the KCR is mostly above ground and its seats are less slippery. KCR fares range between $3-$7.50. Trains usually run every 4-6 minutes between 5:30am-12:25am. The KCR is a good, cheap way to see the New Territories. There are special Sha Tin racetrack tickets on race days.

The KCR has expensive first-class coaches, worthwhile but not necessary even if you are going all the way to Lo Wu. A ticket to that China border port costs $27 and trains run every 6-12 minutes. Although most trains stop at the border, a few express trains go all the way to Canton. Incidentally, you could keep taking trains, including the Trans-Siberian, all the way to Europe from here. *Local enquiries 602-7799.*

For the **LRT (Light Rail Transit)**, see the "New Territories" chapter.

BY TRAM

These old, rattling, double-decker streetcars are unique to Hong Kong. They are often full, but if you see one that's empty hop on! This is one of the best and cheapest ($1.20) rides in town. Go up to the top floor and sit in front and just watch Hong Kong's passing street theater of life.

The trams leave their terminals every 45 seconds. They run from about 6am-midnight from Kennedy Town to Western-Central-Wanchai-Causeway Bay-North Point-Quarry Bay and then Shau Kei Wan. Some detour through Happy Valley. Get on through the back door and pay when you exit through the front. The conductor doesn't give change. Trams are least crowded at night. You can rent trams for private parties. *Call 311-3509.*

BY TOUR

Should you take a tour or go sightseeing on your own? If you are short of time and want to pack a lot into a couple of days, it is definitely worth the expense. Tours give you the lay of the land and you can always go back later on your own if you want.

HKTA

HKTA organizes some very good tours which are sold through travel agents and hotel concierges. There are discounts for seniors over 60.

Guides cannot accept tips, but you might be asked to tip the driver. *For more information, pick up brochures at HKTA or call 801-7390/801-7392.*

Here are some offerings:

The Heritage Tour takes you to the New Territories and some of the oldest Chinese buildings in Hong Kong. Most of these are simple, small but charming. The half-day (five-hour) tour includes a renovated walled village, Man Mo Temple, Tai Po Market, a Chinese mansion from 1865 and an ancestral hall. $280. The full-day tour includes everything on the half-day tour, plus a dim sum lunch, Kun Ting Study Hall and one of the biggest and oldest ancestral halls. $430 includes lunch.

The Land Between Tour goes to the New Territories, to Tai Mo Shan Hong Kong's tallest mountain, to a bird sanctuary near China and lunch. This is a day of relaxing in the countryside away from the bustle of the city (except for the heavy traffic going to and from China). Seniors and children under 16 pay $245. Adults pay $295.

The Family Insight Tour is the only "non-touristy" tour available in Hong Kong. Over 50% of Hong Kong people live in government-subsidized housing. You see two public housing estates, visit a family and a social service organization such as a nursery. You also stop at a market, the Hong Kong Housing Authority's exhibition center and Hong Kong's best temple, Wong Tai Sin. Children under six are free. Children under 16 and seniors pay $170. Adults pay $210.

Come Horse Racing Tour includes transportation, admission and a great buffet dinner in the Members' Enclosure of the Royal Hong Kong Jockey Club, September-June on Wednesday evenings or Saturday afternoons. A guide answers your questions and shows you how to place bets. You have to be over 18 and in Hong Kong 21 days or less. There are no senior's discounts. You pay $468. See also Horse Racing in "Special Interest".

Sports & Recreation Tour heads out to the private Clearwater Bay Golf & Country Club in Sai Kung and includes lunch. You can play golf, tennis, badminton, squash, swim or take a sauna for an extra fee. $330.

Lantau Island Monastery Tour is a relaxing tour that goes through the harbor from near the Star Ferry piers to Mui Wo on Lantau Island. A bus and guide take you to Cheung Sha Beach, the nicest beach in this area. There are no canteens, just a beach with changing rooms, life guards and no time to swim. Up the mountain is a stop at Shek Pik Reservoir and you can look at the maximum-security prison across the road. You can wander around Tai-O fishing village for 30 minutes. There are squid and fish stomachs hanging out to dry and a tiny, human-powered ferry you can ride.

Then you go to the Po Lin Buddhist Monastery for a good vegetarian lunch. You also get a chance to climb up to its 23-meter-high bronze buddha before heading back to the big city. You could go back by regular ferry which is more stable than the tour junk.

The *HKTA Walking Tour Booklets* are great, pocket-sized and cost only $25. There are five covering Central and Western, Yau Ma Tei, Cheung Chau, Lantau and Sai Kung.

Other Tours

The World Wildlife Fund has nature tours to Maipo Marshes and around the 100-year-old Island House in the New Territories, but they are often booked months in advance. *Call 526-4473.* **Gray Line Tours of Hong Kong** *(72 Nathan Rd., Kowloon. 368-7111)* offers a number of different tours including Sung Dynasty Village, a two-hour harbor cruise for $155, Ocean Park in Aberdeen and a four-and-a-half-hour Hong Kong Island Tour for $195. The Island Tour visits the Peak, Aberdeen (where you can pay a little more for a sampan tour but it's worth it), Repulse Bay and Stanley. Discounts are for children under 12.

Gray Line can also arrange a three-and-a-half-hour private tour with a driver/guide by Mercedes Benz for $830 ($1050 for a stretch limousine). This is a good deal considering that a chauffered car rental can be about $770.

MP Tours *(Star Ferry Pier, 366-7024/845-2324/311-3509)*. The English isn't all that great, but MP Tours has six open-top tram tours in antique, double-decker trams. Daytime, evening and cocktail tours are an hour and 10 minutes and cost $110. Children under 12 are $80. A lunch tour with dim sum costs $240. Dinner is $370. There are also 12 harbor cruises on a Star Ferry starting at $110 for one hour and ten minutes. Brochures are available at the entrance to the Star Ferry piers.

Watertours of Hong Kong Ltd *(721-2856/739-3302/367-1970)* has six modernized junks (sorry, no sails). They offer 19 tours ranging from $120 (child $90) for one-hour in the harbor to $470 for the four-hour sunset cruise with dinner in an Aberdeen floating restaurant ($280 without dinner, child $170). Other tours go to Lie Yue Mun Seafood Village ($440 including dinner), Lantau Island Monastery, Cheng Chau Island and Sung Dynasty Village. **Tour East** *(Austin Place, 366-3111)* offers an Island Tour, $160. For touring **Sung Dynasty Village**, see Chapter 14, "New Kowloon."

8. SPORTS
& RECREATION

For upcoming sporting events, the monthly *City News* has the most extensive listing. Hong Kong Tourist Association's *Hong Kong Diary* lists major events. Both are free and available at City Hall in Central and in HKTA offices. If your favorite sport or recreational activity is not listed here, don't despair. HKTA has files on sports and facilities. Call or visit.

BADMINTON

Call the **Hong Kong Badminton Association** *(836-4066)* for facilities and competitions.

BEACHES

Repulse Bay Beach on Hong Kong Island is the most popular, but is very polluted. There are cleaner beaches on Lantau Island and in the New Territories. Opinions vary on water quality. The government tests it regularly and says it's okay to swim. Many foreign residents will only swim in pools, citing skin diseases and ear infections from the ocean. Rare shark attacks in the New Territories should end now that shark nets have been put up. Swim at your own risk. We are divided. Ruth the mother won't risk it, but Linda the adventurous daughter will.

Beaches are closed and a red flag goes up when it is not safe to swim. Locals stop swimming in September, but if you are from a colder climate, you can still enjoy it in early December. Life guards are on duty 9am-6pm, April 1-October 31 at popular beaches.

BICYCLING

You can rent bicycles on Lantau Island. At almost every town along the KCR (especially Tai Wai, Sha Tin and Tai Po Market) you can rent 18 to 21-gear racing or mountain bikes for about $10 an hour, and others for $30 a day. You need identification and a deposit. You might be able to hire a bicycle in Tai Wai and return it to another shop 15 kilometers away in

Tai Po Market. Bicycle tracks shared only with strollers and joggers are beside pretty Tolo Harbour, near Hong Kong University and along Plover Cove Dam. On weekends these areas are crowded. For exact locations of shops, contact HKTA. You could also call the **Hong Kong Cycling Association**, *573-3861*.

BIRDWATCHING

The best aviaries are in the **Zoological and Botanical Gardens** in Central. The walk-in aviary in **Hong Kong Park** is worth visiting. A small one with Southeast Asian birds is on the LRT line in the New Territories. **Maipo Marsh** is a bird sanctuary in the New Territories beside the Chinese border, once blessed by Prince Philip.

BOWLING

Four Seas Bowling Centre charges about $20 and $3 for shoe rental. *4/F, City Plaza I, Taikoo Shing, Hong Kong Island, 567-0703 (Taikoo MTR).*

GOLF

HKTA has a *Hong Kong for Golfers* brochure. The top hotels can arrange for guests to play. The **Clear Water Bay Golf and Country Club** *(Sai Kung Peninsula, New Territories. 719-5936)* has an 18-hole course, among many other facilities. The green fee is over $1,000. HKTA goes there on its **Sports and Recreation Tour** *(801-7177)*.

The **Royal Hong Kong Golf Club** has two locations. Non-members can play weekdays only. In **Fanling**, New Territories *(670-1211)*, there are three 18-hole courses at $1,200/course. The beautiful, old **Deep Water Bay** golf course, *on the south side of Hong Kong Island (812-7070, 9:30am-1:30pm, $350 for 18 holes, $5 for a set of clubs)* has nine holes and a putting green.

The **Discovery Bay Golf Club** *(Lantau Island, 987-7272)* has a 9 and an 18-hole golf course. Non-members can play weekdays ($700) and on the brightly-lit course on any night *(6-10:30pm $1,150)*.

HORSE RACING

The racing season is from mid-September to June on Wednesday nights and weekends. *For information call the Royal Hong Kong Jockey Club at 837-8111 or fax 890-2946. The South China Morning Post* has a racing supplement on race days which lists riders, horses, odds and best bets. Tracks are in **Happy Valley** on Hong Kong Island and **Sha Tin** in the New Territories.

Going to the races is a bright-lights fun thing to do that's also historical. Horses have raced in Happy Valley since 1846. The organizers founded the first jockey club in 1884 with mounts from China. The disruptions of the Boxer Rebellion in 1901 forced the club to look to Australia for mounts. Races continued inspite of a disasterous club house fire in 1918 in which 600 people died. They also continued during the Japanese occupation. The club became **The Royal Hong Kong Jockey Club** in 1960 and racing became professional after a horse-doping scandal was uncovered in the early 1970s. There are no purses. The same jockeys ride several races.

The larger **Sha Tin** race course was built in 1978 with a capacity for 80,000 people and luxury, three-story air-conditioned "apartments" where all the race horses live.

The Jockey Club is the second-largest employer in Hong Kong not counting government. It donates millions of dollars a year to charities, museums, cultural projects, and parks. **Ocean Park** is one of its many successful projects.

The easiest way to go is by HKTA tour which includes transfers from the Excelsior Hotel or any other staging area, admission to the Members' Enclosure which has 13 betting windows (hardly any line-ups), and a great buffet meal. A guide is available to give betting instructions and explanations. The tour leaves the club after the end of the 5th race because of the heavy traffic. Night racing is spectacular with the big screen magnifying the action, instant replays and close-ups of the horses and riders. High-rise buildings ring the course.

Going on your own is interesting and a lot cheaper. You will have to deal with crowds, line-ups and traffic. Betting procedures are the same as elsewhere. One can also bet off-track at branch offices of the club.

HORSEBACK RIDING

You can ride at **Lantau Tea Gardens**, *Lantau Island (985-5718) for $360/hour*. **Pokfulam Riding School** charges $310 per lesson, but there is a waiting list (*550-1359, Pokfulam Reservoir Rd., Hong Kong Island, near Queen Mary Hospital*).

ICE SKATING

Head for **City Plaza**, *Taikoo Shing (Taikoo MTR)* on Hong Kong Island and **Tuen Mun Town Plaza**, New Territories *(Town Centre LRT)*.

JOGGING

Best are the **Peak** and **Bowen Road** in the early morning (See "Central"), **Victoria Park** running track in Causeway Bay, **Kowloon Park** in Tsim Sha Tsui, the **Promenade** along the waterfront between the Star Ferry and Tsim Sha Tsui East. Also good are along the rivers in Sha Tin and Tai Po, and in the New Territories.

LAWN BOWLING

Test your skill at lawn bowling in **Victoria Park**, Causeway Bay.

MARTIAL ARTS

Call the **Hong Kong Chinese Martial Arts Association**, *(687 Nathan Rd, 394-4803)* for upcoming events. You might want to check out **Kung Fu Supplies Company**, *6/F, 188 Johnston Rd., Wanchai. 891-1912.*

MASSAGE AND SAUNA

Sunny Paradise *(339-347 Lockhart Rd., Wanchai. 831-0123)* offers a 45-minute massage and sauna for $195. **VIP Sauna** *(13/F, Autoplaza, Mody Rd., Tsim Sha Tsui East. 311-2288)* has the same deal for $550. Look under "Baths and Saunas" in the yellow pages. Legitimate places will serve both men and women. For more personal services look under "Massage" or "Escorts." Many hotels also provide massage service.

PARACHUTING

The **Hong Kong Parachute Club** *(891-5447)* has a weekend training course for $2,000, which includes one jump.

ROCK CLIMBING

The **Hong Kong Mountaineering Training Centre** *(388-3626)* offers a two-day rock climbing course from $200.

ROLLER SKATING

Head for **City Plaza**, Taikoo Shing, Quarry Bay. There are also small rinks in **Victoria Park** in Causeway Bay on Hong Kong Island and **Tuen Mun Town Park**, New Territories.

RUGBY

The **Rugby Sevens** are three days of fast, exciting 7-a-side international rugby, around Easter (late March, early April). About 40,000 expatriates attend daily. This three-day party is characterized by streakers, body painting, and lots of beer. Tickets go fast. Call HKTA or the **Hong Kong Rugby Football Union**, 566-0719 for more information.

SCUBA DIVING

Hong Kong is not a great place to dive. There is a lot more marine life in the Philippines, but if you insist: **Bunns Divers Institute**, *188 Wanchai Rd., Hong Kong Island, 893-7899*, goes out every Sunday. The boat costs $260 and equipment $280. The **International (Elite) Divers' Training**

Centre, *381-2789/381-1132*, gives a PADI Open Water Diving Course for $3,500/person. **Bunn's Diving Equipment**, *572-1629*, is a dive shop.

SQUASH

The **Hong Kong Squash Centre**, *Hong Kong Park (869-0611)* has 16 courts, open 7am-11pm at the cost of $46/hr. **Victoria Park** *(570-6186)* and some hotels also have courts.

SWIMMING

There is an indoor public pool in Kowloon Park *(724-3577)* and an outdoor pool in Victoria Park *(570-4682)*. See "Beaches" earlier in this chapter.

TAI CHI CHUAN

(**T'ai Chi Ch'uan**) To watch or participate, go in the early morning to **Victoria Park** (Causeway Bay), the **Botanical Gardens** (Central), or **Kowloon Park** (Tsim Sha Tsui). Teachers of *tai chi* believe that good health must be earned. Through slow graceful exercises, the body is brought into harmony with *chi*, the cosmic breath. Known also as shadow boxing, the movements help with circulation, joints, and muscles. They increase oxygen intake, and improve the nervous system. It is relaxing and good for what ails you. It is not as easy as it looks because it requires a lot of balance, a union of the body and the mind.

Tai Chi developed out of the Yin-Yang from the Three Kingdoms period, about 220 AD-265 AD. It started out imitating tigers, deer, bear, apes and cranes. By joining a group you can learn movements, but if you want to learn the background and meaning of what you are doing, look for an English-speaking teacher or a good book.

TENNIS

The **Hong Kong Tennis Centre** *(574-9122, on Wong Nei Chong Gap Road, Hong Kong Island, open until 11pm)* has 17 lit tennis courts. **Victoria Park** *in Causeway Bay, 570-6186,* has 14 lit courts, open 7am-11pm. **Kowloon Park** has some too. Public courts usually charge $23-44/hour.

WALKING

The best walk is around the **Peak**. See "Central". HKTA's free *Country Walks* leaflet describes short, 2-3 hour walks on Hong Kong Island and the New Territories. HKTA also sells excellent walking tour books for $25. Other good books are the three-book *Magic Walks* series by Kaarlo Schepel and the fascinating *Historical Hong Kong Walks: Hong Kong Island* by Madeleine Tang.

WATERSKIING

The **Waterski Club**, *Deep Water Bay, Hong Kong Island (812-0391)* charges $480/hour for boat, driver, and equipment.

WINDSURFING

Pro-shop *(723-6816)* runs three windsurfing centers, where you can rent equipment and wetsuits, on **Stanley Beach** (Hong Kong Island), **Cheung Chau Windsurfing Centre** (Tung Wan Beach), and **Sha Ha Beach**, in front of the Surf Hotel, a five-minute drive from Sai Kung in the New Territories.

9. FOOD & DRINK

Hong Kong is famous for food. It runs the range from cheap, street restaurants on crude folding tables in **Temple Street** to magnificent spreads with silver platters and jade spoons in the **Regent Hotel**. Both can be very delicious and equally satisfying in their own ways. Food also ranges internationally and the first question after someone suggests going out is "What kind?"

CHINESE FOOD

Chinese restaurants are everywhere in Hong Kong. Knives are unnecessary because cooks usually chop food up in thin, bite-size pieces for quick stir-frying, using a minimum of fuel. Chinese food can also appear whole, like fish or pork hocks, but you can easily separate these with chopsticks. Cooks chop up poultry before it appears at the table, the bones deliberately splintered so you can reach the food inside the bones. Do be careful. Chinese cooking reflects the many periods of famine in Chinese history. You eat everything possible and waste nothing, not even chicken feet, duck tongues, jellyfish and sea slugs, all famous delicacies.

For Chinese food, it's usually better to eat in a group to get variety. Ten is ideal. Some restaurants have a set dinner for one with lots of dishes but it can be very expensive. Try buffets. Although the food is not as freshly cooked, there are lots of things to taste. Make note of favorite dishes so you can order them later. Expect cheaper restaurants to be noisy with the chatter of excited Hong Kong people. The more expensive the restaurant, the quieter it'll be. There are many distinct kinds of Chinese food; the most common in Hong Kong is Cantonese.

Beijing Food

Beijing or **Peking** is light with few sauces, some roasts and lots of garlic, leeks and scallions. Dishes are accompanied by buns, and meat dumplings made of flour and baked, steamed, fried or boiled in soup. Peking food is somewhat salty. Famous dishes include Peking duck, pan-fried onion cake, hot-sour soup, sauteed chicken and walnuts, and tiny Tianjin cabbage with black mushrooms.

Cantonese

Cantonese has several sub-groups. You quickly cook stir-fried Cantonese food in peanut oil, garlic, and ginger for crisp vegetables. It is somewhat sweet with starches and sugar in the sauces and uses a lot of oyster sauce and soy sauce. Famous dishes are crisp-skinned roasted goose, steamed chicken, shark's fin in chicken and ham soup, steamed live fish or prawns, stir-fried beef in oyster sauce, and sweet and sour pork spareribs.

Dim sum

Dim sum is a form of Cantonese cooking. You choose from a variety of small pastries or meat dishes usually for lunch and sometimes for breakfast. People will say, *Hui yum cha,* which means go to a tea house for these tiny steamed, fried, deep-fried or baked delicacies. The steamed dim sum arrive in little baskets. You usually also order a dish of noodles or congee (flavored rice gruel) but we prefer gorging just on the pastries. Two or three dishes should fill each person up.

In some restaurants women push trolleys with different dim sum dishes. You wave them down, check out what is available and point to one or two. In more expensive restaurants, you order from a menu. *The Hong Kong Association of Travel Agents' Official Map* book (free) has color photographs of dim sum dishes, with descriptions and names in English and Chinese so you can point to order. Otherwise, try the following:
- *Har gow*: steamed, smoothy-wrapped shrimp dumpling
- *Sui mai*: steamed, minced pork and shrimp dumpling
- *Cha sui bow*: steamed, barbecued pork buns
- *Tsun guen*: deep-fried spring roll with pork, mushrooms, chicken, bamboo shoots and bean sprouts
- *Ho yip fan*: fried rice wrapped in lotus leaf and steamed
- *Pai gwut*: steamed pork spareribs Gai chuk: steamed chicken in bean curd wrapping
- *Daan* tart: egg custard tart.

Chiu Chow

Chiu Chow is a form of Cantonese cooking from **Shantou (Swatow)** in northern Guangdong province. Most restaurants have a little stall with hanging poultry gizzards and liver, pork intestines, or octopus, tinted orange. The emphasis is on seafoods: double-boiled shark's fins with chicken soup, baked lobster with *Cheunjew* sauce and sliced whelk shell fish with ham. Other dishes include fried sliced pigeon with *Cheunjew* sauce, deep-fried spiced goose, and fried shredded pork with pickled cabbage.

Shanghai

Shanghai food is grouped with that of Suzhou, Yangzhou, Wuxi, etc. It is cooked longer in sesame oil, neither sweet nor salty, and not spicy hot. It can be very ornamental. Borscht is on the menu of many Shanghai restaurants because of the many white Russians who once lived there. Among the many Shanghai dishes are shrimp with tomato sauce on crispy rice, West Lake fish, chicken with cashew nuts, lion's head casserole and beggar's chicken.

Szechuan

Szechuan or **Sichuan** dishes are spicy, peppery hot, and oily but there are bland dishes as well. A favorite is smoked duck with camphor and tea flavor, spicy stir-fried prawns, Ma-po bean curd (with a hot meat sauce), and chicken with green onions and cashews.

ORDERING

The secret of successful ordering is to go with at least one Chinese-speaking friend. It makes a difference. Most Hong Kong people are gourmets and know a lot about food.

Frequently, the specials of the day are not on the menu but in Chinese on the wall. Every restaurant also has its own specialties. Ask about them. They will probably be a little more expensive but are usually worth it.

The easiest way to order is to watch the dishes going to other tables then point and say, "I want one of those." Or tell the waiter how much you want to pay and let the cook decide. Meals chosen by cooks are usually very good but you should always ask to approve the menu. You might get something unique and expensive like camel's hump which you might not like.

The proper way to order is to choose a variety of different kinds of dishes, usually one dish per person plus a starch. You can always order more. If you are on your own and want a light lunch, try fried noodles, won ton soup or dim sum.

Hong Kong is the largest importer of sharks' fins in the world, almost a national dish which should be tried at least once even though it is very expensive. You must also try dim sum.

USING CHOPSTICKS

Chinese food is designed to be eaten with these extension of fingers. Restaurants can supply forks if you can't use them. But learning is part of the fun, and most people master them after a few meals. Watch those around you for hints on how to use them properly. You lift a bowl of white rice to the mouth and shovel it in with chopsticks. Long noodles are slurped in and cut with your teeth.

When cooking your own food as in Mongolian Hot Pot, be careful that the utensils you use on raw meat or fish are not the same utensils you put into your own mouth.

HOW TO USE CHOPSTICKS

The bottom stick is held firmly by the base of the thumb and the knuckle of the ring finger. The top stick is the ONLY one that is moved and is held by the thumb and the index and middle fingers. The tip of the top stick should be brought toward the tip of the bottom one. Keep the tips even.

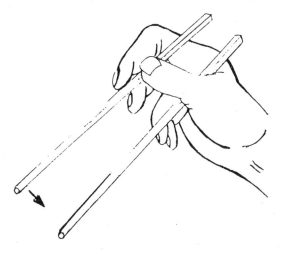

MARTIN MALLOY

EATING CHINESE FOOD

Chinese food is usually served on large platters which ideally arrive one at a time and from which you take a share. You should eat it hot as soon as possible. In very formal meals, an attendant first puts the platter on the table to be admired, and then takes it away to be divided into individual dishes before passing it to each guest. If an attendant doesn't serve the food, your host might pick up the best pieces and put them on your plate or everybody just digs in.

Elaborate banquets can have 12 to 20 courses so you should pace yourself. Eat only one-20th of what you normally eat so you will have room for a taste of everything. If there is something you don't like, just leave it.

WARNING

Hong Kong is not immune to food poisoning even though the tap water is treated and safe. To avoid an upset stomach, eat only hot, cooked foods in restaurants with questionable hygiene, especially in hot weather.

Make sure the meat everywhere is not red and the fish thoroughly cooked. Check the plates and chopsticks for cleanliness. You might want to scald them with hot tea.

If you get an upset stomach, eat rice congee, which is rice cooked to a gruel consistency and flavored with salted egg, fermented bean curd, or whatever. Congee is easy on the stomach. Avoid fried dishes, spices and dairy products until you feel better. Eat dry crackers and toast, arrowroot biscuits, apple sauce and bananas.

Take Pepto-Bismol if the disorder is mild, or something like Imodium or call a doctor if it's severe. China supplies the ingredients for much of Hong Kong's fresh produce. As pesticides are not as carefully monitored there as in North America, don't eat it if something tastes "funny" to you.

MSG

Hong Kong is moving away from the flavor-enhancer monosodium glutamate (MSG), but some of the older, conservative Chinese restaurants still use it. It gives some people headaches, a quickened pulse rate, and sleepless nights. If you don't want any *mei ding*, tell your waiter. It is not used for western food or in any of the major hotels. Some restaurants now advertise "No MSG."

TOASTING

Toasting is an integral part of every banquet. Chinese people do not like to drink alone. The host should give the first toast of welcome. You can respond and encourage the rest to drink too. *Gan bei!* means "Empty your glass!" Chinese people also have drinking games. You might ask your friends to teach you.

TEA

You could be asked your choice of tea with your meal. Many foreigners love jasmine or hung pean and order it all the time. But there are other good teas. *Po li* is good in hot weather and helps you digest grease. *Keemun* is good in wintertime, also for greasy food. *Longching* (dragon well) is a famous delicious tea from Hangzhou, and you can impress the waitor with your knowledge. *Sao Mei* is more bitter than *Po Li* for waking up and cleaning the intestines. A little bitter is **Iron Buddha** tea. **Ti Kuan Yin** is an oolong tea from Fujian.

To tell the waiter you want your tea pot refilled, turn the pot's lid upside down on top of the pot.

NON-ALCOHOLIC BEVERAGES

You can get all the North American stuff here, except Dr. Pepper which Linda only found at Kublai's restaurant in Tsim Sha Tsui. You can find some interesting drinks in 7-11s and other convenience stores, like cold, sweet chrysanthemum tea (Linda' favorite), sugar cane juice, jelly drinks, and exotic fruit juices.

ALCOHOL

The national drink is cognac but there are lots of interesting Chinese or foreign wines. You can buy all kinds of beer: German, Canadian, Chinese, etc. The most popular are Carlsberg and San Miguel, which are good. The government taxes alcohol so be sure to ask the price before you order.

10. WHERE TO STAY

PRICES

Hotels cost about the same or a little more than in New York City. Rooms are generally small. Expect to pay at least $800-$1000 for a decent hotel room. Prices range from $2350 at the famous Peninsula in Tsim Sha Tsui down to $250 in guest houses. Room prices depend on the size of the room and the quality of the view. Hotels add 10% service charge and 5% government tax to your bill. Prices are accurate at press time, but are rising fast. Some hotels have been increasing prices twice a year.

Hong Kong hotels are almost fully booked year round. The only low season are the weeks around the Chinese New Year because stores and offices are closed.

Many hotels have one price for single and double occupancy. Almost all hotels have suites. The most expensive suites range in the Grand Hyatt $5000-22000, Mandarin $4500-22000, The Regent $3600-20000, Ritz-Carlton $7800-20000 and Island Shangri-La $7800-24000.

Most budget and moderate hotels are in Mong Kok and Yau Ma Tei. Moderate hotels can also be found in Wanchai and Tsim Sha Tsui. Expensive hotels are in Central, Causeway Bay, Tsim Sha Tsui and Tsim Sha Tsui East. Guest houses for $450 or less are listed at the end of this chapter.

Local calls from rooms usually cost between $2-4 although they are free in a few budget hotels. Buffet breakfasts in expensive hotels start from about $130.

SAVING MONEY

Is price critical? If so, shop around for the best deal. The Holiday Inn Golden Mile's cheapest available on one specific date in 1994 was US$207.70 for a single. The Holiday Inn Crowne Plaza had a room on the same day for US$134.60, (about 40% off the regular price!) a special. Ask for discounts, there's no harm and you might be pleasantly surprised.

Many hotels have long-staying, meeting, summer and winter packages, and corporate discounts. Check out plans like the Holiday Inn's

Priority Club which gives upgrades and discounts. The Sheraton has special rates with advance bookings. See also Saving Money in Chapter 6.

RESERVATIONS

We strongly recommend that you reserve a room at least two months before you arrive. Hotel occupancy rates are about 90%. Reserve through the North American reservation numbers in the hotel listings or through a travel agent or airline. You can also telephone or fax the hotels directly. Most hotels ask for credit-card secured deposits for arrivals after 6pm.

SERVICES

Generally, the cheaper the hotel, the less English, but in all of these, with patience, you should be able to communicate. If you are having problems, ask for a manager or phone HKTA.

All hotels have private baths, room telephones, air-conditioning, smoke alarms in the rooms, safe deposit boxes in lobbies, laundry services, 110/220 volt outlets for shavers, and televisions with at least two local English-speaking channels. All have money changing (usually at a bad rate), international direct dial (IDD), and postal and laundry services unless noted otherwise. Check out time is usually noon.

In all moderate hotels are a mini-refrigerator and often other facilities found also in expensive hotels. Expensive hotels have pay in-house movies, television remote controls, mini-bars, free daily newpapers, same-day laundry service, business centers, executive floors, hairdryers, free baggage storage and non-smoking floors or rooms. There are peep-holes and double or triple locks in doors. They have concierges with a knowledge of tailors, theater tickets, tours, restaurants and shopping who can also make airline reservations, confirmations and mail packages. Some hotels have fancy room key cards computerized just for your use and secure in-room safes. Many have kettles that you can use for making your own coffee or tea.

Almost all hotels have Cantonese restaurants and western coffee shops. The more expensive hotels also have fine restaurants with European or Japanese food and a variety of Chinese cuisines. Recommended hotel restaurants are listed in Chapter 11, "Where to Eat."

Do you want to watch television while soaking in a tub? Try the Peninsula's new tower. Do you want error-free voice-mail messages? There's the Grand Hyatt, The Peninsula, New World, Sheraton and New World Harbour View. If any of these services are crucial to your choice, ask about them when enquiring about reservations. Services as well as prices change.

Hotels do not pay for inclusion in this book. We have chosen hotels worthy of your consideration because of price, location, and quality.

AIRPORT SHUTTLES & LIMOS

Some hotels including the moderately-priced Wharney in Wanchai and the Metropole in Mongkok have airport shuttle services ($70/$30) and limo ($230/120) services if you request it. The Peninsula can pick you up in a Rolls Royce. At the Regent you can choose a Daimler. The Victoria has Mercedes with mobile phones for the use of passengers.

If you want to save money, take a taxi or better still the Airbus. When you reserve, ask about airport pickup and the cost.

SPORTS

Most expensive hotels have exercise equipment. Some have swimming pools. The largest swimming pool is at the New World Harbour View/Grand Hyatt in Wanchai. The Victoria in Western and the Royal Park in the New Territories have a health club, pool and tennis courts.

The Grand Hyatt and the New World in Wanchai have all of the above plus a jogging track and putting green. The Grand Plaza in Quarry Bay on Hong Kong Island has all that plus squash. The Salisbury YMCA in Tsim Sha Tsui has squash, a health club and a pool.

KIDS

Almost all hotels can arrange for babysitting (about $40/hour) and children under 12 years can share a room with their parents for free. In the Holiday Inns, it's under 19 and at the Sheraton, it's 18. Baby cots are usually available without charge.

BUSINESS

The best hotels for business are the Regent and the Mandarin. All expensive and moderate hotels have business centers with fax, photocopy, typewriter and probably secretarial services. Most can arrange courier service. A few have computers, pagers and mobile telephones for rent.

If you want two telephone lines and conference calls from your room, go to the Grand Hyatt, Mandarin Oriental, Peninsula, Regent and Ritz Carlton. The Holiday Inn Crowne Plaza and others can rent you an office. As for Cable Network News (CNN), can you function without up-to-the minute television news?

If not, check into the CharterHouse, Island Shangri-La, Mandarin, The Ritz-Carlton, Park Lane or Excelsior. Almost all hotels have conference and banquet facilities. Many hotels can put a fax machine into some of their rooms.

THE BEST HOTELS

*The best hotels are the **Regent** and the more expensive, but historical **Peninsula**, both in Tsim Sha Tsui. The **Mandarin** in Central is a close third. Next in line are the two **Shangri-La's** (in Central and Tsim Sha Tsui East) and the **Grand Hyatt** in Wanchai. The **Ritz-Carlton** in Central is the most exclusive and classy.*

*The best moderately-priced hotels are the **Holiday Inn Golden Mile**, **Kimberley**, **Kowloon Hotel**, **New World Hotel**, and the **Park** in Tsim Sha Tsui, the **Majestic** in Yau Ma Tei, and the **Kowloon Panda** and the **Royal Park** in the New Territories.*

*The best budget hotels are the **Garden View International House** in Central, the **Salisbury YMCA** in Tsim Sha Tsui, the **Booth Lodge** (Salvation Army), the **Eaton** in Yau Ma Tei and the **Anne Black YWCA** in Mong Kok.*

*The best view of the harbor is from the **Regent**, then the **Mandarin**, the **Ritz Carlton**, and the **Furama** in Central. The construction in the harbor makes it even more interesting. Also good are the **Hotel Victoria** in Western, the **Grand Hyatt/New World Harbour View** in Wanchai, the **Excelsior** in Causeway Bay, and in Tsim Sha Tsui East, the **Holiday Inn Crowne Plaza** and the **Nikko**.*

*The most gracious and elegant hotel coffee shops are the **Grand Hyatt**, **Mandarin**, **Peninsula**, and **Regent**.*

*The best hotel library is at the **Island Shangri-La**, the room, not necessarily the books.*

CONSIDER LOCATION

The best place for business is Central. Shoppers should head for Tsim Sha Tsui. If they want quality without regard to price, then choose Pacific Place where our favorite hotel of the three good ones is the Island Shangri-La. Kowloon has the airport and railway station and is only seven minutes by Star Ferry or MTR from Hong Kong Island. A taxi through the Cross-Harbour tunnel takes a lot longer and can be overly expensive.

If you're only staying a couple of days and need a taxi to the airport, stay on the Kowloon side. All districts except Tsim Sha Tsui East are on the MTR (subway) line, within 5-20 minutes of each other.

On beautiful, historic **Hong Kong Island**, most hotels are in the four adjoining districts along the waterfront. **Western** is the rapidly changing, traditional Chinese district with lots of antique stores and the Macau Ferry Pier. **Central** is the clean-cut business, financial and government center with tall, modern buildings, wonderful parks, good shopping and Lan Kwai Fong, the most popular eating and drinking neighborhood. **Wanchai** is part business and part old, red-light district. Crowded **Causeway Bay** has the largest park and the most Japanese department stores.

On Kowloon, touristy **Tsim Sha Tsui** is good for shopping, has a great park, the most hotels and museums, but is very crowded. Modern **Tsim Sha Tsui East** has the least air pollution and crowds, but is less interesting with only shopping malls, hotels, expensive hostess clubs and one museum. It is the closest to the railway station. Crowded **Yau Ma Tei** borders Tsim Sha Tsui and Kowloon Park and has two markets. **Mong Kok** is even more crowded, has the worst air pollution, but is an interesting Chinese area with three markets.

There are a few good hotels in the **New Territories**. They are cheaper, but are about a half hour by MTR/KCR from downtown. If you have problems with air pollution, head for the islands. The only decent hotel is the Warwick on Cheung Chau. You might want a vacation flat. Going to China by ship or bus? If so, think about the Royal Pacific, the Omnis or the Hong Kong Renaissance. As for Macau, the Hotel Victoria sits on top of the ferry terminal.

HKTA has the free *Hotels* booklet listing hotels, prices, and facilities.

HOTEL LISTINGS

All hotels take Visa, MasterCard, American Express and some take Diners Club, unless indicated otherwise. Prices are for single or double occupancy of double rooms. Only a few hotels charge less for singles. Phone numbers for reserving rooms in North America are at the end of each listing. All distances (i.e. 5 minutes to MTR) are for walking unless otherwise specified.

HONG KONG ISLAND

Central–Expensive

HOTEL FURAMA KEMPINSKI HONG KONG, *1 Connaught Road Central. 525-5111, fax 868-1768. 517 rooms. $1680-2480 double. Extra bed $250. North American reservations call 1-800-426-3135.*

This comfortable, 30-story, 1973 hotel is in a great location, a few steps from Central MTR station and a two-minute walk from the Star Ferry. It takes mainly individual travelers, and has a good view of Central, the Peak and the harbor, especially from the La Ronda revolving restaurant. Amenities include French and Japanese restaurants, bars, business center, in-room safes, lots of drawer space, scales and two health centers with sizeable gym, sauna, jacuzzi and steam bath. One is for males only.

ISLAND SHANGRI-LA HONG KONG, *Pacific Place, Supreme Court Road. Floors 5-8 and 39-56. 877-3838, fax 521-8742. 575 rooms. $2100-3150. Extra bed $350.*

This 1991 hotel has good Peak and harbor views and is very well located, classy and opulent. It has 500 works of art. The most spectacular is a 14-story, Chinese landscape painting of the Great Wall of China, the largest such painting in the world. It also has oriental antiques and 756 Viennese chandeliers. On top of the giant, upmarket **Pacific Place** shopping mall, it is across the street from Hong Kong Park and Admiralty MTR. There are French and Japanese restaurants, a lobster bar and exceptionally good Cantonese food.

Facilities include a 24-hour business center, a heated outdoor pool, a deli, lounges, 24-hour room service, a wood-panelled, two story-high library for browsing and afternoon tea. It also has a good gym, aerobics classes, tanning machine, massage, steam bath, sauna, jacuzzis, personal training, Daimler limousines and a Roger Craig beauty salon. Spacious rooms have separate shower stalls and tubs, bidets, double sinks, kettles, safes, two desks, three telephones and scales. Reservations in North America 1-800-942-5050.

The **Conrad** and the **Marriott** are also good luxury hotels at the same location.

MANDARIN ORIENTAL, *5 Connaught Road, Central, GPO Box 2623. 522-0111, fax 810-6190. 538 rooms. $2250-3400. Extra bed $500. North American reservations 1-800-526-6566.*

This 1963, 25-story hotel decorated with antiques and sculptures has excellent service, a small lobby and a great location. The MTR is across the street and the Star Ferry is two blocks away. It has big rooms with balconies and a small, beautiful pool, styled after a Roman bath. Its highly-rated French restaurant, **Pierrot**, specializes in Petrossian caviar. Look for the charming ladies on elephants near the **Mandarin Grill**. This was the first hotel in Hong Kong with 24-hour on-command videos. You have a choice of 60. Facilities include a business center, large gym, deli, 24-hour room service and four bars. The figure head in its **Clipper Lounge** is from the movie *Billy Budd*. It also has dancing, deep-tissue massage, sauna, Chinese acupressure, solarium, beauty salon and barber shop, in-room safes, scales and Rolls Royces.

THE RITZ-CARLTON, *3 Connaught Road Central. 877-6666, fax 877-6778. 216 rooms. $2500-3700. Extra bed $500. Reservations in North America 1-800-241-3333.*

This slender, cozy, 1993, tastefully-decorated, 25-story hotel is aimed at an exclusive clientele who want privacy and good attentive service. There is a dress code in the public areas. Facilities include Japanese, Tuscan (Italian), and Asian restaurants, outdoor pool, 24-hour room service, bar, lounge with high tea, free in-house movies, ballroom, business center, executive floors with private elevator, sauna, steam room, massage, jacuzzi, small gym, non-smoking rooms, art gallery, beauty salon and Rolls Royces. Rooms have silk wall coverings, leather-top desks and safes. The Ritz is steps to the MTR and close to Star Ferry.

Budget–Central
GARDEN VIEW INTERNATIONAL HOUSE, *1 MacDonnel Road. 877-3737, fax 845-6263. 131 rooms. $630-740 double. $13,257-15,504/ month.*

One of the best deals in town. The YWCA manages this 1990 hotel, but you'd never guess, when you enter the elegant marble lobby or relax in its large, comfortable rooms with bay windows and mini-refrigerators. The only problem is the location across from the lush Botanical and Zoological Gardens (which is great), but a 20-minute walk down to Central. Public buses are available. There's a restaurant, 24-hour business center with computer rental, outdoor pool, badminton court, gym, chapel and babysitting. There is no 5% government tax nor room service.

Western–Expensive
HOTEL VICTORIA, *Shun Tak Centre, 200 Connaught Road, Central 540-7228, fax 858-3398. 508 rooms. $1650-2550. Extra bed $280. North America reservations 1-800-44-UTELL or 1-800-538-8882.*

This oasis of peace is accessible from the Sheung Wan MTR stop and sits on top of a 160-unit proletarian shopping mall and the busy Macau ferry terminal. 75% of the rooms have a good harbor view and the seven, 40th-floor suites have their own roof gardens. Facilities include an Asian restaurant, deli, bar, lounge with dancing, tea terrace, free 24-hour movie channel, business center with computer and three executive floors with great views. There's also tennis, outdoor pool, golf-driving ranges, massage, sauna, steam room, well-equipped gym, 24-hour room service and a frequent free shuttle bus to Star Ferry and Pacific Place. It has no non-smoking floors.

Wanchai–Expensive
GRAND HYATT HONG KONG, *1 Harbour Road. 588-1234, fax 802-0677. 573 rooms. $1900-2950. Extra bed $350. North American reservations 1-800-233-1234.*

This magnificent, 36-story hotel is indeed grand with a pair of curving staircases swirling down to the impressive black marble lobby. Eight kilometers from the airport and 5.6 kilometers from the railway station, its public areas are works of art and worth visiting, even if you don't stay here. There is an elegant disco, the **Champagne Bar**, a coffee shop with a breath-taking view, and some of Hong Kong's best restaurants. Try the Milanese, Japanese (with extensive sake menu) or Cantonese restaurants. The latter captures the romantic flavor of a 1930 *staipan's* home.

Outdoor recreational facilities on a 11,000 square meter, rooftop terrace include a 335-meter jogging trail, golf-driving range, putting green, two floodlit tennis courts and a sizeable gym. Its 47-meter outdoor hotel pool is Hong Kong's longest. These facilities are shared with the New World Harbour View. There's also 24-hour room service, bar, lounge, business center and executive floors with a split-level lounge. There's a sauna, massage, three jacuzzis, in-room safes, separate shower stalls and complimentry shuttle service by London taxi to Central.

NEW WORLD HARBOUR VIEW, *1 Harbour Road. 802-8888, fax 802-8833. 862 rooms. $1680-2800. Extra bed $250. North American reservations 1-800-538-8882.*

This 42-story, modern, glitzy, comfortable 1989 hotel is less elegant than its sister, the Grand Hyatt next door. It is very good nonetheless. They share the same, great roof-top facilities mentioned above. The **Oasis Bar** has a good view and an all-you-can-eat snack buffet. Well-lit medium-sized rooms have kettles. There is a deli, 24-hour room service, bar, lounge, well-equipped business center with computer rentals and packing service, executive floors, gym, steam bath, sauna, jacuzzi, beauty salon, and BMW and Mercedes limousines. It's about 500 meters by covered walkway to Wanchai MTR and is close to the Wanchai Ferry to Tsim Sha Tsui, Kowloon. A free shuttle bus connects with Central.

Wanchai–Moderate

CENTURY HONG KONG HOTEL, *238 Jaffe Road. 598-8888, fax 598-8866. 511 rooms. $1300-1950. Extra bed $300.*

This slightly over-priced, 1991 hotel is better than the Wharney. Located in a crowded neighborhood close to the Wanchai MTR station, it has small rooms, bathrooms and beds. There's also an outdoor pool, business center, kettles, Italian and Asian restaurants, 24-hour room service, non-smoking floors and well-equipped gym.

CHARTERHOUSE, *209-219 Wanchai Road. 833-5566, fax 833-5888. Rooms $1000-$1400.* You'll find narrow halls, short, thin beds and great dim sum in this good, small, slightly over-priced hotel. The bathrooms and tubs are tiny. Facilities include in-room safes, CNN and kettles. It is on a busy street with small stores within walking distance of the Wanchai and Causeway Bay MTR stops. There is 24-hour secretarial service and a Karaoke lounge. Try to haggle.

EVERGREEN PLAZA HOTEL, *33 Hennessy Rd. 866-9111, fax 861-3121. 296 rooms. $1000-1300.*

This glitzy, 1991 hotel is very popular with Taiwan tourists. It has a business center, heated pool, in-room safes, kettles, four sprinklers per room, poor bedside reading lights and small bathrooms.

LUK KWOK HOTEL, *72 Gloucester Road. 866-2166, fax 866-2622. 192 rooms. Doubles $1200-1300. Singles $920-1080.*

The famous Suzie Wong hotel does not look at all like the rundown girlie bar with the hourly rooms that used to entertain the fleet in the 1960s. The only souvenirs of that era are old photos in its lobby.

SOUTH PACIFIC, *23 Morrison Hill Rd., 572-3838, fax 893-7773. 293 rooms. $980-1700.*

This tall, circular, glass building was built in 1992 and is about a five-minute walk to Causeway Bay MTR station at Times Square shopping mall. It has a restaurant, coffee shop, two lounges and caters mainly to Chinese tourists. Small rooms have hairdryers, kettles, mini-bars and safes.

THE WESLEY, *22 Henessey Road. 866-6688, fax 866-6633. 250 rooms. $900-1500. North American reservations 1-800-44UTELL.*

This is a basic hotel that caters mainly to Japanese visitors. Its pastel-colored rooms have kettles, hairdryers and mini-bars, but the one Linda saw also had a dirty carpet. It is the closest Wanchai hotel to Central and is only a seven-minute walk from Admiralty MTR. It replaced the century-old Soldiers and Sailors Home and is a joint venture of Grand Hotel Holdings and the Methodist Church. It has a restaurant, coffee shop, business center and kettles.

THE WHARNEY, *57-73 Lockhart Rd, 861-1000, fax 865-6023. 335 rooms. $1200-1380.*

This nice hotel is better than the South Pacific, although you can hear street noise in some rooms. It is two blocks to Wanchai MTR. Rooms have kettles and mini-bars. Among its facilities are a tiny outdoor pool, business center (with computer rental), restaurant, coffee shop, bar, gym, steam bath, sauna and a non-smoking floor.

Wanchai–Budget

HARBOUR VIEW INTERNATIONAL HOUSE, *4 Harbour Road. 802-0111, fax 802-9063. 320 rooms. $700-1150. Extra bed $160 for deluxe rooms only.*

This YWCA affiliate is just west of the Grand Hyatt with almost the same, good waterfront view. It has a European restaurant, tours, narrow halls and beds, small televisions, no tubs, just showers, and parcel, fax and photocopying services. Its shuttle to the Star Ferry is free.

HOTEL NEW HARBOUR, *41-49 Hennessy Road. 861-1166, fax 865-6111. 173 rooms. $770-1150. Extra bed $180. Book through China Travel Service in North America 1-800-663-1126, 1-800-332-2831 or 1-800-553-8764.*

This basic hotel with narrow halls is in need of renovating. Use it as a last resort. It is on a busy noisy street.

Causeway Bay–Expensive

REGAL HONG KONG HOTEL, *Paliburg Plaza, 68 Yee Wo Street. 890-6633, fax 881-0777. 425 rooms. $1750-2450. Extra person $300. Reservations in U.S. 1-800-222-8888, Canada 1-800-233-9188.*

Hemmed in by the city, this 37-story, 1993 luxury hotel is actually quite workable. Huge lobby windows, like giant movie screens, show a travelogue of Hong Kong, especially as the trams go by. And yet, you are apart, relaxing on a Louis XIV couch in the lobby, surrounded by a relatively successful attempt at flossy, classical European ambiance. Gold pillars and white marble statues of women in flowing gowns, punctuate the effect. Bed to ceiling oil paintings decorate the rooms and the 31st floor, year-round, outdoor, Roman pool has a good view. You can jog on the street before 7am. Eat at a Mediterranean, Asian, or Chiuchow restaurant with good dim sum.

The business center has computer rental and equipment for meetings. The executive floor comes with free use of a boardroom. Hotel facilities include massage, sauna, 24-hour room service, pub, disco/karaoke, tea lounge, steam bath, small gym, aerobics, in-room safes and Rolls Royce limos. You can walk to the nearby MTR and tram.

Causeway Bay–Moderate

THE EXCELSIOR HOTEL, *281 Gloucester Road. 894-8888, fax 895-6459. 891 rooms. $1200-2200. Extra person $350. Reservations in North America 1-800-526-6566.*

Built on land acquired by Jardine Matheson from Hong Kong's first land auction, this 34-story hotel has been a fixture here since 1970. Close to the waterfront, next door to the World Trade Centre and a couple minutes walk to department stores and the MTR, it is well-located. It does however have a small, crowded lobby and stained carpets. But it has a popular bar with nightly jazz, 24-hour room service, Italian food, and a Cantonese restaurant inspired by the Forbidden City with a 4,000-liter fish tank and dim sum lunch.

It has a non-smoking floor, executive floors, and a business center with encyclopedias. For fitness, there is aerobics, Swedish massage, jacuzzi, steam bath, sauna and two indoor lit tennis courts. In its rooms are small bathrooms, CNN, trouser press and safe.

THE PARK LANE, *310 Gloucester Road, 890-3355, fax 576-7853. 815 rooms. $1500-2650. Extra bed $300. North American reservations 1-800-338-1338.*

Cheaper rooms are subject to availability. It is easy to relax in this very pleasant, unpretentious, family-run, 28-story, 1973 hotel. It has spacious rooms with smallish bathrooms. Formerly named the Park Plaza and Park Radisson, it has a good view from the rooftop **Parc 27** restaurant of

Victoria Park across the street. The executive floors have CD players, free use of conference room and private elevator. Facilities include 24-hour room service, bake shop, bar, lounge, business center, gym, solarium, sauna, steam bath, jacuzzi, massage, beauty salon, in-room safes, scales and non-smoking floors. Park-view rooms have three telephones.

North Point–Moderate City

GARDEN HOTEL, *231 Electric Rd. 887-2888, fax 887-1111. 615 rooms. $1155-1550. Single $1050-1450.*

Use this hotel as a last resort. Service needs work and it's not very convenient. Follow the map in the Fortress Hill MTR station. It's six kilometers from the airport and six stops from Central on the MTR. It has a business center, gym, sauna and pool.

Quarry Bay–Moderate

GRAND PLAZA, *2 Kornhill Rd. 886-0011, fax 886-1738. 250 rooms. $1100-1650. Studio apartments $18,000 a month. One bedroom $28,000. North American reservations 1-800-UTELL.*

This hotel has excellent sports facilities, but is 15-minutes by MTR to Central. It sits on top of Taikoo Shing MTR, near the massive City Plaza shopping mall, which has ice and roller skating. Rooms have kettles and minibars. The hotel has a bar, lounge, business center, indoor pool, four squash courts, tennis, golf-putting green and driving range, jogging track, gym, steam bath, sauna and jacuzzi. The hotel's **Club Grand** also has billiards, badminton and table tennis.

KOWLOON

Tsim Sha Tsui–Expensive

HONG KONG RENAISSANCE (formerly Ramada Renaissance), *8 Peking Road. 375-1133, fax 375-6611. 500 rooms. $1700-2600. Extra bed $380. North American reservations 1-800-228-9898.*

This restful, 19-story, 1989, luxury hotel is in a corner away from crowds and exudes quiet efficiency. The heated, roof-top pool has a bar. Well-lit rooms have wide beds, satellite television, separate shower stalls, scales and three telephones, two with hands-free speakers. Its **Bostonian American Bar and Restaurant** is fun and papered with customer drawings.

The Renaissance has executive rooms with fax machines and in-room safes. The business center rents lap top computers. There is also dim sum, 24-hour room service, lobby lounge, gym, massage, sauna, solarium and squash. It is above the **Mitsukoshi** department store and close to Harbour City mall.

HYATT REGENCY HONG KONG, *67 Nathan Road. 311-1234, fax 739-8701. 723 rooms. $1900-2500. Extra bed $300. Reservations in North America 1-800-233-1234.*

This 1969, 17-floor hotel renovated in 1994, is obviously for shoppers. It is in the middle of Tsim Sha Tsui, next to the MTR. The ground floor is frequently packed with people and 91 jewelry shops, camera shops and tailors. There is no pool, gym nor sylvan view. There is 24-hour room service, Chinese food served in western style, bar, lounge, business center, executive floors, in-room safes, satellite and pay television, emergency flashlights and non-smoking rooms. Halls and beds are narrow.

OMNI THE HONG KONG HOTEL, *3 Canton Road, Harbour City. 736-0088, fax 736-0011. 665 rooms. $1700-3200. Extra bed $300. North American reservations 1-800-THE-OMNI.*

This 18-story, 1970-hotel has a busy lobby, akin to a railway station. It has the best quality and location of the three Omni hotels attached to Hong Kong's largest mall. The 400-room **Omni Marco Polo** (second best) and the 440-room **Omni Prince** are smaller, cheaper and mainly for tour groups. The **Omni Hong Kong** has Chiu Chow, Japanese, and international restaurants. The best is the **Taipan Grill**. It has 24-hour room service, bars, executive floors and a 24-hour business center which can arrange printing jobs. It also has a heated outdoor pool and non-smoking floor. In its big rooms are separate shower stalls and lots of good lighting.

SHERATON HONG KONG HOTEL & TOWERS, *20 Nathan Road. 369-1111, fax 739-8707. 789 rooms. $1950-3100. Single $1850-3100. Extra Bed $200. North American reservations 1-800-325-3535. Reservations are held only to 4pm.*

This 18-story, luxury hotel is aging gracefully in a great location. It is next to the Telecom office, beside a small park, close to the Star Ferry and surrounded by good shopping. Three glass-enclosed elevators, two of them outside, have a good view of the harbor and Hong Kong Island. It has a highly recommended Japanese restaurant. The **Grandstand Grill** with American beef and the Indian restaurant are good.

The business center has viewdata and pager/mobile phone rentals. It has 24-hour room service, dim sum, bars, private karaoke rooms, executive floors with private elevator and a gym with a computerized fitness testing system. It also has a heated, year-round, rooftop pool, jacuzzi, golf simulator, sauna, massage, beauty salon, Reuter's wire, non-smoking floors and a 70-shop shopping mall. It is half a block from a MTR entrance and gives cheaper rates if booked two weeks or a month in advance with one night's deposit. It gives frequent flier points. Its senior's discount is subject to availability.

THE PENINSULA, *Salisbury Road, 366-6251, fax 722-4170. 300 rooms. $2350-3200. Extra bed $300.* This, the oldest, most expensive and most beautiful hotel in Hong Kong is in a great location. It has huge Victorian rooms with dressing rooms, impeccable service and excellent restaurants. It is also a tourist attraction and deserves at least a look. The high lobby ceiling in the original wing has carved gold trim and rams' head pillars.

The new **Rooftop Restaurant** on the 27th and 28th floor of the new tower has an uninterrupted harbor view. Afternoon tea in the lobby lounge, the place to see and be seen, is an old tradition. It has a book written about it. After being commandeered to house British troops, the six-story Peninsula opened in 1928 across from the original railway station. The Japanese invaders made it their headquarters in 1941 and it housed 2000 of their former prisoners of war after the Japanese surrender. In 1969, it added an extension at the back which made it "H"-shaped. In 1994, it completed a 30-story tower with 10 floors of office suites.

The Peninsula's restaurants include **Gaddi's and Chesa** (Swiss). It also has dim sum, a Japanese restaurant with a very extensive wine cellar and a caviar bar. Gilded Chinese wood carvings, T. Allom prints of China, lots of lamps and four telephones decorate each room. Its big bathrooms have separate shower stalls, two sinks and scales. Amenities include 24-hour room service, a bar, dancing in Gaddi's, a business center with teleconferencing, health spa with waterfall, year-round Roman-style pool with retractable screen, steam bath, sauna, jacuzzi, large gym, massage, beauty salon, in-room safe, satellite television and 110-shop arcade. In the new tower, rooms also have private fax machines. It has a fleet of Rolls Royces and a helipad.

THE REGENT, *18 Salisbury Road. 721-1211, fax 739-4546. 602 rooms. $2000-3100. North American reservations 1-800-545-4000.*

This is one of the best hotels in the world. Also known as **Lai Ching Dao Din**, this 17-story, 1980 hotel has two gold Rolls-Royces and the world's largest (23) fleet of Daimler limousines, some with cocktail cabinets and all with mobile telephones. John Kennedy Jr. and Daryl Hannah stayed here. Its famous **La Plume Restaurant** is probably the most expensive in town, but is highly recommended for very special occasions. It has an excellent European and seafood restaurant with live fish, an **Oyster Bar** and a wine cellar with 10,000 bottles. The **Lobby Lounge** has the best harbor view and is worth a visit.

The Regent claims the largest ballroom in the city. Its business center has a Reuters terminal, printing service, fax machines, video-players and mobile telephones for hire. The use of a conference room here is free to guests. Other facilities include 24-hour room service, lounges, poolside bar, large year-round outdoor pool and jacuzzis, steam room, sauna, solarium and Chinese and Swedish massage. Rooms have three two-line speaker telephones, separate shower stalls, in-room safes, satellite television and air-purification systems. There are 230 shops in the adjacent mall. It is close to the Space Museum, Cultural Centre and Star Ferry, but away from crowds.

Tsim Sha Tsui–Moderate

HOLIDAY INN GOLDEN MILE, *46-52 Nathan Rd. 369-3111, fax 369-8016. 600 rooms. $1660-2100. Single $1150-1990. Reservations 1-800-HOLIDAY.*

This is a good hotel in a great location across from the MTR station and in the heart of Tsim Sha Tsui. The only problem is the constant activity in the lobby. Still, one guest stayed here 230 times! It has medium-sized rooms including four designed for female executives. The business center has computer rental and 24-hour cable, fax and photocopying service. The executive floors have CNN. It has two bars, roof-top pool, gym, sauna, beauty salon, 24-hour room service, a German restaurant, a deli and three non-smoking floors. It also has satellite TV and sits on top of a small shopping plaza with a medical and dental center. There are discounts for guests who stay over two weeks.

IMPERIAL HOTEL, *30-34 Nathan Rd. 366-2201, fax 311-2360. 215 rooms. $900-1100. Single $820-1020. North American reservations 1-800-44UTELL.*

This old, dark, musty hotel has peeling wallpaper and the room Linda saw had rotten-egg-bathroom smells. The only thing going for it is a fantastic location across the street from Tsim Sha Tsui MTR in the heart of the Golden Mile shopping district. The budget YMCA is much better. This hotel offers 50% off for day-use before 6 pm. A Spaghetti House and a British pub are nearby.

THE KIMBERLEY HOTEL, *28 Kimberley Rd. 723-3888, fax 723-3888. 496 rooms. $1060-1450. Single $960-1350. Extra Person $250. Obtain reservations in North America through Steigenberger Reservation Service 1-800-223-5652.*

North American shoppers and businessmen on a budget head for this good, 1989 hotel. It has Japanese, American, and Chinese food. The rooms, bathrooms and televisions are small, but there are kettles. It has a sauna, business center and health spa. It is three blocks from the MTR.

THE KOWLOON HOTEL, *19-21 Nathan Rd. 369-8698, fax 369-8698. 707 rooms. $1620-1860; Singles $1400-1780. North American reservations 1-800-262-9467 or 1-800-462-7899.*

The main attraction is a decent but overpriced hotel in a fantastic location. It is right at the MTR, behind the Peninsula and seven minutes walk from the Star Ferry. It has tiny, functional rooms with plastic sinks. Some rooms have computer games. The lobby has a computer that can give you handy printouts of tourist attractions in Chinese and English. The Kowloon lacks the class and quality of its neighbor though it is also part of the same Peninsula Group. It has a pizzeria, lounge, business center, beauty salon, a 30-shop arcade and a fleet of Mercedes.

NEW ASTOR HOTEL, *11 Carnarvon Road. 366-7261, fax 722-7122. 151 rooms. $880-1200. North American reservations 1-800-44UTELL.*

This is a basic, clean hotel in a good location. It has in-house movies on small televisions and is half a block from a MTR station.

NEW WORLD HOTEL, *22 Salisbury Road, 369-4111, fax 369-9387. 543 rooms. $1400-2200. Extra bed $250. North American reservations 1-800-637-7200 or 1-800-44UTELL.*

A modern, unassuming 1978-hotel near the harbor, it has no real harbor views from rooms. It is worth considering because it is away from the crowds, but only a five-minute walk to downtown and the MTR. It has a garden and good security. From its restful, newly-renovated lobby you can go directly into a six-story shopping mall with 230 shops, bars, night clubs and restaurants. A cheaper laundry service is next door.

The hotel has 24-hour room service, karaoke lounge, disco, business center and executive floors with fax machines. You will also find a 20-meter-long outdoor pool heated to 29°C, Fitness and Dance Centre, pay sauna, steam bath, yoga class, aerobics, beauty salon, in-room safes, kettles and non-smoking floors. It is three blocks to the MTR.

PARK HOTEL, *61-65 Chatham Road South. 366-1371, fax 739-7259. 430 rooms. $1100-1300. Singles $1000-1200. Extra person $250. North American reservations 1-800-44UTELL.*

A family owns this modest, 16-story, 1961 hotel which is used to North Americans. It has two restaurants, lounge, bar and small bathrooms. The upper floors have in-room safes. It is on busy Chatham Road, near lots of stores and the Science Museum, but is farther than most (eight-minute walk) from the MTR. There is a small park across the street. It has a substantial tea buffet from 3pm to 5:30pm.

THE ROYAL PACIFIC HOTEL & TOWER, *China Hong Kong City, 33 Canton Road. 736-1188, 738-2222, fax 736-1212. 632 rooms. $950-2280. Extra bed $300. North American reservations 1-800-44UTELL.*

Consider this 13-story hotel if you want to be next to the ferry and bus terminal to China. The small lobby, narrow halls and long, thin rooms in this 1988 hotel make Ruth think of a chicken farm. Rooms are larger in its ten-story tower. The weird canopy of lights above the escalator from the street give an initial amusement park feel. It has a fascinating view of ferries coming and going. It has a Swiss restaurant, bar, business center and gym. Rooms have safes, slender twins, three telephones, separate shower stalls and in-house movies. A small, proletarian mall with restaurants is in neighboring China Hong Kong City. Harbour City is a few steps away in the other direction. An elevated footpath goes to Kowloon Park. The MTR is beyond.

Tsim Sha Tsui–Budget

GUANGDONG HOTEL, *18 Prat Avenue. 739-3311, fax 721-1137. 234 rooms. $1000-1200.* This hotel is on a narrow side street in the eastern part of Tsim Sha Tsui near Canton Road, two blocks from the MTR station. It has a lobby lounge, European restaurant, narrow halls and in the future will have safe deposit boxes in the lobby. Rooms have flasks for drinking water, hair dryers and small bath rooms. It has a business center, looked clean, but something caused a tickle in Ruth's throat here. So it's okay but...

THE SALISBURY YMCA OF HONG KONG, *41 Salisbury Road. 369-2211, fax 739-9315. 398 rooms. $760-950. Single $650-760. Suites $1270-1490. Extra bed $150. Dormitory bunk bed $165. No 5% government tax.*

Everybody knows this is the best deal in town, which is why it is always full. You should book one to three months ahead and have to pay cash or credit card for the first night. It is next door to The Peninsula Hotel, near the Star Ferry and MTR. It has room service, two restaurants, satellite television, in-room safes, two swimming pools, fitness center, squash, hair salon, book store, secretarial and fax services, and piano studios for guest bookings. YMCA membership is not necessary. It first opened in 1924 and is across the street from the Hong Kong Cultural Centre. Reserve directly or through Tour East, Travel Advisers or Hong Kong Student Travel.

Tsim Sha Tsui East–Expensive

HOLIDAY INN CROWNE PLAZA HARBOUR VIEW, *70 Mody Rd. 721-5161, fax 369-5672. 592 rooms. $1600-2360. Single $1500-2250. Extra bed $300. North American reservations 1-800-HOLIDAY.*

This luxury, five-star hotel is popular with business people and has executive floors. Across the road is the waterfront promenade which runs along the harbor and is good for jogging. It offers a 20% discount for people over 65 during low season. Rooms have satellite TV, safes and mini bars with single-use cameras. It has three restaurants, coffee shop, bar, two lounges, business center with computer, outdoor pool, massage, sauna, harbor view and a good Italian restaurant.

KOWLOON SHANGRI-LA, *64 Mody Road. 721-2111, fax 723-8686. 719 rooms. $1950-2800. Extra bed $300. North American reservations 1-800-942-5050.*

A beautiful, magnificent-looking hotel with spacious rooms. It has very good standards, although it is not as polished as the more expensive Island Shangri-La. It has recommended Japanese, Continental, and Californian restaurants. The **Shang Palace** is especially good for Cantonese food and dim sum. It has 24-hour room service, a bake shop, lobby and rooftop lounges, business center, executive floor, small indoor pool, sauna, jacuzzi, massage, solarium, gym, beauty salon, satellite television and kettles. The 14th floor and up have in-room safes. Limousine and car rentals are available.

HOTEL NIKKO HONG KONG, *72 Mody Rd. 739-1111, fax 311-3122. 461 rooms. $1750-2750. Extra Person $350. North American reservations 1-800-NIKKO-US or any Japan Airlines Office.*

This very good, 17-story, 1988 hotel caters mainly to Japanese guests but has hosted British rock stars. Hong Kong's only Japanese-managed hotel, it is the closest to the Hong Kong Coliseum and the Kowloon Railway Station. The hotel has French, Kyoto-style Japanese and south east Asian restaurants and a harbor view that includes the interesting container port. The health club provides exercise clothes and shoes and tailors a fitness program for each guest. The bathrooms have "gold" plated bathroom fixtures and separate shower stalls.

Facilities include lounges, terrace bar, in-room fax machines and video cameras rentals. Its business center rents mobile telephones. There is also an executive floor, aerobics dance classes, roof top pool with swimming lessons, sauna, massage and Rolls Royces. Ask about summer and winter packages.

Yau Ma Tei–Moderate

MAJESTIC HOTEL, *348 Nathan Rd. 781-1333, fax 781-1773. 387 rooms. $980-1280. Extra bed $250. North American reservations 1-800-44UTELL.*

A good deal, it has first class amenities for second class prices. Good-sized rooms have in-house movies, satellite TV, flight information, hairdryers, safes and kettles. In the bathroom, there are lots of free things, usually found only in more expensive hotels, such as a comb, sewing kit, emery board, toothbrush and razor. It has a restaurant, bar, business center, beauty salon and non-smoking floor. On top of a 35-shop mall with two cinemas, it is a block from the MTR.

PRUDENTIAL HOTEL, *222 Nathan Rd. 311-8222, fax 311-4760. 434 rooms. $900-1450. Extra bed $280. North American reservations 1-800-44UTELL*

This hotel is straight out of a science fiction movie. Its outdoor, glass, "bullet-lift" whisks you up to the "observatory tower" and large rooms have clashing red, grey and black furniture. Otherwise, it's a decent hotel on top of the Jordan MTR and about 100 shops. It's nicer than the Imperial, but not as nice as the Majestic Hotel. Facilities include a coffee shop, bar, business center, a long outdoor pool, in-house movies and non-smoking floor.

Yau Ma Tei–Budget

   BANGKOK ROYAL HOTEL, *2-12 Pilkem St. 735-9181, fax 730-2209. 70 rooms. $620-680. Single $540-600.*

   This five-story hotel from the 1950s is in need of renovation and has no babysitting. However, it is two minutes from the Jordan MTR, half a block from Kowloon Park and is not on a busy street. It has photocopying, but no postal service. A noisy restaurant is off to the side of the lobby. It has one of the first Thai restaurants in Hong Kong. The nearby Shamrock is a little better.

   BOOTH LODGE, *11 Wing Sing Lane. 771-9266, fax 385-1140. 52 rooms. $580-780. Extra bed $120. No 5% tax. To reserve, fax or call with credit card number.*

   This is one of the best deals in town. It is run by the Salvation Army, which does an excellent job. The medium-sized rooms are spotless, the staff are friendly and the lobby is huge. There is a gift shop with a photocopying machine. Local phone calls from rooms are free. This hotel is close to the Jade and Night Markets. It has a coffee shop, and is one block from the Yau Ma Tei MTR. It accepts Visa, MasterCard and American Express but not Diners.

   CARITAS BIANCHI LODGE, *4 Cliff Rd. 388-1111, fax 770-6669. 90 rooms. $620. Single $530. Triple $770. Extra bed $150. No 5% government tax. For reservations, call Fair Town Tours (212) 226-2007 in New York, (415) 392-3690 in Los Angeles and Jet Pacific Holidays (604) 732-8874 in Canada.*

   You can feel the springs in the bed. Kids under ten can stay for free with parents. It does not have IDD. This hotel is run by Caritas, an active Roman Catholic charitable organization. It is next to Booth Lodge, but is not as nice.

   EATON HOTEL, *380 Nathan Rd. 782-1818, fax 782-5563. 392 rooms. $950-1100. North American reservations 1-800-44UTELL.*

   This 1990 hotel offers good value for "intelligent luxury" and is popular with Chinese and Japanese businesspeople. Its lobby lounge has a pleasant, outdoor patio, a tiny garden and sits on top of four floors of shops and two cinemas. Rooms have hairdryers, kettles, in-house movies, in-room safe and remote control TV. Local calls cost $4! It has five restaurants, coffee shop, bar, lounge, business center with computer rental and is five minutes from Jordan MTR.

   NATHAN HOTEL, *378 Nathan Rd. 388-5141, fax 770-4262. 190 rooms. $800. Single $650. Triple $950. Extra bed $100.*

   Choose this 1968 hotel only for its location, five minutes from Jordan MTR. The staff are not very friendly. It has three restaurants, business center and 24-hour room service.

   SHAMROCK HOTEL, *223 Nathan Rd. 735-2271, fax 736-7354. 148 rooms. $680-850. Single $580-770. Extra bed $100.*

This 1950, 10-story hotel has a lot of character. The outside of the building is dirty and forbidding, but its small lobby is clean and decorated with gold Chinese carvings and 17 chandeliers. It is half a block from Kowloon Park and a five-minute walk from Jordan MTR. Only kids under three can stay with parents for free. It has two restaurants, a bar and doesn't charge for local calls.

YMCA INTERNATIONAL HOUSE, *23 Waterloo Rd. 771-9111, fax 388-5926. 277 rooms. $620-730. Single $520-630. Extra bed $132.*

This the worst of the YMCA hotels. The small gym has bicycle and rowing machines, but no weight machines. It has small, slightly grubby rooms, an unpleasant lobby, a restaurant, coffee shop, chapel, free local calls, massage, sauna and is one block from Yau Ma Tei MTR.

Mong Kok–Moderate

GRAND TOWER HOTEL, *627-641 Nathan Rd. 789-0011, fax 789-0945. 549 rooms. $830-1100. Triple $1500. Extra bed $230. North American reservations 1-800-44UTELL.*

The Grand Tower is in the heart of Mong Kok, one-minute from Mong Kok MTR and a few minutes from the Ladies Market and the Bird Market. It is a decent good-value hotel, but needs renovating. The rooms have stained carpets and peeling wall paper, but also hairdryers and kettles. There is live piano music in the marble lobby lounge and it has two restaurants, bar and business centre.

THE METROPOLE HOTEL, *75 Waterloo Rd. 761-1711, fax 761-0769. 487 rooms. $960-1150. U.S. reservations (415) 398-6627 and (818) 457-8688. In Canada (604) 837-8787.*

This decent, clean hotel is in a lousy location. It is a 20-minute walk to Mong Kok MTR, but the hotel offers a free hourly shuttle bus to the MTR and Tsim Sha Tsui. A huge, gilded carving hangs in the lobby. Built in 1991, the 22-story hotel is managed by China Travel Service (CTS) and has a direct booking system for visas and train tickets for China. The business center has Lotus and Symphony computers for rent and its two executive floors receive Reuters Newswatch Financial Service. Five rooms are for wheelchair travelers. It has two restaurants, bar, karaoke, business center, small outdoor pool, in-house movies, small televisions, two Japanese channels, an executive and non-smoking floor.

NEWTON HOTEL KOWLOON, *58-66 Boundary Street. 787-2338, fax 789-0688. 176 rooms. $880-1180. Single $800-1100. Extra bed $200.*

Nicely maintained, small, 12-story, 1992 property with small rooms and basic services. The east side has a good view of the sunrise, soccer fields, early morning pet market and tai chi people. Amenities include lounge, karaoke, business center, concierge, in-room safes and limo service. It is three blocks from Prince Edward MTR. A 24-hour convenience store is nearby. An hourly shuttle goes to the airport, 2.5 kilometers away.

Mong Kok–Budget
YWCA ANNE BLACK GUEST HOUSE, *5 Man Fuk Rd., Waterloo Hill Rd. 713-9211, fax 761-1269. 100 rooms. $550-570. Extra bed $100. Single with shared bath $270! Double $7344-7560 a month but only January-August.*

This hotel offers good value and clean rooms, but an inconvenient location. It has a restaurant, coffee shop and is a 20-minute walk to Mong Kok MTR. The small rooms have no bathtub or 110/220 power outlet. There is no money changing.

The Airport, Kowloon City–Moderate
REGAL AIRPORT HOTEL, *Sai Po Road. 718-0333, fax 718-4111. 400 soundproof rooms. $850-1750. Extra person $220. North American reservations 1-800-222-8888 or 1-800-UTELL.*

This modern, lively, 14-story, 1983 hotel is linked by walkway and baggage conveyor belt (with helpful bellman) to the airport, and is better than staying at the airport itself for hours. It is a good place to spend the night before an early morning flight, a stay that could also be productive.

There is a beauty salon, barber, babysitter, clinic, travel service and business center with computer rental and 24-hour fax service. It also has a lot of information about China. Flight information is in all rooms and lobby. Aside from the airport, it is not close to anything else of interest although a six-floor mall is about 10-minutes drive away. The **Roof Top Bar** and restaurant have a great view of the air field.

The Regal has Chiu Chow, seafood, French and international restaurants, a bake shop, 24-hour room service, a British pub, karaoke and lounges. Rooms have safes and satellite television. The concierge can pack and mail. There are rooms for female executives, non-smoking floors and limousine service. A shuttle bus goes to Tsim Sha Tsui.

Tsuen Wan, New Territories–Moderate
KOWLOON PANDA HOTEL, *3 Tsuen Wah Street. 409-1111, fax 409-1818. 1026 rooms, many already booked long term. $1050-1400 but gives discounts if space. Extra person $180. North American reservations 1-800-344-1212.*

This 1990 high-rise hotel is too far out for the short-term visitor. It is fine if you don't mind a half-hour commute on the MTR and a ten-minute walk. A lively, comfortable hotel, its many American guests make it look like something out of middle America. The hotel has *dim sum*, an Italian restaurant, karaoke, bar, lounge, deli, ice-cream parlor, business center and executive floors.

It also has an outdoor pool, sauna and massage. Rooms have kettles and poor reading lights.

The **Yaohan Department Store** is in the same building and gives a 10% discount to hotel guests. There is not much else in the neighborhood. The complimentary shuttle bus to Kowloon Park Drive and Middle Road in Tsim Sha Tsui arrives in 30 minutes if the road is jam-free. The limousine service takes about 25 minutes to the airport.

Sha Tin, New Territories–Moderate

REGAL RIVERSIDE, *Tai Chung Kiu Rd. 649-7878, fax 637-4748. 830 rooms. $1100-1450. North American reservations 1-800-44UTELL.*

The Royal Park is better and more convenient, but the Regal on the river offers a wargames package, a shuttle bus to and from the airport and downtown, and has Hong Kong's only float capsule where you soak in salty water. It has an atrium style lobby, three restaurants, 24-hour coffee shop and room service, bar, lounge and disco. Its **Topform Health Club** has a gym, sauna and jacuzzi. This hotel is a 25-minute walk from Sha Tin KCR.

ROYAL PARK HOTEL, *8 Pak Hok Ting St. 601-2111, fax 601-3666. 448 rooms. $1020-1350. North American reservations 1-800-44UTELL.*

This hotel has some of the largest rooms in Hong Kong at 360 square feet. It is popular with Japanese and Koreans and across from the large, riverside Shatin Central Park and near the massive Shatin Town Centre shopping complex. Its clean rooms have satellite TV. It has four restaurants, lounge, business center, indoor/outdoor pool, tennis court, gym, sauna and 24-hour room service. It is only an eight-minute walk from the Sha Tin KCR.

Outlying Islands– Lantau

As you get off the ferry at **Mui Wo**, to your right are a number of small shops with pictures of apartments for rent. They are pretty cheap ($150-250) during the week. *Call 984-2132/984-2172 for more information.* If you continue along the beach to the right, you will reach the white and orange **SILVERMINE BAY BEACH HOTEL** which has an outdoor pool and two restaurants. *$760-1060 for a double. 30% less on weekdays. 984-8295, fax 984-1907.* **LANTAU TEA GARDENS** has rooms for rent.

Outlying Islands– Cheung Chau

THE WARWICK HOTEL, *East Bay, Cheung Chau, 981-0081, fax 981-9174. $980–1180.* Seventy rooms with balconies. A comfortable but not luxurious hotel above the beach and a five minute walk from the ferry pier. The hotel has a terrace restaurant, bar, coffee shop, karaoke and outdoor pool.

GUEST HOUSES

These are the cheapest places to stay in Hong Kong. They occupy a part of one floor or more in a building and don't usually accept credit cards. You can bargain, especially if you're staying for a few nights. Look at the room first. They vary greatly. Some have no windows! Call first for reservations; they fill up quickly.

Unfortunately, **Chung King Mansion** is still the cheapest place to stay. It is a bizarre and pretty awful building, but has some decent places. **Mirador Mansions**, a block away, is slightly better. Both are in excellent locations in the heart of the Golden Mile shopping district of Tsim Sha Tsui and a block from the MTR. **Noble Hostel** and the **Baccaret** are the nicest. For dorm beds, the best is **STB Hostel**.

What is in a Guest House?

Most guest houses have a refrigerator, phone books and a phone which can be used for free in the "lobby." You can also receive incoming calls. All guest houses listed here have rooms with private bath, color TV, air-conditioner and smoke detector. Most are plagued with street noise, have a table, mirror, trash can and hangers. Most guest houses sell drinks and some will let you send or receive faxes.

In the bathroom there is usually soap, a towel, toilet paper and an exhaust fan. Guest houses have a variety of hot water systems usually involving a switch in the room or down the hall. Most bathrooms are closet-size. In the smallest, you wash by sitting on the toilet and using a hand-held shower head! Just think, many Hong Kong people shower like this all their lives.

English is generally poor but passable. Some places have Filipina employees, all of whom speak good English. Only Chung King House and the STB Hostel are HKTA members.

Women

Linda thinks that all the guest houses mentioned here are safe. Many women feel uncomfortable in the shopping arcade of Chung King mansions, because it is filled with rather aggressive men. However, Linda stayed there for five weeks without any serious problems. Indian men tried to pick her up at the Mirador and New Lucky Mansion. If such behavior is going to disturb you, head for the **STB hostel**, **Noble Hostel**, or the **YWCA** in Mong Kok.

Warning

There are some unscrupulous guest house owners. Beware of places without a sign with the name and phone number above the door. If someone is pushy, leave. Legitimate guest houses will not push you or get nasty if you want to look at other places. It's best to stick to guest houses mentioned in this guide book or recommended by friends.

Beware of the 3/F, A-block guest house in Chung King with no sign. Linda stopped there on the way up to the London. The evil Chinese manager lied and said he was the London's manager and it was full. He got nasty when she told him she wanted to check it anyway. She stupidly let him bully her. He charged her $250 for a tiny room and then got fresh!! By the way, he's married. He told one American man he had to pay three days in advance. When the American found a cheaper place, the manager refused to refund his money. Linda heard that this manager also has a place in Mirador Mansion, again with no sign.

NOBLE HOSTEL, *Head office: 37, Paterson St., Paterson Bldg., Flat C1, 7/F, Causeway Bay. Telephone Mr. or Mrs. Lin for availability and addresses, 576-6148, 890-6218, fax 577-0847. Airbus No. A3. Double rooms with private showers $330-$380. Triple $420. Doubles with shared bath $260-$280. Singles with shared bath $200-$230.*

Rooms here are in four separate apartment buildings with six to eleven rooms in each. Other apartments are at 27 Paterson, 6 Cleveland and 9 Kingston Streets, good locations for this area. There are no signs in English or Chinese. You ring the street-level door and tell the guard what floor you want but the guard does not understand "Noble Hostel." The rooms are clean, small with just the bare necessities including a washing machine. Restaurants are in the neighborhood. This is the only good guest house on Hong Kong Island.

THE BACCARET HOTEL, *11/F, Windsor Bldg, 29-31 Chatham Rd., Tsim Sha Tsui. 366-5922, fax 723-5398. $500. Visa and MasterCard.*

Ten minutes from the MTR near Mody Rd., women run this up-scale, "short-time" hotel with three-star rooms. They're large, modern and each room has a small couch, telephone, desk, sprinkler system, bathtub and large television. It's very nice as long as you don't mind passing embarrassed, well-dressed couples in the hall. A two-hour stay will cost you $180. There are other short-time hotels in the building.

OCEAN GUEST HOUSE, *Flat G, 11/F, New Lucky Mansion, 15 Jordan Rd., Yau Ma Tei. 385-0125/780-7606, fax 782-6441. Eight rooms. $350. Single $300.*

A Chinese family runs this decent place with small rooms, big windows and bedside lamps. The New Lucky Mansion has about seven other guest houses and open hallways. It is right at the Jordan MTR station, exit B1 at the corner of Nathan Rd.

LYTON HOUSE INN, *6/F, Lyton Bldg., 32 Mody Rd., Tsim Sha Tsui. 367-3791/739-0970, fax 724-2685. Eight rooms. $400-600.*

Friendly Filipinas manage these large, simple, run-down rooms with telephone, desk, chair and bathtub (but no shower curtain). Some even have mini-refrigerators! A few other guest houses are in this building.

MAN HING LEUNG, *14/F, Mirador Mansion, 56-58 Nathan Rd., Tsim Sha Tsui. 722-0678/311-8807, fax 311-6669. 20 rooms. $300-360. Single $260-300. Triple $360-450.*

A family runs this guest house of small rooms. Mirador Mansion is set around a courtyard with open-air hallways and several other guest houses.

STAR GUEST HOUSE, *6/F, 20 Cameron Rd., Tsim Sha Tsui. 723-0686, fax 3112275. 13 rooms. $380-420. Single $330-350. Triple $450.*

Two and a half blocks from the MTR in Tsim Sha Tsui, manager Charlie Chan and his Filipina employees offer tiny, clean rooms. They also run the New Star Guest House on the 2nd floor and the 16-room Lee Gardens, across the street on the 8th floor.

STB HOSTEL, *1-3/F, Great Eastern Mansion, 255-261 Reclamation Street, Yau Ma Tei. 710-9199, fax 385-0153. 18 rooms. $400.*

The Hong Kong Student Travel Bureau operates this 1986 hostel, best known for its dorms. The 50 beds (mainly bunks) in air-conditioned, segregated dorms cost $100 each and are four short blocks from the MTR. The rooms are pretty small for the price. Still, unlike most guest houses, they have a closet, peepholes, second locks, room telephones and shower stalls with curtains! The bathroom Linda saw did stink a little. A common room has a travel counter, magazines and a drink machine. Lockers cost $5-10. You can call, mail or fax in reservations. You can use a card to pay for the room but not to secure reservations.

CHUNG KING MANSIONS, *40 Nathan Rd., Tsim Sha Tsui*, offers the cheapest accommodations in Hong Kong. An excellent location across the street from the MTR, it is a 10-minute walk from the Star Ferry. Ironically, it is also a block from the expensive Peninsula Hotel.

Chung King has great Indian food at the **Delhi Club Mess** *(3/F B-block-* see "Where to Eat" chapter), a good exchange rate at the **Wallstreet Money Changer**, and cheap laundry ($20/5lbs.), film processing ($.70/photo) and faxing ($5) services at **A1-Laundry** on the ground floor. In the basement, the dreadful, 24-hour **IFJ Food Plaza** has cheap beer and dim sum. We don't recommend anything else.

Now the bad news. Linda would never recommend this place to her grandmother. This notorius beehive of over 100 guest houses (often several on one floor) is horrible, fascinating, and straight out of Blade Runner. The bottom two floors of the shopping arcade are filled with all nationalities, especially Indian and Nigerian men. People flog guest houses, restaurants and fake "copy watches" at the entrance.

There are six blocks from A to E with separate elevators, all accessible from the arcade. This place used to be a fire trap. However in 1993, legislation required all guest houses to have smoke detectors, fire alarms and extinguishers. So far so good. About once a month, the police raid at dawn looking for illegal aliens and waking up guests at 5am.

Expect long lines at the elevators. If you're going to A-block and you can't take the lines anymore and if you're brave, try the stairs. Walk out to Nathan Road, turn right and right again at the first alley. Take the first, dark, grimy staircase on your right. Be careful. Linda met a man who slipped and broke his leg here. Otherwise it's great exercise! If you can handle the building, there are some decent, clean places.

CHUNG KING HOUSE, *Block A, 4/F and 5/F. 366-5362, fax 721-3570. 75 rooms. $391. Single $276, triple $460.*

This, the king of Chung King has been here since the beginning in 1962. It offers large, dark, musty, motel-like rooms each with incredibly, a bathtub (but no shower curtain), a telephone and a desk. This is a good deal, but a rather forbidding place. This guest house is a HKTA member so charges 15% on top.

FIRST GUEST HOUSE, *Block A, 7/F. 739-5986. Nine rooms. $220-250, single $150. Cheaper rooms without bath.*

Some nice Filipinas oversee this clean place, associated with the **NEW YORK GUEST HOUSE**, *B-block, 7/F. 739-5986.*

LONDON GUEST HOUSE, *Block A, 6/F. 366-5975/366-5010, fax 739-2809. 17 rooms. $190-250. Single $170-200. Air conditioning $20 extra.*

This is Linda's favorite, mainly because of Fresca, the friendly Filipina and Rambo the cat. It is clean, bright and one of the cheapest places to stay. Coffee and drinks $5. Luggage storage $5 a day. Local faxes $5.

WELCOME GUEST HOUSE, *Block A, 7/F. 721-7793, fax 311-5558. 18 rooms. $180-260, Single $180-220. Cheaper rooms without baths.*

This is Linda's second favorite. The father/son managers are very nice and helpful. They have fax, IDD, and laundry service ($8/jeans, $5/shirts) and can arrange China visas ($200-same day, $160-next day).

11. WHERE TO EAT

There are some fantastic restaurants in Hong Kong. Some of the best are in expensive hotels, others in grubby pigeon holes. Fast food places are the cheapest and are described at the end of this chapter. Reservations are necessary at popular restaurants, especially if you want a table with a view of the harbor. Sometimes these are booked months in advance.

THE BEST RESTAURANTS

Expensive: The best Italian restaurants are **Va Bene** in Central and **Grissini's** in Wanchai. The best American is **Dan Ryan's** in Central and Tsim Sha Tsui. There's also **Plume** (European) and **Lai Ching Heen** (Cantonese) in the Regent Hotel, **Chesa** (Swiss) and **Gaddi's** (Continental) in the Peninsula, the **Hunan Garden** in Central, **Amigo Restaurant** (French) in Happy Valley, and **One Harbour Road** (Cantonese) in the Grand Hyatt. We loved the **Unkai Japanese Restaurant** in the Sheraton Hotel. Try also any of the **Mandarin Oriental's restaurants**.

Moderate: **Peking Garden** in Tsim Sha Tsui, **Ah-So Sushi Bar** in Harbour City, **Luk Yu Tea House** (Cantonese) in Central and **Yung Kee** (Cantonese) in Central are good.

Budget: Head to the **Arirang** for Korean barbeque and **Kublai's** for Mongolian barbeque, both in Tsim Sha Tsui. The **Chili Chili Club** in Wanchai has great Thai food, and there's **Delifrance** in Central.

DINING EXPERIENCES

Why eat at an average restaurant when you can have an exotic dining experience? Hong Kong is full of them. But do take care. The Causeway Bay Typhoon Shelter where you eat in a tiny sampan boat from food cooked on another is dirty. And the big pink paddle-wheel ship, the Pearl of the Orient, is not worth considering.

If you want to eat at a street market or a *Dai Pai Dong* stall, make sure the food is thoroughly cooked and piping hot. Decide for yourself if the restaurant is clean or not.

Floating Restaurants

There are two floating restaurants on Hong Kong Island, covered in lights with garish, oriental interiors. They are the **Jumbo Floating Restaurant** and the smaller **Tai Pak**. Both are neat settings in which to eat, but the food is not very good. See Chapter 14, "Aberdeen."

Harbor Cruises

Many tour companies offer day and evening harbor cruises that include dinner usually at the floating restaurants.

Korean BBQ

You have to try this! You cook thinly sliced meat at a grill built into your table. A good place to go is the **Arirang** restaurant in Tsim Sha Tsui or Causeway Bay.

Mongolian Grill

The place for this is **Kublai's** in Tsim Sha Tsui and Wanchai. You create your own stir fry from a buffet of fresh vegetables, meat and 20 sauces. Don't worry, someone else cooks it for you.

Revolving Restaurants

Hong Kong has two revolving restaurants. The best is **La Ronda** in the Furama Hotel in Central. It serves a good buffet and has a fabulous view of the harbor. The food and view are not as good at **Revolving 66** in Wanchai.

Seafood Villages

Here you choose your meal from tanks of live sea food in simple fishing villages. It's best to go with a group of people. Ask the concierge if anyone else in the hotel is interested. Go to Lamma or Cheung Chau Island. You eat in charming, slightly run-down open air restaurants on stilts over the water near the ferry pier.

A step above these is **Lei Yue Mun** in the New Territories along the MTR line. Here the restaurants are a little nicer. And of course, many of the top seafood restaurants like the **Regent Hotel** also have live fish tanks from which to choose. Ruth loves the steamed prawns and the deep-fried squid.

Sung Dynasty Village

This re-creation of an ancient Chinese village has shows and serves food.

WANDERING

You really don't know what you feel like eating. Never fear, there are places in Hong Kong where you can choose from a dozen or more restaurants. Just wander until a delicious aroma or charming decor entices you in. You may find some undiscovered gem to share with us!

Start in **Lan Kwai Fung** in Central. It has Californian, Indian, Lebanese, Italian, Tex Mex, Japanese, German and French food. See "Central" in this chapter. Then there are the shopping malls. **Pacific Place** in Central and **Times Square** in Causeway Bay are both convenient to the MTR. In Tsim Sha Tsui, **Harbour City** has a number of places. Walk along Canton Road from the Star Ferry and peek into the courtyards. We have included all of these areas below.

DRESS

Some expensive restaurants have dress codes. Smart casual generally means no shorts, sandals, collarless shirts and ripped clothing. Rules are less strict for women. Telephone if in doubt.

HOURS

Many restaurants open only for lunch and dinner between 11am-3pm and 6-11pm. Others stay open all day. Some are closed on Sunday.

RESTAURANT LISTINGS

Most restaurants accept major credit cards (Visa, American Express, MasterCard and sometimes Diners Club). If they accept all four we have indicated "All cards," otherwise we only list those accepted. We have also included areas and shopping plazas with a lot of restaurants as well, because their descriptions include directions. All of the restaurants have English menus, except for **Luk Yu Tea House**.

HONG KONG ISLAND

Central

AFRIKAN CAFE, African-inspired nouvelle moderate. *7 Glenealy St., Lan Kwai Fong. 868-9299. A minimum charge of $60 starts after 9pm. Noon-12am, closed Sundays. All cards, no Diners.*

This nice, little indoor 1993 cafe is simply decorated with a few large wood carvings and enhanced by quiet ethnic music and a tiny garden. Kofta sandwiches and salads from $60. It also has desserts, some South African wines, specialty coffees brewed at your table and only two beers: Boags Premium Lager from Tasmania ($30) and Dos Equis.

AL'S DINER, American moderate. *39 D'Aguilar, Lan Kwai Fong. 869-1869. Open 11am-midnight. Sunday from 6pm. Happy hour 5pm-8pm. All cards.* This is a typical American diner (except for jello shots $36) with the obligatory juke box, for the seriously homesick only. You can get the same thing in the U.S. for a lot less.

AMERICAN PIE, American moderate. *4/F, California Entertainment Building, 34-36 D'Aguilar Street, 877-9779. All cards, no Diners.* Small restaurant with great desserts and salads. Try the chicken curry salad. 12 noon-3pm; 6:30pm-10:30pm. Desserts to midnight.

ASHOKA, Indian budget. *57-59 Wyndham St., Lan Kwai Fong. 524-9623. Also in Wanchai. Noon-2:30pm; 6pm-10:30pm. All cards.*

BEIRUT, Lebanese expensive. *27-39 D'Aguilar St, Lan Kwai Fong. 804-6611. Noon-12:30am, open for dinner from 3pm. Closed Sunday. All cards, no Diners.* Good food in cramped quarters.

BOMBAY PALACE, North Indian budget. *Far East Finance Centre, 16 Harcourt Rd. 527-0115/529-3562. Lunch buffet $95. Vegetarian entrees $44. Meat entrees $60-80. Admiralty MTR. It is open noon-2:30pm, 6pm-11pm, closed Sunday. All cards.* This surprisingly elegant restaurant has lace curtains, chandeliers, gold buddhas and good tandoori and biryani. Popular with the office crowd.

CACTUS CLUB, Tex Mex moderate. *13 Lan Kwai Fong. 525-6732. All credit cards accepted only on orders of $200 or more. Monday to Thursday, noon-1am; Friday noon-3am, and Saturday 5pm-3am. Closed Sundays. All cards.* A two-story bar with food. Chili con carne $52.

CALIFORNIA, California nouvelle moderate. *24-26 Lan Kwai Fong. 521-1345. Open noon-3pm; 6pm-10:30pm. Sundays 6pm-10:30pm.* Turns into a popular disco on Friday and Saturday nights after 11:30pm.

CITY HALL RESTAURANT, Cantonese/dim sum budget. *City Hall, low B block, Central. 521-1303. 10am-3pm; 6pm-11:30pm daily.* This modest restaurant has an extensive menu, okay food and dim sum trolleys at lunch.

DAN RYAN'S CHICAGO GRILL, American moderate. *Level 1, no. 114, Pacific Place. 845-4600, 11am-midnight. All cards.* This is the best of the American restaurants. Sandwiches $58-$68. Salads $92-114. Entrees include Maryland crab cakes, spaghetti and barbecued pork ribs $98, $169 and $202; U.S. filet mignon $160-$602; lamb chops $132; nachos $59; potato skins $45; onion rings $28; chicken wings $46; apple pie $37. "Warning: we serve American Portions."

GRAFFITI, American moderate. *38-44 D'Aguilar St., 521-2202. Monday-Wednesday noon-midnight. Thursday noon-2am. Friday and Saturday noon-3am. Sunday 5:30pm-midnight. All cards.* This pleasant place has things like pizza, wings and a small but good salad bar. Fill up a huge bowl for $80. They supply crayons for doodling on the tables.

GRAPPA'S, Italian budget-moderate. *Level 1, no. 132, Pacific Place. 524-7615. Daily 9am-10:15pm.* Favorite appetizers Beef Cappraccio $75 or steamed mussels $85. Pizza are $55-$95 and Lasagne $85.

HUNAN GARDEN RESTAURANT, Hunan and Cantonese expensive. *3/F, The Forum, Exchange Square, 8 Connaught Place. 868-2880. Open daily 11:30am-3pm, 5:30pm-midnight. All cards.* This classy restaurant has pretty pink table cloths, some spicy hot dishes and a good view of the harbor. It is highly recommended. Dim sum costs $20-25 per basket, noodles and rice $28-70, and other dishes $75-150. Popular are fillet of fish with fried minced bean, fried chicken with chili and masked chicken soup. Recommended are the white fish covered with peanuts and minced chicken soup in a bamboo container. Jacket and tie.

From the Star Ferry, head right past the post office. The Forum is between the two towers of Exchange Square.

JADE GARDEN, Cantonese moderate. *1/F Swire House, 11 Chater Road Central. 526 3031. All credit cards. 11:30am-midnight, dim sum 2:30pm-6pm only. The Jade Garden has branches in Lower G/F, Jardine House, 1 Connaught Road. 524-5098; 1/F, 500 Hennessy Road, Causeway Bay. 895 2200; 1 Hysan Avenue, Causeway Bay. 577-9332.* Noodles and rice cost about $70 and entrees $140-170.

JEWISH OR KING DAVID'S CLUB. Mediterranean budget-moderate. *4/F Melbourne Plaza, 33 Queen's Road Central. 801-5440.* Phone first. Depending on who answers, non-Jewish tourists do or do not have to pay the $600 membership. It might be moving to a new location in 1995. $110 for set lunch. Kosher. Coffee shop has Mezze $50, Lentil Rice Mejabarra $22, pan fried mullet $60 and challa and pita breads. The Club can also deliver its good food to hotels.

JIMMY'S KITCHEN, European moderate. *Basement, South China Building, 1-3 Wyndham Street. 526-5293. Open noon daily. Last order 11:30pm. All cards.* One of the few restaurants with British decor, Union Jacks and all, the same family has operated this place by since 1928. Bowl of pickled shallots grace every table. Entrees $98-138. Daily specials $86-128. Vegetarian entrees $80-90. Fresh orange juice $34; tea $24-48. Especially popular with business people, this has a branch called Landau's in Wanchai.

LA RONDA, mixed expensive. *Top floor, Furama Kempinski Hotel, 1 Connaught Rd. Central. 525-5111. Reservations essential. All cards.* The best revolving restaurant in town serves up a great buffet with many different kinds of Asian and western food, with a great view of the harbor. Smart casual.

LA ROSE NOIRE, Western coffee shop moderate. *Shop 301-303, The Mall, 1 Pacific Place. 877-0118, 877-0563.* Good place to rest your feet and rendezvous with friends.

LAN KWAI FONG – the Area. This trendy, upscale hangout of yuppies, chuppies (Chinese yuppies) and Central's office crowd is chockfull of restaurants and bars with a sprinkling of fast food places and flower shops. Restaurants come and go in this fickle place, but there are always a lot of good ones. *To get here, go to Central MTR, take the Pedder St. exit, walk up to Queen's Rd. Central, turn right and then left at Wyndham or D'Aguilar.*

Some good restaurants here are **Beirut**, **Cafe Afrikan**, **California**, **Graffiti**, **M at the Fringe**, **Midnight Express**, **Va Bene** and **1997**. See individual listings for more details.

LUK YU TEA HOUSE, Cantonese/dimsum moderate. *24-26 Stanley Street Central. 523-5464, 523-5463. 7am-10pm; dim sum 7am-6pm. No credit cards.* This is one of Ruth's favorites because all old Hong Kong tea houses used to have surly waiters and spitoons like this. They don't allow photos and have no menus in English. The reproduction of the original 1920s building is a lot brighter and cleaner than it originally was. Go early for lunch. It's always crowded. Oh yes, the food is good too. Try the fried milk.

M AT THE FRINGE, Mediterranean nouvelle expensive. *2 Lower Albert Rd., (at the top of Wyndham St). 877-4000. 12-2:30pm, 7-10pm, closed Sunday. All cards.* Good food in the old Ice House Building now decorated like a Shakespearean theater set.

MAN WAH, Cantonese expensive. *25/F, Mandarin Oriental Hotel, 5 Connaught Road Central. 522-0111. Open noon-3pm and 6:30pm-11pm. All credit cards.* Classical Qing dynasty decor and good food. Jacket and tie. Good wine.

MANDARIN GRILL, Continental expensive. *1/F, Mandarin Oriental Hotel, 5 Connaught Road Central. 522-0111. Open 7am-11am, noon-3pm and 6:30pm-11pm. All credit cards.* The most popular dishes are the Agnollotti pasta appetizer $145, the angler fish with eggplant lasagna $260, and the American Black Angus prime rib of beef $257. Jacket and tie.

MIDNIGHT EXPRESS, Middle Eastern budget. *3 Lan Kwai Fong St. 525-5010. 11am-3am, Friday and Saturday 11am-6am. Sunday 6pm-1am.* Okay, this is a fast food place. But you may need one good, cheap place to eat in Lan Kwai Fong. Midnight Express is a take-out with a few plastic chairs and excellent falafels for $35. Good coffee is $10. It was voted "Best Hole in the Wall" by *Hong Kong Magazine*.

MOZART STUB-N RESTAURANT, Austrian moderate. *G/F, 8 Glenealy Street Central near Government House, Wyndham and Upper Albert Road. 522-1763. 12noon-2pm; 7 pm-10:30pm. All credit cards.* Fantastic, small and exclusive. Ask for the weiner schnitzel or boiled beef.

PACIFIC PLACE, *the Mall at Admiralty MTR*, has some great restaurants in its three luxury hotels. In the mall, try **Dan Ryan's**, **Zen**, and the **Golden Elephant Thai Restaurants**. There's also a fast food court.

PEKING GARDEN, Peking moderate. *3/F, Alexander House basement.* *526-6456.* Downstairs is quieter. The whole Peking Garden chain is good and makes a show of noodle-making by hand, Peking duck carving and breaking the Beggar's Chicken shell. It has dim sum, sizzling prawns, Peking duck, and chicken with walnut in black bean sauce. Try also the onion cakes and minced pigeon. Reservations are necessary. *Branches in Shop 003, Tower I, Basement, Pacific Place, 845-8452; 1/F Excelsior Hotel Shopping Arcade, 281 Gloucester Road, Causeway Bay, 577-7231; Unit 201, Cityplaza II, Taikoo Shing, 18 Taikoo Shing Road, Quarry Bay, 884-4131. All cards.*

PETRUS, French expensive. *56/F, Island Shangri-La Hotel, 2 Pacific Place. 820-8590. Noon-3pm; 7pm-11pm. Closed Sunday lunch. All cards.* Extensive wine list. Modern French food, healthy and back to basics. Classy Thai silk hangs on the walls. Carved ramshead chairs, black marble pillars and a great view add to the class. Set lunch with two courses $240 and three courses $260. Entrees are $200-230. Jacket and tie.

PIERROT, French contemporary very expensive. *Mandarin Oriental Hotel, 5 Connaught Road Central. 522-0111. Weekdays noon-3pm; 7pm-11pm. Weekends and holidays 7pm-11pm. All cards.* Petrossian heads its unique caviar menu (with sharks' fins; with noodles, vodka and cream sauce; with different kinds of potatoes, etc.). Most popular here are the marinated Toro tuna appetizer $155, the roast fillet of seabass $255, and the rack of baby lamb $265. Smart casual for women, jacket and tie for men.

POST 1997, Asian & Continental moderate. *9 Lan Kwai Fong. 810-9333. It is open generally 9am-2:30am weekdays, Friday and Saturday 24 hours. All cards.* This place features good food and artsy decor. This is part of the 1997 group, which includes the popular **Club 1997 disco** and **Mecca 97** which has cute, middle-eastern decor and okay Mediterranean food. The lunch buffet costs $75 and is served 11am-3am.

VA BENE, Italian expensive. *58-62 D'Aguilar St., Lan Kwai Fong. 845-5577. Reservations recommended especially on weekends. Weekdays noon-3pm, 7pm-12pm. Saturday and Sunday 7pm-12pm. All cards.* This great little Italian restaurant has excellent Venetian food. Pasta costs under $100. The set lunch (antipasto, entree and coffee) is $138. Salads start at $60. No shorts or flip flops.

YUNG KEE RESTAURANT, Cantonese moderate. *32-40 Wellington Street Central. 522-1624. From Central MTR Peddar Street exit, head south uphill along D'Aguilar or Wyndham Streets. Make a right on Wellington. Open daily 11am-11:30pm. Dim sum daily 2pm-5:30pm. All cards.* The father of the present owner Kenneth Kam started out over half a century ago with a small shop and a great recipe for a juicy goose with crispy skin. The Yung Kee now has over 200 workers and cooks 300-380 geese a day. You can also get delicious roast pigeon.

ZEN CHINESE CUISINE, Cantonese moderate. *LG1, The Mall, Pacific Place, 88 Queensway. 845-4555. Open 11:30am-3pm; 6pm-11pm. Sunday and holidays 10:30am-5pm; 6pm-11pm. Near the JW Marriott Hotel. All cards.* Good dim sum at $22-$26 a basket and good ambiance. No carts.

PEAK

PEAK CAFE, Pan-Asian.* *121 Peak Rd. 849-7868, Open 10:30am-midnight.* Near the tram terminal in a small, charming old building with a patio. Delightful. It serves delicious, moderately-priced food and is highly recommended.

THE PEAK, European. *100 (2/F, 100 Peak Rd. 849-8883)* Expensive, adequate food with a good view.

THE CAFE DECO, *118 Peak Rd. 849-5111, in the Peak Galleria mall.*

WANCHAI

AMERICAN RESTAURANT, Beijing budget. *20 Lockhart Road near the Evergreen Plaza Hotel. 527-7277. Reservations needed. 11:30am-11:30pm daily. No credit cards.* One of the few old rundown restaurants left, the American's most popular dishes are Beggars' Chicken, ordered two hours before for $270, and Peking duck $220 (medium whole). Entrees range from $31-$66.

ASHOKA, Indian budget. *185 Wanchai Rd. 891-8981. Noon-2:30pm. 6pm-10:30pm.* See also Central above.

CHILI CHILI CLUB, Thai budget. *1/F, 88 Lockhart Road (at Luard Rd.). 527-2872. Noon-3pm, 6pm-10:30pm. All cards.* This popular restaurant features delicious food and simple, hotel-coffee-shop decor. Choose from 58 Thai and Chinese dishes. Try the satay or green mussels and one of the coconut milk curries. No wines.

FOOK LAM MOON, Cantonese seafood very expensive. *Three floors, 34-45 Johnston Road. 866-0663. 11:30am-11:30pm. Dim sum 11:30am-3pm. Branch also at 53-59 Kimberley Road, Tsim Sha Tsui. 366-0286.* The Fook Lam Moon frequently has line-ups. The abalone and birds nest range from $750-$880. Other dishes are $80-$160.

GOLDEN CROWN SHARK'S FIN SEAFOOD RESTAURANT, Cantonese budget to moderate. *2/F Charterhouse Hotel, 209-219 Wan Chai Road. 893-9228. 8am-3:30pm; 5:30pm-midnight. Visa, American Express and MasterCard.* Entrees $48-$80. Dim sum. ($12-16-20 per dish).

GRISSINI'S, Italian nouvelle expensive. *Grand Hyatt Hotel, 1 Harbour Rd. 588-1234. Noon-2:30pm, 7pm-11pm. All cards.* This chic restaurant has a good view of the harbor and excellent Milanese food. They bake their own bread in the restaurant and 1,000 bottles of expensive Italian wines are on display. Smart casual.

HARRY RAMSDEN'S, British budget. *Shops 3 and 4, Wu Chung House, 213 Queen's Road East near Hopewell Centre. 832-9626. Open 11:30am-11:30pm. Visa, Mastercard and American Express.* You get a free meal if not served in 15 minutes, weekday noon-3pm. Famous for fish and chips.

HEALTHY MESS, Vegetarian very cheap. *G/F 51-53 Hennessy Road. 527-3918. Next to New Harbour Hotel. No credit cards.* $2 to $3 for tasty dim sum, but be sure it is hot because this shop could be cleaner. Take-out and few tables.

HORSE AND CARRIAGE, budget pub grub. *117 Lockhart Rd. 528-0430. Open 11am-6am. No cards.* The office crowd heads to this cozy, dark, Tudor-style bar for lunch.

JO JO'S MESS CLUB, North Indian budget. *1/F, 86-90 Lee Tung Street, south of Southorn Playground off Johnson Road. 527-3776. 12am-3pm; 6:00pm-11pm daily. Visa and MasterCard.* Another small cheap restaurant with good food. Entrees $28-$35. Popular are chicken tikka, samosas and chicken tikka masala.

JOHNSTON MESS, North Indian budget. *1/F, 104 Johnston Road. 891-6525. Noon-3pm; 6pm-11pm daily except Sunday which has no lunch. South of Wanchai MTR Station. Takes only Visa and MasterCard.* This tiny modest canteen produces good tandoori and biriyani. Free membership. $50 set lunch; $98 set dinner. Entrees $25-$54.

KUBLAI'S, budget Mongolian grill. *151 Lockhart Road. 511-2287. Packed at lunch and dinner. All credit cards. Noon-3pm; 6:30pm-11pm.*

ONE HARBOUR ROAD, Cantonese very expensive. *Grand Hyatt Hotel, 1 Harbour Road. 588-1234. Noon-2:30pm; 6:30pm-10:30pm. All cards.* This flossy Cantonese restaurant exudes the flavor of a taipan's home on the Peak in the 1930s. It has Italian dinnerware and silver-tipped chopsticks. Sharks' fins $160-340; other dishes $90-180. Smart casual (no running shoes).

REVOLVING 66, European expensive. *62/F, Hopewell Centre, 183 Queen's Rd. East. 862-6166. Noon-midnight. All cards.* La Ronda in Central is a much better restaurant with a better view and tastier food. One fun thing about this place is the outdoor glass elevator, but you don't have to eat here to take it.

CAUSEWAY BAY

Except for Times Square, all these restaurants are north of or on Hennessy Road or Yee Wo Street.

ARIRANG, Korean budget. *11/F, Times Square. 506-3298. All cards.*

BAAN THAI (Thai, Chiangmai style) moderate. *4/F, Causeway Bay Plaza I, 489 Hennessy Road. 831-9155. At Causeway Bay MTR station. 11:30am-3pm; 6pm-11:30pm.* Lovely classy Thai decor. Lunch buffet $135; roast pork chops with sour cream $68; steamed fish in lemon chilis and garlic $159; baked king prawns $138.

CHINA MAX, mixed expensive. *11/F, Times Square, 1 Matheson Street. 9223-7988. Open 11am-2am. All cards.* Adequate Thai, Chinese and American food in a neat environment. Stone buddhas sit serenely beside modern paintings, like a punk version of Chairman Mao with neon lights for hair. The huge Caesar salad is excellent and only $50. Good cheesecake costs $60. Menu mix of western entrees $145-235; Thai $95-175; Chinese $80-165; Pasta and noodles $85-95; Pizza $80 and 85. There's a live band Thursday-Saturday 10:30pm-2pm.

CLEVELAND RESTAURANT, Sichuan moderate to expensive. *6 Cleveland Street. 576-3876. From Causeway Bay MTR stop head east to Victoria Park and north of Park Lane towards harbor. 11am-11:30pm. All cards.* Entrees $66-$72. Smoked duck. Sizzling prawns. English might be a problem.

GRILL ROOM, steaks expensive. *Excelsior Hotel, 281 Gloucester Road. 894-8888. Entrees $325-375. Go east from Sogo exit of Causeway Bay MTR stop and north on East Point Road. Noon-2:30pm; 7pm-11pm. All cards.* Main course $200. Appetizer $100. Soup $50. Most popular are the sirloin steak, rib eye steak and roast prime beef. Smart casual.

MAXIM'S CHINESE RESTAURANT, Cantonese budget to moderate. *1-2/F, Hong Kong Mansion, 1 Yee Wo Street. 894-9933. Part of major restaurant chain, this is open 7:30am-midnight. Dim sum 7:30am-4pm. From the Sogo exit of Causeway Bay MTR, walk east along Yee Wo St. All cards.* There are usually line-ups here for dishes priced from $55-90 not counting delicacies like abalone.

PARK 27, Western expensive. *Top floor, Park Lane Hotel, 310 Gloucester Road. 890-3355. Noon-3pm, 6pm-11pm. All cards.* Good view of Victoria Park and yacht club. Try the grilled prawns with pasta or the beef tenderloin. Smart casual.

PATERSON VIETNAMESE RESTAURANT, Vietnamese moderate. *10 Cleveland Street. 890-6146, 895-2372. 11:30am-3pm; 6pm to midnight. All cards.* Noodle soup $28-45; vermicelli $32-60. White table cloths and pleasant, unpretensious atmosphere.

PEKING GARDEN, Peking moderate. *Excelsior Hotel Plaza. Part of chain, see Central above.*

PHOENIX CONGEE & NOODLES, Cantonese budget. *13 Cleveland Street. 577-7973. 7:30am-midnight. Noodles from 11am.* Small, clean and filling. Congee $19-58; noodle soup $16-19; fried noodles $22-58.

RANGOON RESTAURANT, Burmese budget. *G/F, 265 Gloucester Road. 892-1182. About 35 meters west of the Excelsior Hotel. 11:30am-11:30pm.*

American Express, MasterCard and JCB. For those who don't know Burmese cuisine, there's a menu with photos. The white table cloths are a little stained. The most popular dishes are chili Chin Maung Kyaw (sour leaf vegetable with shrimp), Nga Tha Loud (hilsa fish) and Mon Hin Gar (fish soup). The curry is weaker than India's.

RED PEPPER, Szechuan moderate. *7 Lan Fong Rd. (near Times Square). 577-3811. Noon-3pm, 6pm-11:30pm. All cards.* Although this place is touristy, it has good chili prawns and sweet and sour pork.

TIMES SQUARE SHOPPING PLAZA has a number of good restaurants on its top four floors, including the **Arirang**, **China Max**, and the **Wu Kong Shanghai Restaurant**. *Go to Causeway Bay MTR and take the Times Square exit.*

VEGI FOOD KITCHEN, Chinese vegetarian budget. *890-6660/895-1836. 8 Cleveland Street. 11am-midnight. Dim sum 11am-5pm.* Okay food.

WINDSOR HOUSE, Cantonese/Chiu Chow moderate. *Entrance on Great George Street, west and south of the Park Lane Hotel. 7/F. Open 7:30am-midnight. Dim sum 7:30am-5:30pm daily; 6/F. Chiuchow Garden 11:30am-3pm; 5:30pm-midnight. Sunday and holidays 10am-3pm; 5:30-midnight.* There are several popular restaurants frequented mainly by local people. Dim sum in trolleys. Entrees $60-95. $13-15 for congee; $18 for noodles; $13-26 for dim sum. **Whimsyland** has electric games for children and adults on another floor.

WU KONG SHANGHAI RESTAURANT, Shanghai moderate. *12/F, Times Square, 506-1018. Branch in Tsim Sha Tsui.*

HAPPY VALLEY

AMIGO RESTAURANT, French – very expensive and highly recommended for special occasions. *79A Wong Nei Chong Road. 577-2202. Noon-3pm; 6pm-midnight. All cards.* Tie and jacket. Try the fresh goose liver panfried with Madeira and the roast rack of New Zealand lamb.

ARIRANG, Korean budget. *76 Morrison Hill Rd. 572-3027. Noon-11:30pm. All cards.*

DIMSUM, *63 Sing Woo Rd. 834-8893.* Has dim sum all day, but is a little more expensive than other places. One trusted American gourmet said it is the best in Hong Kong.

JOCKEY CLUB. The easiest way for a visitor to eat at the **Members' Enclosure** here is to take the Horseracing tour. The Chinese food is great.

ABERDEEN

BLUE OCEAN RESTAURANT, Cantonese budget to moderate. *9/F, Aberdeen Marina Tower, 8 Shum Wan Road. 555-9415. Mon-Sat, 11am-*

11:30pm; Sundays and holidays 10am-11:30pm. All cards. Dim sum. Same street as Aberdeen Yacht Club and western entrance to Jumbo Restaurant. Great view of Aberdeen harbor.

NORTH POINT

CASA MEXICANA, Mexican expensive. *Basement, Victoria Centre, 566-5560.* This is a fun place with good Mexican food and a cheerful, Filipino band in ponchos that take requests. There's a $180 minimum at dinner.

REPULSE BAY

THE VERANDAH, French expensive. *1/F, the Repulse Bay, 109 Repulse Bay Rd. 812-2722. Open noon-2:30pm, 3:30pm-5:30pm and 7pm-10:30pm. Breakfast on Sundays and holidays is 8am-10:30pm.* Ruth hasn't forgiven them for tearing down her beautiful wedding-night hotel. She does admit the restaurant is lovely and romantic, they've kept the fans (in spite of the air-conditioning), and the food has a good reputation, but it's not quite the same. The set lunch is $195, entrees $190-200. It serves French food and American lobster and overpriced afternoon tea. (Three scones with cream, jam and tea cost $85, but that's Hong Kong!) Although it's across the street from the beach, it allows no sandals or sleeveless shirts. All cards.

SPICES is downstairs from The Verandah and has more moderately-priced Asian food and an outdoor patio. The set lunch is $118, entrees $190-$240. Sunday brunch is $238. Both restaurants are in a building in front of the huge apartment complex with a giant square *fung shui* hole for dragons.

STANLEY

A number of inexpensive, outdoor Chinese restaurants are in the market below the old police station. For upscale food, try the ones listed here.

STANLEY'S FRENCH RESTAURANT, French moderate/expensive. *86 Stanley Main Street. 813-8873. All cards.* On weekends, the set lunch costs $60-$96 and dinner entrees are $152-166. Popular are the Cajun pomfret at $144 and spring chicken and prawns at $156. Vegetarian and children's menus too. Smart casual.

STANLEY'S ORIENTAL RESTAURANT, Thai, Sri Lankan, tandoori and Creole moderate/expensive. *Next door to Stanley's French Restaurant, reached by the same telephone number.* The set dinner menu all-inclusive costs

$290. Entrees are $123-147. Popular dishes are Kukulmas curry $103, Rogan Josh lamb curry $119, Thai prawn curry $147, and tandoori chicken $102-141.

Both these Stanley restaurants are open at 9am for drinks, lunch 12-2:45pm, afternoon tea 3-5pm and dinner weekdays 7:15pm-10:15pm. Dinner weekends are from 6:30pm-10:30pm. Closed at midnight. These are on the way to the Tin Hau Temple.

TABLE 88, *813-6262. Noon-10:30. All cards.* International moderate. Try the French duck. Smart casual.

KOWLOON

Tsim Sha Tsui

All of the restaurants listed here are within walking distance of the Tsim Sha Tsui MTR stop and the Star Ferry.

AH-SO SUSHI BAR, Japanese moderate to expensive. *159 Ocean Galleries, Harbour City, South Tower, 15 Canton Rd. 2/F near Marco Polo Hotel. 735-2298. Noon-3pm; 5:30pm-11pm. All cards.* No frills. Sushi and sashimi. A favorite is the California roll and the lean tuna. For the uninitiated, the bar has plastic models of different dishes.

ARIRANG, Korean budget. *19 Canton Road, Sutton Court. 730-3667. Noon-3pm, 6-11pm. All cards.* This bright, cheerful restaurant serves Korean barbeque for $70-90, which you cook yourself on barbecues built into the tables. This comes with soup, rice and six side dishes. Try the Modeum Gooi (meat combination).

AU TROU NORMAND, French expensive. *Basement, 6 Carnavon Road. 366-8754. Noon-3pm, 7pm-11pm. All cards.* Simple French farmhouse decor is the setting for good French food and wine. Try escargots de bourgougne, home-smoked Norwegian salmon or grilled lamb. The lunch buffet is only $110 and includes dessert and coffee. Casual.

BARON'S TABLE, German expensive. *Holiday Inn Golden Mile, 50 Nathan Road. 369-3111. Noon-2:30pm, 7:30pm-11pm. All cards.* Pigs knuckles and black forest cake. Smart casual.

BUKHARA TANDOORI RESTAURANT, Moderate North Indian. *Sheraton Hong Kong Hotel, 20 Nathan Road. 369-1111. Major credit cards. 12-3pm; 6:30pm-11:30pm.* Tandoori chicken costs $98, lamb chops $130, whole leg of lamb $190 and other entrees $80-130.

CHESA, Swiss very expensive. *The Peninsula Hotel, Salisbury Road. 366-6251. Open 12noon-3pm; 6:30pm-11pm. All cards.* Appetizers are air-dried meats from Grissons $95, crepes au saumon fume gratinee $95, cheese fondu Vaudoise $115 and emince de veau Zurichoise $155. Entrees $105-180. This restaurant is more homey than the formal Gaddi's, so smart casual is the word.

DAN RYAN'S, American moderate. *200 Ocean Terminal, Harbour City. 845-4600.* See Dan Ryan's in Central.

DELHI CLUB MESS, Indian budget. *3/F, Block C, Chung King Mansions, 40 Nathan Road. 368-1682. Noon-3:30pm, 6pm-11:30pm. No credit cards.* You have to brave the notorious mansions to get here, but it's worth it. The set lunch $36 and dinner $50 are great deals. You get three dishes, nan (bread), and dessert.

GADDIS, Continental very expensive. *The Peninsula Hotel, Salisbury Road. 366-6251. Noon-3pm; 7pm-11pm. All credit cards.* This famous restaurant is for very special occasions. Popular dishes are the smoked Balik salmon and caviar $330; pan-fried goose liver $210; Angus beef tenderloin $330; Scottish rack of lamb $280; steamed filet of sea bass $330; and Balsamico vinegrette and baby mushrooms and herbs. Most dishes cost $250-330. Coat and tie.

GOLDEN BULL VIETNAMESE RESTAURANT, Vietnamese moderate. *101 Ocean Centre, Harbour City, 5 Canton Road. 730-4866. Also in New World Centre L1, 17. From Star Ferry, turn left up the escalator, and ask directions. Noon-11:30pm. All cards.*

GOLDEN ELEPHANT, Thai moderate. *G/F, 17 Canton Rd. near Marco Polo Hotel. 735-0733. Noon-3pm, 6pm-midnight. All cards.* Some people describe this as "Thai fast food" and some as Chinese-influenced Thai food. Either way, the buffet is a pretty good way to sample Thai food. The lunch buffet costs $108, the dinner buffet $188.

GRAPPA'S, Italian budget to moderate. *1/F, Shop 105-8 (next to main escalator), Ocean Centre, Harbour City, 5 Canton Road. 317-288. Arriving on the Star Ferry in Tsim Sha Tsui, turn left to Ocean Terminal and up the escalator. Continue in the same direction into Ocean Centre. It's on the right. Noon-11pm daily.* Favorite appetizers are beef cappraccio $75 and steamed mussels $85. Pizza costs $55-$95 and lasagne $85. No dress code.

GREAT SHANGHAI, Shanghai budget/moderate. *23-26 Prat Avenue. 366-8158. 11am-11pm. All cards.* This is an older tried-and-true-establishment that serves braised eel, sauteed shrimp, and Chung King chicken.

HARBOUR CITY-THE MALL. Don't despair, most of the restaurants here are easily found along **Canton Road**, so you don't even have to go into this confusing shopping mall. Many of the restaurants are in courtyards tucked into, but not inside the mall. If you walk north up Canton Road from the Star Ferry, you will find the **Ah-So**, **Golden Elephant Thai**, **Golden Bull**, **Grappa's** and the **Arirang** among others. Sylvester Stallone's **Planet Hollywood** opened in 1994 here.

JADE GARDEN, Cantonese moderate. *4th floor, Star House. 730-6888. 10am-3:30pm dim sum. Also open 5:30pm-midnight. Part of chain.* See Central.

KUBLAI'S, Mongolian grill budget. *55 Kimberley Rd., 722-0733. 12:30pm-3pm., 6:30pm-11pm.* Fill a bowl with noodles or rice, fresh veggies, meat, toppings and your choice of twenty different sauces. Then bring it to the grill area, where a chef stir-fries your creation. Repeat until your stomach is full. If this is your first time, start off small and keep trying until you get it just right. The trick is to use lots of sauces. Lunch buffet $68. Dinner buffet $98. Caesar salad $38.

LAI CHING HEEN, Cantonese very expensive. *The Regent Hotel, 18 Salisbury Road. 721-1211. 12-2:30pm; 6pm-9:30pm. All cards.* This is where you can use ivory chopsticks trimmed with silver and be served from a jade spoon. This restaurant is lovely and should be used for very special occasions. It is famous for its abalone $360-$5800, bird's nest $300-$1300 and sharks fins $170-$340. Most dishes are cheaper like its deep fried scallops and pears for only $120 but servings are small. Dim sum goes for $22-25-$40 per basket. Smart casual.

LOTUS POND SZECHUAN RESTAURANT, Sichuan and Cantonese expensive. *G/F 006-007 Ocean Galleries, Phase IV, Harbour City, 15 Canton Road. 730-8688.* Ask for the smoked duck and fried egg plant.

PEKING GARDEN, Peking moderate. *A branch of this reliable chain is at 3/F, Star House, 3 Salisbury Road, 735-8211, and 1/F Empire Centre, 68 Mody Road, Tsim Sha Tsui East, 721-8868. Hours for both are 11:30am-3pm and 5:30pm-11:30pm. Sunday and holidays 10:30am-3pm and 5:30pm-midnight. All cards.*

PLANET HOLLYWOOD, American moderate. *3 Canton Road, Harbour City, Tsim Sha Tsui. 377-7888.* Very noisy. Hamburgers with fries, cole slaw and dill pickles $78. 12" pizza $98-$108. Ribs, fajitas, salads, champagne. Think of it more as a tourist attraction.

PLUME, European. Very expensive. *The Regent Hotel, 18 Salisbury Road. 721-1211. At the Tsim Sha Tsui MTR stop you leave by the Sheraton exit. Turn left after the Sheraton Hotel. Open 7pm to departure of last guest. All cards.* With a ceiling to floor glass window, it has a fabulous view of the harbor. 8000 bottles of wine rest in its wine cellar, the oldest from 1820 is only $5600. It also has a tandoori oven. All guests get goose liver and butter free. For $630 per person you get scallops, truffle soup, veal cutlets, French pudding, petits fours and coffee. Coat and tie.

THE SPICE MARKET, Southeast Asian moderate. *3/F Omni Prince Hotel. 736-1888. 6am-2:30pm, 6:30pm-12:30 midnight. All cards.* Asian buffet (Indonesian, Indian, Singaporean, Japanese, etc.). Lunch buffet $88, dinner buffet $150. Try the Tom yam kung soup and $60 nasi goreng.

SPRING DEER, Peking moderate to expensive. *1/F, 42 Mody Road. 366-4012. Noon-3pm. 6pm-11pm daily. All cards.* One of the oldest in Kowloon. Peking duck and Beggar's chicken.

TUTTO BENE, Italian expensive. *7 Knutsford Terrace. 316-2116. Noon-2:30pm; 6:30pm-10:30pm. All cards.* Popular are the veal marsala and chicken with rosemary. Smart casual.

TAIPAN GRILL, Continental expensive, *The Omni Hong Kong Hotel, 3 Canton Road, Harbour City. 736-0088. Noon-2:30pm; 6:30pm-10:30pm. All cards.* Most popular dishes are meat or fish flambe. Fillet $245.

THREE FIVE, Korean budget. *6 Ashley Street. 376-2993. 7am-11pm. No cards.* This is another place for Korean BBQ. Although Linda would recommend the **Arirang** (see above) first, because it's bigger, brighter, slightly cheaper and cleaner, she prefers the beef BBQ sauce a little more here because it's less salty. This is a small, tacky place, whose four large, shared tables are usually full. You get a stick of Wrigley's double-mint gum with your bill. English is a problem.

UNKAI JAPANESE RESTAURANT, Osaka expensive. *3/F, Sheraton Hong Kong Hotel, 20 Nathan Road. 369-1111. Noon-2:15pm; 6:30pm-10:15pm.* Superb sushi, fresh sashimi, teppanyaki and crisp tempura all highly recommended. ANA, its Japanese airline owner, flies ingredients daily from Japan. Smart casual.

WU KONG SHANGHAI RESTAURANT, Shanghai moderate. *Basement, Alpha House, 27-33 Nathan Rd. 366-7244. All credit cards. Hyatt Hotel exit from Tsim Sha Tsui MTR stop. 11:30am-11:15pm.* Dim sum.

Tsim Sha Tsui East

PEKING GARDEN, Peking moderate. *A branch of this reliable restaurant is at 1/F Empire Centre, 68 Mody Rd., Tsim Sha Tsui East. 721-8868. Monday-Saturday 11:30am-3pm and 5:30pm-midnight. All cards.* See review in Central.

SABATINI'S, Italian expensive. *3/F Royal Garden Hotel, 69 Mody Rd. 733-2000. Noon-2:30pm; 7pm-11pm. All cards.* Smart casual. Other outlets in Rome, Tokyo and Singapore. Try the baked sea bass or seafood pasta.

Cheung Chau Island

There are good, open-air Chinese seafood restaurants near the ferry pier. Next to Pak Tai Temple is a good Indian restaurant with reasonable prices. This is a nice place to relax. **GARDEN CAFE**, on the main road from the pier, 300 meters before the beach is an expat hang-out.

BUDGET FOOD

The cheapest places to eat are fast food restaurants and Chinese food stalls. **McDonald's** costs less than in the U.S. If a fast food restaurant is full, customers share tables – a good chance to make friends. These places are in most shopping malls and on the street. The most fun and exotic are the food fairs, with their variety of Asian and western food outlets.

The **Pacific Place Food Fair** in Central is always packed and has stalls that serve Thai, Singapore, Shanghai, Cantonese and American food. The basement of the **Silvercord Mall** at 30 Canton Rd. across from the Marco Polo Hotel offers Indian, Chinese, Thai, Japanese, ice cream and more. Food fairs are usually in the basements of shopping malls.

For lower-priced western food, try the **Mall Cafe** in the **YMCA** *(41 Salisbury Rd., Tsim Sha Tsui)* where the breakfast buffet with bacon and eggs cost $39 and the lunch buffet $44. **Pizza Huts** and the more established **Spaghetti Houses** are more expensive, liquor-licenced, sit-down-and-be-waited-on places, where pizza costs between $50-60. In Pizza Hut, you pay $27 for a small bowl from the salad bar.

Oliver's Super Sandwiches sells good, deli-style sandwiches (about $20), baked potatoes, salads and breakfasts. There are 16 of these around the city, including: *Pacific Place (Lower G/F. 845-6192), The Landmark (basement 877-6631), and Pacific Centre (28 Hankow Road in Tsim Sha Tsui 723-9303).*

You can find McDonald's, Kentucky Fried, Wendy's, and Jack in the Box. Here are a few convenient locations. Each should have a list of branches: ***Kentucky Fried Chicken***, *Pacific Place in Central and 2 Cameron Rd. in Tsim Sha Tsui. In addition to the **McDonald's** at the airport, there are about 65 others including Pacific Place, and 5 and 37 Queen's Road Central. In Tsim Sha Tsui, 21A Granville Rd., and Star House, beside the Star Ferry. **Wendy's**, **McDonald's**, and **KFC** are side-by-side in Causeway Bay on the south side of Hennessy Road at Patterson. A **Jack-in-the-Box** is at 53 Patterson in Causeway Bay.*

For a change, try **Delifrance** which has seven restaurants mainly on the Hong Kong side. *Get a list from 1/F, Worldwide House, 19 Des Voeux Rd. 873-3893.* With soups, baguette sandwiches, and rich cheese pasteries, it is the most interesting and expensive of the fast food chains. There's also **Lucullus Gourmet Shops**, *Shop 249, Ocean Centre, Tsim Sha Tsui. 730-0332, 730-0555, the basement of Sogo Department Store in Causeway Bay, and 10C, Ice House St., Central. 868-0449 and 868-9526.*

There are also a number of Chinese chains. They are not quite as clean as the western ones but they are an equally cheap alternative when you tire of McDonald's and KFC. Generally, they sell western sandwiches, snacks and Western and Chinese entrees. They issue chopsticks with Chinese food and plastic cuttlery with western. The English can be poor, but you can point to the bilingual menu. The coffee is usually terrible, often served with condensed milk. Tourists rarely brave these places.

The best of the Chinese chains is **East East Wanton** which has mainly noodles, **Fairwood Fast Food** with its clown emblem, and then **Maxim's**. **Cafe de Coral** is the most prolific, least clean and doesn't always have

English menus; however, its sizzling plate of noodles with shredded beef in black pepper sauce for $20 is quite good.

The cheapest place to eat is on the street at food stalls. They are usually not hygienic and a few people have gotten sick. Some foreigners eat at them often and have no problem. It's your decision. English is generally not spoken. Look to see what others are eating and point. At lunch time, most people eat soup with noodles, veggies and meat. There are stalls in **Temple Street Night Market** and near the **Ladies Market** in Mong Kok.

See also **Midnight Express** (Middle-Eastern) in Central.

12. SHOPPING

You can get some fantastic deals in Hong Kong. The markets have incredibly cheap clothing, and fashions can be a year ahead of North America. Hong Kong produces a big selection of top-of-the-line western-styled clothes for many foreign companies. Also good buys are high-quality silk, jewelry, gold, jade, gems like opals, diamonds, top-of-the-market watches, leather purses, furs, eye glasses and frames, pirated computers, computer books and some computer software.

Hong Kong has the biggest offering of traditional and modern Chinese products. They're usually cheaper than anywhere else in the world except for China; however, in China you might have to go to several cities to get what you can find in one store here.

Because of the volume selling, there is a wider variety of electronics, computers, stereo equipment and cameras available in Hong Kong. Hong Kong sells models destined for the Asian, European and North American markets. Some of these Japanese and Taiwanese brands don't get to North America.

Don't expect the shopping bargains of the 1970s and 1980s because of the high rents, but there's still a lot around.

THE BEST SHOPPING AROUND

*The best place to shop for high quality goods is Central. **Stanley** and **Granville Streets** are our favorite markets for middle quality clothes; for lower quality we like the markets in **Mong Kok** and **Prince Edward** even though these markets are not consistently good. We also like the **Gurkha Market** but never have time for it. For cheaper Chinese arts and crafts, we head for **Stanley** and **Tsim Sha Tsui**, and then the more expensive Chinese department stores.*

DUTY FREE HONG KONG

Because it is a tax-free port, imports into Hong Kong are duty-free except for alcohol, tobacco, perfume, cosmetics and hydrocarbon oils, like gasoline. Don't be fooled by "duty-free stores". The only real duty-free store is at the airport where these exceptions are truly tax exempt. Hong Kong adds no sales taxes.

SHOPPING HOURS

Convenience stores open later. Supermarkets close about 9pm.
- **Central and Western** – *generally 10am-7pm. A few open to 9pm*
- **Causeway Bay** – *10am-9:30pm or 10pm. A few open to midnight*
- **Tsim Sha Tsui** – *10am-9pm. A few close 8pm or midnight*
- **Tsim Sha Tsui East** – *10am-7:30pm.*
- **Hotel shopping malls** – *9:30-10am to 7-10pm. Some closed Sundays*

THE ART OF SHOPPING

If you know what you want, check out prices at home before you go. Some things are cheaper in Hong Kong and some things are not. If you're after Chinese goods, check out stores in Chinatowns where prices should be lowest.

After your arrival here, for big ticket purchases, telephone the sole agents for electronics, photographic equipment, etc. They can tell you suggested retail prices, accessories and guarantees and give you a list of authorized dealers. We have some sole agents below. More complete lists are available in the Hong Kong Tourist Association's free *Shopping* booklets. Ask your hotel concierge to also recommend nearby stores.

Telephone several dealers and ask about availability, prices and HKTA membership. The telephoned price is still not the lowest but you're getting close. HKTA stores with the red logo of a sailing junk are safer. If you have any problems with them, the Association will intercede.

If you don't know exactly what you want, look around for the best prices and models. These can vary a lot. Write the model number and price on the business card of each store you visit so you won't forget and can compare.

It is always best to get an introduction to a store. If your hotel concierge sent you, the shopkeeper knows he has to make you happy or the concierge might not send anybody else. The same goes for the sole agent or the HKTA. Complain to them if you are dissatisfied. If you find any store in this book not as we mentioned, please let us know and we will take it out of our next edition.

We highly recommend HKTA's free booklets. See HKTA in "Basic Information". The one named *Shopping* lists HKTA member stores and sole agents for everything from electronic and photographic equipment to sporting goods, opticals and porcelain. It has lots of advice and a huge list of stores, but doesn't make recommendations or include descriptions. *Shoppers Guide to Consumer Electronics* helps with VCRs, video cameras, disc players, photography equipment and computers. There is also one for jewelry.

Shopping in Hong Kong can be exhausting and at some point you have to ask yourself how much your time is worth. When you can't look at another shop, retreat to a nearby park, bar or coffee shop to relax and regain your peace of mind. Ruth tries to delay decisions on any big purchases until the next day.

BARGAINING

Hong Kong is no longer a major bargaining place. The merchants have realized that they can make more money if they spend less time arguing. You can still bargain in outdoor markets and in Tsim Sha Tsui, especially the jewelry stores which mark up prices expecting you to haggle. Bargain also in stores that beckon you in. You can dicker in camera shops but never in department stores or supermarkets. Haggling on the Hong Kong side is harder than Tsim Sha Tsui which is more used to tourists. Still, you lose nothing by asking, "Could you offer me a better price?"

Other ploys are: "I am not a rich American" or "I'll tell my friends to come here" or "The store down the street said it was less." Of course they've heard it all before, but it's part of the fun. Start to leave and see how they react.

First decide on a purchase and how much it is worth to you. If you've done the above homework, you know your own bottom line. When you buy more than one item, you have a better chance of success. "If I buy the camera, the zoom lens, and a carrying case, what discount will you give me?" Vendors will usually only go down 10% on their first asking price, more on an outrageously quoted price depending on the kind of goods.

Offer less than you're willing to pay. Most importantly, keep your sense of humor. It's more fun if you make faces or pretend to cry when the price is too high. Getting mad is useless. The Chinese look down on people who can't control their tempers. It should be a game, not a pitched battle. If you think you're getting close to an agreement, say something like "I might be interested if you throw in three rolls of film and a camera strap too."

Haggling is best if there are no other customers in the store. It is best with a manager. Clerks can only go down so far; managers can go further. Some vendors will go down more if you are the first or last customer of the day.

Always ask about discounts even in Chinese department stores like Yue Hwa and Chinese Arts and Crafts. Go to the Customer Service Department and tell them you want to buy a lot of things. It may be worth a 10% discount.

SEALING THE DEAL

Credit cards and travelers' checks are accepted at most stores, but ask first. You are sometimes charged an additional 2-3% for credit card purchases, so you usually get a better deal if you pay cash. The store doesn't want to pay a percentage to the credit card company.

Get a receipt. You can't normally return purchases so make sure the receipt is itemized and the exchange policy is stated in writing. You also want the model number (if any) of the purchase on the receipt.

ELECTRONICS

Be aware that appliances requiring electricity can be in 220 volts. If you want something for use in North America, make sure it is 110 volts. Also be sure to get an international guarantee for purchased electronics with the name and address of a dealer in your own country, hopefully near your home. Be aware that North American agents might not have parts for some models nor any manuals on how to fix them.

CLOTHING

Clothing and shoes could be marked in British, American, European, Japanese or Chinese sizes. Things can get really confusing. Always measure. Hold the tee-shirt up to yourself. Before you leave home, take measurements of people for whom you are buying. Carry a measuring tape. HKTA's *Shopping* booklet has a handy size comparison chart.

Consult a copy of Vogue or other recent fashion magazines to compare prices. Some cottons and woolens made for the local market could shrink. Serious shoppers should aim for the sales seasons: two weeks before Chinese New Year's and in August.

COMPLAINTS

See HKTA and Complaints in the Chapter 6.

DON'T GET RIPPED OFF

Most shopkeepers are honest. They would not stay in business long if they weren't. Be aware of the few who are not. *Bait and switch* is the name of one game, especially in Tsim Sha Tsui. Check each purchase carefully. Don't let store clerks box your purchases in the next room where they could change it for an inferior or broken model. Do not be intimidated by how hurt the shopkeeper appears at your accusation of dishonesty.

One of the most frequent complaints is that shipped goods never arrived or arrived broken. To avoid this, stick to HKTA stores, keep receipts including cost of postage or pay your hotel to do the packing and shipping. You could also post it yourself (cheaper) or courier it. Hong

Kong post offices are as efficient as North American post offices, but do get insurance.

Then there's the good price on the camera, but a rip-off on accessories. Sometimes they sell you old or defective goods as new.

You don't need to give a deposit except for custom-made goods.

SHOPPING TOURS

You might be interested in a human shopping guide customizing tours for you. They are expatriate women who know what some North Americans want. They have their own networks of bargain places and will probably save you a lot of time. They may save you money on purchses, but you pay them alot for their services. You might want to try our list of shops before you hire one. Corporations use them to take care of visiting business people or their spouses.

Because they are working for you, they should not get commissions from stores, and they should try to get you the best deals. Write ahead in plenty of time, tell them what you're looking for and ask for their fees. If you use them, please tell us how satisfactory they were.

Try Helen Giff of **Asian Cajun**, *12 Scenic Villa Drive, Flat 4F, Pokfulam, Hong Kong. 566-9010, fax 855-9571.* Elaine Healey of **SilkRoad International** *(882-4446; fax 882-4470)* says she can arrange custom-made copies of Chanel jewelry for a fraction of the price.

Non-Stop Shoppers Unlimited organizes tours to the New Territories, especially the Gurkha Market (Fridays only). Aimed mainly at local residents, it also goes to carpet outlets, furniture, porcelain, brass, candle, chocolate and rattan factories. *Contact Lyn Hirschhorn, A2601 Queen's Garden, 9 Old Peak Road, Hong Kong, 523-3850 or fax 868-1164.*

WHERE TO BUY
Markets

You can find great bargains in factory overruns of clothing designed for export. These are the extras made for foreign companies as well as rejects with missing buttons or even erroneous labels. Check quality carefully. Be careful of copycats such as Levi Strauz (rather than Strauss). Aim for quality, not the label. It's easy to put a Cassini label on a cheaper shirt. All clothing markets have kids clothes, panty hose, umbrellas, cheap watches and more. Be sure to bargain.

Be aware that signs in markets can be confusing. A cart of socks may have a sign that says 3/$10, but the Chinese writing might say white socks only. If you see lots of Chinese people clustered around a stall in a market, it's probably a good deal. There are permanent street markets and illegal street markets, one or two isolated carts. Stock is inconsistent. Sometimes there are good buys, sometimes nothing. Owners of the unlicensed carts might pick up and disappear when an uncooperative policeman approaches. Buyers need not worry.

Buyers do need to worry about labels. Do not believe "100% silk." Look carefully at Rolex imitations which should cost no more than $100. The watch will work but the "gold" wears off.

Factory Outlets

In addition to the markets, individual factories have fancy, air-conditioned outlets in Central and on Granville Rd. in Tsim Sha Tsui. They also sell at the factories themselves but that's too much of a hassle and time consuming. Not only are the factories hard to find, but they are dirty and you might not find a range of sizes and styles nor matching tops and bottoms. Get a copy of Dana Goetz's *Hong Kong Factory Bargains* from a bookstore. It's the bible. See Pedder Building in "Central" below.

Malls

Air-conditioned malls are great places to go during the sweltering summer, in rainy weather, or on cold days. If you are in a hurry, be sure you have explicit directions to the store you want. It is easy to get lost. Malls have maps at their information desks. Prices are generally the same as in North America with similiar stores like the Body Shop and Esprit.

The best mall is **Pacific Place** in Central at Admiralty MTR. The largest and most confusing is **Harbour City** in Tsim Sha Tsui near the Star Ferry. The newest and least confusing is **Times Square** at Causeway Bay MTR. The best for kids is **Taikoo Shing City Plaza** at Taikoo MTR stop, because it has roller and ice skating. The most upper-class are the **Landmark** in Central and the **hotel arcades**.

Almost all malls have fast-food eating places, most have decent restaurants and some have movie theaters (good for non-shopping companions). Floor numbers are usually the first number of the unit address. For example 274 would be on the second floor.

Hotel Arcades

You can find designer fashions and jewelry in convenient, exclusive, usually over-priced hotel malls like those in the Regent and the Peninsula in Tsim Sha Tsui and the Mandarin in Central.

WHERE TO FIND MARKETS AND MALLS BY DISTRICT

HONG KONG ISLAND

Central

Where do you start? There's so much. **Li Yuen Street East** and **West** are inexpensive clothing and purse alleys. The **Prince's Building** (*open*

11am-5pm) is good for silver, antiques, linens and middle-quality art objects. **The Landmark, Pacific Place,** and the **Mandarin Hotel Arcade** are also in Central. See "Factory Outlets" below for the Pedder Building.

Western – Hollywood Road/Cat Street

The first district west of Central is one of the best places to look for Chinese antiques. It has about 80 tiny shops around the Man Mo temple on Hollywood Road and in or around the **Cat Street Galleries** at 38 Lok Ku Road and on **Upper Lascar Row**. One can spend a productive day window-shopping, if not buying. Most stores here open 11am-6pm daily.

Cat Street Galleries offers free car service with Central, *Monday-Saturday 10am-6pm. 541-8908.* You can also take a taxi from Sheung Wan MTR stop or the long escalator from Central Market to Hollywood Road, and walk west six short blocks. Antique shops are all along this street and in the Galleries. From the temple, go down the Ladder St. steps and then one block west to the Galleries.

Western - Western Market

You'll find this market one block west of the Sheung Wan MTR stop *at 323 Des Veoux Road West; shops 10am-7pm, restaurant 11am-11:30pm.* Follow the signs to the Macau Ferry but get out on the south side of Connaught Rd. Go west to the end of the foot bridge at Morrison Street to the Market. This old produce market is now a tourist market with relatively inexpensive wares and restaurant. It has tagua nut (vegetable ivory) carvings, antique embroidery, rock shop, leather craft, cloth, old photos and art gallery. No name brands. This is also on the tram line.

Wanchai

In South Wanchai on Queen's Road East, west of the Hopewell Centre, you can find shops for toys, rattan and rosewood furniture (a good buy) and picture frames. East of the Centre is the bustling Wanchai food market. The **New World Harbour View Hotel arcade** has two shops of the **Design Gallery**, *833-4333*. It has unusual but interesting Hong Kong-designed clothes and electronics. A large Chinese arts and crafts store is in the **China Resources Building** a block to the east.

Causeway Bay-North

This is the second most touristy shopping area after Tsim Sha Tsui and equally crowded. Many foreign residents find it cheaper to shop here than the big malls, but large, western sizes are rare. It has the small, cheap **Jardine's Bazaar** (clothes and accessories market). See "Causeway Bay." There are five, large, upmarket Japanese department stores nearby with great sales, and two China products stores. On dry evenings, about

10:30pm stalls magically appear here usually around the **Sogo Department Store** MTR exit, the **Pearl Theatre**, and sometimes in the **Excelsior Hotel plaza** on East Point Road. We have found silver jewelery, belts, tee shirts, ties, underwear, belts and purses.

STANLEY MARKET

Though a little more expensive than other markets, the quality, styles and variety here is better. Going to Stanley makes a pleasant half-day excursion to the lush green side of the island. It has leather, down, silk, cashmere and cotton clothing, lots of linens, Chinese arts and crafts, watches and souvenirs. Check quality and cleanliness of goods carefully. See also "Stanley."

Ruth's favorite shop here is **Best Price** with lots of good labels. From the bus stop, head downhill past Wellcome supermarket as far as you can go and then turn left along Stanley Main St. Walk through the market comparing prices. Turn left up the hill at Ann & Albert's and China Town. The Best Price is on the right, one floor up. The **China Products Store** on Stanley Main St. has better clothing styles than most other Chinese stores. Across from the bus stop is Ellis Jewelery which has been there for decades.

KOWLOON

Tsim Sha Tsui

This is shopping heaven or hell, depending on how you look at it. It has a huge number of stores, but is one of the biggest tourist traps. Some stores have no price tags, and bargaining is done everywhere except in the malls. The two main areas to shop here are **Harbour City Mall** (see "Tsim Sha Tsui"), and **Nathan Road** and surrounding streets from the harbor to the north end of the park. The **New World Centre** is a smaller mall with a lot of good stores too.

Nathan Road (aka the Golden Mile) has hundreds of camera, crafts and clothing shops. It is very crowded with narrow streets, but prices here can be the equivalent of the street markets. You can find $10 T-shirts and $25 silk blouses. Granville and Kimberley Rds. are known for fashionable clothes and name brands, and Granville has factory overruns with labels like Bloomingdale's and Sak's and big sizes. Check quality. The prices are good.

There is an interesting little alley between Hankow and Lock Roads, parallel to Haiphong Rd. It has traditional Chinese crafts at reasonable prices. Be sure to bargain. A line of name-brand boutiques (Park Lane Shoppers Boulevard) fringes the east side of Kowloon Park and you can find cheap silk blouses and boxer shorts on the south side, along Haiphong Rd.

Tsim Sha Tsui East

This is the least crowded, least interesting shopping area in Hong Kong with several malls, but prices are the same as elsewhere.

Yau Ma Tei

The **Jade Market** and the fascinating **Temple St. Night Market** (for cheap everything) are here. Gap, Liz Claybourne, etc. have been at Temple St. but don't count on it. You can get three pirated CDs for $100, but the selection is not very good. *8pm-11pm.*

Mong Kok

Shop here for inexpensive stereo equipment and the four-block-long **Ladies Market** on Tung Choi St, which has clothes for men and women and a huge selection of sleazy lingerie. Linda bought Calvin Klein jeans for $90. Check out the Bird Market when you're in the area.

Prince Edward Market

Ruth's favourite has mainly clothes and handbags for great prices. Lots of seconds so be careful. Go to Prince Edward MTR station and take the Allied Plaza exit. Cross the street and walk straight ahead. At the light, turn left for two short blocks. Then right to Fa Yuen St. where there are stalls in front of the stores. Shopping is best in the dumpy-looking shops and only for the first block. It has primarily clothes and bags. A flower market is nearby. *Open 9:30am.*

New Territories

Large malls are in Sha Tin, Tuen Mun, and Tsuen Wan with the same prices and many of the same stores as downtown. The **Sha Tin mall** has Toys R Us.

The **Gurkha Market** on Fridays is in Sai Kung near the British military base and usually has some great clothing factory overruns. A bus leaves on Friday mornings ($32) at 8:30am from the Star Ferry, Central. It returns at 1 pm. Call HKTA to confirm.

SHOPPING BY SUBJECT
ANTIQUES AND REPRODUCTIONS

Unlike China which restricts exports of antiques older than 1795, Hong Kong sells a whole range. For anything older than 1795, look here. Prices are lower in China for anything younger. Hong Kong has a lot of variety but there are also reproductions, so be careful.

Stores here can tell you about restoration, refinishing and repairs of antiques. Many stores do not keep all their valuable pieces out. You have to ask. If an object is over 100 years old, you don't have to pay customs duty on it when you return to the U.S. or Canada. Most stores can give you a certificate to that effect if an object costs more than $1,000.

The art auction houses of **Christie's** and **Sotheby's** hold auctions once or twice a year. **Christie Swire's** address is: *28/F, 2804-6, Alexander House, 16-20 Chater Rd., Central. 521-5396.* Sotheby's address is: *Room 309-310, Exchange Square II, 8 Connaught Rd. Central. 524-8121.* Look in the newspapers for auction dates.

Hollywood Road in Western has the most number of shops and they vary from cheap to very expensive. You have to do a lot of walking and haggling. There are some other upscale stores with fancy rents that have been in business a long time.

Here are some of our picks:

Altfield Gallery, *45 Graham St. Central, 524-4867, fax 524-5676. All cards.* Above Hollywood Rd., it has reproductions of Ming and Qing furniture, and Chinese and Tibetan carpets. It is also sole agent for Jim Thompson Thai silk. *Also Rooms 220, 248-249 Prince's Building. 524-7526; fax 524-0510*

Charlotte Horstmann & Gerald Godfrey, Ltd. *Shop 104, Ocean Terminal, 730-9412. All cards.* This is for serious, wealthy antique fans. Where else can you get a full 18th century Qing dynasty bannerman's ceremonial costume?

C.P. Ching Fine Oriental Art, *319 Pacific Place, 88 Queensway, Central. 810-9033. All cards.* South East Asian, Japanese and Chinese textiles, sculptures and Buddhist art.

Eastern Dreams, *47A Hollywood Rd. 544-2804. All cards.* Ceramics, furniture and antiques from neolithic to Qing are here. *Shop also on G/F, 4 Shelley Street, Central. 524-4787.*

Flagstaff Museum of Teaware *(529-9390).* Buy reproductions of unusual tea pots at a fair price. See "Central."

Hollywood Galleries, *G/F, 175 Hollywood Road, 541 6338. All cards.* Here are jade carvings and Buddha statues.

Honeychurch Antiques, *29 Hollywood Rd. 543-2433, fax 541-3683. All cards.* American couple Glenn and Lucille Vessa have been here over 20 years. They sell European and Asian antiques, furniture, carpets, silver and maps.

Lun Chai Curios Store, *22 Hollywood Rd. 544-1138 and 142 Hollywood Rd. 540-4772. All cards.* Porcelain, carvings and gilt bronzes.

Yue Po Chai Antique Co., *8-10 Hollywood Rd. 540-4374.* Porcelains, bronzes and ceramics are here.

Zee Stone Gallery, *11, Forum, III Exchange Square, Central. 845-4476. Fax 877-2859.* They sell antique Tibetan and Xinjiang carpets.

ANTIQUE APPRAISERS

Lammert Bros. Auctions, *545-9859;* **Sotheby's (HK) Ltd.**, *524-8121;* *Hong Kong Artcraft Merchants Association 368-2347.*

ART GALLERIES

Paintings are for sale in stores in the Ritz-Carlton Hotel, the Mandarin Hotel, and City Hall in Central. **Alisan Fine Arts** has modern Chinese oils and watercolors *at 315 Prince's Building, Central. 526-1091.* Zee Stone Gallery (see above) also has contemporary Chinese art.

ARTS AND CRAFTS

Mountain Folkcraft, *12 Wo On Lane, Central. 523-2817.* To find this funky little shop, take the third road to your right up from Queen's Rd. Central, off D'Aguilar St. in Lan Kwai Fong. There is a small shrine at the end of this deadend. You can find clothing, batik, carvings, embroidery and furniture from Chinese and South East Asian minorities here.

Banyan Tree, *214 Ocean Galleries, Harbour City. 730-6631; 214 Prince's Building, Chater Rd. Central 523-5561; No. 112, The Repulse Bay, 109 Repulse Bay Rd. 592-8721.* This charming upscale shop has rattan, wicker, baskets and gifts from Asia.

BOOKS

See Chapter 6, "Basic Information."

CARPETS

Tai Ping Carpets, *Shop 110, G/F, Hutchinson House, Central. 526-6231; Wing On Plaza, G/F, 62 Mody Rd., Tsim Sha Tsui East. 369-4061.* Can also custom-make carpets in 4-6 weeks with New Zealand wool.

Oriental Carpet Palace, *G/F 61 Wyndham St. Central. 845-4747.* Tribal, Iranian, Kashmiri, wool and silk. All cards.

Zee Stone Gallery. See Antiques above.

See also "Chinese Arts and Crafts" below.

CHINESE ARTS AND CRAFTS

We have included Chinese products stores here that sell everything including wrenches and televisions and are essentially department stores. They take credit cards. Their handicrafts are more expensive than in Tsim Sha Tsui and Stanley markets, but the quality and selection is better. It's fun just to look around, especially at the elaborately carved jade sculptures, the giant cloisonne vases, the red lacquer and crazy gold filigree. They tend to price non-Chinese goods higher than the Japanese department stores.

China Arts & Crafts Stores have high quality silk, embroidered table cloths, jewelry, stone carvings, etc. from China. Other Chinese department stores are **China Products**, **Chinese Merchandise Emporium**, and **Yue Hwa China Products**. They are all crowded on weekends. The small **Welfare Handicrafts** stores and **Caritas** sell crafts for charity.

On Hong Kong Island

Caritas, *2 Caine Rd., beside the Botanical Gardens in Central. No cards.*

China Arts & Crafts, *Pacific Place, Central. 523-3933.*

China Arts & Crafts, *24-28 Queen's Rd (near Pedder St.), Central.*

CRC Department Store, *92-104 Queen's Rd. across from Central Market, near Queen Victoria St., Central.*

China Arts & Crafts, *China Resources Bldg, 26 Harbour Rd., Wanchai. 827-6667.*

China Products, *488-500 Hennessy Rd. (by Percival St.), Causeway Bay. 572-0222.*

CRC Department Store, *31 Yee Wo St., Causeway Bay at Victoria Park. 890-8321.*

Oriental Handicraft. Co. *1/F, 106 Prince's Bldg., Chater Rd. Central. 524-1868.* Embroidered table cloths, silk kimonos and blouses.

Welfare Handicrafts, *Basement, Jardine House (port-hole building) by Star Ferry, Connaught Rd., Central. 524-3356.*

In Kowloon

China Arts & Crafts, *Star House, 3 Salisbury Rd., Tsim Sha Tsui, 735-4061.*

China Arts & Crafts, *30 Canton Rd. (near Haiphong Rd.), Tsim Sha Tsui, 375-0155.*

China Arts & Crafts, *New World Centre, Salisbury Rd., Tsim Sha Tsui, 369-7760.*

Chung Kiu Chinese Products Ltd., *17 Hankow Rd. (at Peking Rd.), Tsim Sha Tsui, 723-3211.*

Welfare Handicrafts, *Salisbury Rd., between Canton Rd. and Kowloon Park Dr., Tsim Sha Tsui. 366-6979.*

Yue Hwa Chinese Products, *54-64 Nathan Rd. at Mody Rd., basement, under Mirador Mansions, Tsim Sha Tsui. 368-9165.* This is usually quiet and has a few bargain bins. Linda found a silk dress shirt here for $125, but found the same for $40 on Haiphong Road, south of Kowloon Park.

Yue Hwa Chinese Products, *Park Lane Boulevard, 143-161 Nathan Rd., Tsim Sha Tsui. 739-3888.* This is touristy and not very interesting.

China Arts & Crafts, *233-239 Nathan Rd, Yau Ma Tei. 733-0061.*

Yue Hwa Chinese Products, *301-309 Nathan Rd, Yau Ma Tei. 384-0084.*

CHILDREN'S CLOTHES

Available in all of the clothing markets, malls, and department stores.

CIGARS

Divan, *G/F in Mandarin Oriental Hotel. 522-0111. 11am-10pm.* Cigars here have good storage and real Cuban clerk Abel Ortega.

CLOTHES

Cheapest are the markets. Best value for money are the factory outlets below. The malls have good quality, but North American prices. You can buy designer clothes used once or twice by rich local women (small sizes) at **Donna's**, *503 Lyndhurst Tower, 1 Lyndhurst Terrace, Central; Phoenix Fashion, 1/F, 10 Wellington St., Central; Le Place, Shop 203A, Pedder Building, Pedder St. Central.* See also Tailors and Shoes below.

COMPUTERS

These are cheaper than you'll find in North America. Clones or copies can be less expensive here, but the Hong Kong government has been cracking down. Besides, you might not be able to get counterfeits into your own country and pirated software may not be compatible with your system. Do also be aware of pirated software with viruses that could contaminate your computer. Do look for cheaper genuine software.

If you want to see what's available try: **Golden Shopping Arcade**, *156 Fuk Wah St., Shamshuipo, Kowloon.* This is famous for cheap computer clones and pirated books. Take the MTR to Shamshuipo, north of Tsim Sha Tsui, and leave by the Golden Shopping Arcade exit. Walk for one block. There is a sign.

It's a dirty, crowded, fire-trap of a three-story building on the first corner but what do you expect of a market? Oxford English? Incidentally, if you're lucky, in winter, outside the main entrance on Sundays, peddlers sell snakes. One peddler swings a live snake in the air, catches it in his teeth and bites off the head. What other computer center has this kind of entertainment?

Groups of computer shops are also in the **Computer Mall**, *11/12/F, Windsor House, 311 Gloucester Road, Causeway Bay. 895-4998, 865-5266;* **Admiralty Centre** *across from Pacific Place in Central* has a row of 10 or 15 small computer shops downstairs. You can buy computer software at two shops in **Times Square** at Causeway Bay MTR. If you need the name of one reliable shop, try **A-1 Electronics Co.**, *Holiday Inn Golden Mile, Shop B 117A, 50 Nathan Rd., Tsim Sha Tsui. 366-6552. Branch at 48 Lockhart Road, Wanchai. 861-3218.*

Sole Agents: For Apple, **Gilman Business System**, *893-0303; for IBM, IBM China/HK Corporation 825-6222*; for Canon, **Jardine Office Systems**, *565-2011.*

DEPARTMENT STORES

Except for the Chinese department stores above, these carry big international name brands like Lanvin and Chanel and have North American prices. Phone for branches near you or check the phone book.

The main locally-owned Hong Kong department stores are the middle-priced **Dragon Seed**, *39 Queen's Rd. Central. 524-2016.* This has conservative styles), **Sincere**, *173 Des Voeux Rd. Central. 544-2688.* Cheaper prices; **Shui Hing**, *23-25 Nathan Rd., Tsim Sha Tsui. 721-1495* and **Wing On**, *Des Voeux Rd., Central and 361 Nathan Rd., Yau Ma Tei. 780-4341.*

Lane Crawford is the best, most expensive and has a history of more than 100 years in Hong Kong. The main store is *at 70 Queen's Rd. Central. 526-6121.* It has branches in Pacific Place and Times Square.

Marks & Spencer is British with branches in *Quarry Bay, Excelsior Plaza (Causeway Bay), and Pacific Place and the Landmark in Central, 869-0976.* It has larger clothes sizes and the same price range as the Japanese stores.

Japanese department stores have smaller-sized clothes and also the whole range of name brands. There are three in Causeway Bay: **Daimaru**, *Great George St. 10:30am-9:30pm. 576-7321*; **Matsuzakaya**, *2-20 Paterson St. 890-6622. Stores also in Admiralty Centre and Tsim Sha Tsui. 10:30am-9:30pm;* and **Sogo**, *555 Hennessy Rd., Causeway Bay 833-8338. 10am-10pm.* Reasonably priced.

Seibu, *Pacific Place, Central. 868-0111* is the most expensive with unusual items. **Isetan of Japan** is the cheapest and is in the *Sheraton Hotel Shopping Mall, 20 Nathan Rd., Tsim Sha Tsui MTR. 369-1111, and Aberdeen Centre. 814-7406.* **Yaohan** is at *G/F and 1st Basement, Site 576, Whampoa Garden, Hung Hom. 766-0338. A branch is also at the Panda Hotel in Tseun Wan. 409-0339.*

DRUG STORES

Pharmacies are much like North America's with many of the same name brands. There are Manning's and the much bigger Watson's chains. Not all have pharmacists.

Manning's, *Shop B, 22-23, 1st Basement, The Landmark, 12-16A Des Voeux Road, Central. 524-9855;* **Watson's** (with pharmacist), *Shop 31, Paterson Plaza, Paterson St., Causeway Bay. 895-4008; Haiphong Mansion, 101 Nathan Rd., Tsim Sha Tsui. 369-2011.*

FACTORY OUTLETS

Here you find the best deals on brand-name clothing. We urge serious bargain hunters to read Dana Goetz's book *Hong Kong Factory Bargains*. She has been updating it regularly for years, lives in Hong Kong, and knows her subject thoroughly. HKTA also has a factory outlet guide. Call outlets for their hours and directions before you head there.

Among the best and most convenient are those listed below, all within a few blocks of each other in Central. The Pedder Building is across from the Landmark on Pedder St. From the Pedder Building to the Grand Progress Building, go uphill to Queen's Rd., turn right then left up D'Aguilar St. Make a second left from Queen's Road, then right on Lan Kwai Fong to 58. Stock changes constantly.

Ca Va, *7/F. Pedder Bldg., 12 Pedder Street, south entrance. 537-7174. 10am-6:30pm.* This has had some silk and cotton knits depending on the season. Some brands have been over half the U.S. price.

C.C.C., *3/F, Grand Progress Building, 58-62 D'Aguilar St., Lan Kwai Fong. 530-1536.   10am-5:30pm.* This has had big-sized cotton shirts, trousers, etc.

Shopper's World-Safari, *1/F, Pedder Bldg., 12 Pedder St. 523-1950. 9:30am-6:30pm. Open Sundays.* This has had $260 sweaters and woolen pants.

Whispers, *9-A, Grand Progress Building, 58-62 D'Aguilar St., Central. 877-9590. 10am-6pm. Saturday 10am-5pm. Closed Sunday.* This has had great evening wear in good styles. It has new stock every Friday and specializes in linens and uncrushables.

Wintex/Lisa Ferranti, *4/F. Pedder Bldg., 12 Pedder St. 9:30am-6:30pm. Closed Sundays.*

FABRICS

Chinese arts and crafts stores above have silk, cashmere, wools and cotton. Li Yuen alleys, and Cloth Alley on Queen's Rd. East in Western have limited supplies but are cheaper. For unusual fabrics see interior decorator stores like the **Altfield Gallery**, *45 Graham St. Central, 524-4867,* which has Thai silk.

FOOD STORES

Supermarkets are similar to North America's, with most North American brands and British ones as well, but the shops are smaller. The chains are **Park 'N Shop** and **Wellcome**. Some have delicatessens. There are also 24-hour **7-11's** and **Circle K's**.

FUR

Hong Kong is one of the largest fur exporters in the world. Furs come mostly from Scandinavia and the U.S. and much is re-exported to China. Furs can be 50% cheaper here. Be careful of furs from China usually sold in China products stores. They might not be properly cured and could produce a bad odor when wet. Among the largest and longest-established stores (1935) are the **Siberian Fur Stores** *at 29 Des Voeux Rd., Central. 522-1380. 9:30am-6pm and 21 Chatham Rd., Tsim Sha Tsui. 366-7039. 9:30am-6:30pm.* Two stuffed lions are in the front window of the Tsim Sha Tsui store.

GLASSES

They are cheaper than in North America, and finished in four to five days. The **Optical Shop** is a reliable chain with about 19 stores in Kowloon and 13 on Hong Kong Island. Try *117, Prince's Building, 10 Chater Rd. Central 523-8385.* It has brands like Armani and Dior. **Optical 88** has 11 outlets. Try *G/F, 65 Percival Street, Causeway Bay. 891-7316 or 161, Ocean Terminal, Harbour City, Tsim Sha Tsui. 736-2973.* There's also **Mandarin Optical Co.**, *51 Queen's Road Central. 522-7944.*

IVORY

It is illegal to take out elephant ivory, unless you have an import permit from your own country and an export permit from Hong Kong. *Call the Hong Kong Agriculture and Fisheries Department at 733-2283.*

JEWELRY

Hong Kong is a great place to buy locally-made jewelry and carved gems. It has more jewelry stores than any other city in the world. It is the world's third largest diamond trading center and a major center for gem cutting and polishing, especially opals. The selection is especially good for pearls, rubies, sapphires and emeralds. You can also buy agate, jasper, amethyst, aquamarine, cat's eye chrysoberyl, citrine and coral. Then there's garnet, goldstone, lapis lazuli and malachite. There's also peridot, sodalite, topaz, tourmaline and turquoise. These can be carved or made into jewelry.

Like most everything else, jewelry is free of sales taxes! Competition between the thousand jewelry stores keeps down the prices. And like other countries, there are synthetics and imitations, which are fine unless they're sold to you as the genuine article. Most jewelers are honest about these clones. If you want to buy gems here, we suggest you learn as much about them as possible before you arrive. Take an introductory course on this very complicated subject. Read books on how to buy.

Tourists have complained that later appraisals indicated a poorer quality of stone than they were led to believe. Ruth's experience with two major gems has been the opposite. After they arrived in North America, appraisers found them better than expected. You do need to be careful, especially in Tsim Sha Tsui and Mody Road.

To be safe, stick to stores recommended in this book. Otherwise, make sure the dealer is a HKTA member and in the case of diamonds, one that has been referred by the **Diamond Importers' Association** (DIA). Avoid higher-priced department stores and those that entertain a lot of tour buses and have price tags in US dollars. That usually indicates higher mark-ups. Do shop where local residents shop. Ask your hotel concierge or trusted Hong Kong friends for suggestions.

If the price tag is a whopper, you might want to take the gem to an independent gemologist for an appraisal. Make sure "return-for-full-refund" is written on the receipt, in case the gemologist disagrees with the store. Your receipt should also have the dealer's name and address, the type of stone, origin of gem, dimensions, its carat size, color, and any unusual qualities. It should mention the setting, gold content and any flaws. You probably do not want "return for exchange". For appraisals contact the **Gemological Association of Hong Kong**, *366-6066*. Certified gemologists who are members of this association have stickers to this effect displayed in their stores. They usually charge by the carat. Appraising 1 to 1.5 carats could cost $700.

Among the appraisers suggested by the DIA and whose wares are probably also reliable are:

Hong Kong Gems Exchange Ltd., *Room 102 & 103, Baskerville House, Central. 522-5007;* **Asian Gemological Laboratory**, *7/F, 11 Lock Rd., Tsim Sha Tsui. 723-0429;* Henry Cheng, FGA, **President Jewellery Co. Ltd.**, *G/F, no.11, Chung King Arcade, 36-44 Nathan Rd., Tsim Sha Tsui. 366-7085/723-4522.* There's also Alex Chan, FGA, **Premier Jewellery Co. Ltd.**, *G16 Shopping Arcade, Holiday Inn Golden Mile Hotel, 50 Nathan Road, Tsim Sha Tsui. 368-0002/368-0003.*

The non-profit DIA can give tips and names of outlets for diamonds. It was first established here in 1972. *Write to Room 1102, Parker House, 72 Queen's Road Central or call 523-5497/526-0561.* They will give you the full list of gem-testing centers, an introduction, and a list of member retailers and wholesalers. The introduction should give you an automatic discount but you can still haggle. It also gives a bank reference. You might want to check to be sure the store will still be in business for the duration of any guarantee. The DIA can't give you prices.

Prices should be reasonable on settings as well as gems because of lower labor costs. Might we suggest you bring jewelry to Hong Kong for repairs? Ruth has had rings expanded here. Every jeweler has a loup magnifying glass you can borrow for a close-up look. Do be prepared to haggle. If you've read this far, you might also want to read HKTA's booklet *Shopping Guide to Jewelery*.

Diamonds

The markup for diamonds in Hong Kong is 10%; in New York 50-100%. The variety in Hong Kong is enormous and the workmanship is usually good. Stones are good quality. Be sure to check the 4 C's of diamonds: carats, color, clarity, and cut. Expensive diamonds come with certificates. Be sure to ask for them.

Gold

Hong Kong people love gold. Many have seen paper money become worthless. But gold is not meant for sitting in bank vaults. Gold jewelry is status and as much as possible is worn, especially at weddings. Most gold in Hong Kong is 24 carat or 99.9% pure. HKTA member stores must stamp the fineness and an identifying mark on each piece of gold. For jewelry, 24 carat is too soft and has a different color than that used in North America. Some 24 carat necklace clasps are "S" shaped and can be bent sideways to open. Eventually some of these break so be careful. You can also buy other gold alloys like 22, 18, 14 and 10 carats. 22 carats means 22 parts gold to two parts of other metals. 14 carats means 14 parts gold to 10 of other metals.

Prices are decided by the weight of the gold. To compare prices here with other countries, multiply the number of taels by 1.20337 to get the troy ounces used in newspaper price quotes for gold.

Designers– International

International designs have been pirated here, although the government has tried to stamp out counterfeiting. Look for good fake Chanel jewelry in Stanley Market for a fraction of the cost of the real thing. Shopping is done clandestinely. You look for a store selling jewelry, make sure no one is looking and quietly ask, "Do you sell Chanel?" A pair of earrings can be $150. For obvious reasons, we can't give an address, and don't tell anyone we told you. For the real thing try places like **Les Must de Cartier** in the Regent and Peninisula hotel arcades in Tsim Sha Tsui.

Designers – Local

Hong Kong has a lot of good jewelry designers. The most famous internationally is Kai-yin Lo. She has stores in several shopping malls with her imaginative Asian designs. She uses good quality gems. Cheaper are May and Virginia Ng of Itre Decor Ltd. who also work with semi-precious stones. For plain necklaces of only stones, try Lo & Rador below.

Jade

The Chinese word for jade is *yu*, and it's applied to most hard green stones. The word makes no distinction between jadeite and nephrite as North Americans do, and "jade" could be serpentine, chrysoprase, or even soft, breakable soapstone. For the Chinese, jade is special and magical. It keeps people especially children healthy and brings them luck. It protects the dead from evil spirits. Jade can be that lovely imperial green, or a wide variety of colors. Valuable are multiple colors in one stone which the carver has worked into the carving.

The open-air **Jade Market** is fun to browse in, but vendors will tell you that glass and a lot of other things are jade. See "Yau Ma Tei, Kowloon." Good jade is not cheap. Some of it is treated to enhance the color and a year or so after you get it home, the colors could separate. They glue two or three stones together with an imperial green jelly-like substance that is seen through the almost translucent stone on top. This deception is hidden by a bezel setting. Be aware that the popular miniature trees labeled "jade" are other kinds of stone, neither nephrite nor jadeite.

Opals

Opals are a good buy. Many Hong Kong companies have their own mines in Australia and polished opals have been cheaper here than there. The **Opal Mine** (free) across Nathan Rd. from the mosque in Kowloon Park is a good place to start if you know nothing about quality and color. But check other stores before you buy.

Pearls

Pearls and Hong Kong are almost synonymous. Cultured and fresh-water pearls, of all kinds and quality, are sold by the ton. See Amerex, Elissa Cohen, Pearl Gallery and the high-end Trio Pearl below.

JEWELRY STORES

Larry's, **Henry's**, **Chow Tai Fook**, **King Fook** and **Tsei Sui Luen** are chains that sell mainly Chinese-style gold jewelry. We have listed a few of their convenient locations below.

Amerex Jewellery, *702 Tak Shing House, 20 Des Voeux Road, Central. 523-9145.* One of the best for pearls. A 12" 8mm. strand of pink Mikimoto cultured pearls costs about US$4100.

Chaumont International (factory outlet), *Room 1003, 10/F, Metropole Bldg., 57 Peking Rd. Tsim Sha Tsui. 368-7331.* Fresh water pearls. Colored stones. All cards.

Chinese Products stores above are good for jewelry but the settings might be too conservative for western tastes. The branch in Star House, near the Star Ferry in Tsim Sha Tsui, has a big selection especially of jade.

Chow Sang Sang is a chain of traditional Chinese gold stores. *G/F, 72 Queen's Rd. Central. 526-2009; 501 Hennessy Rd., Causeway Bay. 893-3677; 229-529 Nathan Rd., Yau Ma Tei. 730-3241/332-0633.*

Chow Tai Fook's largest store is *at 44-46 Queens Rd. Central. 524-3374; also Causeway Bay Plaza, 489 Hennessy Rd. 838-6222.*

Dehres International Limited, *2018 St. George's Building, 2 Ice House St. Central. 521-3411, fax 845-0506.* Primarily diamond wholesalers. 1ct-40ct. sizes. Serious buyers who want to pay over US$10,000 should call for an appointment.

Elissa Cohen, *209 Hankow Centre, 5-15 Hankow Rd., Tsim Sha Tsui. 312-0811 or 312-0820. All cards.* Cultured pearls, ready-made and Italian jewelry. Not cheap. Different designs. Good quality broaches. Ask for Eliza.

Henry's, *43-45 Queen's Rd, Central. 526-5233; 29 Nathan Road, Tsim Sha Tsui. 368-3101.*

Itre Decor Ltd., *B-2-18, New World Centre, Tsim Sha Tsui. 722-4617. Visa and MasterCard only.* Mainly jewelry with semi-precious stones.

J.A. Windsor & Co., *111 G/F, Prince's Building, 10 Chater Rd., Central. 522-1719. Also Shop 266 Ocean Galleries, Harbour City. 735-2150, 10am-6:30pm. Monday-Saturdays. Kowloon shop also Sunday noon-5pm.* Ask for 10% discount.

Jenny Jewellery Company, *G06-07, Regal Kowloon Hotel, 71 Mody Road, Tsim Sha Tsui East. 721-8569.* Gold chains, diamonds and gems.

Just Gold, *G/F, 47 Queen's Road Central. 869-0799; 452 Hennessy Road, Causeway Bay. 891-9183. Visa and MasterCard.*

Kai-Yin Lo, *Shop 373, The Mall, Pacific Place, Central. 840-0066; Mezzanine floor, Mandarin Oriental Hotel, 5 Connaught Road Central. 524-8238; BE-11 Peninsula Hotel Arcade, Salisbury Road, Tsim Sha Tsui. 721-9693.*

King Fook Gold & Jewellery, *Shop 216-217, The Mall, Pacific Place, 88 Queensway, Central. 845-6766; King Fook Building, 30-32 Des Voeux Road Central. 822-8500; Hong Kong Mansion, G/F, 1 Yee Wo Street, Causeway Bay. 576-1032.*

Larry's, *G47, The Landmark, Central. 521-1268; Shop 232, Pacific Place, Level 2, Central. 868-3993; Shop 239, Ocean Terminal, Harbour City, Tsim Sha Tsui. 730-8081; 33 Nathan Road, Tsim Sha Tsui. 721-8133.*

Les Must de Cartier, *Prince's Building, 8A Chater Rd. Central. 522-2963; Pacific Place, Level 3, 88 Queensway, Central. 523-1852; Shop L1 & W10, Peninsula Hotel, Salisbury Road, Tsim Sha Tsui. 368-8036; Shop R133, Regent Hotel Arcade, 18 Salisbury Road, Tsim Sha Tsui 311-5911.*

Lo & Rador International, *#27 Far East Mansions, 5-6 Middle Rd., Tsim Sha Tsui. 367-1655.* Great for gemstones and gemstone carvings.

The Opal Mine, *Burlington House Arcade, 92 Nathan Rd. Tsim Sha Tsui. 721-9933, 9:30am-6:30pm.* Free. Across the street from the Kowloon Park mosque, this replica of an Australian mine is worth seeing. Prices marked in US dollars.

Pearl Gallery, *1/F, New World Tower, 16-18 Queen's Road Central. 526-3599.* Cultured, fresh water and South Sea.

The Showroom, *1203 Central Bldg. at Pedder St. and Queen's Rd. Central, 525-7085.* Small good shop with gold, pearls, diamonds and emeralds.

Trio Pearl, *Mezzanine floor, Peninsula Hotel Arcade, Salisbury Road, Tsim Sha Tsui. 367-9171.* Jewelry and pearls.

Tse Sui Luen Jewellery, *Commercial House, 35 Queen's Road Central. 524-0094; Park Lane Square, 132-134 Nathan Road, Tsim Sha Tsui. 739-6673.*

IN THE MOOD TO BROWSE!

Just feel like wandering? The greatest concentrations of HKTA-member jewelry shops are the half-dozen on Queen's Road in Central between #16-82, and the four in the Prince's Building on Chater Road and Ice House Street. In Tsim Sha Tsui, from #25A-130 Nathan Rd, you can find 64 stores, mainly in shopping malls. There are 18 in the Hyatt Hotel and 12 in the Holiday Inn Golden Mile across the street. Please be careful even in HKTA stores. We repeat, Tsim Sha Tsui is a tourist trap and Tsim Sha Tsui East is worse but has about 42 stores in malls like the Peninsula Centre and Empire Centre, from 25A-40 Mody Rd. You can find Chinese-style jewelry from #315-343 on Nathan Rd. in Yau Ma Tei, and from #610-644 on Nathan Rd. in Mong Kok.

LEATHER - PURSES

Try markets like Li Yuen Streets, Central, for imitations and purse factory overruns at reasonable prices.

MEDICINES - CHINESE

Try Chinese products stores. See Arts and Crafts above. Herbal medicine stores are all over. See our tour of Western.

PERFUMES

Try **Victoria Dispensary**, *Luk Hoi Tong Bldg., G/F, 31, Queen's Rd. C., 522-9479.* Unusual and charming shop.

PHOTOCOPYING

Cheapest are tiny, little stationary shops. Next are fancy printing centres, and most expensive are the hotels. Clerks in tiny shops speak little if any English. We suggest places like **CopyKat Printing Centre**, *Shop 342, 3/F, Prince's Building, Chater Rd. Central. 522-6191.*

PHOTOGRAPHIC EQUIPMENT AND SUPPLIES

See advice above in Art of Shopping. For stores, try:

Broadway Photo Supply, *Times Square 714-715. 506-1350; 3 Lee Tong St., Wanchai. 865-2127; 78 Queen's Rd. Central. 523-5513.*

Fuji Image, *next to HKTA, Shop 1, Lower G/F, Jardine House, Central. 523-8662. 17 other outlets around the city including Park Lane Square Shopping Centre, Shop 1003, 132-134 Nathan Road, across from Kowloon Park. 368-4128.* Does very good developing but their price for film is high.

Kinefoto Ltd., *27-29 Pottinger St. Central. 523-2087.*

Mark's Photo Supplies, *G/F Tak Shing House, 20 Des Voeux Rd. Central. 523-5273. 9:30am-7pm.*

Photo Scientific Appliances, *G/F 6 Stanley Rd. Central. 522-1903.* Several photo shops also on this street.

Selected sole agents:
- **Canon** – *529-7921,* Jardine Consumer Electronics
- **Fuji** – *406-3226,* Fuji Photo Products Hong Kong
- **Kodak** – *564-9333,* Kodak (Far East) Ltd.
- **Konica** – *827-7288,* Konica HK Ltd.
- **Minolta** – *565-8181,* Minolta Ltd.
- **Nikon** – *524-5031,* Shiro Ltd.
- **Olympus** – *730-5663,* Kingstone Development Co.
- **Pentax** – *873-7923,* Jebson & Co Ltd.
- **Vivitar** – *363-6313,* Hanimex Vivitar
- **Yashica** – *544-6171,* Wing On Cheong Emporium Ltd.

PORCELAIN, CERAMICS, AND CHINA

Try the China products stores under Arts and Crafts above and the following: **Non-stop Shoppers**, *523-3850,* has tours to the New Territories that sometimes includes **L.& E. Porcelain** and **Overjoy Porcelain**. You can design your own at Overjoy and shipping service is available.

For British brands, there's **Craig's Ltd.**, *G/F., St. George's Building, 2 Ice House St. Central. 522-8726.* For Waterford, **Wedgwood**, *Ocean Terminal 1228, Harbour City, 2/F. 730-8930.*

SKIN PRODUCTS

The **Body Shop** has stores *in the Landmark 9221-8316 and Ocean Centre 9227-8700.* China products stores (see Arts & Crafts) have creams made from pearls used since ancient Chinese times for beauty. See Drug Stores above.

SHOES

You can get cheap shoes in the Li Yuen Streets in Central. You can have shoes and boots made in Happy Valley. There are several stores along Leighton Rd. and Wong Nai Chung Gap Rd.

Try **Nancy Shoes and Bags** for women's, *G/F, 173 Wong Nei Chung Rd., Happy Valley. 576-3633.* There's also **Lee Kee Boot & Shoemakers**, *19-21B Hankow Rd. 375-1098. (Only men).* The problem with most ready-made shoe stores here are the small sizes. For large sizes, there's **Edinburgh/Vincci** in *Pacific Place (251)* and the shoe shop in the Star Ferry after you pay your fare. Stanley Market has a shop for sneakers. Large sizes are cheaper in North America.

SILVER

J.A. Windsor, *111 Prince's Bldg., Chater Road. 522-1719.* Jewelry, frames, and cutlery.

The Jubilee Silver Shoppe, *U-14, Man Yee Bldg., 60-68 Des Voeux Rd. Central. 525-0622.*

SILK

For silk yard goods, the Chinese products stores above are good. The branch in Star House, near the Kowloon Star Ferry, has a big selection. Check along Peking Rd., Granville Rd. and Haiphong Rd. for clothing.

STAMPS AND COINS

You can pick up new stamps at the Philatelic Centre in the main post office, by the Star Ferry in Central. **New Century Collections** has a philatelic shop *in the Star Ferry Pier, Kowloon and in Shop 217 for coins, 2/F, Causeway Bay Centre, 19 Sugar St., Causeway Bay at Victoria Park. 890-5539.* In Western, visit **Wah Hing Stamps and Coins**, *192 Queen's Road Central* and **Man Fung Coins**, *227 Queen's Road Central.* The shopkeepers don't speak much English, but they have some interesting stuff, such as stamps with half nude women from Ajman and Yemen.

SUITCASES

For cheap ones but not name brands try *G/F, Chung King Mansions, 36-44 Nathan Rd., Tsim Sha Tsui.* China products stores have China-made brands (with help from Japanese partners). Strong red, white and blue plastic bags almost a meter long with zippers only cost about $20. They are good for taking purchases home and later for storage.

TAILORS

The days of tailoring clothes within 24 hours are long gone. Tailors need time for two fittings for a suit, or only one for a shirt. If you want it to fit right, it takes at least three full days.

For tailoring, you need to give a non-refundable deposit, sometimes 50%. It helps if you have a picture of what you want or pick one from the tailor's catalogue. They can also do mail order but we don't recommend it. Too many things could go wrong. Some of the following tailors will go to your hotel room for measurements and fittings.

A-Man Hing Cheong Co., *M10, Mandarin Oriental Hotel Arcade, Central, 522-3336.* This shop has been there 30 years.

Ascot Chang Co., *Shop 143, Prince's Building, Chater Rd. Central. 523-3663; fax 861-0426.* Shops also in the Peninsula and Regent Hotels. This company has been making shirts for years. They need three to five days and a minimum order for three shirts at $700-$800 each. This is very expensive and other shops can do shirts for less.

William Chang and Son, *8/F, Hankow Mansion, 38 Hankow Rd. (near the Hyatt Regency), Tsim Shat Sui. 366-0709.* Cheapest and recommended.

Juliette Li, *Flat C2, 5/F, Man Wah Heights, 30 Inverness Road, Kowloon City. 336-2861. Pager 1101-36118.*

Poon Kee Tailor, *1/F, Flat D, 65 Wellington St. Central. 524 3742.*

TEA

For Chinese tea, the cheapest are the supermarkets and Chinese products stores. For fancier teas, go to **Fook Ming Tong Tea Shop**, *G/F, 15C, Prince's Bldg., Ice House St. entrance. 521-0037. 9:30am-6:30pm.* Here you can find neat tea tins, and taste tests. There is also a small, similiar shop in the basement of Pacific Place.

TOYS

Toys R Us, which takes all cards, have branches in: *G/F Ocean Terminal. 730-9462. Open 10am-8pm; Windsor House, 311 Gloucester Rd. Causeway Bay, 881-1728. 10am-10pm.* Ruth likes the locally-owned **Wing Wa Toys**, *G/F, 156 Queen's Rd. East, on the north side towards the Hopewell Centre from Central. 528-1090. No cards.* Toys R Us has more variety. Many prices are higher than in the U.S.

VIDEO & AUDIO

See Art of Shopping above. Linda found some things like Walkman speakers cheaper and other things like tapedecks more expensive. You have to work for your bargains. There is more variety than in North America.

With VCRs and televisions, make sure what you buy is compatible with one of the three broadcasting systems. North America uses the NTSC system; Europe and Hong Kong use PAL, and France and Russia use Seacam. If you have a multi-system TV, get a multi-system VCR preferably of the same brand. Read HKTA's free *Shopping Guide to Consumer Electronics*.

For the latest in electronics, see **Fortress Premium Shop**, *G6/G7, China Bldg., 29 Queen's Rd, Central. 868-3428. All cards.* Also **Chung Yuen Electronics Co.**, *308 Ocean Centre, Harbour City. Sony dealer. 736-8323.*

Selected Sole Agents:
- **Aiwa** – *787-0838*, Aiwa/Dransfield & Co. Ltd.
- **Bose** – *760-7818*, Pacific Audio Supplies Ltd.
- **Hitachi** – *780-4351*, Hitachi Ltd.
- **JVC** – *722-0320*
- **Kenwood** – *410-4567*, Kenwood & Lee Electronics Ltd.
- **National Panasonic** – *733-3833*, Shun Hing Electronic Trading Co.
- **Philips** – *821-5888*, Philips HK Ltd.
- **Pioneer** – *521-8020*, Shinwa Engineering Co.
- **Sanyo** – *507-2997*, Tatt Sing Sanyo Electric Co.
- **Sony** – *543-1227*, Fook Yuen Electronic Co.
- **Toshiba** – *723-9932*, Man On Toshiba Ltd.

WATCHES

Watches are no longer great bargains except for very expensive ones. Peddlers sell fakes on the street in Tsim Sha Tsui and in the markets but they usually work and make fun souvenirs.

For genuine brands, phone the Sole Agents for Rolex, Seiko, etc. Get numbers from HKTA.

13. ENTERTAINMENT & NIGHTLIFE

ENTERTAINMENT

There is always something going on in Hong Kong: from ballet to Cantonese opera to drama and pop stars, like David Bowie. Local and foreign talent from all corners of the world entertain here. Pick up *Hong Kong Diary* and *Hong Kong This Week* at an HKTA office, which lists everything going on in town. For other useful publications, see Chapter 6.

Hong Kong frequently has festivals, such as the arts, film, food and fringe festivals. The **Hong Kong Arts Festival** has everything from ballet to belly dancers (January-February) and the biennial Festival of Asian Arts runs October-November. The **Hong Kong Fringe Festival** (January-February) begins with street theater in Central.

Dance groups include the **Hong Kong Ballet**, the **Hong Kong Dance Company** (Chinese-oriented), and the **City Contemporary Dance Company**. For drama, check the **Fringe Club**, the **Hong Kong Academy of the Performing Arts**, and the **Hong Kong Arts Centre**. Keep an eye out for **Zuni Icasehedron**, a radical, political performance art group.

The main orchestras are the **Hong Kong Philharmonic** and the 85-piece **Hong Kong Chinese Orchestra** which uses traditional Chinese and western instruments. The **Hong Kong Cultural Centre** and the **Hong Kong Academy of Performing Arts** sometimes have free recitals.

Tickets for most shows are available through **URBTIX**. *For information call 723-7713, for reservations 734-9009.*

HONG KONG ISLAND

City Hall, *beside the Star Ferry terminal, Central* has a concert hall, recital hall, theater hall, art gallery and restaurants. It has orchestras, plays, ballets, occasionally Cantonese opera and more. City Hall publishes *City News*, which lists events.

Fringe Club, *2 Lower Albert Rd. Central. 521-7251.* You'll find films, plays, music, musicals and a good restaurant in the old Ice House Building, above Lan Kwai Fong. See M on the Fringe in "Where to Eat."

Hong Kong Academy for Performing Arts, *1 Gloucester Rd. Wanchai. 584-1500.* Its four theaters are home to dance, theater, recitals and in 1994, Andrew Lloyd Weber's musical Cats.

Hong Kong Arts Centre, *2 Harbour Rd. Wanchai. 582-0200.* Films, dance, music and plays are in the two theaters here. There are also two art galleries. The Arts Centre publishes *Artslink* which lists upcoming shows and is available free at HKTA offices.

Hong Kong Stadium, Hong Kong's largest (40,000 seats) opened in March 1994 to instant controversy. Nearby residents complained about noisy concerts. There was talk of keeping it exclusively sports, but we doubt it. It is the location for the annual rough and rowdy Rugby Sevens.

Queen Elizabeth Stadium, *18 Oi Kwan Rd. Wanchai. 575-6793.* This 3,500 seat stadium has mainly sports events such as the Harlem Globetrotters.

KOWLOON

Academic Community Hall, *224 Waterloo Rd. Kowloon Tong. 338-6121.* This used to be the main venue for big pop stars, before the Hong Kong Coliseum. Now, anything goes; movies, music, drama, etc.

Hong Kong Coliseum, *9 Cheong Wan Rd. Hung Hom, next to Tsim Sha Tsui East. 355-7215/765-9215.* 12,000 seats for shows by major pop and rock artists like Eric Clapton and David Bowie. It looks like a giant inverted pyramid.

Hong Kong Cultural Centre, *10 Salisbury Rd. Tsim Sha Tsui. 734-2010/734-9009.* Dance, dramas, musicals, operas and recitals take place in the Concert Hall (2,100 seats), Grand Theatre (1,750) and the Studio Theatre.

CANTONESE OPERA

Although not very popular with foreigners, it is definitely worth seeing once, for the incredible costumes and the experience. It is nothing like western opera. There are many kinds of Chinese opera and Hong Kong's is from south China, a very stylized art form with slow-moving plots, long monologues, weird make-up, wonderful costumes and high-pitched singing. The fighting scenes are thrilling, full of sword play, acrobatics and action punctuated by cymbals. But it is difficult for the uninitiated to understand.

If you saw the movie *Farewell My Concubine*, you should appreciate the painful discipline of its actors. The symbolism is important and audiences usually know what is good and express their appreciation loudly. The stories are ancient. The Chinese used opera to communicate history to an illiterate audience, and of course, distorted the facts in the interest of holding their interest.

The villian is always known near the beginning from the white patch on his nose. A **black face** is an honest but uncouth character. A **white face** shows a treacherous, cunning, but dignified person. **Red** is for loyalty and sincerity, black for honesty and all-around goodness. **Yellow** is for impulsiveness, and gold and silver are for demons and gods.

Settings are usually symbolic and simple. Two bamboo poles with some cloth attached could be a city wall or gate. A chariot is two yellow flags with a wheel drawn on each. A couple of poles on either side of an actor is a sedan chair. Anyone with an oar is on a boat. A man lifting up his foot as he exits, is stepping over the high threshold of a door.

Costumes are ornate and colorful. A hat with two long, dangling pheasant or peacock feathers is worn by a high military officer, usually a marshal; a hat with wobbling wings out to the sides just above the ears belongs to a magistrate. Generals have flags matching their costumes and mounted like wings on their backs. The flags are distributed to identify imperial messengers.

The acting too is symbolic. Crossed eyes mean anger. Walking with hands extended in front means it's dark. A man holding a riding crop is riding a horse, or sometimes he is a horse. A particularly well-executed swing of long hair (anguish) or prolonged trembling (fear) might elicit gasps of appreciation and applause. Check HKTA Information for upcoming events which are usually around Chinese New Year's.

The **Temple Street Night Market** has casual street performances on the weekend, but alas no costumes. There are sometimes shows at **City Hall** in Central and **Sha Tin Town Hall** in the New Territories.

MOVIES

Sometimes you just need to relax or maybe your companions want to shop and you don't. How about a movie? First, the bad news. Movies get here later than the States and cost the same. Censors often cut them brutally because of time restrictions. Also, the popcorn is sometimes sweet. The good news is you usually get a choice about the popcorn and thre are good cinemas with reserved seats.

Hong Kong makes some hilarious, slap-stick movies and kung-fu costume dramas with lots of supernatural events and great acrobatics. This is Bruce Lee-land. Check the English-language newspapers for listings. These will also tell you about sub-titles. The **International Film Festival** runs from March to April.

NIGHTLIFE

There's much to do. Hong Kong never sleeps. Go on a sunset harbor tour (see Tours in Chapter 5). Head up to the Peak for the sunset and a staggering view of the harbor (see Central).

Walk along the waterfront promenade from Tsim Sha Tsui to Tsim Sha Tsui East for a breathtaking view of the ships and Hong Kong Island. Take the Star Ferry from Tsim Sha Tsui, or ride a tram (see Getting Around Town). Go to the Sung Dynasty Village in New Kowloon for the dinner and show or go to the horse races. Go shopping in Tsim Sha Tsui until midnight or at the Temple Street Night Market in Yau Ma Tei, which stays open even later and has Cantonese street opera on weekends. Head over to the Space Museum in Tsim Sha Tsui for an Omnimax film on the ceiling of the ball-shaped planetarium.

How about golf? Yes, Hong Kong has golf at night under lights. Then there's tennis, squash, bowling, ice-skating or rollerskating. See Sports. Or head to one of Hong Kong's many lounges, pubs and discos.

Hong Kong people work hard (some 60 hours a week!) and play hard in Hong Kong's huge assortment of drinking establishments. Want to relax in luxury soothed by soft, live music? Head to a first-class hotel lounge, like the **Champagne Bar** in Wanchai. Would you like a fantastic view to go with that? Check out the **Regent's Lobby Lounge** in Tsim Sha Tsui, the **Tiara** in Tsim Sha Tsui East or the **Harlequin Bar** in Central. If you like watching airplanes land and take off in comfort, there's the bar on the top floor of the **Regal Airport Hotel.**

Night Clubs & Live Music

Asia has a big entertainment industry of its own with music and stars of whom most North Americans have never heard. You might want to sample it. Popular Cantonese singers are at the **Ocean City** and **Ocean Palace Restaurants and Night Clubs**.

For live music go to **Ned Kelly's** in Tsim Sha Tsui or the **Jazz Club** and **Hardy's Folk Bar** in Central. For the British pub experience try the **Bull and Bear** in Central or **Mad Dogs** in Tsim Sha Tsui. Into dancing? Well, hop over to **JJ's** in Wanchai, **Jump** in Causeway Bay, **Club 1997** in Central or the **Catwalk** in Tsim Sha Tsui.

THE BASICS

The drinking age is 18, but few places ask for identification. Drugs and unlicensed gambling are illegal. Most establishments are open later on weekends and covers (admission costs) are higher. Saturday nights are the busiest. Most places are open for public holidays, but telephone ahead to be sure. Many luxury hotels have popular bars, lounges and/or discos, and tend to be expensive. Most places take credit cards. The action starts after work at the pubs and after 10 or 11pm at the discos. Many British, Canadians and Americans work in the larger pubs and discos.

Beer

Beer usually costs $30-$50, except at happy hour, when drinks are usually half price. Happy hours are very popular. The most common beers are **San Miguel** and **Carlsberg**. **Tsingtao**, a Chinese beer, is sometimes available, but is not as good. The cheapest beer is one you buy in **7-11** and bring home.

Dress Code

Some of the more expensive places have a dress code, usually smart casual. This usually means no shorts, collar-less or sleeveless shirts, ripped jeans or track pants. In most cases the rules are more relaxed for women.

Food

Most bars and pubs (except hostess bars) serve reasonably-priced food. If a bar opens at 8am, it serves breakfast. If it opens before 11am, lunch is probably available. Pub grub includes things like fish and chips, and steak and kidney pie. The **Oasis Bar** in the New World Harbour View Hotel has a hungry hour offering a very substantial all-you-can-eat buffet for the price of a drink.

Singles

It can be hard to make friends here. The best spot for the under-40 traveler is **Lan Kwai Fong**, Central. You could also try discos like **Jump** in Causeway Bay. You can sit and chat with the bartender and your neighbors at pubs like **Mad Dogs** in Tsim Sha Tsui. Most people meet at work, during the day, on tours, walks and in fast food places.

NIGHTLIFE HIGHLIGHTS

In this section we've listed some of Hong Kong's nightlife highlights. In the next section we list your options in detail.

Central

The **Mandarin Hotel** has good bars, but **Lan Kwai Fong** is the place to go. This trendy night (and day) time hillside hang out is usually crowded after 10pm. Well-dressed people bar hop and people-watch from open-air pubs. Most places have British staff. Check out **Club 1997** disco, **Hardy's Folk Bar**, the **Jazz Club**, **Mad Dogs** or **Schnurrbart** pub. This area has a reputation for drugs (mainly among expatriate teenagers with rich parents), but it's busy and quite safe.

Wanchai

Head here for traditional British pubs, topless bars and tattoo parlors. The best tattoo parlor is **Ricky's** *at 79 Lockhart Rd., 527-8908.* Wanchai has been Hong Kong's red light district since World War I, but is gradually becoming more of a business district. This was the setting for the famous book and movie *The World of Suzie Wong.* Walk along Lockhart Road from Fenwick St. east to Tonnochy for a taste of the old Wanch.

Friendly Filipina maids flock here to relax, to places like the **Neptune** on Saturday nights. Ironically, one of Hong Kong's most impressive luxury hotels, the **Grand Hyatt**, is also in Wanchai and has a good disco and a champagne bar. But it's on the better side of Gloucester Road.

Causeway Bay

Check out **Jump**, the friendly restaurant/bar/disco or the bars and lounges at the **Excelsior Hotel**.

Kowloon

Tsim Sha Tsui has everything; luxury lounges in the **Regent** and the **Sheraton**, the **Hong Kong Renaissance's** lively **Bostonian**, **Ned Kelly's** Australian fun pub with live jazz, **Mad Dogs** British pub, **Canton Disco**, not to mention hostess clubs and topless bars. Tsim Tsa Tsui East has luxury hotel bars and expensive hostess clubs.

HONG KONG ISLAND

Central

The Bull & Bear (pub), *G/F Hutchinson House, 10 Harcourt Rd. 525-7436. Happy hour 5-8pm. Open 11am-midnight.* Padded wooden benches line the walls of this large, popular, noisy, Tudor-style pub. In this comfortable place, you can loosen your tie.

California (disco), *G/F, California Tower, 24-26 Lan Kwai Fong. 521-1345. Happy Hour 5-8pm.* This popular restaurant turns into a disco after 11:30pm. $80 cover.

Captain's Bar (live music), *Mandarin Oriental Hotel, 522-0111. Open 11am-2am.* A Filipino and occasionally a jazz band plays Monday-Saturday, 9pm-midnight. This small bar is popular with 30-plus professionals. On Sundays, there's a piano player. Buffet lunch 12pm-2:30pm. Smart casual.

Chinnery Bar, *Mandarin Oriental, 5 Connaught Rd. Central. 522-0111. Open 11am-11pm, closed Sunday.* Business men frequent this small, clubbish bar, decorated in rich wood, wine racks and Chinnery reproductions. Chinnery was a famous painter from the 1880s. There's a good whisky selection. Smart casual.

Club 1997 (disco), *9 Lan Kwai Fong. 810-9333. Happy hour 5pm-9pm. Open 5pm-5am, Sunday 8pm-2am.* This small, popular disco is part of the 1997 complex that includes the restaurants **Mecca 97** and **Post 97**. Cover charge on weekends. Smart casual. Beer $44.

Cyrano (live jazz and dancing), *56/F, Island Shangri-La Hotel, Pacific Place, (Admiralty MTR). 820-8591. Open 6pm-2am.* This luxury music lounge is the highest and often has jazz. Smart casual.

Go Down (restaurant, bar, good live jazz on Wednesdays after 10pm), *G/F, Admiralty Centre, 18 Harcourt Rd. (Admiralty MTR) 866-1166. Happy hour 5-7pm and 11pm-midnight. Open 10am-2am.* Business people come here to wind down amid modern music and attractive European waitresses. The decor is Canton go down (warehouse), with long wooden tables and a few old barrels. They have an extensive drink list that tells you exactly what is in those enticing cocktails. Beer $32-35. Coffee/coke $22.

Hardy's Folk Club (live music), *35 D'Aguilar St. Lan Kwai Fong. 522-4448. Happy hour 5:30-8:30pm.* Beer $35. No cover.

Harlequin Bar (lounge), *25/F Mandarin Oriental, Hong Kong, 5 Connaught Rd. 522-0111. Open 11am-1am.* This romantic, roof-top bar has piano music and a great view of the harbor. Petrossian caviar is available between noon-2pm and 5:30pm-11pm. Smart casual, no sneakers.

The Jazz Club, *34-36 D'Aguilar St. Lan Kwai Fong. 845-8477.* The live jazz begins between 9:30pm-10:30pm. There's no cover for local bands.

The Jockey (pub), *1/F Swire House, 11 Chater Rd. 526-1478. Open 11am-11pm, closed Sunday.*

Mad Dogs (British pub), *33 Wyndham St. 810-1000. Open 11am-3am.* (above Lan Kwai Fong) See Tsim Sha Tsui for review.

Pomeroy's Wine Bar Ltd., *Shop 349, Level 3, The Mall, Pacific Place, 88 Queensway, Central. 523-4772. Happy Hour 5-7pm, 10-11pm. Open 11am-midnight.* A branch is at *G/F, On Hing Bldg, On Hing Terrace (off Wyndham St.), Lan Kwai Fong. 810-1162.* This dark, cozy place has 13 kinds of beer and 32 kinds of wine. Its lunch buffet ($125) includes a drink. Entrees cost $70-90, but you can get onion rings for $25 and soups from $40. Beer $36.

Schnurrbart (pub), *29 D'Aguilar St. 532-4700.* German beer and food.

Wanchai

Champagne Bar (lounge), *Grand Hyatt Hotel, 1 Harbour Rd. 588-1234. Open 5pm-2am.* The Grand Hyatt describes this place as "a corner of Paris circa 1920". This small, romantic lounge, done in modern art-deco, boasts the "most extensive champagne list in Hong Kong," caviar and a pianist and with a female singer from 10pm nightly. Beer $46. Smart casual, no sneakers.

J.J.'s (entertainment center), *Grand Hyatt. 588-1234. Happy hour 5:30pm-8:30pm. Open 5:30pm-2am.* This large, popular, fun, upscale place has two floors featuring American rhythm and blues band CC Riders and a really good disco (after 10pm). The pizzeria lounge has billiards, darts, sandwiches and pizza. The well-dressed, under-40 crowd flock here. Smart casual, no sneakers. Cover $110, $170 Friday-Saturday after 9pm. Beer $46.

Joe Bananas (restaurant/bar/disco), *G/F, Shiu Lam Building, 23 Luard Rd. 529-1811. Visa and MasterCard only. Open 11:30am-5am. Sunday 6pm-4am.* This large American-style restaurant attracts the under-40 expat crowd. At 11pm, the dance floor is cleared of tables and chairs for the popular disco. JBs has the same management as Mad Dogs, so no shorts, shirts without collars (after 6pm), hats or fur. Women can wear whatever they like. Beer $38. Happy hour 11:30am-9pm. On Friday and Saturday there is a cover charge of $100, which includes two standard drinks. The cover starts at 9pm for men and 11pm for women.

Horse and Carriage (pub), *117 Lockhart Rd. Open 11am-6am. Happy Hour 11am-8pm. No cards.* This is more popular as an afternoon restaurant. See "Where to Eat." Beer $29-30.

Horse & Groom (pub), *161 Lockhart Rd. 507-2517. Happy hour 10:30am-8pm.* A black panther scupture dominates this quiet, two-story bar, populated with a few Chinese and a sprinkling of expats. The wood-panelled walls feature beer ads from the 1920s. Beer $31-36. Beer is $19-24 during Happy Hour.

Old China Hand (traditional English pub), *104 Lockhart Rd. 527-9174. No cards.* British expats frequent this smoky, cafeteria-like pub that has Filipino staff, and beer for $28-30. Authentic, greasy, British breakfast available from 7-10am. Entrees $50-60.

The Wanch (live music), *54 Jaffe Rd. 861-1621. No cover.* Folk and rock music Wednesday, Friday and Saturday starts at 9pm.

Causeway Bay

Dickens Bar (pub, live music), *basement, The Excelsior Hotel, 281 Gloucester Rd. 894-8888.* There's a $20 cover for good jazz from 3pm-6pm on Sundays. Monday-Saturday, there's a Filipino band from 9pm. Curry buffet lunch $85. Smart casual. Beer $38. Open 11am-2am.

Jump (restaurant/bar/disco), *7/F, Causeway Bay Plaza II, 463 Lockhart Rd. (at Percival St. near Wanchai). 832-7122. Happy hour 5-8pm. Open noon-2am and Friday and Saturday until 4am.* This large, American-style restaurant has good food, friendly service and ice-cream cocktails. Performance bartenders (like in Tom Cruise's movie Cocktail) serve the under-40 crowd. After 11pm, there's a popular disco. It's packed on Friday and Saturday nights, when there's a $100 cover charge after 11pm. They have Molson Golden. Smart casual, no sneakers. Most people wear jeans. Beer $36-43.

Noon Gun Bar, *3/F The Excelsior. 894-8888. Open 12pm-3pm, 5pm-12am, Saturday 5pm-2am.* Jardine's Noon Day Gun across the road opens this bar that features live piano music. No Happy Hour. Smart casual.

Talk of the Town Cocktail Lounge, *34/F, The Excelsior. 894-8888. Open 5pm-1-2am.* Live music and harbor view.

KOWLOON

Tsim Tsa Tsui

Bar City (Entertainment Center), *New World Centre. 369-8571. Open 9pm-2:30am.* This place is divided into three environments: the Zodiac disco, the Crazy Horse Saloon, and Country & Western with live bands. The first two have a $100 cover, which includes one drink. Country & Western charges a $10 cover.

Catwalk Nightspot (disco, salsa band/karaoke rooms), *18/F, New World Hotel, 22 Salisbury Rd. 369-4111. Open 9pm-3am.*

Chin Chin (bar), *Hyatt Regency, 1/F, 67 Nathan Rd. 311-1234. Open 11am-2am.* A statue of Buddha guards this small, dark bar that has lounge singers from 5pm. The set lunch is $95 and available Monday-Saturday, noon-3pm. Beer $30.

Kangaroo Pub & Windjammer Restaurant, *35 Haiphong Rd. 376-0083.* Chinese cluster around tables and gwailos cluster around the bars in this large, two-story pub. Snacks can be had for $20-30. Lunch is from 11am-3pm.

Mad Dogs (British pub), basement, *32 Nathan Rd. 301-2222. Visa and MasterCard only. Happy hour 4-7pm. Open 7am-3am.* Nice basement bar with friendly British staff. However, it is a tad pompous with rules such as no sleeveless shirts, shorts, fur, or hats except on the statue of the bulldog behind the bar. In addition, beer is $42! but it comes with potato chips. Single men line the bar at lunch time. Occasional live music.

Ned Kelly's Last Stand (The fun pub, live music), *11A Ashley Rd. 376-0562. No cards. Open 11am-2am.* This friendly Aussie pub was named after an Australian bandit and is usually packed after 9:30pm, when the 7-piece band starts to jam some great "good-time Dixieland jazz".

Ocean City Restaurant & Nightclub (dinner/dance), *Level 3, New World Centre, 18 Salisbury Rd. 369-9688. Open 8am-1am.* One of the world's largest Chinese restaurants featuring Cantonese singers and set menus.

Ocean Palace Restaurant & Nightclub, *4/F Ocean Centre. 730-7111. Open 7:30am-2am.* A set dinner, magicians, acrobats and local singers cost $100. Both of the Ocean's are popular with groups of local Chinese.

The Regent Hotel Lobby Lounge, *18 Salisbury Rd. 721-1211. Open 8am-12:30am.* This lounge has a spectacular view of Hong Kong island. It is popular and the only lobby lounge that Linda has seen line-ups for.

Drinks come with almonds. Beer $44-45. Soft drinks $37. Mixed drinks $65. The **Mezzanine Lounge** (above the lobby) has live music and is open 9pm-2am.

Someplace Else (bar/restaurant), *Sheraton Hotel basement, 20 Nathan Rd. 369-1111. Popular happy hour 4-7pm. Open 11am-1am.* This place is popular with foreigners and proud of its daiquiries ($55). Dress code "not naked." Beer $35.

Sky Lounge, *18/F, Sheraton Hotel, 20 Nathan Rd. 369-1111. Minimum charge. Open 11am-1am.* Great view of Hong Kong island.

Tsim Tsa Tsui East

Golden Carp Bar (lounge/disco), *Holiday Inn Crowne Plaza, 70 Mody Rd. 721-5161. Open 11pm-1am.* Harbor view.

The Music Room (bar, dancing), *Shangri-La Hotel, 64 Mody Rd. 721-2111. Happy hour 5pm-9:30pm. Open 5pm-2am.* Right now, this place offers theme nights; Sunday is ballroom dancing. Monday is two for one. Tuesday is oldies. Wednesday is Chinese pop. Thursday is ladies night. Friday and Saturday there's a disco (min. charge $118). Call first. Theme nights can change.

Tiara Lounge, *21/F, Shangri-La Hotel, 64 Mody Rd. 721-2111. Open 5pm-2am.* Piano music and a great harbor view.

HOSTESS CLUBS

A hostess club is where men pay for female company. Most of them are luxurious nightclubs with tasteful cabaret acts. Hostess clubs are unique to Hong Kong, Singapore, and Japan. Local business people bring their Japanese clients here for entertainment. The biggest and most famous hostess club is **Club Bboss**. **China City** is second. Both are in Tsim Sha Tsui East. Couples are usually welcome.

You should know that if you talk to a hostess, you are charged for every 15 minutes or less. Bouncers make sure that you pay. You're safest sticking to clubs recommended in this book and the free HKTA *Dining and Entertainment* booklet.

What Happens in a Hostess Club

1) Sit down and order a drink. 2) If a woman is requested, a mama-san will discuss the kind you want. 3) The woman will come, sit with you and talk. You can buy her a drink, but it's not required. 4) The mama-san will check if you are happy with her selection. If not, she will bring another. 5) If you like her, you can take her out of the club, but have to pay for her time. 6) More personal services are discussed with the woman and have nothing to do with the club. Very personal services will usually cost between $2,000-$5,000.

China City Night Club, *4/F Peninsula Centre, 67 Mody Rd. 723-3278. Open noon-4am.* This club is usually mentioned after Club Bboss. It is also expensive and has fountains, dancing, live music and hundreds of girls.

Club Bboss, *basement, Mandarin Plaza, 14 Science Museum Rd. Tsim Sha Tsui East. 369-2883. Happy hour 2pm-9pm. Open 2pm-4am.* One of three red-turbaned Sikhs opens the door and a dozen attractive Chinese women in purple suits greet you at the world's largest hostess club. Club Bboss can accommodate 3,500 guests and has 1,000 registered hostesses. There are usually only about 400 to 600 available. This place used to be named Club Volvo, until the car company complained.

There is a dance floor, Las Vegas-style shows, 60 private VIP/karaoke rooms, "Romantic World" and a gold fish pond. The hostesses are mainly Chinese and South East Asian. A few are European. They wear cute little cocktail dresses or slit Chinese cheongsams. 20 employees work from 4am-2pm, just shining the brass!! Visitors have included Latin American presidents, Arab princes and Sylvester Stallone.

So what does all this cost? There's a minimum charge of $450. Most people order a bottle of X-O Cognac for $1350-2100 and regulars leave unfinished bottles in the bottle keep for next time. There are mini-computers that keep track of drinks and hostesses. Each hostess has a card that she uses to clock in. 15 minutes with a hostess costs $53. If you want to take her out, you pay $37 for every 10 minutes, until 4am. Karaoke is $350/hour. Beer $110.

Club Deluxe, *L-301, New World Centre Office Building, 18 Salisbury Rd, Tsim Sha Tsui. 721-0277. Open 9pm-3am.* This small hostess club doesn't come close to the others in terms of decor and atmosphere. However, if you're real curious and can't afford to shell out $450, this may be the place. There's live music and dancing. There's also a putting green and a billiards table in two of the nine VIP rooms, which you must reserve two days in advance. A cover charge of $100 applies if you don't hire a hostess. Hostesses are $234/hour. No shorts or flipflops. Beer $70.

Club Metropolitan, *311-1111. Open 8pm-4am.* Across from Club Bboss and is almost the same, except it's a little more fantastical, decorated with thousands of little lights.

New Tonnochy Night Club, *1-5 Tonnochy Rd., Wanchai. 575-4376. Open 1pm-4am.* This luxury hostess club boasts 200 girls and live entertainment. It is slightly cheaper than Bboss, China City and Metropolitan.

TOPLESS BARS

Beware, these bars can charge you a fee for conversing with the staff like in the hostess bars. Generally, these places are a rip-off. If you're heading to Thailand or the Philippines, wait.

Bottoms Up, *basement, 14 Hankow Rd., Tsim Sha Tsui. 721-4509. Happy hour 4:30-8:30pm. Open 4:30pm-3am.* This is the most respectable and popular. You can't miss the sign outside. It is a collage of buttocks. Topless European and Asian women sit inside circular bars and bend low to get drinks. Thus the name. Bottoms Up appears in a very short scene in the James Bond movie *Man With a Golden Gun.* Couples are welcome, but single women aren't. Beer $58.

Red Lips Bar, *1a Lock Rd, Tsim Sha Tsui. Open 11am-4am.* This is a sleezy, well-established, green-velvet, topless bar with a small stage, that hasn't changed much in the past 30 years. It is not a member of HKTA. Couples are welcome, single men more so. Beer $44. Tsim Sha Tsui MTR.

Lockhart Rd. and **Fenwick St.** This is the heart of Wanchai's formerly topless scene. Nowadays, most are conservative, Thai-style bars, with women in bikinis and bodysuits, dancing around brass poles on small stages. Some clubs even have video screens outside, so you can see the action within!

The most famous bar is the **Suzie Wong Bar and Night Club**, *21 Fenwick St*, named after the hooker with a heart of gold in Richard Mason's 1957 novel. Unfortunately, it looks pretty pathetic; six bored women in a small, dark bar. Instead, check out **Club Pussycat**, *3 Fenwick St.* or any of the others in this area.

180

14. SEEING THE SIGHTS

Hong Kong is small and easy to get around, but there is much to see and do! Explore ornate temples and monasteries, fascinating markets, large museums, handsome British colonial buildings, beautiful city parks and interesting little shopping alleys. For the adventurous, there are traditional Chinese walled villages, small fishing villages and large country parks.

ORIENTATION

Hong Kong is made up of **Hong Kong Island**, **Kowloon Peninsula** (across the harbor on the mainland), the **New Territories** to the north, and the **outlying islands**. The three important places that you need to remember are **Tsim Sha Tsui** (the tourist center on the tip of Kowloon Peninsula), **Central** on Hong Kong Island, (across the harbor from Tsim Sha Tsui), and wherever you are staying.

Some tourist sights are closed for public holidays especially Christmas, New Years Day and Chinese New Years. If the pollution gets to you, head to the south side of Hong Kong island or the outlying islands where cars are banned. Lantau has only a few buses and taxis.

SIGHTSEEING HIGHLIGHTS

- *The Peak and the Peak Tram, Central, Hong Kong Island*
- *The Star Ferry that runs between Central and Tsim Sha Tsui*
- *Stanley Market, Hong Kong Island*
- *Ocean Park, Aberdeen, Hong Kong Island*
- *The Night Market, Yau Ma Tei, Kowloon*
- *The Bird Market, Mong Kok, Kowloon*
- *Sung Dynasty Village, New Kowloon*
- *Wong Tai Sin Temple, New Kowloon*
- *Ping Shan Heritage Trail, along the LRT line, New Territories*
- *Big Buddha, Lantau Island.*
- *Macau*

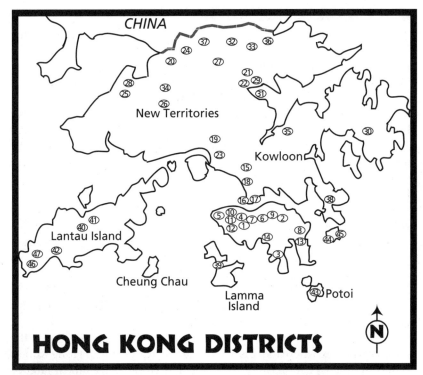

HONG KONG DISTRICTS

1. Hong Kong Island
2. Tin Hau Temple-Causeway Bay
3. Old Stanley Police Station
4. Former Supreme Court
5. Main Building, Hong Kong University
6. Flagstaff House Cotton Tree Drive
7. Former French Mission Building-Battery Path
8. Law Uk-Chan Wai
9. Wan-Chai Post Office 221 Queen's Road East
10. Western Market Central District
11. Old Pathological Institute
12. St. Stephen's Girls' College
13. Ancient Rock Carving-Big Wave Bay
14. Rock Carving-Wong Chuk Hang
15. Lei Cheung Uk Tomb
16. Former K.C.R. Clock Tower
17. Former Kowloon British School
18. Royal Observatory-Tsim Sha Tsui
19. Sam Tung Uk Village
20. Man Lun Fang Ancestral Hall
21. Man Mo Temple / Tai Po Market
22. Old Tai Po Market / Railway Station
23. Old House-Hoi Pa Village

24. Tai Fu Tai-San Tin
25. Kun Ting Study Hall-Ping Shan
26. Kat Hing Wai-Kam Tin
27. Tang Chung Ling Ancestral Hall
28. Tsui Shing Lau Pagoda
29. Old District Office North
30. Sheung Yiu Village
31. Island House (Yuen Chau Tsai) -Tai Po
32. Liu Man Shek Tong Ancestral Hall
33. Kun Lung Gate Tower
34. Yeung Hau Kung
35. Old House Wong Uk Village
36. Kang Yung Study Hall
37. Hau Kui Shek Ancestral Hall
38. Rock Inscription Joss House Bay
39. Ancient Rock Carving-Cheung Chau
40. Tung Chung Fort
41. Tung Chung Battery
42. Ancient Rock Carving-Shek Pik
43. Ancient Rock Carving-Po Toi
44. Ancient Rock Carving-Tung Lung
45. Tung Lung Fort
46. Fan Lau Fort
47. Stone Circle-Fan Lau-Lantau

ONLY HAVE A FEW DAYS!

If you have only one day, take a half-day Hong Kong island tour in the morning. Then go to Wong Tai Sin Temple, the Bird Market and/or the Jade Market and finish off the evening with a sunset cruise. You could also take the fascinating Sung Dynasty Village Dinner Tour. The adventurous may want to head off for an evening at the Night Market.

If you don't like tours, you can do your own Hong Kong Island tour, but it will take longer. Hop on a taxi or bus to Aberdeen and hire a sampan for a short tour of the harbor, where people still live on boats. Then take a bus or taxi to Stanley Market and explore. After that, head back to Central and take the Peak Tram up to the Peak for Hong Kong's most famous view of the harbor.

If You Have Two Days

What to do on the second day depends on what you like. The market person should go to Mong Kok and Yau Ma Tei, if you haven't done so already. For Chinese culture head to the Sung Dynasty Village or the Middle Kingdom. If you want to just have fun, how about Ocean Park in Aberdeen? You can find fresh air, on the islands. The most famous attraction there is the Big Buddha on the largest island, Lantau.

If you want to get off the tourist track, head out to the LRT line in the New Territories, where there is a heritage trail with many of Hong Kong's oldest buildings, a monastery, a temple and Hong Kong's most famous walled village.

If You Have Three Days

Go to Macau for at least one. It is only one hour by ferry away, but it's a different country. Europeans have lived there for 300 years longer than in Hong Kong, and there are alot of charming old buildings. The pace is slower, the air is cleaner and the Portuguese and Macanese food is fabulous. There are eight casinos and everything is cheaper. Please consult Chapter 8 and later sections of this chapter for attractions that are tailor-made for you.

Warning: consider the weather. If you're doing hiking, carry water.

HONG KONG ISLAND

Hong Kong Island, the most beautiful part of the territory, is exquisite. It is mostly mountainous, a giant amphitheatre of high-rise buildings, trees and crags sloping down to the harbor. You may be surprised to discover that the center of the island is covered by several large country parks. A fifty-kilometer nature trail with glorious views winds through them, around peaks and reservoirs.

Early settlers started today's practice of filling in the harbor with land and setting buildings on it. They also started the funicular tram up to the Peak in 1888. The tram lines which run between Shaukeiwan in the east and Kennedy Town in the west were laid in 1904.

The founding fathers chose Hong Kong Island over Lantau as the site of the first settlement because there was no water on Lantau. They built a ring of water catchments around the mountains leading into several reservoirs. These paved ditches are over a meter deep and many kilometers long. Hong Kong still uses the reservoirs but imports 70% of its fresh water from China.

The various districts of Hong Kong Island are actually joined to each other without definite breaks. Along the northern harborfront from west to east are **Western**, **Central**, **Wanchai**, and **Causeway Bay**. **Aberdeen**, **Repulse Bay**, and **Stanley** are on the less populated southside.

CENTRAL DISTRICT

Once called **Victoria**, **Central** was the British district of Hong Kong. The sidewalks used to be covered in the south China style by arcades as protection from the elements. Today, Central is the business center and the historical heart. Originally on the waterfront, **Queen's Road** was the first one built in the colony.

Central is home to huge, modern, architectual wonders, glass towers, Asian trading companies, international banks, shopping centers, parks and luxury hotels. It does, however, have the oldest colonial buildings.

Central has the highest commercial rents in the world. They are so high that the Hilton Hotel, a fixture here for many decades, will probably be replaced with an office block. Central is the insurance and banking center. The impressive headquarters of the competing Bank of China and the Hongkong Bank are here along with the Stock Exchange. The City Hall, the headquarters of the British Navy, the Legislative Council Chambers, the Star Ferry and some government offices are also here. Good for upmarket shopping, Central also has its bargains.

It is small; Pacific Place in the east to Central Market in the west is less than a mile or a little over one kilometer. Stores here close early evening and all is quiet except for the Lan Kwai Fong restaurants and bars.

But on Sundays and holidays, Central becomes mini-Manila. Thousands of Filipina women (mainly domestic servants) take over on their only day off work. The area roars with Tagalog and laughter. The women have picnics, look at photographs, sell Filipino food from duffel bags, and do their nails in a carnival-like atmosphere. The almost one million Filipinos are the largest expatriate group.

The buildings in Central are connected by a vast network of elevated, covered sidewalks and air-conditioned underground MTR walkways. One such sidewalk runs along the waterfront westward from Exchange Square to the Hotel Victoria. A branch on the way hooks up with the Midlevel's escalator through Central Market. One can usually avoid the crowded sidewalks and lorries below and stay dry in rainy weather.

MTR
Central station has the most exits:
- **A – Exchange Square**
- **B – World Wide House**
- **C – Li Yuen Street**
- **D – Pedder Street and Lan Kwai Fong**
- **H – Alexandra House**
- **J – Chater Garden**
- **K – Statue Square**

Admiralty MTR stop is also in Central to the east. This is the stop for Pacific Place mall and Hong Kong Park.

CENTRAL HIGHLIGHTS
You must ride the famous Peak Tram to the Peak for the finest, most famous view of Hong Kong. The Botanical Gardens and Hong Kong Park are the territory's best. The Li Yuen Streets are fun alleys in which to shop.

SUGGESTED CENTRAL ITINERARY
For a good **four to six hour itinerary**: take the free double-decker bus or walk from the Star Ferry to the **Peak Tram** station. This open-top shuttle bus from the east side of the Star Ferry, goes daily every 15 to 20 minutes, between 9am and 7pm.

Once there, ride up to the **Peak**, wander around and then come back down by tram or bus. If by bus, you can stop at the **Botanical Gardens**. It's a 15-minute walk back up Garden Road from the Tram Station. After the Gardens, walk down the hill to **St. John's Cathedral** for a rest in its lovely old pews. To get to **Hong Kong Park** from here, go back to Garden Road and look for an overpass. Take this overpass across Garden Road into the well-marked Citibank building. Go up the escalator. Follow signs to Hong Kong Park and the tea ware museum. You will pass a plaque to the memory of soldiers who defended Hong Kong during World War II.

Collapse at **Pacific Place** or picnic in the park. There are plenty of restaurants, including one in the park called the **Park Inn Restaurant**, which is great for children. The time depends on how long you linger and whether you go by bus or walk.

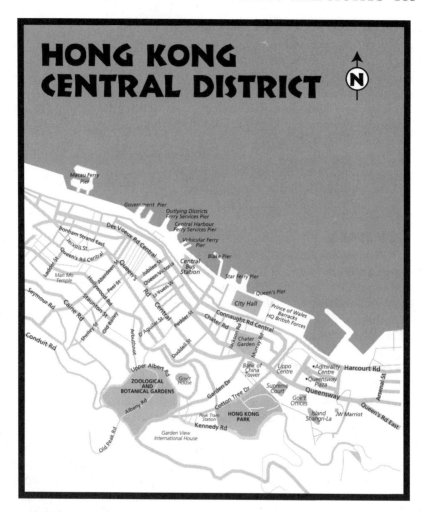

ORIENTATION

You can get to Central by taking the Star Ferry from Tsim Sha Tsui or the MTR to Central station. As you leave the Star Ferry, to your right is the **General Post Office**, **Jardine House** with its distinctive port-hole-shaped windows and an HKTA office in its basement, **Exchange Square** with the **Hong Kong Stock Exchange** and the main bus terminal underneath, and then the **Outlying Districts Ferry Services Pier**. To your left is the bus stop for Ocean Park and the free Peak Tram bus.

Beyond that is **City Hall**. Straight ahead and a touch right is the underpass to the **Cenotaph**, **Statue Square** and the MTR. If you keep on going you get to the Hongkong Bank and up the hill to the Peak Tram station, **Cathedral**, and **Zoo**.

HONG KONG STOCK EXCHANGE

It is best to telephone ahead to make an appointment to see this exchange, one of the most important in the world. Its tiny first floor Viewing Gallery has tape-recorded descriptions of the history and background. If you don't phone, you might only be allowed to see the trading floor from its front door. The exchange is a room of staggering proportions with neat, orderly rows of computer terminals. It is not chaotic and frantic like that of New York.

You'll find the Exchange in Exchange Tower One on the first floor. The main entrance is across from World Wide House on Connaught Rd. off the elevated walkway. *Trading hours are 10am-12:30; 2:30-3:30pm. Telephone Public Affairs 522-1122.*

CITY HALL

People pose for wedding pictures in the small, enclosed **Memorial Garden** with its Henry Moore sculpture. A theater, cafe (set lunch $58), restaurant, and the Urban Publications office are also in the low block and one can book theater tickets here. In City Hall high block, at Connaught Rd., there's the **Exhibition Hall**, **Marriage Registry**, and a large **public library**, *open 10am-6pm daily, Sunday 1pm-6pm and closed Thursday.*

STATUE SQUARE

The only statue is of a banker, of course. **Sir Thomas Jackson** was Chief Manager of the Hong Kong-Shanghai Banking Corporation between 1876 and 1902. Across Chater Road is the **Cenotaph**, a memorial to Hong Kong's war dead.

To the east of the square lies the **Legislative Council**. There are two to five legislative meetings a month. *You can reserve public seats; call 869-9492.* Smaller daily meetings of groups like the financial committee are open to the public on a first-come basis. This handsome, columned, late-Victorian building, was formerly the Supreme Court. A carving of Blind Justice stands on the Chinese-tiled roof.

On the other side of Des Voeux Rd. is the impressive headquarters of the **Hongkong Bank**, *1 Queen's Rd.,* with 62 escalators. At the entrance to this unusual glass building lie two bronze British lions that have guarded the bank since 1935. Their placement in 1985 after this new building was completed, was the result of expert, and highly-paid fung shui expertise. Here you can buy four post cards for $2 each.

This building looks almost like it was made with an Erector set. Guides joke that it can be dismantled and moved in a hurry. Its two cannon-shaped structures on top are pointed at its rival, the Bank of China. But the Bank of China is higher, has sharp points, "like a knife cutting into the heart of Hong Kong."

Next to and east of the Hongkong Bank between Des Voeux Rd. and Queen's Road Central is the tiny, largely unknown **Tsui Museum of Art** in the old Bank of China building. The entrance is in the alley on the west side of this conveniently-located building. It has 2000 antiques, mainly ceramics.

From the back of the Hongkong Bank, cross Queen's Road Central and climb up the staircase. Go up past the old, red-brick French Mission buildings to **St. John's Cathedral**, *4-8 Garden Road. 523-4157.* This is probably the oldest Anglican Church in the Far East. The beige-colored gothic building with green shutters was opened in 1849. With its windows open at times to the outside, its wicker seats and its ceiling fans, St. John's still gives a feeling of an era when air-conditioning didn't exist. You can enjoy Wednesday recitals 1:20-1:50pm and lunch here. Look for the carvings topped by poppy flowers.

Daily Communion is at 7:15am; public holidays at 8am. Post cards are cheap at the church store. It is just a bit downhill and across Garden Road from the Peak Tram station.

THE ZOOLOGICAL AND BOTANICAL GARDENS

A wild, lush, subtropical, hillside garden of ferns, palms, pines, hibiscus, azaleas and more, this is a lovely place to stroll and relax. The zoo has a playground at the top, a small greenhouse, formal garden, refreshment stand and a large number of aviaries with hundreds of bird species. A tunnel under Albany Road takes you to the small zoo with lots of monkeys and three overweight jaguars. The zoo's successful breeding program is helping to save endangered species.

The Gardens were established in 1864 on six hectares of land. This was expanded to include the zoo in the 1970s. People practice *tai chi* here in the morning.

There is a good view of **Government House** (the home of Hong Kong's Governor) which was built in 1855 and was the only building restored by the Japanese during the occupation. The tower was a Japanese addition. Once a year (usually the first Sunday in March), the public is allowed into the grounds to see the azaleas in bloom. *Phone 842-8777 for the exact date and time.* To get to the Gardens: from St. John's Cathedral, the Botanical Gardens are a 15-20 minute walk up Garden Rd., past the Peak Tram Station and Government House. An alternative route is to take a taxi or the Central-Midlevels Escalator. But more about the escalator later.

PEDDER BUILDING

Pedder Building has factory outlets. See Shopping.

LAN KWAI FONG

From Pedder St. MTR exit walk up the hill, turn right on Queen's Rd. and take the first street left (Wyndham St.). This is the trendiest area to eat and drink. (See also "Where to Eat" and "Entertainment & Nightlife") Near the top of Lan Kwai Fong is the **Fringe Club** *at 2 Lower Albert Rd.*, Hong Kong's alternative theater arena with a good restaurant. The club is housed in the old ice house which dates from 1913 and before. This is where an enterprising American stored Hong Kong's first ice, which he shipped from lakes in the U.S.

LI YUEN STREETS EAST & WEST, & THE ALLEYS

Two busy, parallel alleys full of shops and street stalls sell clothes, silks, accessories, make-up, cloth, underwear, etc. almost like they did 100 years ago. To get here, take Central MTR exit C-Li Yuen St. to Des Voeux Rd. To your right is the upscale Landmark shopping mall and across the street is the cheaper World Wide House.

Turn left. They're the 4th and 5th alley on your left. Beyond them is **Pottinger Street**. A block up the hill, Pottinger Street becomes a set of stairs lined with stalls (most closed Sundays) that sell mainly ribbons, buttons and bows, another example of the past. Three blocks up the stairs is the **Central Police Station**, a group of Victorian buildings dating from 1919 on Hollywood Road. Turn right here for antique shops and the Central-Midlevels Escalator. Turn left for Lan Kwai Fong.

Theatre Lane

This alley is off Queen's Rd. Central west of Pedder St. and has shoe shines, shoe repairs, locksmiths and engravers.

CENTRAL MARKET

Located between Queen's Rd. and Des Voeux Rd., at Queen Victoria St. Open 6am-8pm daily, sometimes closed Sundays. Not for the squeamish. The main entrance is on Queen's Road. Look for giant prawns, chickens and pigeons being plucked by hand or machine, and geese being inflated with air. The ground floor has chickens. The first (which is the ground floor from Queen's Rd.) has pork, and bloody (ugh) skinned water buffalo heads. Halal/Muslim meat stalls have signs in Arabic.

This market is also the starting point for the **Central-Midlevels Escalator**, a series of escalators and walkways. It is the longest in the world at 800 meters and takes about a half hour, running downhill from 6am-10am and uphill 10:20am-10pm. You will cross the antique shop area of **Hollywood Rd.** and go past the green and white **Jamia Mosque** which is straight out of 1,001 Nights. Then you cross Mosque St. and Robinson

Rd., the home of the **Ohel Leal Synagogue**, *70 Robinson Rd., 801-5442*, built in 1902 by Lord Kadoorie for his mother. The escalator ends at the residential area of Conduit Rd. Children should be fascinated.

To return to Central, you can catch a taxi or a #3 minibus going left. From Conduit Rd., it's only a ten-minute walk to the top of the Botanical Gardens. Walk left, go down the stairs, along a curving walkway, down more stairs and follow a winding, cement path through the park.

HONG KONG PARK

Inside the park you'll find the white **Flagstaff House**, built in 1846 and is Hong Kong's oldest colonial building. It was originally the home of the Commander-in-Chief of the British Forces. Opened to the public in 1991, it now houses the **Flagstaff House Museum of Tea Ware** with about 500 tea cups and pots in many different sizes and shapes. It is a good place to learn about tea. *Open 10am-5pm, closed Wednesday. Free.*

The Chinese have been drinking tea for about 2000 years. Popular at first only in the south, it became a national drink during the Tang dynasty. Here, you can see how and where Japan's famous tea ceremony started with its powdered tea and bamboo whip. And it was during the Yuan dynasty of the Mongols that the Chinese first added flower petals. The museum has changing exhibitions.

Hong Kong Park *is open 7am-11pm and is free.* Follow signs uphill from the museum to the greenhouse Conservatory with its orchids, Cactus Room, and Humid Room. Egyptian papyrus grows outside. The huge walk-in aviary has fancy blue and red Victoria Crowned Pigeons, long-red-tailed Birds of Paradise and hundreds of others.

The ten-hectare park is inviting, manicured and modern with lots of fountains, flowering trees and bushes. It is a good place to take photos of such architectural marvels as the Lippo Centre and the Bank of China building rising out of the greenery to the north.

You can also reach Hong Kong Park by escalator through **Pacific Place**, a large shopping mall at Admiralty MTR. The park is outside the front door of the Island Shangri-La Hotel on Supreme Court Road. You should be able to get a taxi at the entrance to this hotel.

THE PEAK TRAM

The tram operates 7am to midnight. A trip is made every 10-15 minutes and costs $10 or $16 return. Telephone 849-7654. Go only if you can see the peak clearly from below; clouds could obscure your view. Avoid 10-10:30am when all tour groups arrive. There is plenty of time the rest of the day. For the best view, sit on the right side on the way up or at the very back window. The tram does not stop at Barker, May, Macdonnell and Kennedy Roads unless someone sounds the bell. This is a public means of transportation as well as a tourist attraction.

The Peak Tram takes five to eight minutes to whisk you straight up to 334 meters above sea level, about 200 meters below the top of Victoria Peak. Don't worry, they've had no accidents in the past 100 years. This used to be the only way to the exclusive residences on the mountain before they built the road. The tram cars themselves are Swiss with a capacity of 120 people each trip. Tours usually go one way – up. Their bus drivers meet them at the top and thence to Aberdeen.

In 1993, progress destroyed one of the most desirable apartment buildings in the city, attached to the top terminal building. It had a ghost story. One day the tram inexplicably stopped running. The crew started investigating and discovered that a new tenant had insisted on opening the maid's room that came with his flat. That room had been sealed for decades after a servant had committed suicide there. After the Canadian tenant obliged and paid for ceremonies to appease her spirit, the tram started working once more.

The modern, three-story **Peak Galleria** building beyond the terminal has restaurants and upmarket stores. The best view is still below it outside, at the pavilion where you can see the white governor's mansion between the high rises. This is to the left as you leave the tram terminal. From here, you can watch the planes arriving or leaving every two minutes.

The lower **Peak Tram Station** is on Garden Road, across the road between St. John's Cathedral and the Botanical Gardens.

An incredibly beautiful mountain road also goes to the Peak, past some of Hong Kong's wealthiest homes. #1 minibus connects with the Star Ferry, #15 double-decker bus with Exchange Square ($5.20) and #15B bus with Causeway Bay. To get to the bus station on the peak, walk down Peak Road two minutes from the Peak terminal.

VICTORIA PEAK

This has always been the most fashionable and expensive address in Hong Kong. Not only is the Peak a few degrees cooler, but the view is one of the best in the world. The British prohibited Chinese people, aside from servants, from living here until 1930. In 1994, a two-story house here broke home price records by selling for US$2,000 a square foot for a total of US$32.7 million.

Walks

Harlech and **Lugard Roads** circle the peak for a view of the entire island, the harbor and Kowloon. It takes about one hour. Try it at dusk. If you want to get away from the crowds, you can also head up **Mt. Austin Road** to **Victoria Peak Gardens**. This is actually a large public park set in a valley and the former site of the Governor's Lodge which was demolished by the Japanese in World War II. From here you can head up to Victoria Peak itself for a fabulous harbor view or take the **Governor's walk** to a viewing pavilion of the southern side of the island.

THE POLICE MUSEUM

27 Coombe Rd. at Wan Chai Gap. 849-6018. Open 9am-5pm, Tuesday 2pm-5pm, closed Monday. Free. This small, fascinating museum in a park setting is too often overlooked. On weekdays, you may have it all to yourself. Highlights include photos from the late 1800s to the present (including before and after pictures of decapitated pirates), a heroin manufacturing workshop, a bomb disposal wheel barrow, a triad (Chinese mafia) gallery and a narcotics gallery with examples of different drugs and related paraphernalia. You can see free video programs from 1956 to the present. Postcards and Royal Hong Kong Police souvenirs are on sale. Take CMB bus 15-Peak from Exchange Square, Central. Look for the museum's sign on the left side, at the junction of Peak and Stubbs Roads.

From the playground nearby, across Coombe Road, there's a great view of **Aberdeen Reservoir**. This is also the top of **Aberdeen Country Park**, and you can walk down Aberdeen Reservoir Rd. to the reservoir and Aberdeen. It takes about an hour and a half.

You can also backtrack, cross Stubbs Road and take the steep cement path down about 10 minutes. Turn right at the playground and you will be on **Bowen Rd**. It's a 35-minute walk (past Lover's Rock) to Stubbs Rd. where you can get any bus going to Central.

BOWEN ROAD

Take CMB bus 15, 6, 61 or 262 from Central. The bus will go through Wanchai and past the graveyard. Get off near the Adventist Hospital at the junction of Stubbs Road, Wong Nai Chung Gap Rd., and Tai Hang Rd. Bowen Road starts behind the Stubbs Road bus stop.

This vehicle-free road is set among trees and bushes and is a favorite of joggers. It's easy going and charming, except for the inevitable trash. There are great views of Happy Valley Racetrack and some large mansions.

But the main attraction is **Lover's Rock**, about a 20-minute walk. Climb the stairs on your left. This large, red-painted rock is surrounded by small statues of **Kwan Yin**, the Buddhist goddess of mercy, and **Kwan Kung**, the red-faced god of war. There are also incense spirals, pictures of a man and woman holding hands and a great view. Another 10 minutes takes you to Wan Chai Gap Rd. where you can walk down to Queen's Rd. East, Wanchai.

PING SHAN MUSEUM

This small museum is at **Hong Kong University** in Pokfulam, not Central. While it should not have top priority in your sightseeing, it is worth visiting if you are interested in ancient Chinese-Christian history. It has 966 tiny bronze Nestorian crosses from the 13th century including some swastika designs, the largest such collection in the world from this Christian sect. Found in China, there are no duplicates. The museum also has exquisite mirrors, some over 2200 years old, Qing and Shang bronzes, and 5000-year old Yangshao neolithic pottery.

Take #3 bus from Central outside the main bus terminal heading east. The bus winds past Government House then west past Caritas House on Caine Rd. and along Seymour Rd. Alight at 94 Bonham Road. 859-2114. Open 9:30am-6pm Monday-Saturdays. Closed Sundays and public holidays.

WESTERN DISTRICT

Known popularly as **Western**, **Sheung Wan** was the old Chinese settlement. Though a great deal has been torn down and rebuilt as office and apartment blocks, you can still find much of the traditional here like decades-old stores selling live snakes and herbal medicines.

Western is almost all concrete now. The older part with Hollywood Road and its antique shops, and the Man Mo Temple are partway up the mountain. It is a good place to see bamboo scaffolding on buildings under construction.

Closer to the harbor, you could see the offices of the compradores only a few years ago. These were the middle men doing business between the foreigners and the Chinese. They worked on Des Voeux Rd. and Connaught Rd. Central. There were also the "provision" stores here for the ships. Most have now been replaced by supermarkets.

The luxurious Hotel Victoria is almost on top of the Macau ferry pier with its helicopter pad. Between Sheung Wan and Central are ferries to some outlying islands and the Harbour Building with a tower overseeing traffic in the whole harbor. The harborside is flat with land-fill. Almost across Connaught Rd. from the Hotel Victoria is Western Market. Joined to this hotel by an underground passage is the Sheung Wan MTR stop.

WESTERN HIGHLIGHTS

Western is full of antique stores, little alleys, ladder streets and Man Mo Temple, Hong Kong Island's most famous.

SUGGESTED WESTERN ITINERARY

The more interesting walk is along Hollywood Road in and out of tiny antique stores, to the **Man Mo Temple**. Start from the Li Yuen Streets in Central and climb the stairs of Pottinger Street. Turn right on Hollywood Road. The area around the Cat Street Galleries used to be the red light district with boarding houses for seamen.

Ruth used to walk through Western west from the Central Market along Queen's Road looking for lingering bits of old Hong Kong. They are increasingly difficult to find. Streets up the mountain are still mostly staircases, as they have been for over a hundred years. In dried food stores and herbal medicine stores (try 125 and 152 Queen's Rd. Central), there are still dried sharks' fins, birds' nest, mushrooms, abalone, insects, sea horses and the penises of some animals. You can also find ginseng, goats' horns, sea cucumbers and cashews. Ruth looked for the controversial seals' penises exported from Canada but couldn't see any. And clerks still do not speak English.

In **Man Wah Lane**, an alley on the north side, a street stall sells bolts of cloth and another chops. These fancy-handled rubber stamps were once used legally in place of a signature. You should be able to order a chop for yourself now and come back for it later. Tea shops are at 153 and 290, still selling tea in bricks, the old way with no cup-size bags.

Where Queen's Rd. West becomes Bonham Strand, go off to the left onto **Jervois** for old shops full of dusty bolts of textiles. Shops of the same goods tended to stick together. Ruth did find live snakes at 58-60 Jervois. Snake bile is used in cough medicines and aphrodisiacs and snake is also a favorite wintertime dish. Back on Bonham, she couldn't find addresses from the HKTA book on Western. The buildings were torn down.

MAN MO TEMPLE

Open 7am-5pm. This is the best temple on Hong Kong Island and is dedicated to **Man Cheong**, the god of literature (with calligraphy brush in hand) and **Kwan Kung**, the god of war and patron saint of policemen and their enemies, the triads. It is also one of the oldest and largest temples on the island. Kwan Kung was a third century warrior whose exploits were immortalized in the classic Chinese novel *The Three Kingdoms.*

Inside are brass and pewter incense burners, incense spirals (which can burn for up to three weeks!), and carved wooden sedan chairs used in processions of the gods. A variety of lesser gods line the walls. The rooms are very smoky. Behind is a repository for human ashes.

LADDER STREET

Many of the streets up the mountain here are staircases. Any of them could be called a ladder street, but the designated one is in front of the Man Mo Temple.

CAT STREET

Also known as **Lascar Row**, this is a small, open-air flea market. Nearby are the **Cat Street Galleries**, a collection of anique stores *at 38 Lok Ku Rd. and at Upper Lascar Row.*

POSSESSION STREET

Towards the western end of Hollywood Rd. is where the British prematurely raised the Union Jack on January 26, 1841, and claimed Hong Kong island as theirs. The view is now blocked by high-rises.

WING SING STREET

Also known as **Egg St.**, this is a narrow lane specializing in preserved or salted duck and sometimes quail eggs. The duck eggs are soaked in tea leaves and straw for a month or so and hatched in restaurants with a yucky green yoke and transparent green "egg white" and misnamed 100 or 1000-year old eggs. They are delicious with pickles and rice! Honest! *The street, if it still exists, runs north of Des Voeux Rd., and east of Man Wa Lane.*

WESTERN MARKET

323 Des Veoux Rd. West. This used to be a produce market. It is now a handsome market for tourist wares. If you are in the vicinity, it is worth a stop just to window shop and look at this fascinating old building with 1920s decor. It is one block west of Sheung Wan MTR station. See also Chapter 12, "Shopping."

WANCHAI DISTRICT

This has been a red light district since World War II. It was notorious from the fifties to the mid-seventies when thousands of foreign service-men flocked here for Rest and Recreation during the Korean and Vietnam wars. Richard Mason immortalized Wanchai in his 1950s book *The World of Suzie Wong.* The **Suzi Wong Bar**, named after the heroine, is still here.

Although a few tattoo parlors and topless bars remain in "the Wanch," this area has become more respectable but is still dumpy. Because of ridiculously high rents in Central, businesses and hotels have spread here, many of them to North Wanchai beside the harbor, a site conveniently close to the Cross-Harbour Tunnel to Kowloon.

One of the joys of north Wanchai is being able to walk along its network of elevated sidewalks, even through buildings, without concern about crossing busy streets. One of the disadvantages is the constant roar of traffic from dawn to almost midnight on Gloucester Road. South Wanchai still has a lot of fascinating, narrow, crowded streets and lanes.

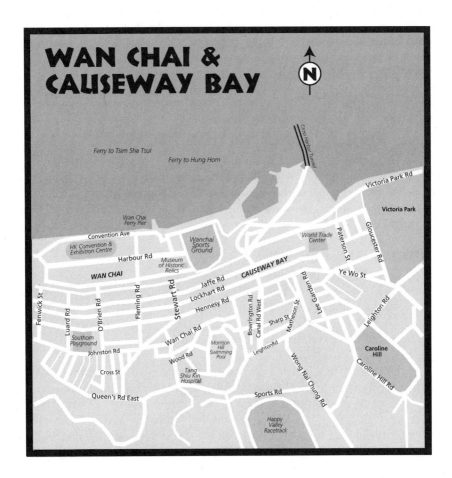

ORIENTATION

You can reach north Wanchai by MTR or tram. Take the O'Brien Road exit of the Wanchai MTR station and follow signs to the Convention Centre and the elevated walkway over Gloucester Road, through the

Immigration Building and elegant, crystal-chandeliered Central Plaza. From Tsim Sha Tsui or Hung Hom it is more pleasant and more direct to take the Star Ferry and then a right.

You can reach south Wanchai by MTR or tram. From the Wanchai MTR station, take the O'Brien Rd. exit. Walk south a half block, cross Johnston Road, jog right and continue straight on Tai Yuen St. two blocks, through the bustling **Wanchai Market** (clothes, food and flowers) to Queen's Road East. Cross the road to the **Old Wanchai Post Office**. To your right, one and two blocks respectively are the **Hopewell Centre** and **Tai Wong Temple**.

QUEEN'S ROAD EAST

This used to be the old waterfront of Wanchai. It now has lots of good rosewood and rattan furniture shops.

OLD WANCHAI POST OFFICE

This small, whitewashed building was built in 1913 and operated as a post office for 77 years. It still houses the old wooden counter, postboxes, and now also the **Environmental Resource Centre**. Wanchai's current post office is next door and open 10am-5pm, Wednesday 10am-1pm, closed Sunday.

HOPEWELL CENTRE

This tall round building is nicknamed "the stone cigar" and resembles one. A *fung shui* master advised that a swimming pool be built on the roof, to keep the building from burning down. A pool was built (but not open to the public) and the building hasn't had any fires. The Hopewell Centre is Wanchai's main landmark and was Hong Kong's tallest building until the Bank of China Tower.

There's not much to do here, except ride up and down in the outdoor glass elevator from the 17-56th floor for a good view of the harbor. The Revolving 66 restaurant is at the top (see "Where to Eat"). A car park is on the 17th floor, accessible from the hill behind it. Harry Ramsden's British restaurant is on the ground floor. If you walk east 600 meters on Queen's Rd., there's the Sikh Temple at the corner of Stubb's Rd. and beyond to the south east, the interesting cemeteries of Happy Valley.

TAI WONG TEMPLE

129-131 Queen's Road East. This small temple from the 1860s open 7am-6pm is dedicated to Hung Shing, a Tang dynasty official (618-907 AD) who promoted astronomy, mathematics and geology and could predict the weather. Fisher folk of course worship him.

NORTH WANCHAI

Here you'll find the **Hong Kong Academy for Performing Arts** *at 1 Gloucester Rd., 584-1500* and next door **The Hong Kong Arts Centre**, another venue for performances and art gallery. See Chapter 13, "Entertainment & Nightlife."

The seven-story glass-wall **Hong Kong Convention and Exhibition Centre**, *One Harbour Rd., Wanchai, 582-8888,* has 7 1/2 acres of exhibition space, two theaters and a number of restaurants. It is worth a visit if only for the view through its huge harborside glass windows. The work in the harbor here is an extension to the convention center.

The **Museum of Chinese Historical Relics**, *28 Harcourt Rd., in the China Resources Building, 574-2692, open 10am-6pm; 1pm-6pm Sundays,* only has occasional exhibitions of Chinese handicrafts and paintings.

CAUSEWAY BAY & HAPPY VALLEY DISTRICTS

Much of **Causeway Bay** used to be a bay until they threw mountains of dirt and rubble into it. It is now primarily a shopping and residential area, the street names reflecting the early British merchants who worked here.

The company **Jardine Matheson** has always had its Hong Kong headquarters here with wharfs, warehouses and employee homes. Its trade name in Shanghai was *Yee Wo*, hence the name of the main street.

ORIENTATION

Except for **Times Square**, a large mall accessible from Causeway Bay MTR station, most hotels and shopping are north of or on Hennessy Rd./Yee Wo St. on a small area of reclaimed land. It is one of the more pleasant places in which to stay as it is close to the water and the vast Victoria Park.

Most of the sightseeing here is south of Hennessy Rd. and up the mountain away from the water. The **Happy Valley Jockey Club** and the Football Stadium are to the south. You reach Causeway Bay from the Causeway Bay MTR station and the tram. A second MTR station, Tin Hau, is to the east at other side of Victoria Park. It is close to the Cross-Harbour Tunnel entrance.

BOAT LIFE

The Causeway Bay Typhoon Shelter is not just a shelter, it is the permanent home of a few families living on junks. You can get a sampan ride but we don't recommend eating on a floating restaurant. Also across Gloucester Rd. from the Excelsior Hotel is the flossy Royal Hong Kong Yacht Club on Kellet Island which is no longer an island.

THE NOON DAY GUN

Jardine Matheson first fired this cannon as a salute to its taipans coming home. The British navy objected as it felt the right to fire ceremonial cannons was solely its own. In punishment, it demanded that the trading company fire it at noon each day instead. Other people and groups can also do this now for a fee to charity; telephone the Office of the Company Secretary 843-8243. Accessible by a tunnel door in the west side of the World Trade Centre on Gloucester Road, the gun is across the road from the Excelsior Hotel. You can hear reference to it in Noel Coward's famous song *Mad Dogs and Englishmen.*

JARDINE'S BAZAAR

This small, cramped, open-air clothes market is only a block long. The alley turns into a food market and ends at **Jardine's Bazaar Road**, where you can see people making *dim sum.* To get to the market, take the Jardine's Crescent exit from Causeway Bay MTR. The alley is across the street.

VICTORIA PARK

Head here to get away from the city's confusion. Its 50 acres has lots of grass. The design is not as interesting as other parks but it is a great place to people-watch especially on weekends. It has swimming pools, a football field, jogging track and a small rollerskating rink. There is squash, basketball, volleyball and 13 tennis courts. Maybe you can join a game.

Between 6am and 8am, you can watch people practicing *tai chi chuan.* Huge flower and plant markets make it very colorful during the **Chinese New Year's Flower Festival**. It is also a popular moon-watching place during the **Mid-Autumn Festival**. As the largest park in town, it is the staging area for many political demonstration and fairs.

TIN HAU TEMPLE

Take the MTR to Tin Hau station and the Tin Hau Temple exit. Cross Causeway Rd. Turn right and then left onto Tin Hau Temple Road. This small temple, built in the late 18th century, has two levels and used to be on the waterfront. On the second level are dozens of small, ash-covered statues.

The Hakka ancestors of the Tai family which currently manages it, built this temple. The even smaller, octogonal **Lin Fa Kung Temple** is a five-minute walk from the Tin Hau temple. Turn left, left at Causeway Road, left on Tung Lo Wan Rd and left at the second street.

AW BOON HAW GARDENS

(aka **Tiger Balm Gardens**) *At Tai Hang Rd, open 10am-4pm. You can visit the jade collection by appointment 576-0467.* Aw Boon Haw made a fortune selling Tiger Balm, an analgesic rub similiar to Vicks Vapor Rub. In 1935, Aw Boon Haw built these "gardens," an artificial landscape filled with colorful plaster animals, birds, and people. Some visitors find it charming and imaginative; others think it gaudy and in bad taste. Kids usually enjoy the artificial tunnels and caves. Take a taxi from Causeway Bay or bus 11 from Exchange Square, Central.

HAPPY VALLEY

Malaria or "bad air" made the British abandon this valley as a residential area. Luckily malaria no longer exists in Hong Kong. One hillside is covered with cemeteries from early colonial times. In 1846, they held the first horse races here and still do. Take a taxi or a tram marked "Happy Valley" from Causeway Bay.

ABERDEEN DISTRICT

This former fishing village with a well-protected harbor, still moors fishing boats, but now also pleasure craft. Many people still live on boats here. On land Aberdeen is an industrial center and the site of Ocean Park, the best amusement park in the city. It is located on the south side of the island, west of Repulse Bay.

A fresh sea food market operates after 9am all day. You can smell shrimp paste everywhere. Look for drying squid and air-conditioned junks. 5000 boat people live in Aberdeen; some also have apartments on land. Most do not fish any more. A higher percentage of authentic boat people live on Cheung Chau island.

Take bus #70, 6A, 260 or 262 from Exchange Square in Central. Get off at the first stop after the Aberdeen Tunnel and walk about 20 minutes or grab a taxi.

AP LEI CHAU

(**Duck's Tongue Island**) is across from Aberdeen, joined by a bridge that offers a good view of fishing boats and yachts. The island is covered with highrises, but its shore has boatyards for building and repairing junks.

Aberdeen Power Station is also here with its five huge chimneys. Because the word for "four" sounds like the Chinese word for "death" and is a very unlucky number, it built a fifth fake chimney. People take superstitions very seriously here.

FLOATING RESTAURANTS

The food in these huge, gaudy, three-story barges covered in lights and dragons, is not great. Seafood is cheaper and better on Cheung Chau or Lamma Islands. However, the garish oriental interiors and exteriors make the boat trip out to the restaurants a worthwhile experience. The biggest is the Jumbo, then the Tai Pak and Sea Palace. You can always get a sampan to Lamma Island for about $60 or eat at the Blue Ocean Restaurant described below. For the best photos of these unique restaurants, get there before 10am when the sun is on the front.

You can go to the pier and hire a sampan for a 20-minute tour of the harbor, available from the main seawall opposite Aberdeen Center. 9am-5pm, $40, child: $30. For a free trip on the harbor, take Jumbo Restaurants ferry, look around, and take another ferry back or onward to "Shum Wan" and the Blue Ocean.

ABERDEEN COUNTRY PARK

Above the town at the end of Aberdeen Reservoir Rd., this has a visitor's center with the area's history, plants and animals. There are fitness trails, nature trails and World War II relics.

OCEAN PARK/WATER WORLD/MIDDLE KINGDOM

Three amusement parks are in one location *(873-8888)*. There is something for every one here. **Ocean Park**, *Open 10am-6pm, 9am Sunday. Admission $140, child $74*, the largest in Southeast Asia, has two parts. In the lower, there is a house with free-flying butterflies, an artistic exhibit of goldfish (black ones absorb evil spirits; gold ones attract wealth), otters, playground, petting zoo, orchid house, etc. Then you take the cable car to the top part for dolphin, killer whale and high diving shows, a shark tunnel and an aviary. Don't miss Atoll Reef, a three-story salt-water aquarium full of fish, sea turtles, etc. with different fish at different levels.

The shows are in an incredibly beautiful setting at the tip of the peninsula jutting into the South China Sea. The cable car is not for those with a fear of heights. A special Citybus leaves from Admiralty MTR station every half hour from 8:45am. The price includes admission. No. 6 minibus goes from the Star Ferry in Central to the main entrance, daily except Sundays and public holidays for $9 one way or $16 return.

Water World, *open 10am-5pm with admission $60, child $40,* is a large water park that has a wave pool and water slides and operates May to October.

Middle Kingdom, *open 10am-6pm, admission $140, child (6-7 yrs) $70,* is a living lesson in Chinese history and culture with replicas of famous

Chinese temples, palaces, pagodas and street scenes. You can learn to make paper here and have your fortune told — in English. There's also a variety show with acrobats. The only restaurant, beside the food kiosks in Ocean Park, is inside the Middle Kingdom which is attached to Ocean Park by escalator and has a separate entrance at Tai Shue Wan.

THE SOUTH SIDE: REPULSE BAY & STANLEY DISTRICTS

Take the twisting, turning, cliff-side road to see the other side of the island, where rocky hillsides alternate with white sand beaches and luxury highrises. Mansions and luxury apartments dot the green mountainside. From Central, it's about 30 minutes to Repulse Bay and another 15 to Stanley, depending on the traffic.

This is our favorite bus ride in Hong Kong for both the breathtaking views and the speed that the bus drivers take the corners on the skinny, cliff-hugging roads. You can also count the times you hit tree branches.

Hop buses from Central (Exchange Square bus terminal) or Admiralty MTR (use the Queensway Plaza exit and walk right to the bus stop on the Queensway). You can go through the Aberdeen tunnel and past Deep Water Bay Beach or over the mountain, which only takes 10 minutes more. It's best to go both ways, preferably in a double-decker bus (#6, 6A, 61). Buses cost between $6-$10. A taxi to Repulse Bay can cost $60.

Buses
6-Central-mountain-Repulse Bay (RB)-Stanley Market-Stanley Prison
6A-Central-Aberdeen Tunnel-RB-Stanley Market-Stanley Fort
61-Central-over mountain-Repulse Bay
260-Central-Aberdeen Tunnel-RB-Stanley Village-Stanley Prison
262-Central-Aberdeen Tunnel-RB-Chung Hom Kok

REPULSE BAY

The most notable thing in Repulse Bay is its very large and popular beach. There's standing-room only on summer weekends. There are changing facilities, rafts, lifeguards, a large McDonald's and a Maxim's restaurant (the Chinese fastfood kind). On the beach are two large recent statues of Tin Hau and Kwan Yin, protectors of fishermen, and a pavilion. You can walk from the other end of the beach along the waterfront to Deep Water Bay and Aberdeen.

Above the beach, across from the main bus stop, at 109 Repulse Bay Rd. is a life-size replica of the old Repulse Bay Hotel. The original was torn down in 1982, but this copy of the building was built four years later. The fountain is from the original. It's quite beautiful and houses some shops, a drugstore and two good, very expensive restaurants: **The Verandah** and **Spices** (see Chapter 11, "Repulse Bay").

STANLEY

Stanley is most famous for its market although the original village is still a dirty, fascinating shanty town. Surrounding these are expensive residential areas. The beach is popular for windsurfing year-round.

Stanley has a long history. It was one of the largest villages on the island when the British arrived in 1841. One of the first things that the British built was **Stanley Fort**, which then and now houses the British military. There is also a large maximum-security prison and a small, old graveyard on Stanley Peninsula. The Japanese kept mainly British expatriates in an internment camp here during the occupation.

STANLEY MARKET

Open about 10:00am-5:30pm, depending on the season. This is a popular, pleasant, open-air market with factory over-runs, silks, arts and crafts. It has some of the best quality goods of the markets, but also in some cases, higher prices.

TIN HAU TEMPLE

To get there from the bus stop, walk back and head downhill to the water. Turn right at Park 'N Shop past the fruit and then the meat stalls. Bear left past Stanley's French Restaurant then right along Stanley Main St. past the Hongkong Bank along the waterfront for a block to the fishing village. Follow the pavement to the right to the temple. Don't bother with signs to "Fashion Factory" or Richard's Studio.

This tiny temple was built in 1767. During World War II, people sought refuge here. A bomb landed nearby but did not explode, thanks to **Tin Hau**, goddess of the sea, patroness of fishermen. People at the temple say the skin of the tiger shot during the Japanese occupation is in a side room. From outside you can see a temple on the hill above.

This is the **Kwan Yin Temple**. If you have lots of time head up the main path through the village maze. The Kwan Yin temple is modern and medium-sized with a large (about seven meter) statue of Kwan Yin looking mercifully over the village. There is a small garden, good view and tile paintings of her life. Above the temple is the road entrance to Ma Hang Village. From here you can catch a bus to Central or a minibus to Aberdeen.

OLD STANLEY POLICE STATION

This small, two-story, white-washed building from 1859 used to be Hong Kong's oldest police station and now houses the good restaurant Tables 88 with its movie-set interior. It is located above Stanley Market almost across from the bus station at lucky 88 Stanley Village Rd. Feel like walking? Continue along this road, take Wong Ma Kok Rd. right at the fork, past the playing field, to Stanley Military Cemetery (30-minute walk). On the other side of the road and down is St. Stephen's Beach.

STANLEY BEACH

There are several beaches in the area. The better one is on Tai Tam Bay, a five-minute walk from Stanley Village. It has windsurfing, showers and changing rooms.

NEAR STANLEY

Tai Tam Country Park has a huge reservoir, views of the ocean, lovely walks and World War II pillboxes. Take bus #14-Sai Wan from the bus station at the market about 10 minutes past the American Club. The entrance is just before the large reservoir on your left. To the left of the reservoir is a cement catch water with a thin concrete path beside it. If you climb up the stairs, you can walk along this, past a small, clean fresh water pool, back to Stanley or all the way to Repulse Bay.

HONG KONG ISLAND COUNTRY PARKS

The fifty-kilometer Hong Kong Trail passes through Hong Kong Island's four country parks: Pok Fu Lam, Aberdeen, Tai Tam and Shek O Country Parks. For more information, please see Parks in Chapter 6, "Basic Information."

KOWLOON

Kowloon is a 12-square kilometer peninsula. China handed over this and Stone Cutter's Island to the British in 1860. Stone Cutter's is occupied now by British military and eyed enviously by the mainland Chinese navy. Boundary Street was the border between Hong Kong and China until 1898. It is seven blocks north of Argyle Street in Mong Kok.

The hills behind Kowloon gave it its name, Gow Lung (nine dragons). The Chinese believe that hills are dragons. The story goes that the young, last Sung (Song) Emperor pointed out the eight dragons (hills), but his diplomatic minister said "Oh no sir, there are nine, for you are also a dragon".

TSIM SHA TSUI DISTRICT

The name means *sharp sandy point* in Cantonese. It is shopping heaven and Hong Kong's tourist ghetto. It is almost impossible not to shop here when signs on "silk" ties read "$10." The main road is **Nathan Rd.** (known at the south end as the **Golden Mile**). Governor Nathan built this large, straight road initially in the middle of nowhere and it became known as Nathan's folly. Today it is the heart of Tsim Sha Tsui.

Along Nathan Road and its side streets, you can find inexpensive clothing, an unbelievable number of camera shops and good restaurants and bars. One of Hong Kong's largest and most confusing shopping centers is here, **Harbour City**. Attractions for non-shoppers include the delightful **Kowloon Park**, the **Hong Kong Cultural Centre**, the **Museum of History**, the **Space Museum** and the unforgettable **Star Ferry**.

ORIENTATION

You can get to Tsim Sha Tsui by Star Ferry from Central or Wanchai and MTR (Tsim Sha Tsui station). To get to the Star Ferry from the station, take the exit E-Star Ferry. Walk straight on Nathan Rd. (The needle-shaped building across the harbor rising up in front of you is Central Plaza office tower, Hong Kong's tallest and most expensive building.) Turn right on Salisbury Rd. and walk four blocks. To your right will be the Peninsula Hotel and left, the Hong Kong Space Museum. The Star Ferry and the bus terminal are between Harbour City and the Hong Kong Cultural Centre.

STAR FERRY

The ferry runs every 5-10 minutes from 6:30am-11:30am, 366-2576. This is one of the most memorable ferry rides in the world, spectacular day or night, when the city turns into a glittering jewel. It began in 1898 and is a great way to get a good conception of the city's layout and a close up of the busy harbor. First class is cleaner, more comfortable and has a better view. Second class is more interesting, can smell of diesel fumes, and is $.30 less.

The ride to Central takes about eight minutes. You can also take a ferry from here to Wanchai. It costs $1.50 for adults, $1 for children and people over 65 ride free. If you need change, there is a change-given turnstile.

By the Kowloon Star Ferry terminal, the 45-meter-high **Clock Tower** from the 1910s is all that remains of the original Kowloon-Canton Railway Station torn down in 1978. They have replaced the tracks with the Hong Kong Cultural Centre.

HONG KONG CULTURAL CENTRE

Open 10am-6pm daily, Sunday and public holidays 1pm-6pm. Closed Thursday. This distinctive modern, 1989, beige building has a curved roof and three theaters. *All three can be reached at 734-2009.* You can pay for a tour of the theaters. It also houses the **Museum of Art**, *734-2167,* which

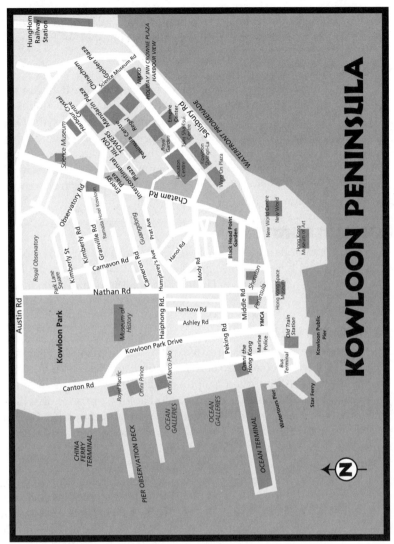

has six galleries with modern art, Chinese antiques and famous paintings of early Hong Kong and Canton. It also has a restaurant and a small shop.

HONG KONG SPACE MUSEUM

Open 2pm-9:30pm. Closed Tuesday. Free. The planetarium show costs $20. (734-2722). Try a moonwalk at 1/6 gravity or spin in a multi-axis chair in this large 1980 museum with displays, videos and a few hands-on exhibits. This museum has an Exhibition Hall, Hall of Solar Sciences and one of the world's largest planetariums. It shows Omni-max films on the ceiling of this dome-shaped building. Sit in the back to avoid neck cramping. Some shows are in English and you get free English-translation headsets for the ones that aren't. Make sure your headset works before the show starts.

HARBOUR CITY

Hong Kong's largest shopping mall has 600 stores. It began with Ocean Terminal in 1966 as a dock and shopping area for cruise ships and has grown with the addition of **Ocean Centre**, **Ocean Galleries**, the **Omni** hotels and pedestrian links to other shopping centers. You can walk from the Star Ferry to Kowloon Park in this thing without seeing natural daylight. Ocean Terminal is to the left in front of the Star Ferry. Sylvester Stallone's **Planet Hollywood** is here with lots of props from famous movies like an alien from Alien.

PENINSULA HOTEL

The most famous and historic hotel in Hong Kong used to be on the waterfront. Stop here for an expensive cup of coffee in its lobby to experience old world elegance. High tea is from 3pm-6pm and will cost (gulp!) $110.

KOWLOON PARK

This modern city park is fun to explore and a great place for kids. There are fountains, a flamingo and duck pond, an aviary with hornbills, toucans and assorted parrots, a sculpture walk with 17 modern sculptures by local artists, and Scotland's Sir Eduardo Paolozzi's bronze of William Blake's "Concept of Newton". There's also an unimpressive Chinese garden and a totem pole presented to Hong Kong by Canada's most unpopular prime minister, Brian Mulroney.

The park is liberally landscaped in pink cement. There is a lot of greenery and benches, but few grassy areas. People practice tai chi chuan in the mornings and sometimes men walk their birds here. This park used to be a British military headquarters. Near the entrance is **Kowloon Mosque**, *724-0095*, Hong Kong's largest. Built in 1984, it replaced the original building from 1896, which served the British Army's Indian soldiers. Visits are by appointment only.

The park's **Sports Complex** (*open 6:30am-midnight; the Aviary closes at 8pm; entrance free*) has many, modernistic wading pools, squash, tennis, restaurants and ice cream. Take MTR exit A1-Kowloon Park.

HONG KONG MUSEUM OF HISTORY

Open 10am-6pm, Sunday 1pm-6pm and closed Friday. 367-1124. The Park is also home to this excellent museum. Photographs, paintings, models, maps and archaeological finds illustrate Hong Kong's history in two barracks buildings from the late 1800s. Look for the women with tiny bound feet and the men wearing their hair in long pigtails as a sign of respect to the Manchu rulers. It also has a life-size reproduction of an old street and is well worth visiting.

ANTIQUITIES AND MONUMENTS OFFICE

136 Nathan Rd., 721-2326. Open 9:30am-12:30pm, Saturday 9:30am-noon and 2-4:30pm. Closed Sunday. Free. This small, historical building houses changing exhibits and a small, permanent collection of pictures and descriptions of Hong Kong's 50 historical monuments. Free brochures on some historical sights are available. A small, one-story brick building across from Kowloon Park, it is the Former Kowloon British School built in 1900 with donations from Mr. Ho Tung (later Sir Robert).

TSIM SHA TSUI EAST DISTRICT

This area used to be mainly water, but thanks to modern land reclamation, it is now the site of luxurious hotels, fancy restaurants, sophisticated shopping arcades and expensive hostess clubs. It's a nice, clean, artificial area that's not crowded. The main attraction here is the fabulous **Science Museum** (see below).

You can get to Tsim Sha Tsui East by walking along Cameron Rd., 15 minutes from the Tsim Sha Tsui MTR (B-Cameron Rd. exit). Or take a taxi or #1 minibus from Kowloon Star Ferry. There is also a hoverferry from the East Ferry Pier (Edinburgh Place) in front of City Hall, Central. It leaves every 20 minutes, 8:10am-8:10pm.

HONG KONG SCIENCE MUSEUM

Science Museum Rd. at Granville and Chatham Rds. 732-3232. Open 1pm-9pm, Saturday and Sunday 10am-9pm, closed Monday. Admission $35, children and seniors (over 60) $20. This unusual pink building (1991) with a gray stripe has four floors of 500 mainly hands-on exhibits. The center piece is the Energy Machine, a giant four-story track for balls with twists, loops, drums, chimes, etc. This is a great place for the kids and the kid in you. Operate a robot arm, play with lasers or make waves.

WATERFRONT PROMENADE

This lit, cement walk borders the entire Tsim Sha Tsui and Tsim Sha Tsui East waterfront and provides great views of Hong Kong Island, and the harbor. You can follow it back to the Star Ferry. It's popular with joggers in the morning.

YAU MA TEI DISTRICT

Starting north of Kowloon Park, the British first developed Yau Ma Tei in 1860 after they acquired Kowloon. Shanghai Street was the main road before they built Nathan. Today, the highlight of this area is the fabulous **Temple Street Night Market**. There is also a large **Tin Hau Temple** and Hong Kong's only **Jade Market**.

TEMPLE STREET NIGHT MARKET

Opens about 6pm, is busiest 9pm-11pm, and closes around 1am. Hong Kong's biggest (about one kilometer long) and best open market is large, inexpensive and has almost everything from clothes, kerosene lanterns, and cordless phones to Nepalese handicrafts, fortune tellers, and Cantonese opera. It's best on the weekend.

Go to Jordan MTR, exit A. Walk right on Jordan two and a half blocks, turn right onto Temple St. The first couple blocks are mainly clothes (jeans from $75, T-shirts 3/$20, CDs 3/$100) and food stalls. Temple Street continues slightly to the right and you can find palm and face readers, bird fortune tellers, sidewalk medicine men and Cantonese street opera, mainly on weekends. Beyond this are more clothes, the Tin Hau temple (closed at night), household goods, mahjong halls and more food stalls. The market ends at Man Ming Lane, so turn right. Yau Ma Tei MTR is only a block or two away.

This is one of the cheapest places to go shopping but there are many fakes. And remember you get what you pay for. If you buy a winter jacket for $70, don't expect the zippers to last. You can find great bargains here, but check quality carefully. Be careful of pickpockets. Try the food stalls at your own risk. Just point to the displayed item you want.

TIN HAU TEMPLE

Open 8am-6pm. This one-hundred year old temple actually houses four small temples. They are all full of spiral incense. Beware of falling ash. The largest is the Tin Hau temple with gaudily painted figures. The three smaller ones are more traditional and are dedicated to **Kwan Yin** (Goddess of Mercy), **Shing Wong** (City God), and **To Tei** (Earth God). Donations are appreciated.

You enter via a small park full of poor, old and middle-aged men shuffling about and sitting on the pavement playing traditional card games with long, thin, paper cards that resemble dominos. A few men look a little crazed, but seem pretty harmless.

Go to Yau Ma Tei MTR, C-Man Ming Lane exit. Walk right three blocks along Nathan Rd. and turn right on Market St.

JADE MARKET

Open 10am-3:30pm. This covered market has about 450 jade dealers, each with a small table. They sell mainly jade, but also some antiques, jewelry and other stones. It's an interesting place, but unless you know what you're doing, buy for desire, not investment. There are a lot of fakes. Bargain like crazy.

This is where Chinese dealers meet to negociate sales. You might see them touching each other's hands as they communicate prices secretly that way.

Children and old people wear jade as an amulet. If they fall, their jade pendants should break instead of the wearer. Carved jade figures represent many things: dragon-power, deer-wealth and tiger-good fortune. The market is located under the Kansu Street overpass. From the Tin Hau Temple, continue south on Nathan Rd. and turn right at Kansu St.

MONG KOK DISTRICT

This is a fascinating market area. On the streets, you can spot huge brass urns in tea houses, snakes, herbal shops and fortune tellers with tortoise shells. The area's military history is reflected in street names like **Waterloo**, **Nelson**, and **Argyle**. This is one of the most densely populated places on earth.

Go to Mong Kok MTR, take the E-Bank Centre exit. Turn left for the **Ladies Market**, *noon-10:30pm*, or right for the **Bird Market**, *Hong Lok Street*. Walk for one and a half blocks in either direction.

BIRD MARKET

There's every kind of bird in this charming, old, one-lane market; cockatoos, budgies, finches and birds you've probably never seen before. You can also pick up bird food and accessories, such as lovely, carved bamboo cages, porcelain feeders, live crickets and meal worms. There are rumors that this place may be moving.

Birds are the most prized pet in traditional Chinese homes, and are valued for their singing. Men walk their birds (rather than dogs) and show them off in tea shops. Dedicated bird owners feed their feathered friends live grasshoppers with chopsticks.

If you continue straight on Nelson St., past **Shanghai St.** (where there are a few interesting shops that sell traditional red Chinese wedding dresses and incense), you'll arrive at the large, bustling **Mong Kok Market** with live snakes and seafood, some clothes, fruit, flowers and bizarre dried things like sharks' fins and sea horses. You can explore here for hours.

LADIES MARKET

These six blocks of stalls and stores are on **Tung Choi St**. They sell inexpensive, women's, men's and kid's clothing and an unusual amount of skimpy women's underwear. It is open in the afternoon. The prices are a tad higher than elsewhere, but the quality is too.

FOR A QUIET ESCAPE ...

*Okay, you've been through three markets, forgot the time and are now exhausted and can't face the MTR at rush hour. Head for the **Grand Tower Hotel Lobby Bar** (5/F) for a $25 coke, clean bathrooms and a little sanity. It's at 627 Nathan Rd.*

NEW KOWLOON DISTRICT

This is the area north and east of Boundary St. and south of the New Territories. It is made up of a number of different areas, all developed and easily accessible by MTR.

LEI CHENG UK MUSEUM

At 41 Tonkin St, Sham Shui Po, 368-2863. Open 10am-1pm, 2pm-6pm. On Sundays, it's 1pm-6pm. Closed Thursday. Free. This will only interest archaeological types. The museum has a 2,000-year old tomb from the Han dynasty (25-220 AD) that was accidently discovered in 1955, during the construction of the housing estates nearby. The small, domed-brick chamber with three side chambers is protected by glass. The museum displays bronze and pottery found in the tomb and pictures of its excavation. Go to Cheung Sha Wan MTR, turn left on Tonkin and walk 10 minutes.

SUNG DYNASTY VILLAGE

Lai Chi Kok, *741-5111*. This is a charming living museum of China's Sung (Song) Dynasty (960-1279 AD). "Villagers" in costume make incense, umbrellas and candy the old-fashioned way. There is an acrobat show, kung fu display, a traditional wedding, a rich man's manor, tea house, tavern, restaurant and Hong Kong's largest wax museum. Wood carvers from Fujian province helped to build this place in 1979. It is older and more worn than the Middle Kingdom at Ocean Park, but that gives it a more authentic feeling.

The village has four tours daily of about four hours each for $165 (children 3-11 $90). This includes coach service from six hotels. Lunch and dinner cost $75 and $121 more. *For reservations call 741-5111 or contact tour desks in the Kowloon Hotel, the Furama Hotel or the Excelsior.*

WONG TAI SIN TEMPLE

Open 7am-5pm. $1 donation. This is the ultimate temple complex. It is usually full of worshippers, offering fruit and small, red, barbecued pigs. There's over a dozen structures here including the colorful main temple, ancestral and Confucian halls, library and a Buddhist shrine (even though this temple is Taoist).

There's a free herbal medicine clinic, a number of temple stalls selling joss sticks and souvenirs and a fortune-telling hall with over 100 fortune tellers (some speak English). There is also a traditional Chinese garden with pavilions, a waterfall, fish pond and a replica of the famous Nine Dragon screen from the Imperial Palace in Beijing. An additional $2 donation is requested for the garden.

The current temple, built in 1973, replaced one from 1921. The image of Wong Tai Sin was brought from China in 1915. The temple receives three million worshippers a year. Blessed, curative waters run from taps. The soothsayers are famous for making horse racing and other predictions. The temple is surrounded by housing estates. It is right at Wong Tai Sin MTR.

LIE YUE MUN

This is a small seafood village beside the Shau Kei Wan Ferry Pier. Shops are full of tanks of all kinds of live seafood (geoducks, parrot fish, crab, etc). Choose your favorite and have one of the many nice restaurants cook it up. It's best to go with a group. Linda went by herself and although she found one place that would serve just one person, the waiters and the seafood shop owner found the idea hysterically funny. If you want to try it, it's the **Sea King Garden Restaurant** ($90 for a small lobster, $40 to cook).

This is an interesting area for walks. A tiny **Tin Hau Temple** is 10 minutes along the water. The harbor here is at its narrowest; you can get a good look at passing cargo ships and tugboats and the eastern side of Hong Kong island. This is also where the Japanese first invaded Hong Kong Island in World War II. Take a taxi ($11.50) or KMB 14C bus from Lam Tin MTR.

KOWLOON WALLED CITY

There's no real reason for you to go here but you may have heard of its fascinating history. The Chinese never officially handed over this tiny area and a Chinese mandarin governed it until his death. After that China largely ignored it. The Hong Kong police did not like to enter it because they feared China would object. The walled city became a refuge for wanted criminals, drug addicts, illegal businesses and prostitutes. The original walls disappeared in the 1920s and 30-story apartment buildings mushroomed.

Linda visited once, walking through the narrow alleys, across thin boards set over mud, and under a tangle of pipes and electrical wires that blocked out the sun. There was no natural light. The government destroyed the city in the 1980s and in its place is building a park with a traditional Chinese garden. It should be finished in 1996.

LION ROCK COUNTRY PARK

In the hills that separate Kowloon and the New Territories, the 3.2-kilometer **Nest Nature Trail** begins near the **Kowloon Hills Country Park Management Centre**. You can sometimes see wild monkeys here. It is next to **Kam Shan Country Park**.

KAM SHAN COUNTRY PARK

Long-tailed macaque monkeys live in its **Monkey Hills** and a 6.4 kilometer trail (section six of the **Maclehose Trail**) ends near World War II fortifications. Take KMB bus 81 from Jordan Ferry. Contact HKTA for more detailed directions.

NEW TERRITORIES

This is a different Hong Kong. The British leased it in 1898 for 99 years. You can do a lot of great things out here: hike, climb deserted mountains, soak in panoramas of the sea, visit monasteries, temples, museums and historical buildings. They're almost all free!! We have divided up the New Territories into three parts, according to the train lines.

NEW TERRITORIES HIGHLIGHTS

*The highlights are the temple complex, monastery and walled village near Tsuen Wan MTR station. On the KCR you have to stop at **10,000 Buddha Monastery** in Sha Tin. And we highly recommend that you head to the LRT for the **Ping Shan Heritage Trail**, the **Ching Chung Koon** temple complex and **Mui Fat Monastery**.*

There are a lot of country parks in the New Territories. The 100-kilometer **Maclehose hiking trail** runs through eight of them, from **Sai Kung** to **Tai Lam Country Park** which stretches to **Tuen Mun**. This winds through rural areas where people live as they have for hundreds of years. The lifestyle is changing quickly as huge housing projects shoot up and industries move in. Go now before it completely disappears. Most of the areas along the train routes are already built up. If you want to see rice fields, go to Kam Tin, eight minutes from Yuen Long LRT, and walk.

HKTA's **Land Between Tour** is the fastest and most convenient way to see this area. See Chapter 7. Sha Tin has two good hotels. See "Where to Stay". Buses mentioned here cost between $2-$6. Green New Territories taxis are cheaper than red ones from Kowloon, but cannot go out of the territories.

Five clans settled this area, led by the Tang in Kam Tin in the tenth century. The Hau in Sheung Shui and the Pang in Fanling arrived in the 1100s. In the 14th and 15th centuries, the Liu came to Sheung Shui and the Man to San Tin.

ALONG THE TSUEN WAN MTR LINE

Tsuen Wan means shallow bay. Originally the site of a few Hakka villages, today developers have filled in the bay and covered it with large residential and industrial projects. The population is around one million. Tsuen Wan is the last station on the red MTR line (only 25 minutes from Tsim Sha Tsui) and has a charming, restored walled village, a monastery and a temple complex.

In the city itself, on the way to the **Tsuen Wan Ferry Pier** (follow the signs) are noodle shops, **Tsuen Wan Town Hall** and a shopping mall. Most maxicabs (minibuses) are at **Shui Wo St**. To get there, take exit B (from Tsuen Wan MTR), turn left at the carpark building (you can get taxis below), turn right and cross the six-lane road. Go down the stairs at the next road.

SAM TUNG UK MUSEUM

Open 9am-4pm and closed on Tuesday. Free. Come and explore this simple, whitewashed, walled village and step back two hundred years. Peek into the ancestral hall, three furnished traditional houses, a display hall and a changing exhibition hall. The Chan clan founded the village in 1786 and sold it to the government in 1981. It was declared a historical monument and opened in 1987. Go to Tsuen Wan MTR station. Take exit B and walk left five minutes.

CHUK LAM SHIM YUEN

(1927, aka **Fu Yong Shan and Bamboo Monastery**) This small, charming temple complex includes a Thai-style four-faced Buddha shrine, two large temples (one with the three large, gold, Precious Buddha statues) and a tiny, miniature landscape populated by statues of Kwan Yin, the goddess of mercy and friends. Try to land a coin in the center house for luck. In the smaller temple behind, you could find Buddhist nuns kneeling and chanting. Please do not disturb. Unusual is the proliferation of gaudy art-deco chandeliers.

The monastery is a short cab ride or twenty minutes walk up hill from Tsuen Wan MTR. Take exit A, sharp right and walk down to the walkway over the MTR tracks. Cross it, follow the cement path straight, turn right, cross the road, go up the stairs and follow the main road up. You can also take maxicab 85 from Shiu Wo St.

YUEN YUEN INSTITUTE

This spectacular temple complex is dedicated to Buddhism, Taoism, and Confucianism. Set on a hill, it is away from the bustle of the city and is full of ornate, decorated buildings. Two unusual, modern versions of the Chinese stone lion guard the main circular temple. On the ground floor, 58 fascinating, painted, male statues, each with a different face and antique costume (mostly warriors and scholars) line the walls. The upper floor has lovely, intricately-carved gilded altars. There are also a few ponds with turtles, fish and ducks. Mourners burn paper cars and houses for the use of the dead in the large brick incinerator near the ancestral hall.

A smaller monastery is next door. The Institute is a 15-minute taxi ride from Tsuen Wan MTR or maxicab 81-Lo Wai Village ($3) from Shui Wo St.

TAI MO SHAN COUNTRY PARK

Tai Mo Shan (*Big Misty Mountain*) is Hong Kong's highest mountain at 958 meters. Across the road from the entrance of Tai Mo Shan is the entrance to **Tai Lam Chung Country Park**. This large country park stretches almost to Tuen Mun and includes Tai Lam Chung Reservoir, built in 1952. Take bus 51-Kam Tin from Tsuen Wan Ferry Pier and walk up a few minutes from the village of Chuen Long. The signs for both parks face each other across the road.

SHING MUN COUNTRY PARK

This park contains one of Hong Kong's oldest reservoirs (1936), abandoned lead mines and World War II fortifications around Smuggler's Ridge (unsafe, do not enter). A museum is in the visitors' center. You can walk via **Lead Mine Pass** to **Tai Po Kau Nature Reserve** or **Tai Mo Shan Park**. Take maxicab 82-Jubilee Reservoir from Shui Wo St. or a 20-minute taxi ride. You can also walk from Sha Tin KCR station.

SAI KUNG PENINSULA

This beautiful area in the eastern New Territories has wild grass lands and dramatic seascapes. Take bus 92, 40 minutes from Choi Hung MTR,

Ngau Chi Wan Civic Centre exit. It leaves every 15 minutes and passes Hebe Haven, an upscale housing and marina area. Go to the end of the line at **Sai Kung Village** where you can find a Tin Hau temple and seafood restaurants in this former fishing community.

SAI KUNG COUNTRY PARK

Open 9:30am-4:30pm, closed Tuesday, and is free. Closing off the two ends of the channel that separated High Island from the mainland and replacing the sea water with fresh created the High Island Reservoir. The **Visitor Centre** displays the history of the peninsula and has hiking trail leaflets.

Pick up a leaflet about the 30-minute **Pak Tam Chung Nature Trail** which teaches you about ancient village life. See a lime kiln and **Sheung Yiu Folk Museum**, *open 9am-4pm, and closed Tuesday and Chinese New Year. 792-6365. Free.* This former Hakka village has traditional furniture and exhibits. Like many New Territories' villages, this one was deserted in the 1800s, after the young men of the town went off to England to open Chinese restaurants.

Take the hourly 94-Wong Shek Pier bus from Sai Kung bus stop, 20 minutes to Pak Tam Chung.

CLEAR WATER BAY PENINSULA

This hilly area is rapidly becoming home to wealthy commuters. It has good beaches, a country club and a Tin Hau Temple. Take 91 bus (45 minutes) from Choi Hung MTR (Ngau Chi Wan Civic Centre exit). It leaves every 15 minutes.

CLEAR WATER BAY SECOND BEACH

This nice, large beach has changing rooms, lifeguards, snack bars and rowing boats in the summer.

CLEAR WATER BAY COUNTRY PARK

It's a 30-minute walk through this park, over Junk Peak to **Clear Water Bay Golf and Country Club**. You can visit the club with HKTA's Sports and Recreation Tour. Direction signs at the club's entrance point to the Tin Hau Temple.

TIN HAU TEMPLE IN JOSS HOUSE BAY

This medium-sized temple dedicated to the Taoist sea goddess Tin Hau hasn't had much luck with the elements. Two shipwrecked brothers, who attributed their survival to the Tin Hau statue they carried, built the original temple in 1012. A typhoon later destroyed it. Descendants of the brothers rebuilt it in 1266 at its present site. Typhoon Wanda badly damaged it and it was restored in 1962. It comes alive on Tin Hau's birthday when sea-faring worshippers pack the place for the colorful ceremony and fill the bay here with fishing boats bedecked with flags and lion dancers. The boats circle three times in homage. A path up hill, on the right side of the temple, leads to an 108-character glass-protected rock inscription from 1274 AD.

Walk from the Country Club or 25 minutes along Tai O Mun Rd. from Clearwater Bay Bus Terminus.

ALONG THE KCR LINE

The KCR is almost identical to the MTR and has only one line (see Transportation). Take the MTR to Kowloon Tong and switch to the KCR.

SHA TIN DISTRICT

There's a lot to see and do around here and it's only 30 minutes from Tsim Sha Tsui. The most famous and best attraction is the **10,000 Buddhas**. Nearby is the large **New Town Plaza** (a shopping center with an electronic, musical fountain) and the lovely riverside **Sha Tin Central Park**, about a 10-minute walk from the MTR station. The population of this well-developed area is 700,000 and growing. *Sha Tin* means sandy plain and used to be a rice growing area.

10,000 BUDDHAS MONASTERY

(Shatin KCR) Actually there are 12,800 small, individual Buddha statues in the large temple. Someone has colorfully painted the nine-story pink pagoda, statues of **Tin Hau**, 18 of Buddha's followers and a large green dog. There are three smaller temples above. The one on the right contains the body of the founder, a monk named **Yuet Kai** who died at age 87 in 1966. He's encased in gold leaf, sits in a glass case and appreciates donations. This is a 20-minute climb above the Sha Tin KCR station.

To get to the monastery, take the left exit from the Sha Tin station, turn left and follow signs past the district map and the red and white buildings of Po Fook Ancestral Hall, and through a squatter village (five-minute walk). Then climb up about 400 steps. There is a drink stand at the top. The District Map Board shows seven walks from 1.1-5.3 kilometers long to **Shing Mun Country Park** and **Jubilee Reservoir**.

On the main road on the way to the monastery you will pass **Po Fook Ancestral Worship Hall**. This complex of buildings on the hill is a modern Chinese cemetery. Only 20 steps up from the main entrance is a little pond with symbolic fish and turtles. However, it's 200 steps to the tasteful temple with three large, gold Buddhas, a small courtyard and a pagoda.

Beyond that are simple ancestral halls and buildings with little cubby holes for human remains. You cannot climb on to the 10,000 Buddha Monastery from here.

CHE KUNG TEMPLE

This large, white building with a black-tile roof is surprisingly simple and houses a large (seven meter) fierce-looking statue of **Che Kung**. He was a Sung dynasty (960-1279 AD) general who appeared to a villager in a dream during a plague which soon ended. In gratitude, the villager built a temple. Peddlers aggressively sell red paper blessings outside. Don't take one unless you agree on the price beforehand (usually $1-$2).

The temple is an eight-minute walk from Tai Wai KCR. If you continue along Che Kung Miu Rd. three minutes, you'll find a gate with a swastika (a Buddhist good luck symbol) above it. Beyond is a **Four-faced Buddha Shrine** and a small temple with many small gold buddhas. Do not enter wearing shoes.

TSANG TAI UK WALLED VILLAGE

(aka **Tsang's Big House**) This large, gray-brick, walled village has four corner watch towers crowned with tridents to keep away evil spirits. A group of Hakkas built it in the mid-1800s. There are some deteriorating carved lintels and paintings in the ancestral hall. The village is still inhabited. Please respect "Private no entry" signs. One of the most authentic of the walled villages, there are a few modern additions. Although the villagers were very nice, Linda still felt she was intruding.

From the Four-Faced Buddha Shrine, continue along Che Kung Miu Rd. for fifteen minutes. Walk under the first road, over the second and turn right on Sha Kok St. The village is down the road on the right.

SHA TIN RACECOURSE

This racecourse is newer and larger than its Happy Valley counterpart. It has room for 70,000 spectators and cost $60 million to build. All of Hong Kong's racehorses are kept here in three-story, air-conditioned, "apartment" buildings. Special KCR trains on racedays stop at Fo Tan station.

The main non-racing attraction here is Penfold Park (695-6189) in the middle of the race course. This lovely, well-landscaped park has large grassy areas (rare in Hong Kong), three artificial ponds with fountains, ducks, geese and the occasional swan, a small aviary, peacocks, a marble statue of three nude women and a refreshment stand. It is open 9:30am to 30 minutes before sunset and is closed Monday and racedays.

From Tai Wai KCR walk five minutes to Jubilee Garden (the first building on the right). Take the second entrance and follow the walkway between blocks 1 and 2 and follow the signs. You may feel a little uncomfortable on your own, because the walkways and the park are sometimes deserted.

CHINESE UNIVERSITY ART GALLERY

Open 10am-4:30pm, Sunday 12:30pm-4:30pm. Free. 695-2218. This medium-sized, modern museum has a large collection of Chinese paintings, calligraphy, bronze seals and jade flower carvings. When Linda saw it, there was a visiting Japanese treasures exhibit. Take the free shuttle bus from University KCR station. Seven minutes later get off at stop number 3. It takes longer to get back.

TAI PO

This was originally a Tanka village. A thousand years ago the natives were forced to become pearl fishermen and an imperial garrison was later established to keep an eye on them. Eventually they fished out all the pearls and the Tang clan became dominant. Today Tai Po is a well-developed town.

HONG KONG RAILWAY MUSEUM

Open 9am-4pm and closed Tuesday. Free. Located in the traditional Chinese Tai Po Market railway station built in 1913, this has a restored waiting room, ticket office and a history of Hong Kong's railway in photographs. You can climb on two old circa-1911 coaches. Take a taxi from Tai Po Market KCR or walk about 10 minutes.

MAN MO TEMPLE

This modest 100-year-old temple (renovated in 1983) is set in bustling Taipo Market and dedicated to the gods of literature and war. Old men play mahjong in the courtyard and throughout the market. Behind the temple is a traditional coffin shop. The ends of the wooden coffins are shaped like four-petalled daisies. The more famous Man Mo Temple is in Western on Hong Kong Island. The recently-restored **Tin Hau Temple** on Ting Kok Rd. is across the river. Take a taxi from Tai Po KCR station to Man Mo or the Railway Museum or walk 20 minutes.

PLOVER COVE RESERVOIR

This 12-square kilometer, man-made lake has a water sports center, park, youth hostels and nature trails. The main dam took seven years and was completed in 1967. Walk up Bride's Pool Road to **Tai Mei Tuk**

Visitors' Centre. Bride's Pool Waterfalls, two sets of small waterfalls set in the woods, is on the same road. The legend goes that bearers accidently dropped a sedan-chair-borne bride into the pool and she drowned. She became immortal and made the pool her home. She uses the waterfall as a mirror for brushing her hair. Take bus 75K-Tai Mei Tuk from Tai Po KCR.

FANLING DISTRICT

This district is in the center of the New Territories. There is not much here except the traditional **Luen Wo Market** which sells mainly food (five minutes by taxi or 78K bus from Fanling KCR, open 10:30am-noon), the **Royal Hong Kong Golf Club** a five-minute taxi ride from the KCR (See Sports-Golf) and the **Tang Chung Ling Ancestral Hall**. This large, basic hall dates from around 1525 but has been restored many times. Take a taxi or 54K minibus, 10-15 minutes from the KCR. The hall is on your right. A temple is across from the KCR station.

SHEUNG SHUI DISTRICT
LOK MA CHAU LOOKOUT POINT

People used to go here to look at China, when China was closed. You can see the skyscrapers of Shenzhen, China's most successful economic zone. Few people go here now, but it still has restrooms and a souvenir stall with a pest of a peddler. It is a 10-minute taxi ride from Sheung Shui KCR or a 30-minute walk from the Lok Ma Chau Rd. and Castle Peak Road junction reached by bus 76K-Sheung Shui from Yuen Long.

LIU MAN SHEK TONG ANCESTRAL HALL

This basic, worn ancestral hall is the main hall of the Liu clan. It was built in 1751 and restored in 1985 and is open only to the Hong Kong Tourist Association (HKTA) Heritage Tour.

SAN TIN

The Man clan settled here in the early 15th century.

TAI FU TAI

(Important Person's House, 1865) Step into this lovely, old home and into the past. Admire the family portraits and the rich blackwood furniture in the Main Hall. Peek into the old bathroom and the kitchen, which has nine separate stoves, because the eight daughters-in-laws and the wife didn't get along (and you thought you had problems!) Doors are decorated with painted wood carvings, walls with plaster moldings and the front of the house with a border of ceramic figures. Can you find the European influences? The original owner was surnamed Man, a mandarin of the seventh rank and a trader. The Man family has lived here since the 1400s and still owns a number of old buildings nearby.

Aside from the HKTA Heritage tour, you can also get here by taxi from Sheung Shui KCR or the 76K-Yuen Long bus from Sheung Shui Bus Terminus. Tai Fu Tai is open 9am-1pm and 2pm-5pm and closed Tuesday.

MAN LUNG FUNG ANCESTRAL HALL

This simple, worn ancestral hall was built in the late 1600s by the Man Clan. It is a short walk from Tai Fu Tai.

ALONG THE LRT

The **LRT** (**Light Rail Transit**) operates in the far western side of the New Territories, beginning in Tuen Mun and ending at Yuen Long. It is only 40 minutes from Central by hoverferry, but this wonderful area is too often overlooked.

HIGHLIGHTS ALONG THE LRT

*Ching Chung Temple, Mui Fat Monastery, and the fabulous **Ping Shan Heritage Trail**. This trail is only a kilometer long and passes by two temples, **Kun Ting Study Hall**, two large ancestral halls, a walled village and Hong Kong's only ancient pagoda. It is an excellent introduction to ancient Chinese culture.*

You can cover all three highlights in one day. Start at Ping Shan (30 minutes from Tuen Mun), then Miu Fat and Ching Chung.

USING THE LRT

This train system is very similar to the MTR and KCR and equally easy to use. It has short, above-ground trains that run on a web of seven, often-overlapping routes. Admission is based on the honor system. You buy a paper ticket from a machine and hop on. Hold on to your ticket because there are random checks. You can change routes, as long as it is in the same direction within two hours. Prices range from $3-4.30, less for children 3-11 and seniors over 65. Machines give change for coins. Trains run from 6am-midnight, every 6-12 minutes.

*The small, orange and white booth at Tuen Mun ferry is the **LRT Customer Services Centre**. You can get a free LRT map and advice here. An LRT map is also included in the MTR/KCR Tourist Guide, free at all MTR, KCR and LRT stations. The LRT Enquiry Hotline is 468-7788.*

TUEN MUN

(**Channel Gate**) This used be an imperial outpost. It briefly was occupied by the Portuguese long before the arrival of the British. Today it is one of the rapidly growing new towns. To get here, take a hovercraft from the Outlying Ferry Pier. It costs $12-15 and leaves every 15 minutes. The trip through the harbor and past the islands takes about 40 minutes. If you get seasick very easily, don't take the ferry on a rough day; instead take bus 59M from Tsuen Wan MTR (40 minutes).

TUEN MUN TOWN PLAZA

Go to Town Centre LRT about 10 minutes by LRT from Tuen Mun. As you climb up from the platform, Tuen Mun Town Plaza is on your right after Trend Plaza. It is a large shopping mall with a musical fountain, an ice-skating rink and about 300 shops like Esprit, Yaohan Department Store, and Kentucky Fried Chicken. Tuen Mun Town Park is left. The Park has paddle boats, a cafe and a rollerskating rink.

MUI FAT MONASTERY

From the outside, this looks like a gaudy, five-story Chinese restaurant with two large, gold dragons and stone elephants guarding the entrance. Inside, on the top floor, the temple is amazing. Thousands of tiles with embossed gold buddhas cover the walls.

Three large, gold buddha statues smile benignly between two towers of hundreds of little gold buddhas, under three huge crystal chandeliers. On the ceiling are scenes from the life of Buddha in Thai-style and below in Chinese style, with English captions. Behind the main altar are ancestral tablets and a many-armed buddha. The temple faces a charming, little grotto with a buddha behind an artificial waterfall. Some lovely old buildings and a massive banyan tree are nearby.

Take the LRT to Lam Tei station about 22 minutes from Tuen Mun. There's an armchair grave at the station and most nearby buildings are under five stories. Walk out to the main road. The monastery is the gold-roofed building to your left across the road.

CHING CHUNG KOON

(**Green Pine Temple**, 1949) *Open 7am-7pm.* This wonderful Taoist temple complex has hundreds of *penjings* – Chinese bonsais. There is also a temple, two large ancestral halls, a senior citizens' home (the residents survive on temple donations), a delightful ceramic mural and a small, traditional Chinese garden. The garden has a pavilion, crooked bridge, moon gate and pond with traditional turtles and goldfish.

The main **Worship Hall** is incredibly ornate and houses many treasures including a 1,000-year-old jade seal, lanterns from Beijing's imperial palace and two beautiful, 300-year-old stone carvings of goddesses. The central altar features the striking statue of **Lu Sun Young**. He was born in 798 AD and was one of the eight immortals who helped spread Taoism and rid the world of evil. If you find nuns and monks dressed in yellow, chanting in an ancestral hall with paper cars and houses outside, do not disturb. This is a funeral.

The temple is across the road from Ching Chung LRT station, about five minutes from Lam Tei and 15 minutes from Tuen Muen.

PING SHAN HERITAGE TRAIL

This is a fun, one-hour self-guided tour through Hong Kong's history and it's all free! It passes through some of the oldest buildings: two temples, an old study hall, the largest ancestral hall, a walled village and the only ancient pagoda. The one-kilometer trail winds through several tiny villages. Historical plaques on all the important buildings indicate that the Tang Clan, who came to Ping Shan in the 12th century, built them. You can pick up a free guide to this trail (with histories and map) at HKTA or simply follow the signs and our directions.

Go to Ping Shan LRT station (about 30 minutes from Tuen Mun), turn left, walk to Pingha Rd., turn right and walk about 15 minutes. The first stop is the small **Hung Shing Temple** on the right side of the tiny Hang Mei Village Park. The temple was built in 1767, rebuilt in 1866 and renovated in 1963. Hung Shing was a Tang dynasty official who used astronomy to predict the weather. He is worshipped by fisher folk.

Continue along Pingha Rd., about two minutes and turn right to the **Kun Ting Study Hall**. This beautiful building is decorated inside and out and was built in 1870 and restored in 1991. The study hall has an ancient desk and chairs, a 100-year-old book, an ancestral hall, wall paintings and lovely painted and carved doors. Scholars prepared here for the imperial examinations to become mandarins or representatives of the emperor. Next door is the attached **Ching Shu Hin**, a richly-decorated guest house for visitors built in 1870. Restoration work began in 1993.

Continue on the same path for a few minutes to the main **Tang Ancestral Hall** of the Tang clan. Built some 700 years ago, it is still used today. The Tangs renovated the hall in 1990-91. Next door is the **Yu Kiu Ancestral Hall** which functioned as a school in the early 1900s. It was built in the 1500s and renovated in the late 1800s.

Keep on the path until it splits. Continue straight for the small, old **Yeung Hau Temple** (aka **Hau Wong**) and left for the **Old Well**, believed to be about 200 years old.

From the Old Well, go straight to **Sheung Cheung Wai**, a 200-year-old walled village on your right. Some of the houses have been replaced by modern ones. A few steps beyond (bear left) is the **Shrine of the Earth God**, represented by two stones on a simple brick altar. Continue along the path five minutes to **Tsui Shing Lau** (Pagoda of the Many Stars). This small, three-story pagoda was built in the 1300s. A typhoon probably destroyed its top four stories a long time ago.

This is the end of the trail. If you don't want to backtrack all the way, you can walk back two minutes to the road going up, on your right (before the pond), turn left and walk to the Hang Mei Tsuen LRT station.

YUEN LONG TOWN PARK

This large park has a nine-story modern pagoda on a hill. The ground floor is a small walk-in aviary with 54 species of South East Asian birds. You can climb up the inside of the pagoda for a great view of Yuen Long. Go to Shui Pin Wai LRT.

YUEN LONG

This built-up town at the end of the LRT line has a small, old **Yeung Hau Temple**. It is dedicated to Hau Wong. *For more information pick up a brochure at the Antiquities and Monuments Office, 136 Nathan Rd., Tsim Sha Tsui.*

KAT HING WAI

This is the most famous and touristy of the walled villages although a lot of the buildings have been modernized. Old women in Hakka hats sell souvenirs and pose for pictures. Settle on a price first. This village was built in the 1600s and is in Kam Tin. The distinctive iron chain link gates were taken by a governor to Ireland in 1898 but were returned to the village in 1925. Two other walled villages are in the area, but they are more modern. The area around nearby Shui Tau is more interesting.

If you have the energy and time, walk out of the village, turn left, walk along the road five minutes and turn right before the school. This is a delightful area to explore. There's old houses, garden plots, a duck pond and a nearby "tree house" (Shu Uk), an ancient house that has been taken over and in some areas replaced by the roots of a great tree. Beyond this are rice fields, vegetable plots and Shui Tau, a fascinating village area with lots of ancient buildings dating from the 17th to 19th centuries.

This area is not set up for tourists.

To get to Kat Hing Wai, go to Yuen Long LRT, take the exit to the left of the train (not to the bus terminus) and cross the street to Long Yat Rd. bus stop. Take bus 54, 64K or 77K about 10 minutes. On your right you'll see the tall, grey brick walls, crowned by short, square watch towers on the four corners. This is Kat Hing Wai. Pay $1 donation to enter. You can also take bus 51 from Tsuen Wan Ferry Pier (50 minutes).

KADOORIE EXPERIMENTAL FARM

Lam Kam Rd, 488-1317. (1951) Terraces of experimental crops, trees and livestock climb the slopes of **Tai Mo Shan**. Call for an appointment two days in advance.

ISLANDS

You will find small fishing villages, white sand beaches, parks, temples and monasteries. There are bare hills with great views, no cars, a slower pace and much to appreciate on the outlying islands. Hong Kong has 235 of them. Most are small and uninhabited. Others are more interesting, especially Lantau, Lamma and Cheung Chau. Locals go there to get away from the city and go to the beach. During weekends, the islands are packed and ferries, buses and hotels cost as much as 100% more.

If you only have time for one, **Cheung Chau** is the best and has good seafood, **Lamma** is the closest, and **Lantau** is the biggest with 144 square kilometers, the best beaches and big buddha. The best hotel is on Cheung Chau and there is an adequate one on Lantau.

Lantau is the only island that allows cars and you need a special permit for one. Many commuters live here to get away from the pollution and high rents. The ferry trip can be a highlight. In the harbor, you can see massive cargo ships, tugboats, luxury yachts, small fishing boats, jetfoils, sea birds and occasionally an American aircraft carrier or submarine.

Hoverferries are faster, but leave less frequently and their windows get covered in mist. Most normal ferries have a more expensive first class on the top floor. There are a few ferries that run from Peng Chau to Mui Wo (Lantau) to Cheung Chau.

All ferries except one leave from the Outlying Districts Services Pier, which is a five-minute walk to your right, along the water, as you leave the Star Ferry in Central. They cost between $5-$15. *For ferry schedules visit or call a Hong Kong Tourist Association (HKTA) office (801-7177) or the ferry company at 542-3081.* We have included some times here for reference, but they are always changing.

LANTAU ISLAND

Lantau or *Tai Yue Shan* in Chinese, is twice the size of Hong Kong, but only has a population of about 30,000. While Hong Kong has more people than trees, Lantau has more trees than people.

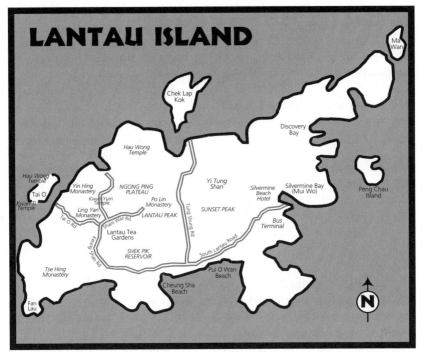

There are lots of monasteries, nice beaches and the world's largest outdoor buddha. Lantau is more than 50% parkland and 70 kilometers of paved trails runs through it. This is also the site for the new airport. If you want to hike, get a detailed map from HKTA or the Government Publication Office.

To get to Lantau, take the hourly ferry (from 8:30am-11:10pm, $7 for ordinary/deluxe classes) from the Outlying Districts Services Pier to Mui Wo (Silvermine Bay). It takes about one and a quarter hours; some go via Peng Chau. Hoverferrries take 35 minutes and leave every 2-3 hours. Buses and taxis wait for the ferries. Lantau taxis are the cheapest in Hong Kong and cost $8 for the first two kilometers. Air-conditioned coaches cost more than regular buses. Call the Lantao Island Bus Company (984-8361) for exact schedules. All of the places mentioned below except for Discovery Bay and the Trappist Monastery can be reached by bus from Mui Wo.

MUI WO

(aka **Silver Mine Bay**) This town is named after the two abandoned silver mines nearby. The silver was poor quality. As you leave the ferry, to your right is the orange and white **Silver Mine Beach Hotel**. You can rent bicycles in front for $10/hour. The beach is polluted.

CHEUNG SHA AND PUI O BEACHES

These two adjacent beaches are 3.2 kilometers of white sand and are pretty clean. Both have lifeguards, changing rooms and refreshment stands. Take bus 2 or 4 from Mui Wo about 15 minutes.

NGONG PING PLATEAU

This is an interesting area, but it's very touristy even on weekdays. Most people come here to see the world's biggest outdoor bronze Buddha. It's 34 meters high and weighs 250 metric tons. It was unveiled in December 1993 and has six much smaller bronze statues of goddesses around it. You climb 250 steps up to the **Big Buddha** who sits on a lotus and belongs to **Po Lin Monastery**. Three monks objecting to Manchu rule in China started this monastery in 1905, the biggest in Hong Kong.

Nearby are the **Lantau Tea Gardens** where you can ride horses, go roller skating or stop at the tea house. They also rent small, air-conditioned, double rooms for $150-190.

Feel like walking? From the Gardens you can follow the signs up to Pa Lam Zen Monastery and the Youth Hostel or walk down two hours to Tung Chung. From Po Lin you can walk one hour to Yin Hing Monastery, via Kwun Yum Temple (see map) or 3-5 hours to Tai O. The HKTA *The Lantau Island Explorer's Guide* ($25) shows you how. You can hike up to Lantau Peak, 934 meters above sea level, Hong Kong's second highest.

On the way to the monastery you will pass **Shek Pik Reservoir** on your right where 6500-year-old pottery has been found. To your left are a maximum security prison and a simple, ancient rock carving. From Shek Pik Reservoir, you can walk two hours to the 18th century **Fan Lau Fort**, a simple structure with a nearby Tin Hau Temple. *For more information, pick up a pamphlet at the Antiquities and Monuments Office, 136 Nathan Rd, Tsim Sha Tsui. Bus 2 runs every hour between 8:20am-6:35pm and costs $8.50, $14.50 on weekends. There are also organized tours.*

TAI O

This large, slightly grubby, fishing village has houses on stilts and has been dubbed Little Venice. It is inhabited mainly by about 6,000 Tanka people, most old. The young people have left. It once attracted pirates who were forced away by the British. It is known for its salted fish. On weekends there's irregular ferry service from Central.

Take a hand-drawn ferry to the island which has two temples and lots of quaint stores. Walk straight, turn right at the second road (Kat Hing Back St). On your left is the small **Kwan Ti Temple**, dedicated to the God of War and Righteousness. It was built in the Ching Dynasty (1644-1911) and has been renovated a lot. A bronze bell from 1793 and statues of Kwan

Ti's and his emperor's horses, Wah To (physician god) left, and Choi San (god of wealth) all inhabit this temple. Further along the same road (bear right at the pond) is the **Hau Wong Temple** which was built in 1699. It has a shrine to the Earth God inside. Outside of the village is an 80-year-old **Kwan Yin Temple,** which was reopened in 1993. Look for restaurants serving snakes.

Take bus #1 to Tai O. It runs every half hour between 6am and 12:30am.

TUNG CHUNG

This is where the last Sung boy emperor stayed with his court. The continually, controversial new airport is being built on the island of **Chek Lap Kok**, opposite **Tung Chung Village**.

The main attraction here is **Tung Chung Fort** (1817). It was built as a defense against coastal pirates and to stop European opium traders. It now houses a primary school and six cannons from 1805. From here you can walk down to the **Hau Wong Temple**. The ruins of **Tung Chung Battery** (1817) are on a hill above the bus terminal. The L-shaped wall of rubble was found in 1980. You can pick up a pamplet about Tung Chung from the Antiquities and Monuments office in Tsim Sha Tsui.

Take the hourly #3 bus from Mui Wo about 45 minutes to Tung Chung. It runs from 9:30am-4:30pm. The last bus from Tung Chung is at 7:15pm. Taxis are rare.

TRAPPIST MONASTERY

This is a pretty, quiet place. The monks have taken a vow of silence. The Trappists were established in the 1600s and are one of the strictest Roman Catholic orders. Take a kaido, a motorized boat, 15 minutes from Peng Chau Island and follow the 14 stations of the cross up hill. You can also walk 45 minutes from Discovery Bay or an hour from Silver Mine Bay. If you want to walk to Discovery Bay, take the path right at the 5th station of the cross as you go up hill.

DISCOVERY BAY WALK

This is a community/residential area with 40% expatriates that is growing like mad. It has a McDonald's, a bar, a 7-11, a good Korean restaurant and the Discovery Bay Golf Course. It is not yet connected by road to the rest of Lantau. Fast ferries leave every 20-30 minutes (less frequently between midnight and 6:30am) from the Star Ferry Pier in Central, cost $22 and take 30 minutes. Follow the crowd quickly from the ferry to the bus stop. Take a #4 bus about two stops to just past the International School. Walk back past the school and head uphill at the stone stairs. Climb up about 20-30 minutes past the path to the left. A second path goes to the left and ultimately to a pavilion with direction posts. This is one of Ruth's favorite hikes because of the great views of the ships, Hong Kong, the Disco Bay ferry pier and the beautiful buildings. Five ferries ply daily between Discovery Bay and Mui Wo.

LAMMA ISLAND

This is the closest and third largest island (13.5 square kilometers) after Hong Kong and Lantau. It has seafood restaurants, good beaches, a population of 3,000 and no cars. Neolithic settlements have been found here. There is a popular walk (one hour and a half) on a concrete path across the island from Sok Kwu Wan to Yung Shue Wan, passing by two good beaches, that both have lifeguards and changing rooms. Unfortunately, there is trash along the trail. A lot of expats have moved to Lamma because it's a lot cheaper than Hong Kong. Take the ferry to either Yung Shue Wan or Sok Kwu Wan.

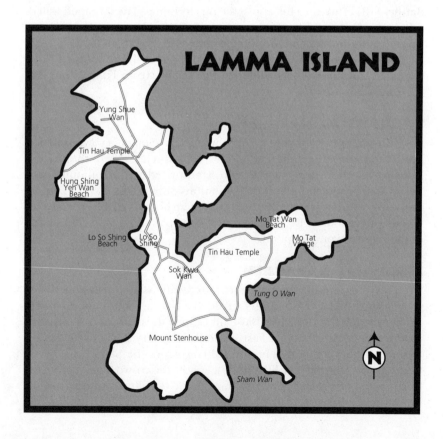

YUNG SHUE WAN

(**Banyan Bay**) This is Lamma's main town. It has traditional stores (incense, candles, dried fish, herbs) and bicycle rentals off Main St. on the way to Hung Shing Ye beach. On Main St. you can find some good seafood restaurants and at the end, the small, hundred-year-old **Tin Hau Temple**. Granite lions guard the entrance. The statue of Tin Hau is in the center, with To Tei, the city god left, and Muen Kuen who guards against evil on the right.

A little further is a shrine to the **Three Mountain Kingdom King**, a local god. **Hung Shing Yeh Wan Beach** is a 25-minute walk. The ferry leaves every 1-2 hours, between 6:50am-10:35pm and takes 45 minutes.

SOK KWU WAN

(**Picnic Bay**) This town is famous for its seafood restaurants along the waterfront. The bay is full of floating fish farms. There's also a **Tin Hau Temple** and the nearby **Lo So Shing beach**. You can walk 25 minutes or take a kaido to the good **Mo Tat Wan Beach**, which has a 400-year-old village behind. It takes about an hour to struggle up **Mt. Stenhouse** (353 meters). The ferry takes 50 minutes and runs every 2-5 hours, between 8am-10pm. There are eight ferries a day from Aberdeen, a 30-minute ride.

CHEUNG CHAU ISLAND

(**Long Island**) This small island, a former pirate base, is only 2.4 square kilometers. It is one of the most crowded with a population of 30,000, many of them commuters. However, it still has a fishing village atmosphere and traditional shops. Cheung Chau has some great seafood restaurants, ship building (junks), fish processing, two beaches, walks and bicycles for rent. Some people still live on boats in Sai Wan. An easy family trail, 2 and 1/2 miles long passes traditional Chinese shops; jade, gold and porcelain. Pick up the *Cheung Chau Walking Tour* book ($25) at HKTA.

To get to Cheung Chau, take the hourly ferry from the Outlying Districts Services Pier. The ferry takes one hour and runs from 6:25am-11:30pm. The five daily hoverferries take 35 minutes.

If you get to Cheung Chau early, you can visit the **Morning Market** which is busiest around 10:30am and is left from the pier. Continue along the waterfront to the playground. Beyond that is **Pak Tai Temple** (aka **Temple of Jade Vacuity**), the most famous of the island temples – mainly because of the colorful **Bun Festival** that is unique to Cheung Chau. Two granite dragons guard the temple and two others decorate the roof. Inside are a 1,000 year-old sword that was found by a fisherman and images of **Favorable Wind Ear** and **Thousand-Li Eye**, who can hear and see at any distance. The temple was built in 1783.

The Pak Tai image was brought from China in 1777 to drive away the plague. Later, fishermen found a black, wooden Pak Tai image, which is still on the main altar. When a plague hit in the 1800s, they carried the image through the street and it was very effective. This was the beginning of the Bun festival.

Pak Tai means Supreme Emperor of the Dark Heaven. He was a prince who became an immortal and defeated the Demon King and his friends, a tortoise and a serpent. These animals are under the feet of the Pak Tai images. He was also considered a god of sea.

If you walk from the ferry pier straight across the island you will come to **Tung Wan Beach**. This is the most popular beach and has lifeguards. To the right is the Warwick Hotel and underneath it a Bronze Age carving. Past the hotel is **Kwum Yum Wan Beach**, and on a hill behind it is a tiny **Kwum Yum (Kwan Yin) Temple**.

SAI WAN

From the Ferry Pier, take a sampan marked *Sai Wan* (five minutes which runs 7am-8pm. $2 for foreigners) or walk 45 minutes along Sun Hing St. past a Tin Hau Temple. The sampan is more interesting, because in Sai Wan many people still live on boats. From Sai Wan Pier, you can walk right, along the waterfront to another **Tin Hau Temple** or go straight and take a path to **Cheung Po Tsai Cave**.

This cave was probably a hide-out of Po Tsai, a pirate from the 1800s. He commanded 600 junks and 40,000 people and had an English mistress. After he surrendered, he helped the government catch other pirates. The cave is not as impressive as its history. You have to climb down through a narrow crevice. An old lady rents flashlights at the entrance.

You can also go to Sai Wan by walking up **Peak Rd.**, which starts as a lane near the fire station. This Peak, like Victoria Peak on Hong Kong Island, was also under Residence Ordinance. You will pass **Kwun Kung Pavillion** (1973) dedicated to the red-faced god of war and righteousness, and the **Meteorological Station** which has a good view. Then head down past a graveyard, the CARE village and arrive at Sai Wan Pier.

PENG CHAU ISLAND

This tiny island between Lantau and Cheung Chau has several thousand people. Near the pier is the 200-year-old **Tin Hau Temple**. You can also take a kaido to the **Trappist Monastery** on Lantau. The 50-minute ferry from Central to Peng Chau runs hourly from 8:15am-11:30pm. The hoverferry takes 25 minutes.

OTHER ISLANDS

There are a lot of other islands to explore but most of them are difficult to get to, unless you have access to a boat. For more information contact HKTA. **Ping Chau** is almost uninhabited with white sand beaches and an abandoned village. It takes about two hours to get to. There are one or two ferries on Saturday and Sunday ($50-70) return, from Ma Liu Shui, near University KCR, New Territories.

Tung Lung Chau has an early 18th century ruined fort and pre-historic rock carvings. Ferries only run Saturday, Sunday and public holidays from Sai Wan Ho Pier, near Sai Wan Ho MTR, Hong Kong Island. Pick up a pamphlet from the Antiquities and Monuments Office.

15. EXCURSIONS & DAY TRIPS

You've come half way around the world to Hong Kong, but did you know that there are some other wonderful places to visit nearby? **Macau** is only an hour away (see Chapters 16–25). **China** is even closer and you are in an excellent position to visit other countries in Asia.

INTO CHINA

Here you are, less than forty kilometers away from the huge, mysterious land of China. Should you go visit? Definitely! It's easy and prices are cheaper. We recommend at least popping over for a day tour of Shenzhen or Zhongshan. If you have more time you can't miss Beijing and Guilin. If you are of Chinese ancestry, do go to the area where you have roots. Read Ruth's book, *China Guide*, published by Open Road Publishing.

If you don't speak Mandarin Chinese, aren't good at charades, and don't want the hassle of making reservations, take a pre-paid tour. It is possible to make all your own arrangements but make them as soon as possible. Transportation is booked full.

In the pages that follow we've listed some basic information about places in China and how to get there.

LO WU

The border of China at **Lo Wu** is only about 40 minutes or $27 (ordinary class) from Kowloon Tong MTR station by KCR. It runs every 6-10 minutes and you can hop on at any KCR station. However, it's not really worth just going to the border to look, because it is not much different from Hong Kong.

SHENZHEN

There are a lot of fun things to do in **Shenzhen**, about one hour by bus from Hong Kong. We recommend **Splendid China** and the **Folk**

Culture Village because they are uniquely Chinese. Windows on the World is adjacent to both. Be ready for a lot of walking.

Folk Culture Village is about 20 kilometers west of the railway station. Here you can get an introduction to the architecture and culture of many of China's 54 minority groups. Among these are the **Miao** with their incredible embroidery, the former headhunting **Wa**, the Europe-conquering **Mongolians** and the religious **Tibetans**. Real people in their distinct costumes can explain (in Mandarin Chinese) about their own unique customs and pose for photos. You can arrive as late as 4pm. and explore until the 7:30pm parade with its 300 performers, which is not to be missed. Afterwards, you can dine at the **Shenzhen Bay Hotel** or stay overnight. It is a comfortable hotel.

Splendid China, *open 8am-5:30,* is a delight, albeit a static display of over 80 miniatures of China's major tourist attractions. Thousands of tiny ceramic people, each different, in period or ethnic dress and in scale, add liveliness. They include Mongolian wrestlers in their leather vests and baggy pants and emperors paying homage at the temple of Confucius. A lot of walking is involved.

Windows on the World has the likes of the Golden Gate Bridge and Eiffel Tower in miniature. **Safari Park**, in another part of the city, is good for children. This wild animal park at 4pm has a parade of animals and clowns. You take buses through the various habitats. Among the 150 species are pandas, golden monkeys, Asian elephants, red-crested cranes and Asian tigers.

Shekou

In the western part of Shenzhen and about 50 minutes by hovercraft from Hong Kong, you will find the **Terracotta Warriors and Horses Exhibition** from Xi'an. The **Nanhai Hotel** is a good place just to relax and sit around a pool by the sea. Shekou is about 15 km from the Splendid China theme park.

GUANGZHOU

About 182 kilometers from Hong Kong, this is a 3.5 hour non-stop train ride. If you don't have time to see anything else, do see the highly recommended 2000-year old **Han Dynasty Mausoleum Museum** behind the China Hotel on Jiefang Road with its delightful history. Not much further is the **Guangzhou Museum** in the Zhenhai Tower in Yuexiu Park, and in another direction, the nine-story **Flower Pagoda**.

There is also the lovely **Chen Family Temple** with its beautifully-carved stone pillars. It now contains an arts and crafts museum and a display of miniature potted plants. You can also visit **Dr. Sun Yatsen Memorial Hall** and **Guangzhou Zoo** and shop.

ZHONGSHAN

Going to the birthplace of the father of republican China, **Dr. Sun Yat-sen**, gives you an opportunity to see the south China countryside, the land from which the first wave of Chinese immigrants to North American came. Tours go direct or via Macau, which is close to Zhongshan and Zhuhai.

GUILIN

Head here for some of the most specatacular scenery in the world. Guilin is famous for its **Li River** boat trip through incredible mountains which you've probably seen in Chinese landscape paintings. You can relax in this charming little tiny town and walk or bicycle. Hotels are good. One can go to Guilin from Guangzhou by train, but it is the same price as a plane and takes a lot longer.

BEIJING

The capital city is only three hours away by plane and has spectacular monuments. Climb the **Great Wall**, visit the **Ming Tombs** and explore the luxurious **Forbidden City**, home to China's emperors for thousands of years.

GETTING TO CHINA ON A TOUR

Here's a sample of what's available: **Arrow Travel Agency** in the Kowloon Hotel (*734-3823*) has a one-day tour to Splendid China and the China Folk Culture Villages in Shenzhen ($690-750). It also has one-day tours to Guangzhou and Shenzhen ($1075) and to Zhongshan and Macau ($900-915).

China Travel Service (*853-3533*) has lots of tours, from the one-day tours to Shenzhen and Guangzhou to a six-day tour to Guilin and Beijing to an eight-day tour to Tibet. Its four-day land tour to Shenzhen and Guangzhou is a good introduction to south China. CTS also has cycling and scuba tours.

Gray Line Tours has a lot of China tours. **New World Hotel Tour Counter** (*734-6653*) can hook you up with the **Hong Kong Ferry Companies'** one-day tour to Shekou and Guangzhou. It also has three-day tours to Guangzhou-Foshan-Zhaoqing and Guilin and a four-day tour to Beijing. They only need 48 hours advance notice. **The Travel Advisors** (*375-0628*) has a seven-day tour to Beijing and Shanghai for US$459-995.

You can book individual travel and tours through **China Travel Service**, **China International Travel Service**, many Hong Kong travel agents, or directly at the ferry pier in China Hong Kong City, Canton Road, Tsim Sha Tsui. See Travel Agents at the end of this chapter.

We suggest you check the comparative price of booking China tours with your travel agent in North America before you go. It could be cheaper.

GETTING TO CHINA ON YOUR OWN

To Shenzhen by Land and Sea

You can take the train from Kowloon to the Chinese border at Lo Wu, and walk to China, but there could be long lineups in the Customs House. You can obtain entry visas in Shenzhen at the railway station border post between 7:30am and 10pm or in Hong Kong. The border is open from 6am-11pm daily. A good time to leave Kowloon is at 9pm so you can cross the border about 10pm. There are usually no lineups then. Later than that, you run the risk of Chinese border officials being unavailable to grant visas. Another good time to cross the border is early morning before the rush. There are many commuters. Make sure you have a secure hotel booking for late evening arrivals.

Citibus 500 goes from China Hong Kong City in Tsim Sha Tsui, eight times a day with stops at City One Shatin, Sha Tau Koh border point, Shenzhen city, Honey Lake, Shenzhen Bay, Xili Lake and Hot Spring Lake. The last bus returns from Shenzhen Bay to Hong Kong at 17:30, too early alas, for the parade at the Folk Culture village. It costs $75 to $95 each way. 745-8888 or fax 786-5876.

Some hotels like the Shangri-La Shenzhen have their own buses, usually one a day. China Travel Service has a bus to the Shenzhen Bay Hotel from which you can walk to three of the theme parks.

To go to the Shenzhen airport from Hong Kong, there is a ferry from China Hong Kong City Port to Fuyong and then bus.

To Guangzhou and Foshan by Train

A non-stop train leaves the Kowloon Railway Station in Hung Hom (near Tsimshatsui East hotels) daily at 7:50, 8:35, 12:25 and 14:10, and costs $200. One train a day goes directly to Foshan.

By Bus

There are direct express buses from Hong Kong to Foshan, Fuzhou, Haikou, Quanzhou, Xiamen, Shantou, Zhaoqing, and Zhanjiang. From Guangzhou or Shenzhen, you can make train or bus connections with other parts of China.

By Sea

There are many ferries from Hong Kong to various parts of China. Destinations include: Guanghai (Taishan), Guangzhou, Haikou, Ningbo, Sanya, Shanghai, Shantou, Shekou, Shenzhen, Wenzhou, Xiamen,

Zhaoqing, Zhongshan and Zhuhai.

These ferries are not fancy cruise ships. Like Chinese trains, passengers are assigned to cabins if overnight, irrespective of sex. If you object to being the sole woman in a cabin of three men or vice versa, you can try to ask for a change. But such bookings are the custom and we have heard of no problems.

For overnight rides, do take your own towel, mug, soap and snacks in case you don't like the food or the lineups. The top first or second class should have towels and soap.

By Air

Be aware that you have to book flights for individuals at least a month in advance, and several months before holidays and trade fairs. One can easily fly to Beijing (three hours) and Shanghai (two hours) if you want big cities and great monuments. Or take a tour to the colorful minorities outside of Kunming, Guiyang or Nanning. There are also direct flights to Xi'an, the home of the Terracotta Army, and Hangzhou, the city of silk and West Lake. One can even fly directly to Ningbo for a Buddhist pilgrimage. It is close to the island home of the Goddess of Mercy.

AIRLINES

Dragonair and Chinese airlines have regularly scheduled flights which can be booked in North America through Cathay Pacific for Dragonair, and through Air China or China Eastern. Dragonair is the best airline.

China Travel Air Service Hong Kong Limited has chartered flights. If these cannot be booked in North America through your travel agent, try any of the China Travel Service offices in North America (Vancouver 872-8787 or 1-800-663-1126 or San Francisco 398-6627, 1-800-332-2831 or 1-800-553-8764).

Dragonair hopes to include Qingdao and Wuhan in its Hong Kong-China destinations this year. It currently flies to Beijing daily; Changsha 2,5; Chengdu 2,3,7; Dalian 4,6; Guilin daily; Haikou daily; Hangzhou 1,2,3,5,6,7; Kunming 2,4,7; Nanjing 1,2,3,4,6; Ningbo 5,7; Shanghai daily; Tianjin 5; Xiamen daily; Xi'an 3,6. (Monday is 1, Tuesday is 2, etc.)

Chartered flight schedules from Hong Kong booked through Hong Kong travel agents: Beihai (2,6); Changchun (2); Changsha (1,4,6); Chengdu (1,3,4,6); Chongqing (1,2,3,4,6); Guilin (daily); Guiyang (1,5); Haikou (daily); Harbin (1,3); Hefei (1,5); Huangshan (5); Jinan (2,5,7); Lanzhou (2); Luoyang (1,4); Meixian (1,4,5); Nanchang (2,4,5); Nanjing (daily); Nanning (2,5,7); Qingdao (1,2,3,4,6); Taiyuan (2); Wuhan (daily); Zhanjiang (1,3,5); Zhengzhou (3,5,7). Sample Fares in Hong Kong dollars have been one way Guilin $1150; Haikou $1050; Harbin $2520.

Reconfirmations are required for onward or return flights at least 72 hours before scheduled departures for most Chinese destinations.

We recommend that you fly to the interior of China from Hong Kong; in fact, it is the safest way to go. The standard of domestic air travel within China needs a lot of work. In 1993 there were ten hijackings and 1994 has had some accidents. Air safety standards, in short, need a lot of work. If we had a choice, we would fly only from Hong Kong to China's interior. We would plan our China trips to minimize air travel, but we would still go.

For Cheap Air Tickets
Shoestring Travel, *Flat A, 4/F, Alpha House, 27-33 Nathan Road, Tsim Sha Tsui. 723-2306.*

Time Travel, *Block A, 16/F, Chung King Mansion, 40 Nathan Road, Tsim Sha Tsui. 723-9993/366-6222.*

SAMPLE AIRFARES

Here are some examples of return fares from Hong Kong in early 1994. The cheapest airfares are for Taiwan, Japan, Thailand, and the Philippines. You can also get one-way tickets for about 60% of the round trip price and there are some one-way combinations, like Hong Kong-Manila-Bangkok for $1350.

Australia	*$5500*	*Nepal*	*$3200*
Europe	*$5500*	*Singapore*	*$2200*
Japan	*$3750*	*Taiwan*	*$1350*
Korea	*$2300*	*Thailand*	*$1650*
Manila	*$1400*	*US* West Coast	*$5150*
New York	*$6950*	*Vietnam*	*$3050*

VISAS

The cheapest Chinese visas are from the Ministry of Foreign Affairs of the People's Republic of China. 835-3657. The office is in the southwest corner of the China Resources Building, 27 Harbour Rd., Wanchai. It takes two business days to process.

Travel agents can get visas more quickly but they cost more. Be sure to specify how many days you want and then add on some extra days in case you are delayed. Your travel agent can arrange a visa as part of a package tour.

You can get individual visas, especially to Shenzhen, Zhuhai and Haikou on arrival at those cities but these are not good for the rest of China.

IMMUNIZATIONS

None are required for China unless you have been in a cholera or yellow fever area prior to visiting. As a precaution, travel clinics in North America have been recommending immunizations against typhoid, tetanus, polio and Hepatitis A. If you are going to Hainan and areas bordering on Laos, Burma, and Vietnam, consider precautions against malaria.

TRAVELING IN CHINA

Unlike Hong Kong, one should not drink the tap water. Bottled and boiled water is available. The standards of English, efficiency, services, maintenance and cleanliness are lower than Hong Kong's.

Hotels in China run the range from excellent and world class to grubby no-star efforts Hong Kong wouldn't allow. Many of the good ones are joint ventures managed by Hilton, Westin and Shangri-La. Services are slightly behind Hong Kong, but so are the prices. The restaurants are not as varied but the food is almost as good and much cheaper.

Getting travel tickets might be a problem because of language and demand but there are travel agencies to help you. Prices for goods made in China are much cheaper than in Hong Kong but they are harder to find.

Aim for street markets for the best bargains in antiques and clothes – but be careful. China doesn't have anything like the Hong Kong Tourist Association to help travelers and keep merchants honest. Still one should be able to haggle more successfully than in Hong Kong. Start at half the quoted price.

TRAVELING TO OTHER COUNTRIES IN ASIA

Hong Kong is a good place from which to visit other Asian countries. Flight tickets usually cost slightly less than in North America. The best places for vacationers are **Thailand** and the **Philippines**, less than three hours away.

Head to Thailand for exotic hill tribes, ancient Khmer ruins, Buddhist temples and white sand beaches. Popular resort areas are Pukhet and Koh Samui. The Philippines is the cheapest place to visit. It has great diving, waterfalls, volcanos, friendly people and thousands of islands. Just don't spend any time in dirty, polluted, crowded Manila. Resorts are in Boracay and Cebu.

TRAVEL AGENTS

There have been problems with agents ripping off tourists. The most common ploy is to ask for a non-refundable deposit and when you return they say the price of the airline went up. We've never had any problems, but be careful. The following Travel Agencies in Hong Kong have been in business a long time. They will not run off with your money. The English is good. *The South China Morning Post* lists cheap air tickets daily.

China Travel Service and **China International Travel Service** specializes in China but other agencies can book China too. With most you can join a group tour or go individually.

Abercrombie & Kent, *27/F Tai Sang Commercial Bldg., 24-34 Hennessy Rd., Wanchai. 865-7818. Fax 866-0556.* They'll book even obscure, out-of-the-way places in China for small groups.

American Express, *G/F, New World Tower, 16-18 Queen's Rd.C., Central. 844-8668.*

Arrow, *Room 2101 Alexander House Central. 523-7171.*

China International Travel Service, *5/F, Tower II, South Sea Centre, 75 Mody Rd., Tsim Sha Tsui. 721-0388.*

China Travel Service, *4/F, CTS House, 78-83 Connaught Rd. Central. 853-3773, 853-3533. Branches are at 2/F, 77 Queen's Rd. Central. 525-2284; 1/F, Alpha House, 27-33 Nathan Rd. (entrance on Peking Rd.). 721-1331.*This has local tours, day tours to Macau and tours all over China.

Dodwell, *Room 1303, Evergo House 38, Gloucester Rd., Wanchai. 866-6699.* Ask for Isabel Quintos.

Gray Line Tours, *Cheong Hing Bldg. no. 501, 72 Nathan Rd., Tsim Sha Tsui. 723-1808.* They offer local tours and day trips to China and Macau.

Hong Kong China Youth Travel, *Room 606, Wing On House, 71 Des Voeux Rd. Central. 525-9075.*

Hong Kong Student Travel, *Room 1816, National Argyle Centre, Mongkok. 390-0421.*

Hong Kong Four Seas Travel, *102, 12/F Tung Ming Bldg., 40 Des Voeux Rd., Central. 523-2065. Fax 868-4995. They also have offices in Kowloon (722-6112/366-3996/311-1312), Causeway Bay (881-0373) and the New Territories.* Four Seas can get cheap airplane tickets.

Hong Kong Student Travel Bureau, *10/F, Rm 1021, Star House, Tsim Sha Tsui. 730-3269.*

International Tourism, *M/F, Flat B, Cheong Tai Comm. Bldg., 60-66, Wing Lok St., Hong Kong. 541-2011/3.* Tours to Macau and day tours to China.

Moon Skystar Ltd., *Chung King Mansion, Nathan Rd., 136-44, E-block, 4/F, Flat 6, Tsim Sha Tsui. 723-1376. Fax 723-6653,* can book the trans-Siberian train.

Thomas Cook, *18/F, Vicwood Plaza, 199 Des Voeux Rd. Central. 545-4399.*

Travel Advisers, *outbound 375-0628, 11006 Silvercord, Tower I, 30 Canton Rd., Tsim Sha Tsui, Kowloon.* They offer tours of Macau, China, Singapore, Thailand, the Philippines, Malaysia and Korea.

16. MACAU - HISTORY, LAND, PEOPLE

HISTORY

Macau's long and colorful history is also part of Portugal's, China's, and Japan's. It was the first European colony in China and the center of the China trade for 300 years until Hong Kong was established. However, compared to Britain, Portugal's relations with China were relatively peaceful and characterized by compromise and cooperation.

Long before the Portuguese arrived, a typhoon blew some Fukinese fishermen off course. They prayed to the goddess **A-Ma** and miraculously survived, landing in Macau. They named the place **A-Ma Cho Kau** (Bay of A-Ma) and later settled there. The Portuguese arrived and shortened the name to **A-Ma Kau** and later to **Macao** or **Macau**. The **A-Ma Temple** in south Macau is its most famous.

But Macau's European history started before the arrival of the Portuguese. It began with **Marco Polo**, who from 1275-1292 stayed in the court of **Kublai Khan** when the Mongols ruled China (aka Cathay). Two hundred years later, Europeans began to search for this rich and exotic land that had almost faded into myth. Among them were Christopher Columbus and John Cabot. Portugal's **Vasco Da Gama** went the other direction and sailed around Africa to India in 1498 and thus opened the first sea route to Asia. In ten years, the Portuguese had established a chain of forts along the coasts of Africa and India.

MILESTONES IN MACAU'S HISTORY

1513 – Jorge Alvares landed in Hong Kong and saw Macau, becoming the first European to set foot on the south China coast. In 1517, Portuguese ambassador **Tome Piras**, tried unsuccessfully to negotiate a trade agreement with China for several years. Then a Portuguese ship attacked Canton (Guangzhou) and the Chinese executed the frustrated Piras.

1542 – **Fernao Mendes Pinto**, a Portuguese trader, accidently became the first European to discover Japan, when he was blown off course. Portuguese missionaries went to work converting the Japanese. Because of China's mistrust of Japan, Portuguese traders were able to completely monopolize all trade between the two countries. However, China did not officially allow the Portuguese to trade with it. Several times, the Chinese attacked and imprisoned some of them.

1557 – The Portuguese defeated some pesky pirates and partly because of this, the Chinese allowed the Portuguese to settle in China. Macau was strategically situated so that the Portuguese could defend the mouth of the Pearl River, the waterway to Canton. Thus Macau was born, the only gateway to China until the 1700s and the only place for European women and children to live until the mid-1800s.

The Chinese officials did not allow Chinese from China to live in Macau unless they were westernized Christians or long-time resident Fukinese fishermen. Many Chinese came across the border daily to work and trade in Macau. Some returned home at night; others hid in their employers' basements.

There were very few Portuguese women, so some of the men married or lived with Malaccan, Japanese and Chinese Christians. The Portuguese also imported African slaves.

Traders ruled this independent little colony. Later they began to pay taxes or rent for Macau and the Chinese built the **Barrier Gate** in north Macau to keep the Portuguese barbarians out. China controlled Macau by stopping the flow of food, water and servants whenever the Portuguese annoyed them. As Macau had little agriculture and no water source, this was highly effective.

1569 – The **Santa Casa da Misercordia**, the first charitable institution in Macau, was founded. It had an orphanage, leprosarium, hospital, supported widows and gave dowries for orphaned women. The old building still sits on Leal Senado Square in central Macau.

1580 – Spain conquered Portugal and ruled it for sixty years. Macau remained loyal to Portugal, but Spain later administered it.

1596 – **Shogun Hideyoshi**, the ruler of Japan, heard of a Spanish sailor boasting about Christian missionaries spearheading invasions. The Shogun began to persecute the Christians. He started by crucifying 26 of them in Nagasaki. Japanese Christians fled to Macau.

1604-1627 – The Dutch tried unsuccessfully to conquer Macau. The attack in 1622 was the most famous battle. The Chinese fled and less than 1,000 Portuguese and Eurasians defended the colony. The Dutch almost captured Macau, until a lucky cannon ball shot from Monte Fort turned the tide. The black slaves who had fought alongside their Portuguese masters got drunk and a little carried away. Since it was St. John the Baptist day, they went around decapitating the enemy. The Portuguese freed many slaves during the euphoria that followed the Dutch retreat.

1623 – Spain's headquarters in **Goa** (India) sent the first governor to Macau. The traders did not welcome him or give him lodging. He forcibly took **Monte Fort** and made it his own residence.

1636 – Meanwhile in Japan, the new Shogun, **Iemitsu**, a friend of the Dutch, expelled other foreigners from Nagasaki. A year later, he responded to an uprising in the Christian town of Shimabara by ordering the execution of thousands more Japanese Christians. The persecution continued for four years. Those who refused to give up their religion for Buddhism, were crucified, burned alive, or worse.

1640 – A sixty-man Portuguese mission went to Japan to plead for the Christians and Iemitsu executed almost all of them. Relations and trade between Macau and Japan came to an end and Japan shut herself off to the outside world for over 200 years.

Because a British gun ship ran amok and attacked Chinese towns, the Chinese forbade the Portuguese from trading in Canton. Macau stagnated after its two main sources of income stopped. Portugal became independent, but also stagnated as the Dutch and the British took over the Asian trade.

1642 – **Joao IV** became king and impoverished Macau sent a gift. Touched, the new king dubbed Macau: *City of the Name of God, None Other More Loyal.*

1700s – The Chinese opened Canton to European traders who settled their families in Macau and made it their base during the off-trading season. Macau prospered.

1810 – The notorious pirate **Cheung Po-tsai**, master of about 200 junks, surrendered in Macau. Other pirates flourished until the Communist takeover in 1949.

1821 – Macau stopped dealing in opium because of Chinese threats.

1842 – The British won the first opium war and many traders moved to Hong Kong, replacing Macau as the most important European port on the China coast. Part of the problem was the silt in Macau's harbor which made it difficult to shelter large ships. To compensate for the loss of income, Macau legalized and licensed gambling in the late 1840s. Macau became the Monte Carlo of the Far East, notorious for gambling, drugs, and prostitution. It never again achieved its former economic glory. This is lucky for us, because unlike Hong Kong, many of the old buildings from Macau's heydays in the 1600s and 1800s have survived.

1844 – On July 3, the United States and China signed their first treaty in Macau. **Caleb Cushing**, American envoy for President John Tyler, and **Viceroy Kiyang** signed the trade-friendship treaty in the **Kun Iam Temple**

in north Macau. Today, you too can sit at the granite table where this historic event took place.

1846 – Joao Ferreira do Amaral became governor. The Portuguese naval captain imposed unpopular taxes, dug up Chinese graves while building roads, and closed the Chinese customs house. The Chinese government was furious.

1849 – A strange year in Macau's history. Hong Kong's **James Summers**, a Protestant teacher, refused to remove his hat during the Corpus Christi procession, despite warnings. He was arrested, hat intact. Amaral refused to release him. A few British marines rescued Summers from jail, killing a Macanese man in the process. Amaral was furious and almost started a war with Britain. The Chinese realized that the powerful Brits and the weaker Macanese weren't best buddies, so the Chinese issued a reward for the troublesome Amaral's head.

On August 22, seven men attacked Amaral when he was out riding. The one-armed Amaral defended himself valiantly, but the men killed him, cut off his only hand and his head, and took them to China. The Chinese refused to give them back and fired on Portuguese troops. Three days later, 36 volunteers and **Lieutenant Vincente Nicolau de Mesquita** took a nearby Chinese fort as an amazed Macau watched. British, Americans, French and Spanish, shocked at Amaral's gruesome assassination and impressed by the bravery of Mesquita, came to Macau's aid with warships and troops. China backed down and never messed with Macau again.

1850 – Chinese refugees fled into Macau during the **Taiping Rebellion**. Like Hong Kong, unrest in China resulted in waves of Chinese refugees, especially during the **Boxer Rebellion** in 1900, the Chinese civil wars in the 1920s and 1940s, World War II and the Communist upheavals in the 1960s. For more information, please see Chapter 3.

1910 – Portugal became a republic after the fall of the monarchy.

1941-45 – Portugal and Macau were neutral in World War II. Macau selflessly helped Chinese and Hong Kong refugees, who fled there for safety, and more than doubled the population. The beautiful Bela Vista Hotel offered emergency accommodations and refugees crowded in the rooms, the lobby and wherever there was space.

1949 – The Communist revolution closed China to the outside world for almost thirty years.

1962 – **Stanley Ho** and his company **Sociedade de Turismo & Diversoes de Macau** (**STDM**, or **Society of Tourism and Amusements of Macau**) bought the gambling monopoly for $3 million from the goverment. This changed the face of Macau and today STDM directly or indirectly employs over 50% of Macau's population and supplies just under 50% of its revenue.

Mr. Ho and STDM have probably affected everything major that has happened in Macau in the past 30 years. Mr. Ho introduced western gambling to Macau and opened the first western-style casinos. To help tourism, he cleared Macau's silted harbors and introduced the first hydrofoils to Asia, cutting Hong Kong-Macau travel time from four hours to 75 minutes. Stanley Ho and STDM made Macau the tourist destination that it is today.

STDM works with the **Macau Government Tourism Office** and charities, such as public housing and the renovation of landmarks. It owns all the casinos, the **Jockey Club**, the golf course and all or a percentage of most of Macau's first class hotels.

STDM is involved in the new airport, the second Taipa bridge, helicopter and jetfoil service to Hong Kong and the US$1 billion **Nam Van Lakes project** in south Macau that will add about 20% more land to Macau's mainland.

1966 – Pro-communist **Red Guard riots** in Macau prompted the Portuguese to return Macau to China, but the Chinese refused. China feared a panic in Hong Kong, on which they were dependent for trade.

1974 – Portugal's new socialist government again offered Macau to China and again the Chinese refused. The **Taipa bridge** was built and the island was linked to the mainland.

1987 – A few years after Britain agreed to hand Hong Kong back to China, agreement was reached to return Macau to China.

1995 – Macau's first international airport on Taipa island will open. Unlike Hong Kong's, Portugal's negotiations with the Chinese on this joint project went smoothly.

December 20, 1999 – Macau will become a **Special Administrative Region of China**, with no major changes made for fifty years.

LAND & PEOPLE
Land

Macau is a small place. It is only 17.5 square kilometers, of which the **mainland peninsula** is 6.5 square kilometers, **Taipa Island** is 4.4 square kilometers, and **Coloane Island** is 6.6 square kilometers. Taipa is attached to the peninsula by two three-kilometer bridges and Coloane is attached to Taipa by a two-kilometer causeway.

Macau is 60 kilometers west of Hong Kong on the opposite side of the mouth of the **Pearl River**, 165 kilometers from **Guangzhou**. It is on the southeastern coast of China and is attached to **Guangdong** province. **Zhuhai** in China is adjacent to Macau.

People

Macau's 500,000 people are 95% Chinese, 3% Portuguese and

European, and 2% other. They are mainly Buddhists, Catholics, and Protestants.

Portuguese and **Mandarin** are the official languages, but **Cantonese** is most widely spoken. The main exports are textiles, clothes and toys. The silk flower industry and tourism are also important to the economy.

Government

Macau is a Chinese territory under Portuguese administration. It is and always has enjoyed relative autonomony from both China and Portugal. The President of Portugal appoints the governor, who works with the advice of the **Advisory Council**. The **Legislative Assembly** is appointed by the governor and elected.

MACAU SKYLINE

17. PLANNING YOUR TRIP TO MACAU

You can book hotels, car rentals and tours in Hong Kong before you go. Hong Kong phone numbers are included in this section, where available.

WHEN TO GO

Try to go during the week. On weekends, the place is packed. The prices of hotel rooms, ferries, rental cars, etc. go up. Macau is also busy in the summer, when Hong Kong locals come here. The climate is basically the same.

FESTIVALS AND HOLIDAYS

Not only does Macau celebrate Portuguese, Catholic and Chinese holidays, but it has its own unique festivals as well. Unlike Hong Kong, fireworks are legal and Macau's Chinese festivals are noisier.

For the festivals lsited below, a "+" sign denotes public holidays and an "*" means that dates are not the same every year. See Chapter 5.

January: 1, +New Year's Day

February: *+Chinese New Year, Procession of Our Lord of Passos occurs forty days after Good Friday and is unique to Macau. A quiet, evening procession bears a statue of Christ carrying the cross from St. Augustine's Church to the Macau Cathedral. The following day, the statue returns via the stations of the cross with much ceremony.

February:-March: Macau Arts Festival

April: *The Birthday of Tin Ha at A-Ma Temple in the south. +Easter Holidays; *+Ching Ming Festival; 25, +Anniversary of the 1974 Portuguese Revolution.

May: *A-Ma Festival, *Feast of the Drunken Dragon, *Feast of the Bathing Buddha, *Tam Kong Festival on Coloane; 1, +Laborers' Day; 13, Procession of our Lady of Fatima. The image is taken from Sao Domingo Church to Penha Church in celebration of the day that three children saw the Virgin Mary in 1917 in Fatima, Portugal.

June: *+Dragon Boat Festival; 10, +Camoes Day and Portuguese Community Day; 24 +Feast of Macau's patron saint, John the Baptist

July: 13, Coloane celebrates the 1910 defeat of pirates.

September-October: International Fireworks Festival *+The day after Mid-Autumn Festival

October: 1, +National Day of the People's Republic of China; 5, +Portugal Republic Day *+Festival of Ancestors (Chung Yeung)

October-November: International Music Festival

November: The Macau Grand Prix. This international race with cars and motorcycles, is held in the third week. Everyone goes to Macau and prices go through the roof. Visitors book hotels months in advance; 2, +All Soul's Day; 30, Feast of Battle (holiday on islands only)

December: Macau Marathon, early December; 1, +Portugal's Independence Day; 8, +Feast of the Immaculate Conception; 22, +Winter Solstice; 24-25, +Christmas

WHAT TO PACK

The same as for Hong Kong, except that Macau is not as formal. There are virtually no dress codes. Beer and cigarettes are half the price.

GETTING TO MACAU

The best way to get here is by boat from Hong Kong. You have a choice of five different kinds. The fastest and the most comfortable is the **jetfoil**. It rides above the water on three blades and feels like an airplane.

All ferries leave from the Macau Ferry Terminal in Shun Tak Centre, 100 Connaught Road, Central, at Sheung Wan MTR, Hong Kong Island. You can buy tickets there, but it is better to book in advance, especially for weekends. All prices are for one-way trips. Prices are generally higher on weekends and at night.

You can also take a **helicopter** from Hong Kong or enter **by land** from Zhuhai, China. Macau's international airport should open in July 1995.

By Jetfoil

Takes 60 minutes from Hong Kong. They run every 15 minutes from 7am to 3 am with 280 seats. Weekdays $105, weekends $115, and night $138. Lower deck: $90, $100 and $117. *Call 859-3333. You can make credit card reservations 28 days in advance by calling 859-6596.*

By Jumbocat

Takes 65 minutes. These big catamarans have 306 seats. They leave every half hour, 7:30am-6pm. $95. Weekends $110. *Call 859-7168.*

By Turbo-cat
Takes 75 minutes. 266 seats. 11 roundtrips daily between 6am and 5pm. Main deck $85-193. Superdeck $119-256. VIP cabins cost $1110-1158.

By Hoverferry
Takes 75-80 minutes. *Call 542-3081.*

By Hi-speed ferry
Takes 95 minutes. This 650-seat craft makes five round trips daily between 7:30am and 8pm. They cost between $35-95. *Call 815-3043.*

By Helicopter
Takes 20 minutes. Nine daily, eight seats. $1086. weekends $1189. *Call Hong Kong 859-3359, in Macau 572-983.* Charter $7,000-7,700 per hour. **East Asia Airlines** operates the helicopters from the ferry piers.

By Tour
You don't really need to take a tour to Macau. It is small and easy to get around and is a wonderful place to explore on your own. However, most tour operators, like Gray Line and China Travel Service offer day trips for about $700-800. Please see the list of travel agents in "Excursions".

VISAS & CUSTOMS
This is easy. Make sure you have your passport. Citizens of the United States, Canada, the United Kingdom, Australia, New Zealand, South Africa, the European Community and about 12 others don't need visas and may stay for 20 days. Hong Kong residents may stay for 90. Almost all others can buy a visa ($175) on arrival or from a Portuguese consulate.
There is a $26 departure tax from Hong Kong and a $22 tax from Macau. You can bring anything in within reason (no heavy artillery or drugs). Returning to Hong Kong, you can take 200 cigarettes and one bottle of wine duty-free and no firecrackers. Hong Kong residents can only import 100 duty-free cigarettes.

FOR MORE INFORMATION
Call or visit the **Macau Tourist Information Bureau (MTIB)**, *3704 Shun Tak Centre, Sheung Wan, Hong Kong Island. 540-8180, fax 559-6513.* There are also information desks in Kai Tak Airport and the Macau Ferry Terminal in Macau. MTIB has offices in the United States, Europe, Australia and Asia. See "Addresses" in the back of this book.

ARRIVALS & DEPARTURES

All ferries and helicopters leave fromHong Kong's **Macau Ferry Pier** in the **Shun Tak Centre** and arrive at the new **Macau Ferry Terminal** in Macau. There's a tourism office for maps and brochures and a snack bar. From the ferry terminal, you can take a taxi, bus, or hotel shuttle. It is only a few minutes to downtown. The hotel shuttles are straight ahead when you exit the terminal (there is no sign) and public buses are to your right.

BACKGROUND BOOKS

Non Fiction: *A Macau Narrative* by Austin Coates is the book on Macau's fascinating history and is a good read. *Macau Miscellany* is by Shann Davies, an authority on Macau, who has lived there for decades. It is a series of entertaining articles about Macau's main tourist attractions.

Fiction: *City of Broken Promises* is a good, historical novel by Austin Coates. *The Jade Pavilion* by Martin Boothe is a novel about an unlikeable Irish gambler and his Eurasian girlfriend in Macau before and during World War II.

EXCURSIONS TO CHINA FROM MACAU

You can easily take a day trip into China. It's best to go with a tour, unless you know some Chinese. You can walk across the border at the **Barrier Gate**, the only point of entry to China. It is open from 7am to midnight daily. You can get a limited visa there. Buses and taxis are available on the China side. Boats go to Guangzhou.

An international airport is planned for 1995 on Taipa Island with service to China. It should be linked directly by one of Asia's longest bridges to the Barrier Gate so that China-bound passengers need only go through immigration once.

Tours

Travel agencies can arrange day tours to Zhongshan and Zhuhai within 24 hours. Call the above agencies or **China Travel Service**, *700-888*. They have offices in the ferry terminals in Macau *(378-837)* and Hong Kong *(540-6333)*.

18. MACAU - BASIC INFORMATION

Many things like electricity, manners and typhoons are the same in Macau as in Hong Kong.

AQUARIUMS

The **Maritime Museum** has a small one.

ART GALLERIES

The **Camoes Museum** in the west has changing art exhibits.

BOOKSTORES

The **Tourist Office** sells some books on Macau. A tiny bookstore is in the **Hyatt Regency Hotel** on Taipa Island. Larger Portuguese book stores have some books in English.

BUSINESS & BUSINESS HOURS

Call the **Macau Business Center**, *881-949*, or the **Export Promotion Department**, *378-221*. **Banks** are open *9am-4pm, Saturday 9am-noon. Closed Sundays*. **Government** is open *8:40am-1pm and 3-5pm, Saturday 8:40-1pm. Closed Sundays*. Private businesses may stay open longer.

EMERGENCIES

Dial 999. You can also call the **police**, *573-333*, **ambulance**, *577-199/ 378-311*, and **fire**, *572-222*. **Kiang Wu Hospital** is on *Geral Coelho Amaral, 371-333/382-816*.

GARDENS

Don't miss the traditional, Chinese **Lou Lim Ieoc Gardens** in east Macau. Other gardens include the **Camoes Gardens** and the tiny **Carmel Church Garden** on Taipa Island.

HEALTH CINCERNS

The water is okay, but to be really safe drink bottled water.

HISTORIC BUILDINGS

Macau has many beautiful old buildings. The most famous is the facade of **Sao Paulo** and the best example of Portuguese architecture is the **Leal Senado**, downtown. The line of 1920s buildings in Taipa, including the **Taipa House Museum** are exquisite.

Sao Domingo Church downtown is the most beautiful church. Most pink and white or yellow and white buildings belong to the government. Macau has several forts like **Guia Fort** and **Monte Fort**, and two beautiful historic hotels with great restaurants.

KIDS

Take them to the **Maritime Museum** in the south, the **Grand Prix Museum** in the east, and the beaches and park on **Coloane Island**.

MAIL

Macau mail is not as reliable as Hong Kong's. The main post office is at **Leal Senado Square**, downtown.

MAKING FRIENDS

If you want to reach below the surface of Macau and make some friends, you might want to volunteer. **Mother's Choice of Macau** which cares for abandoned babies can use help. *Contact Ruth Billet at 550-525, fax 332-840. Hong Cheung Building, 2W, Taipa (near the Hyatt Hotel).*

MONEY

For simplicity's sake, we've used the $ sign to indicate **patacas** (normally **M$**). Macau's pataca equals 100 **avos** and 1.03 Hong Kong dollars. The Hong Kong dollar is accepted at par everywhere, although you will probably get change in patacas. Slot machines take HK$2 coins. If you're only going to be here for a few days, you don't really need any patacas. Try to get rid of your patacas before you leave.

MUSEUMS

The best is the **Maritime Museum** in the south. The **Grand Prix Museum** is also good.

NEWSPAPERS

There are no local English newspapers, but Hong Kong and international papers are available.

PARKS

Stroll in **Coloane Park** on Coloane Island and the **Camoes Gardens**, west.

PHOTOGRAPHY

Foto Princessa, *55-59 Avenida do Infante D'Henrique*, (one block east of Rua da Praia Grand), sells cameras and develops film.

PRECAUTIONS

Macau is even safer than Hong Kong, but you should be careful with your valuables. Beware of pickpockets in crowded places. Look both ways when you cross the street. Avoid the Barrier Gate, the border with China, at night.

SAUNA AND MASSAGE

Hotel Lisboa, *577-666/377-666, extension 1129*; **Hotel Sintra**, *710-111, extension 1841/1842*. About $200/hour.

TELEPHONE

Phone numbers in Macau usually have six digits. Public phones are in Leal Senado Square and in major hotels. Calls cost $1. Local calls are free on other phones. All pay phones have IDD.

To call information for Macau and Hong Kong, dial 181. To call Hong Kong dial 01-852 + number. For all other countries dial 00 + country code + number. To call Macau from Hong Kong dial 01-853 + number.

You can buy **Stored Value Phone Cards** in denominations of $50, $100 and $200 from the telephone office and from stores with a telephone sign outside. The telephone office is in the post office building on the Leal Senado Square, downtown. You can make long distance calls there.

TELEVISION

The local government station is on two channels with English, Portuguese and a little Cantonese. You can also get Hong Kong television, but you can't get Macau television in Hong Kong.

TEMPLES

The **A-Ma Temple** in the south is the most popular and convenient, but the **Kun Iam Temple** in north Macau is nicer, more interesting and less touristy. Both are hundreds of years old.

TIPPING

Expensive restaurants and hotels charge 10% for service. Tip more if you feel the service is good.

TOURIST OFFICE

The **Macau Government Tourist Office**, (**MGTO**), *315-566, fax 510-104, is at 9 Largo Senado (Leal Senado Square), downtown.* The staff is friendly and helpful. There is also a branch in the Macau Ferry Terminal. At both, you can pick up the free pamphlets, maps and Macau Travel Talk which lists hotels, travel agencies, restaurant reviews, etc.

VIEWS

Penha Church in the south has the most pleasant view. **Guia Fort** is the highest point and has the best view.

THE BEAUTIFUL LOU LIM IEOC GARDENS

19. GETTING AROUND MACAU

Macau is a small place. Most of it can be explored on foot, by taxi or buses or a combination of all three. To visit the islands, you may want to rent a car or moke.

We highly recommend that you get a map from the Macau Government Tourist Office with street and attraction names in both English and Chinese. You can also ask hotel staff to write the names and addresses of your destination in both languages. Most people are very helpful with giving directions, especially English-speaking Filipinas.

BY FOOT

The best way to go. Macau is small, interesting, and a lot less crowded than Hong Kong.

BY TAXI

Most taxis are black and have meters. There is a surcharge for baggage and trips to Taipa and Coloane Islands. There is no extra charge to go from the islands to the mainland. Drivers speak less English here than in Hong Kong.

The flagfall is $7 for the first 1.5 kilometers and $.90 for every 250 meters after. Sometimes a driver may not give change and assume that you have given him a tip. Like elsewhere he may not take you the most direct route. You can get cabs at hotels, on the street, or *call 519-519.*

BY RENTAL CAR

You should rent a **moke**, a small, electric jeep-like car. They are fun to drive and are cheaper than regular cars. They cost $280-$310 per day. *Call Avis at the Mandarin Hotel 336-789, in Hong Kong 541-2011.* Television's Martin Yan of the *Wok With Yan* cooking show recently cooked a meal in a moke.

Americans, Brits, and Australians can drive with their own driver's license. Canadians must have an international drivers license. *If you need one call 378-851.* Cars drive on the left side here and on the right side in China. It's a wonder that there aren't more accidents.

BY BUS

Buses cost $1.80-$3.30 and run 7am-midnight. The tourism office has a pamphlet on public buses.

Some useful routes are:

• **3A**: Jetfoil Pier-Lisboa Hotel-Sintra Hotel-Metropole Hotel-Leal Senado-Peninsula Hotel-London Hotel

• **3**: Jetfoil Pier-Lisboa Hotel-Leal Senado-Barrier Gate

• **9**: Maritime Museum-Leal Senado-Lou Lim Ieoc Garden-Barrier Gate-Sun Yat Sen House-Leal Senado-Pousada de Sao Tiago

• **10**: Lisboa Hotel-Barrier Gate

• **12**: Jetfoil Pier-Lisboa Hotel-Lou Lim Ieoc Garden-Kun Iam Temple

• **11**: Leal Senado-Lisboa-Hyatt-Taipa Village-Jockey Club

• **21**: Floating Casino-Lisboa-Hyatt-Coloane Park-Coloane Village

• **21A**: Same, but continues to Coloane's beaches

• **28A**: Jetfoil Pier-Lisboa-Hyatt-Taipa Village-Jockey Club

• **14**: Taipa Village-Coloane Village-Hac Sa Beach

BY PEDICAB

These bicycle-rickshaws can get expensive. Agree on the price first. Make sure it is not per person and includes waiting time, if you want to stop and take pictures. It should cost about $15 for a short ride or $50-60/hour. Bargain fiercely.

BY TOUR

A city tour is generally three to four hours and cost $80 including lunch. It will take you to A-Ma Temple, the Maritime Museum, the facade of Sao Paulo and Monte Fort. Bus tours of the islands generally last only one to two hours and cost $30. There has been sightseeing by ultra-light plane. 10 minutes costs $300. Check it out at 307-343.

Tour Agencies

Most tour agencies also have offices in Hong Kong. International Tourism (see below) is most able to handle English-speaking travelers.

• **Estoril Tours**, *710-462/710-373; Hong Kong 540-8028*

• **International Tourism**, *975-183/567-880; Hong Kong 541-2011*

• **Macau Tours**, *710-003; Hong Kong 542-2338*

20. MACAU - SPORTS & RECREATION

AUTOMOBILE RACES

The **Macau Grand Prix** is one of the most famous races in the world. See Festivals in Chapter 17. There is a **Grand Prix Museum** in east Macau.

BEACHES

Macau is not noted for its beaches. There are two on **Coloane Island**. **Cheoc Van** is the nicest, but **Hac Sa** is larger and has more facilities. They have lifeguards from May 1 to October 31. The water is checked daily for bacteria and is closed if the count is too high. The water here is full of silt, so it looks dirty, but isn't.

BIRDWATCHING

A walk-in aviary is in **Coloane Park**. People walk birds in the **Camoes Gardens** in the west and the **Lou Lim Ieoc Gardens** in the north.

HORSE RACES

On Taipa Island, see Chapter 24.

BICYCLING

You can rent bicycles on Taipa Island, in the village in the main square. You can't ride across the island bridges.

GOLFING

The **Westin Resort** on Coloane Island has a golf course. Before that was built, golfers had to drive an hour and a half into China to Zhongshan or Zhuhai.

HORSEBACK RIDING

On Hac Sa Beach, **Coloane Island**. *Call the Macau Horse Riding Centre, 328-303. It's closed on Mondays.*

JOGGING

Guia Hill is popular with joggers.

MINI-GOLFING

See Hac Sa Beach, Coloane Island.

RUNNING

The **Macau International Marathon** takes place the first Sunday in December. *Contact the Macau Sports Institute 580-762, fax 343-708.*

SWIMMING

There are public pools at both of **Coloane's** beaches.

TAI CHI CHUAN

From 6am-8am, you can probably see practitioners in the **Camoes Gardens** or the **Lou Lim Ieoc Gardens**.

TENNIS & SQUASH

You can play at the **Hyatt Regency**, *831-234, extension 1866.*

WINDSURFING

Head to **Cheoc Van beach** on **Coloane Island** from May to September.

GRAND PRIX RACING MACAU-STYLE

21. MACAU - WHERE TO STAY

The most romantic and interesting hotel is the Pousada de Sao Tiago and then the Hotel Bela Vista. Sporting types should stay at the Westin Resort or the Hyatt Regency on the islands. Gamblers will love the Lisboa, Macau's best entertainment hotel. The closest major hotel to the ferry terminus is the Mandarin Oriental.

Hotel rates go up on weekends and Chinese holidays. Always ask for discounts on weekdays. Local calls are free from most hotel rooms. Hotels add a 10% service charge and 5% government tax to your bill. We have included Hong Kong phone numbers when possible so that you can make reservations. Prices are for doubles unless otherwise indicated. *Pousada* means inn in Portuguese.

Expensive

HOTEL BELA VISTA, *8 Rua do Comendador Kou Ho Neng. 965-333, fax 965-588. Hong Kong 881-1288, fax 576-6006. Eight rooms. $1,700-$3,500. All cards. North American reservations 1-800-44UTELL.* Add $200-500 on weekends and holidays. Extra bed $300. This is a beautiful hotel from the 1800s. Walk into the reception area with its Roman columns, archways and interior balcony, and be transported back to the past. Each of its rooms has a different name. Some of the richly-decorated rooms with high ceilings have a fireplace, a balcony and/or a view of the bay. All rooms have in-room safes and 24-hour room service. Eating on the veranda is an experience not to be missed.

A ferry captain built the hotel and named it the *Boa Vista* (good view). The Macau government took it over in 1901 and it was bought and sold several times. It served as a school, a boarding house, and a haven for refugees during World War II. In 1988 the government bought it again and renovated it. The Mandarin Oriental Hotel Group now manages it. Top Portuguese officials stay here. Guests can use the facilities at the Mandarin Oriental.

HYATT REGENCY MACAU, *2 Estrada Almirante Marques Esparteiro, Taipa Island. 831-234, fax 830-195. Hong Kong 739-1234/559-0168, fax 830-195. 326 rooms. $990-1380. All cards. North American reservations 1-800-233-1234.* A few minutes drive from downtown, this first-class luxury hotel has lots of sports facilities in the attached Taipa Island Resort. The heated pool has a swim-up bar and is set in a tropical garden with a small waterfall. Drop the kids off at the summer camp and sign up for tennis lessons. A free shuttle service goes every half hour to the Lisboa Hotel (downtown) and the ferry pier, or you can rent a moke next door.

There's a good view of Macau, two nearby temples, 24-hour room service and the good Flamingo restaurant. Facilities include three restaurants, coffee shop, bar, business center, outdoor pool, garden and small casino. It also has four lit tennis courts, two squash courts, gym, steam bath, sauna, jacuzzi, solarium, ping pong, billiards, beauty salon, baby sitting and an in-house nurse six days a week.

MANDARIN ORIENTAL MACAU, *Avenida de Amizade. 567-888, fax 594-589. 437 rooms. $1080-1680. Suites $3500-17500. Extra person $320. Hong Kong 881-1288. North American reservations 1-800-526-6566.* This is on the water, close to the ferry terminal. The large, heated outdoor pool has a poolside bar and a view of the harbor. Facilities include a small casino, two restaurants, coffee shop, bar, 24-hour business center, tennis, squash, harbor view, fitness center, massage, solarium and beauty salon. It also has satellite television, car hire, executive floors and honeymoon and conference packages. All cards. We would dub this the top hotel, but we found a gambler sleeping in the white marble lobby here which doesn't do much for an otherwise classy image.

POUSADA DE SAO TIAGO, *Avenida da Republica, Fortaleza de Sao Tiago da Barra. 378-111, fax 552-170. Hong Kong: The Imperial Hotel 739-1216, fax 739-1198. 23 Rooms. $1118-1418. Extra bed $200. All cards.* A romantic fantasy, the pousada was carefully built into the ruins of an old fort. Even the large trees that had overgrown it were incorporated. More so than the Bela Vista, it is full of antique Portuguese furniture, carved wooden beds and chests, fancy, old-style telephones, and blue and white Portuguese tiles. It does have a television and minibar in each room. What's more, this tiny inn has a genuine stone cliff and waterfall as a wall. Its entrance is through a real cave. Rooms are smaller than the Bela Vista's, cosy and romantic. With no elevators, you have to climb three or four levels but it's worth it.

The Portuguese began building the fort in 1616 and completed it in 1629. The small chapel dates from 1640 and is dedicated to Sao Tiago, the patron saint of the Portuguese army. The hotel was completed in 1981. It is generally available except summers, New Years, Christmas and Grand Prix time. It overlooks the inner harbor, is near the Maritime Museum and has a tiny outdoor pool. The staff can arrange for golf, squash and tennis. It has honeymoon, birthday and anniversary packages.

POUSADA RITZ, *Rua da Boa Vista. 339-955, fax 317-826. Hong Kong 739-6993, fax 369-7133. 31 rooms. $1280-1380. Suites $1880-9880. Extra bed $250. American breakfast $52. All cards.* This is a guest house for visiting Chinese officials located above the Bela Vista and open to the public. Over 50% of its rooms are suites, most with verandas and views of the harbor. It has a good Chinese restaurant and a European one with a terrace. There is a beautiful, indoor, heated pool and gym, sauna, jacuzzi and beauty parlor. Rooms have wide twin beds. This hotel expects to change its name to the Ritz Hotel in 1995 when its new extension opens.

WESTIN RESORT, *Estrada de Hac Sa, Coloane Island. 871-111, fax 871-122. Hong Kong 803-2015, fax 857-9688. 208 Rooms. $1200-1550. All cards. North American reservations 1-800-228-3000.* This large Cancun-style resort opened in 1993 on the undeveloped Hac Sa beach and is made for sports enthusiasts. It is built up a hill and has Macau's only golf course (18 holes) at roof level. Swim in one of its three pools. Two are outdoors and one is indoors. There's also eight flood-lit tennis courts, two squash courts, a bowling green, a gym and a large garden. It is about 20 minutes by car from the ferry pier. All rooms have large (270 square foot) balconies, in-room safes, 24-hour room service and satellite television. Other facilities include two restaurants, bar, lounge, business center, whirlpool, sauna, steambath, massage and juice bar. There is no extra charge for kids under 18 sharing a room with parents. Playing on the new, golf course costs $600 per day and $800 on weekends. Electric carts are $150 and caddies $120.

Moderate

HOLIDAY INN, *Macau Rua Pequim, Ed. Yee Chan Kok, 8-B. 781-707, fax 781-711. Hong Kong 810-9628, fax 810-7683. 435 Rooms. $805-1380. Suites $2760-11,040. All cards. North American reservations 1-800-HOLIDAY.* This has a good Chinese restaurant, Oscar's pub, a lounge, Italian restaurant with Italian chef and coffee shop. Rooms have satellite television, movies, kettles and 24-hour room service. The heated indoor pool is T-shaped and you can drop the kids off at the supervised play room for no extra charge.

The Holiday Inn is within walking distance of the Lisboa and is two blocks from the waterfront and close to a small shopping mall. It is across the street from the police station. Facilities include a business center, small casino, 14-piece gym, sauna, steambath, jacuzzi, cold plunge and a shuttle bus to the ferry terminal. Partially opened in 1992, the grand opening should be 1995. Lots of sprinklers everywhere. Breakfast buffet $75.

HOTEL BEVERLY PLAZA, *Avenida do Dr. Rodrigo Rodrigues. 782-288, fax 780-684. Hong Kong: New Astor Travel Service 540-6333, fax 548-0487. 300 rooms. $740-900. Extra bed $160. All cards.* A clean, adequate 19-story hotel with a business center, two restaurants and a bar.

HOTEL FORTUNA, *Rua de Cantao. 786-333, fax 786-363. Hong Kong 559-2010, fax 858-9347. 368 Rooms. $700-980. Extra bed $200. All cards.* Italian marble and Chinese antiques decorate the uncluttered lobby. The rooms are smallish but pretty. It's a three-minute walk from the Lisboa and has a restaurant, lounge, and large nightclub with 30 VIP karaoke rooms.

HOTEL LISBOA, *Avenida de Amizade. 577-666, fax 567-193. Hong Kong: Florinda Hotel International 546-6994, fax 546-7118. 1,050 rooms. $600-850. Extra bed $100. All cards.* Although this is in a great location, you could survive in this fun, bizarre hotel for months without going outside. The space-age roof, shaped like a roulette wheel contrasts with the worn, elegant rooms and the many antiques and massive chandelier in its lobby. It is in a fantastic location downtown across from the Taipa Island bridge, 15 minute walks to the tourist office and the ferry terminal.

The Lisboa has Macau's largest casino, its only Las Vegas-style show, a small shopping arcade and lots of restaurants for Portuguese, Cantonese, Shanghainese, Chiu Chow, Japanese and western food. For the kids, there're bumper cars, pinball machines and video games. You can buy delicious chocolate truffles for only $2.50 at the Pasteleria (cake shop). Facilities include a 24-hour coffee shop, bar, business center, outdoor pool, gym, sauna and beauty salon.

HOTEL PRESIDENTE MACAU, *Avenida da Amizade. 533 888, fax 552-735. Hong Kong 857-1533, fax 559-9445. 318 Rooms. $660-920. Extra bed $200. All cards. North American reservations 1-800-44UTELL.* This has a good Korean restaurant, a lounge, coffee shop, Chinese restaurant, sauna and the Skylight Disco and Nightclub with a cabaret show. Rooms have 24-hour room service and a shuttle bus goes to the ferry pier. It is a few minutes walk from the Lisboa.

HOTEL SINTRA, *Avenida de D. Joao IV. 710-111, fax 510-527. Hong Kong 546-6944, fax 546-7118. 242 Rooms. $560-820.* In a good location, this is managed by the same company as the Lisboa. It has three restaurants, bar, 24-hour room service and shopping arcade.

NEW WORLD EMPEROR HOTEL, *Rua de Xangai. 781-888, fax 782-287. Hong Kong 731-3488, fax 721-0741. North America 1-800-44UTELL; in the U.S. 1-800-538-8882. 405 rooms. $780-980. All cards.* Within walking distance of the Lisboa and part of the well-known, Hong Kong-based New World hotel chain, this glitzy, hotel has a bare lobby of polished, grey stone. Rooms have mini-bars and in-house movies. The hotel has a restaurant, coffee shop, lobby lounge, non-smoking floor and a free shuttle to the Lisboa and ferry pier.

POUSADA DE COLOANE, *Cheoc Van Beach, Coloane Island. 328-143, fax 328-251. Hong Kong 540-8180, fax 559-6513. 22 rooms. $550-580. Extra bed $100. Visa and MasterCard.* If you want to get away from it all come here, except in the summer when the beach is packed. All of the smallish rooms have balconies overlooking the water. The hallways are dark and narrow. There is a large terrace with a patio restaurant, outdoor pool and a tiny playground. The pousada also has a sauna.

Budget

The Macau Govenment Tourist Office has a pamphlet on budget accommodations. Most budget hotels are located near the Floating Casino, downtown. All the hotels below have airconditioning, telephones, private bath and color TV. We would especially recommend the **East Asia** and the **Hotel London**.

EAST ASIA, *1 Rua da Madeira. 922-433, fax 922-430. Hong Kong: New Astor Travel 540-6333, fax 548-0487. 98 rooms, $360-450. Single $230-320. Triple $450. Extra bed $60. All cards.* This is good value inspite of a crowded lobby, two blocks from the waterfront. One of the two elevators wasn't working when Linda visited.

HOTEL LONDON, *Praca de Ponte e Horte 4. 937-761. 46 rooms. $230-276. Triple $391.* Small clean rooms have bathtubs with hand-held shower heads. The English is passable, the lobby tiny and it has no restaurant. It is on a square, by the waterfront, south of Rua do Gamboa.

HOU KONG, *Rua das Lorchas. 937-555. 53 rooms. $280.* This has clean, medium-sized, simple rooms with high ceilings. The bathrooms have tubs with hand-held shower heads. The staff speaks adequate English. It is in an alley across from the Floating Casino.

PENINSULA HOTEL, *Rua das Lorchas, Ponte Cais 14. 318-899, fax 344-933. 123 rooms. $400-500. Single $350. Extra bed $80. Baby cot $20.* Clean rooms in a relatively new building, next to the Floating Casino. The staff speak poor English.

22. MACAU - WHERE TO EAT

One of the best things in Macau is delicious Macanese food. It is Portuguese with influences from China and Portugal's former colonies in Africa, South America, India and Malaysia. Food in Macau is considerably cheaper than in Hong Kong and jackets aren't required anywhere. However the service is slower, but that's what Macau is all about. It's relaxed, sociable, civilized eating. Most restaurants take credit cards.

You should eat at the **Bela Vista Hotel** and, if you have time, the **Forteleza Grill** for the history, atmosphere, and of course the food. Other good restaurants are **Afonso III** and **Bar de Montanha Russa**. Macau's islands also have some great restaurants, like the **Flamingo** and **Fernando's**. They are listed at the end of this chapter.

WHAT TO DRINK

Beverages are also a lot cheaper in Macau, especially Portuguese wine. Some say it's cheaper here than in Portugal. **Mateus** is the best known, but try **Juan Pires** (white), **Convento de Tomar** (red), sparkling **Vinho Verde** or ask for a recommendation. If you're a coffee lover, head for the **Pokka Cafe Restaurant** in the Yaohan Department Store (we're not kidding), on Avenida Amizade.

WHAT TO EAT

Eating anything other than Portuguese and Macanese food is a crime in Macau. The penalty is usually regret. Many restaurants serve a mixture of Macanese and Portuguese prepared in the chef's unique style.

Macanese specialties are African chicken, curried crab, grilled prawns with garlic and chili, cod fish, grilled sardines, pigeon, quail, *minci* (fried minced beef, pork, potatoes and onions in soy sauce), tacho (meat, veggies and Chinese sausage), *caldo verde* soup (potatoes and sausage) and Brazilian *feijoados* (stews).

A good introduction are the two Macanese buffets: **The Pousada de Mong-Ha,** part of the Hotel and Tourism Training School, has a US$12 dinner buffet on Friday and the Pousada de Coloane has a Sunday lunch buffet for $90. When you've had enough Portuguese and Macanese food, the **Loong Inn,** the **Plaza,** and **Lijinxuan** are good Cantonese restaurants.

FOOD TALK IN PORTUGUESE

Most restaurants have menus in English, but just in case: **ameijo** *is clam,* **camarao** *is shrimp,* **carangueijo** *is crab,* **carne de vaca** *is beef,* **cozido** *is stew,* **galinha** *is chicken,* **gamba** *is prawns,* **guizado** *is octopus and* **peixe** *is fish.*

A GALERIA, Macanese/European expensive. *3/F Lisboa Hotel, downtown. 577-666, extension 3152. Open 12:30-2:30pm, 7-11pm. All cards.* This small, simple, elegant restaurant has a decadent dessert trolley, dark lighting and good food.

A LORCHA, Macanese/Portuguese moderate. *289 Rua do Almirante Serigo, south. 313-193. Open 12:30-3:30pm and 6-11:30pm. Closed Tuesdays. MasterCard and Visa.* You get big portions and good food at this restaurant near the Maritime museum. It is noted for its charcoal grilled codfish ($70), seafood rice ($60), stuffed squid ($50), roast Portuguese sausage ($20) and clams ($45). Most customers are tour groups.

AFONSO III, Macanese moderate. *11 Rua Central. 586-272. This serves good, authentic Macanese food near the Leal Senado, downtown. Open 1-3pm, 7-11pm.* Ask for the special.

BAR DE MONTANHA RUSSA, Macanese budget. *Parque Russa, Estrada Ferriera de Amaral, north. 302-731. Open 10am-11pm.* This delightful, outdoor patio restaurant is set in a park and has very good food. It is very popular at lunch with local Portuguese. Order one of the daily specials. Chocolate mousse is only $11.

BELA VISTA, Portuguese/Macanese moderate. *8 Rua do Comendador Kou Ho Neng. 965-533. Open noon-3pm, 7pm-midnight. All cards.* You just have to eat here. The Bela Vista is one of the most beautiful hotels in Macau and has some of the best food. The dining room is lovely with tall French doors, but for a real treat sit on the balcony, under the lazily spinning ceiling fans overlooking the harbor. The Bela Vista is 120 years old. A meal here transports you to a more gentile time, when women with lace parasols strolled along the praia. Order a huge cup of coffee for $20 or a dessert for only $25-40. Entrees cost $80-90.

EASE GARDEN RESTAURANT, Cantonese moderate. *11-13 Rua Dr. Pedro Jose Lobo. 562-328. All cards.* This is famous for dim sum, has no menu in English and is close to the Lisboa Hotel.

FAT SIU LA (House of the Smiling Buddha), Macanese/Portuguese moderate. *64 Rua da Felicidade, downtown. 573-585/573-580. Open noon-12:30am. No cards.* This is the oldest restaurant in Macau. It started in 1903 and is famous for its roast pigeon. The building and the atmosphere are nice, but the food is only adequate.

FORTELEZA GRILL, European/Macanese expensive. *Pousada de Sao Tiago, Avenida da Republica. 578-111. Open 7am-11am, noon-3pm and 7pm-midnight. Reservations recommended for dinner. All cards.* Eating in this 17th century fort is a lovely experience. The Forteleza is decorated with blue and white Portuguese tiles and crystal chandeliers. It has a good view of the harbor and there's candle light at night. The **Garden Terrace** restaurant is also good, but the coffee shop isn't.

HENRI'S GALLEY, Portuguese moderate. *4 Avenida da Republica, south. 556-251. Reservations are required on weekends. Open 11am-11pm. Mastercard and Visa.* The specialties are African chicken, fresh curry crab and huge spicy prawns at this small, modest restaurant with plastic top tables, nautical decor and affable host Henri Wong. The local prawns are cooked with chili peppers, garlic, tomato catsup and black pepper. He uses peanut butter in his African chicken. Canton-born Henri learned to cook during his six years on a Dutch boat as a merchant marine. He opened his restaurant in 1976. Desserts are only $22. It is located below the Bela Vista on the waterfront.

LIJINXUAN, Cantonese/Szechuan/Peking/Hunan. *Pousada Ritz, Rua da Boa Vista, south. 339-955. Open 11am-11pm. No credit cards.* A bright classical Chinese restaurant with good *dimsum*.

LONG KEI, Cantonese moderate. *7 Largo do Senado, downtown. 573-970.* This has okay food and dimsum in a simple setting.

LOONG INN, Cantonese. *Holiday Inn, Rua Pequim. 781-707.* This restaurant serves great dim sum and is near the Lisboa.

PEP 'N CHILI, Szechuan moderate. *9-13 Rua Gago Coutinho at 123 Avenida Ferreira de Almeda. 515-151. Open 10am-3pm and 6pm-midnight. All cards except Diners.* Soft carpets, good service, and fancy prices. It has a menu in English but spoken English needs work. Dishes cost between $40-$48 except for abalone ($130) and prawns (which are up to $88). There is also a branch in Hong Kong.

PLAZA RESTAURANT, Cantonese moderate. *2 Andar, Edificio Xinhua, Rua da Nagasaki. 706-623/705-656. Open 8am-midnight. All cards.* This is Macau's biggest Chinese restaurant. This huge, noisy, popular dining hall has dim sum and very good food. Dishes start at $42. It is across from the Mandarin Hotel in the China Travel Service Building south of the ferry pier.

PORTUGUES, Macanese budget. *16 Rua do Campo. 375-445. No cards.* An old, worn, restaurant with cheap, good food.

PIZZERIA TOSCANO, Italian budget. *28B Rua Formosa, downtown. 592-267. Open 8am-midnight. No cards.* A nice little Italian restaurant with pizza ($34-45), pasta, sandwiches ($11-16), wine and beer ($13).

PRAIA GRANDE, Portuguese. *10 Praca Lobo D'Avila. 973-022. Open noon-4pm, 7-11pm.* This opened in 1991 and is run by two women Cramilda Antonio and Anna Tavares. They serve codfish, sardines, pan-fried baby shrimps with garlic sauce, and baked crab stuffed with shredded ham, onions and garlic. Their grilled jumbo prawns are marinated in white wine with garlic, then topped with cheese and baked. If you eat here, you might find yourself rubbing elbows with the governor of Hong Kong.

RIQUEXO (**Rickshaw**), Macanese budget. *69 Avenida Sidonio Pais. 565-655. No credit cards.* Lunch only in this basic restaurant.

SHANGHAI 4,5,6. Shanghainese moderate. *Lisboa Hotel. 388-404. All cards.* This is a bright, popular, noisy restaurant.

SOLMAR, Portuguese\Macanese expensive. *8-10 Rua da Praia Grand. 574-391. Open 11am-11pm. No cards.* Older gentlemen pass the time sipping brandy in this older restaurant. It is a good place to meet for coffee and a snack across from the Metropole Hotel downtown. It has good food but slow service.

THAI WAI ,Thai budget. *Rua Nova A. Guia 10 R/C, the same street as the Royal Hotel. 325-207/325-568. Open from 8:30am-7:30pm.* As yet undiscovered by tourists, this tiny restaurant does not quite have its act together but it does have highly recommended Thai food. It currently has only six tiny tables and is near Guia Fort. Most entrees cost $40 to $80.

TAIPA ISLAND

FLAMINGO, Asian/European/Macanese moderate. *Hyatt Regency. 831-234. All cards.* Sit on the terrace beside the pond and feed the ducks. At night a group of wandering Filipino minstrels take requests for English, Cantonese, Mandarin and Japanese songs. Start off dinner with fried chili shrimps or the traditional flambeed sausage. Then try the tender, sauteed crab with ginger and spring onion or the thick veal stew. Soups are only $16.

GALO (**Rooster**), Macanese/Portuguese budget. *47 Rua do Cunha at Rua dos Clergos. Taipa Village. 827-318. No cards.* Chinese and Portuguese nicknacks decorate the whitewashed walls of this simple, home-style restaurant. Start off with warm rolls and a photo-album menu. The steak with black pepper sauce is delicious and a big bottle of Tsingtao beer costs only $12.

PINOCCIOS, Portuguese, *4 Rua do Sol, 327-128/327-328. No cards.* This was once a popular restaurant near Galo, but when it expanded, it lost its atmosphere and then the food went down hill.

TEE JEI KITCHEN, Indian budget. *Estrada Nova Edificio Va Fai Un. 320-203. No cards.* The best Indian food in Macau, near the Hyatt Hotel.

COLOANE ISLAND

BALICHAO, Macanese/Portuguese moderate. *Parques de Seac Pai Van, Coloane. 870-098/870-099. Open noon-11pm. All cards except Diners.* This fun restaurant used to be called 1999.

CARACOLA, Portuguese/Macanese moderate. *8 Rua das Gaivotas. 328-226. Open 12:30pm-11pm. Closed Mondays. No credit cards.* One of the best of the island restaurants. It serves good, authentic food, off the main square.

FERNANDO'S, Portuguese moderate. *9 Hac Sa Beach. 328-531. No cards.* This nice, little place with checkered table cloths is one of Macau's most popular restaurants. It offers big portions and country cooking. The food is simple, but pretty good and the menu is only in Portuguese and Chinese. Someone is around to translate. You have to try the delicious house-style clams (ameijos a casa) $58. Entrees cost $70-80.

LA TORE, Italian moderate. *Praia de Cheoc Van, Cheoc Van Beach. 880-156.*

POUSADA DE COLOANE, Macanese/Portuguese moderate. *Cheoc Van Beach. 328-143. MasterCard and Visa.* Sit inside this charming restaurant or outside on the patio overlooking the beach. The restaurant has a buffet on Sunday for $90.

FAST FOOD

MCDONALDS, *17-19 Rua do Campo, 46-48 Avenida da Horta e Costa, Yaohan Department Store Complex and 6-8 Praca de Luis de Camoes.*

PIZZA HUT, *Ave Infante D. Henrique, Hotel Lisboa.*

CAFE E NATA BAKE SHOP, *is in a square with outdoor tables behind the United Colors of Benetton on Rua do Dr. Pedro Jose Lobo 22. 710032.* This place has super egg tarts and good sandwiches.

23. MACAU - SHOPPING

Yes, you can shop in Macau, but don't expect the variety and abundance of stores of Hong Kong. Residents here go there to shop. Jewelry here is the best buy, especially gold. You can sometimes find good Chinese antiques cheaper than Hong Kong but not as cheap as China. Macau makes clothes, silk flowers and toys. One of the best buys is Portuguese wine. Mateus is $38 per bottle. Wages and rents are lower than in Hong Kong and some prices are cheaper. Sales staff are usually more friendly.

If you have problems with stores selling you goods not as represented, the Macau Government Tourist Office should try to mediate. Send it a copy of your receipt and a letter with the details and what you would like them to do. Unlike Hong Kong, Macau's consumer organizations are still in the developing stage. Don't expect too much.

Like every gambling city, Macau has its share of interesting pawn shops. Whether you are buying a camera or selling a diamond, remember bargain, bargain, bargain. There is a street market off Leal Senado Square, downtown. The Macau Government Tourist Office nearby has T-shirts ($25), maps, postcards, books, umbrellas, etc. The Lisboa hotel has some interesting shops and is a fun place to wander.

Yaohan, *open 11am-11pm*, Macau's first international department store, opened in 1993. It is four stories tall with many brand names including The Body Shop, Lancome, Princess Marcella Borghese, and the Optical Shop. You can walk to it from the ferry pier along elevated walkways.

ANTIQUES

You won't find any real treasures in the street, souvenir stalls around the ruins of Sao Paulo in west Macau, but this is a fun place to browse. Down the hill, there are a few antique and curio stores. Buy things you fall in love with, not for investment, unless you really know what you're doing. That way you can't lose. The **Mandarin Oriental Hotel** has a good but very expensive shop. **Wing Tai Curios Centre** *at 1-M Avenida Almeida Ribeiro (573-651)* is also good.

JEWELRY

Gold can be cheaper here than most other places in the world. 18 and 24 carat are available. There are jewelry stores on **Avenida Almeida Ribeiro**, northwest of the tourist office. You can also find some on **Avenida Infante D. Henrique** between Rua Dr. Pedro Jose Lobo, and **Avenida D. Joao IV**, two blocks northwest of the Lisboa Hotel. All jewelry stores are registered with the government.

On Avenida Almeida Ribiero, try **Chow Sang Sang** *at #58, 921-048 or Chow Tai Fook at #54, 573-278.*

CLOTHES

There is a street market with clothes and purses beside the Tourist Office. Another is **Lan Kwai Lou**. The only factory outlet for clothes made locally for export is **Polymax**, *open Saturday and Sundays only, 481-433,* for silk garments. This small store has some good things but unusual sizes. Blouses cost $250, skirts, dresses, pyjamas and ties $48. $90 for a beautiful sandwashed long sleeve shirts.

24. MACAU -
ENTERTAINMENT & NIGHTLIFE

The main entertainment here is gambling. Macau has eight casinos. Most gamblers come from Hong Kong and mainland China where casinos are illegal. There is also a horse racing track on Taipa Island. For other daytime entertainment ideas see Chapters 18, 20, and 25.

CASINOS

Gamblers can play 11 different games, including ancient Chinese ones. The casinos are not glamorous. There are no free drinks. In fact, this may be the only place in the world where you can't gamble with a drink in your hand. You should definitely take a peek. Everyone is serious and quiet and an amazing amount of money is bet. People are usually dressed in their everyday clothes. Slippers and shorts on men are not allowed. The casinos are almost always full, 24-hours a day. The atmosphere is electric as everyone is totally focused on the turning of a card or the rolling of the dice. Wealthy Chinese will off-handedly brag as much about losing a million dollars as winning.

Gambling is usually carried out in Hong Kong dollars and patacas, except in some Lisboa Hotel VIP rooms where they use U.S. dollars. Croupiers usually take 5-10% of the winnings of each bet. Luckily, there are no taxes on winnings. Casinos are open 24 hours-a-day, except the Victoria. They may close when typhoon signal #8 rises. They prohibit cameras, guns and cellular phones inside the casinos and you have to pass through a metal detector. These were installed after three casino robberies in 1993. The legal gambling age is 18 for tourists and 21 for locals. The casinos are popular with people from all walks of life.

Macau legalized gambling in the 1800s but the games were all Chinese until 1962 when Stanley Ho introduced modern, western casinos to Macau. Today Mr. Ho and his company own all eight casinos. These usually have slot machines which the Chinese call "hungry tigers". One paid out one million U.S. dollars in 1992 to an older mainland Chinese woman who was thrilled. There is also baccaret, black jack, roulette, tambola and traditional Chinese games.

The largest and most popular casino is the Lisboa in the **Lisboa Hotel**, downtown. The **Hyatt Hotel** has six tables and no slot machines and the **Mandarin Hotel** has a tiny, luxury casino. The **Kingsway Hotel** has a large casino. The most famous Chinese casino is the two-story **Floating Casino** (aka **Macau Palace**). It is near the inner harbor downtown and is covered with lights and dragons. Its tables are always full, but the slot machines aren't.

The **Kam Pek** on Avenida Almeida Ribiera is another Chinese casino, where the Lisboa's staff is trained. The large **Palacio Pelota Basca**, formerly the jai alai complex, is attached to the ferry pier. There is also the **Victoria**, a small casino at the Jockey Club on Taipa Island, open during horse races.

GAMBLING

Good luck! Don't bet more than you can afford to lose. Watch the games first to make sure you understand them. They play most western games here but sometimes the rules are a little different. For example, in black jack if a side-better bets more than a player, he can call the player's hand. Rules are sometimes posted.

The most popular game is **baccarat** and is played at 66% of Macau's 181 tables. The player can't take the bank, the dealer has the shoe at all times and the minimum is $100-$500. There is also **mini-baccarat**. **Blackjack** is the second most popular and the third is *dai siu* (big and small or cussec), a Chinese game. You bet on whether the total of three rolled dice will be under 10, over 10 or combinations.

TRY YOUR LUCK AT THE TABLES!

Other western games include **slot machines** and **roulette**, which is played only in the Lisboa and the Mandarin. There is only one zero and bets are collected, not frozen at zero. There is also **boule**, a French game, similar to roulette. **Tambola** is played Tuesday to Friday, 8pm-11:30pm at Jai Alai Palace and Saturday and Sunday, 3-6:30pm in the Mona Lisa Hall, Hotel Lisboa, New Wing.

It takes a lifetime to learn how to win Chinese games but some are easy to play. In **fantan**, the croupier starts with a large pile of porcelain buttons. He separates an unknown amount under a cup and then removes four buttons at a time from the remaining pile. You bet on whether 1, 2, 3 or 4 buttons will remain, also odds, evens, corners and three of a kind. **Pai kao** (sometimes spelled pai gow)is complicated Chinese dominos, played with long, thin cards with red and white dots. **Mahjong pai kao** is a variation. All of the games mentioned above are at the Lisboa.

Maximums and **minimums** are usually posted and vary between tables and casinos. Generally, the minimum bet is between $20-$100 and the maximum is $60,000, however this may be extended. In the Lisboa VIP rooms the minimums are higher and the maximum for VIP baccarat is $800,000 and can be extended. One person won $10 million on a single bet on VIP baccarat; another walked out with $20 million at the end of one night.

HORSE RACING

Go to the **Macau Jockey Club** on Taipa Island, *631-317*. The racing season is from September to June. A free shuttle bus goes from the Lisboa Hotel. The minimum is $10 and there is no maximum. October 1992 was an exciting month, when somebody won $1.8 million on a double trio (a record) and $700,000 on a double quinella. The Jockey Club replaced the Macau Trotting Club in 1989. One thousand imported horses live here. The small **Victoria Casino** is also here. The British East India Company held the first horse race on Hac Sa Beach, Coloane Island, in the 1790s.

NIGHTLIFE

Most people head to the casinos or for dinner. The most famous night time entertainment is the risque Crazy Paris Show. Many nightclubs have cover charges that may include a drink or two. Besides Chinese Tsingtao beer, you can also try the Portuguese Sangres and Super Bock, which are better.

The Bar, *Hyatt Regency, Taipa Island. 831-234*. This small, dark, cozy bar is popular before and after the horse races. A half pint of beer costs $17, coke $16.

The Crazy Paris Show, *Mona Lisa Hall, Hotel Lisboa. 377-666 extension 1193. Admission is $200, cheaper on weekdays. Shows are at 8pm and 9:30pm* *nightly*. Fourteen nude and semi-nude, mainly French women dance in a burlesque-style show. This is not as lavish as a Las Vegas show, but it's all Macau has. The show began on a ferry (when the trip from Hong Kong used to take a lot longer) and has been in Macau for fourteen years. 99% of it is in good taste, as close as you can get to wholesome in a strip show. The women are dressed at times in bands of light! The show is popular with both male and female tourists and especially with mainland Chinese who have never seen anything like it.

Mondial Disco, *Hotel Mondial, Rua da Antonio Basto. 566-866. Oscar Bar, Holiday Inn, Rua Pequim. 783-333.*

Portas da Sol (supper club), *2/F, Hotel Lisboa, Old Wing, 377-666 ext.1101 (3101).*

Skylight Disco and Nightclub, *2/F, Presidente Hotel, Avenida da Amizade. 553-888.* Cabaret show and disco.

HOSTESS CLUBS

Hostess clubs and massage parlors are confined to one building, the **Edificio Comercial Sitoi** *on Rua Praie Grande near Almeida Ribeiro, above the main office of the Hong Kong Bank.* The neon in the night is unmistakeable. Although it is not blatantly advertised, prostitution is legal.

25. MACAU - SEEING THE SIGHTS

There is much to see and do in Macau. To simplify matters, we have organized Macau into **south**, **downtown**, **east**, **west** and **islands**. West is actually north of downtown, in the western half of Macau.

If you have a lot of energy, you could see all of Macau's major sights in one day. You should go to the heart of Macau, the square across from the **Leal Senado** which has lots of old colonial buildings, churches, the tourist office and a market. Stop at the Hotel Bela Vista or the Pousada de Sao Tiago for a memorable lunch. Then head south to the **Maritime Museum** for some background and visit Macau's most famous temple across the road. After that, go to Macau's most famous monument, the ruins of **Sao Paulo** in the west. It is surrounded by antique and souvenir shops and is below **Monte Fort**.

SEEING THE SIGHTS BY BICYCLE RICKSHAW

If you have two days or more consider yourself lucky. Macau should be savored like a good wine. It is a wonderful place to explore. Once you have seen the required attractions, head for the more magical. The lovely **Lou Lim Ieoc Garden** and the wonderful **Kun Iam Temple** are in the east. The **Camoes Museum and Garden** and the **Protestant Cemetery** are in the west, north of Sao Paulo. On the islands, head for **Taipa Village**, to a short cobblestone street of pastel-colored 1920s houses, including the **Taipa House Museum**. This is one of the most beautiful places in Macau.

SOUTH

MARITIME MUSEUM

Open 10am-5:30pm, closed Tuesday, and costs $5. This good introduction to Macau is situated in a large, modern building. It has lots of real and replica boats, a history of the A-ma temple, a few hands-on displays, fish tanks, shell displays and a model of Macau in the 17th century. At its drink stand and patio you can relax and watch life in the inner harbor. Near the museum, at pier 1, you can take a half-hour cruise of the fascinating harbor and see China on the other side. The boat leaves at 10:30am, 11:30am, 3:30pm and 4:30pm, Saturday to Monday and costs $15.

A-MA TEMPLE

(aka **Ma Kok Miu**) *Open dawn to dusk.* This four-building temple complex is the oldest and most famous in Macau. It is across from the Maritime Museum. It was built 400 years ago. The story goes that a beautiful, young woman needed to go from Fujian (Fukien) to Macau. A number of wealthy ship owners refused her request, but a poor family took her in their boat. During the journey, a storm hit and all of the boats sank except for the poor family's. When it arrived in Macau, the young woman walked up a hill and disappeared into a bright light. It is believed that the woman was A-ma, also known as Tin Hau in Hong Kong. The temple was built on the place where she alighted from the boat.

As you enter, put your hand into the lion's mouth and spin the ball inside three times to get rid of bad luck. Three of the temples here are dedicated to the Taoist A-ma and one is for the Buddhist goddess of mercy Kwan Yin.

PENHA CHURCH

Open 9am-4pm. This simple, Jesuit church is next to the former bishop's residence. It was built in 1622 and renovated in 1837 and 1935. The area is full of lovely, old colonial buildings including the impressive, pink and white Governor's Residence which you can see from here. Below

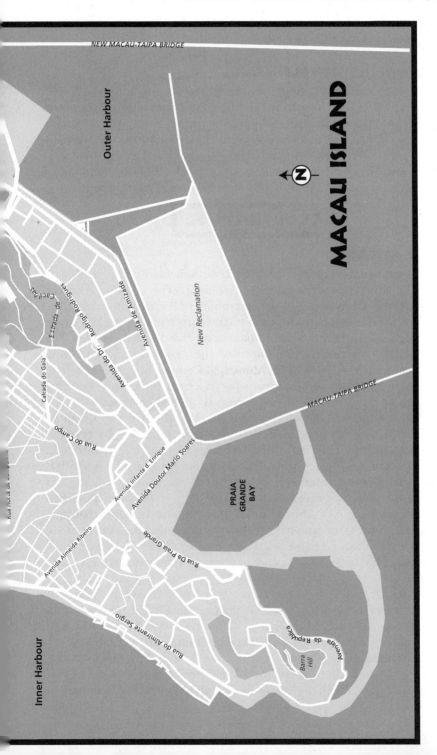

NEW MACAU-TAIPA BRIDGE

Outer Harbour

MACAU ISLAND

New Reclamation

MACAU-TAIPA BRIDGE

Estrada de Cacilhas

Avenida do Dr. Rodrigo Rodrigues

Avenida de Amizade

Calçada do Gaia

Rua do Campo

Rua Nova à Campina

Avenida Infante d' Enrique

Avenida Doutor Mario Soares

PRAIA GRANDE BAY

Avenida Almeida Ribeiro

Rua Da Praia Grande

Rua do Almirante Sergio

Avenida da República

Inner Harbour

Barra Hill

the church is Macau's most pleasant view of the bustling inner harbor with the green hills of China behind it.

HISTORICAL HOTELS

Macau's two most famous historical hotels are also in the south. The impressive **Barra Fortress** from the 17th century houses the **Pousada de Sao Tiago**. Walk through an underground tunnel of cut rock to Macau's most spectacular inn. It is south along the waterfront from the Maritime Museum.

Below Penha Church is the **Bela Vista Hotel**. This beautiful, colonial hotel is from the late 1800s. Both hotels have excellent restaurants.

DOWNTOWN

LEAL SENADO

(**Loyal Senate**) Located on Avenida de Almeida Ribeiro, the Portuguese built this large yellow and white building across the street from the square in 1784. It is one of the best examples of Portuguese architecture in Macau. Take a look inside at the small courtyard. Like the rest of the building it is partially covered in blue and white Portuguese tiles. The building also has an old public library on the second floor, open 1-7pm. The Leal Senado is home of the **Municipal Council**, but previously held the Senate, a group of Macanese who governed the colony, ignoring Portuguese officials and especially Spain-appointed governors.

When you come out of Leal Senado, cross the street to **Largo de Senado** (Senate Square), an L-shaped square bordered by restored colonial buildings. The **Post Office** is the large grey building to your right. Walk straight. On the left, you will pass Rua Sul Do Mercadores which is part of **Sao Domingo Market** and then the yellow and white building that houses the Tourist Office. At the end of the square is **Sao Domingo Church** (St. Dominic). This is one of Macau's most beautiful, baroque churches, built three hundred years ago and only open for services. However, you can ring the bell at the side to enter. There is a small museum in the back. A wide range of restaurants are next to the Tourist Office.

From the Leal Senado, it's a few minutes walk to another cluster of renovated old buildings. As you leave the Leal Senado, turn left, left again and up, bear left on Calcada Tronco Velho to **Sao Augustino Church**. It was built in the early 1800s. Beyond is the **Dom Pedro V Teatro**.

This beautiful, green and white theater, built in 1872, was the home of the Crazy Paris Show in the early 1980s until it moved to the Lisboa Hotel. The Jesuits built the nearby **St. Joseph's Church and Seminary** in the 1700s on Rua do Seminario. It has a small museum open 10am-4pm, closed Wednesday. Walk down toward Rua Central and turn right on Rua de Sao Lourenco to **Sao Lourenco Church** (St. Lawrence). This pretty little church was built in 1846 on Rua de Sao Lourenco. If you walk down Travessa Padre, you will reach Government House and Rua da Praia Grande. Turn right and walk along the waterfront *praia* to the **Bela Vista** on the hill. Much further on is **Barra Fortress (Pousada de Sao Tiago)** and beyond that is the **Maritime Museum.**

WEST

CITADEL DE SAO PAULO DO MONTE

Open 7am-6pm. The Jesuits built **Monte Fort** in the 1600s. It has 200-year-old cannons. The old colonial building in the center houses the Weather Observatory and has a small garden. Monte Fort took its place in history, when in 1622, the Dutch tried to invade Macau. A Jesuit priest fired a cannonball that exploded a Dutch powder keg on June 24, 1622, St. John the Baptist Day. This helped to turn away the Dutch and St. John became Macau's patron saint.

The unwelcome first Spanish governor made his home here when the Jesuits invited him for dinner. After the meal, the governor kicked his hosts out and took over the fort. It takes 5-10 minutes to walk down to Sao Paulo below.

RUINS OF SAO PAULO

This handsome facade is the most famous of Macau's landmarks and dates to 1602. Italian Jesuits designed it and exiled Japanese Christians helped build it. The facade formerly fronted the Church of the Mother of God now known as St. Paul's. The wooden church burned down in a typhoon in 1835. Recent excavations have revealed the remains of an altar.

From the top of the facade down, there is a carving of a dove representing the holy spirit and a statue of the infant Jesus encircled by crucifixion instruments (whip, hammer, thorns). Below is the Virgin Mary surrounded by angels with peonies to represent China and chrysanthemums to represent Japan. The impaled skeleton to the right represents victory over death. Below are statues of four Jesuit saints.

LUIS DE CAMOES MUSEUM

This beautiful, colonial building has a small, formal garden and rotating art exhibits. It belonged to the British East India Company in the 1700s. Camoes was Portugal's most famous poet, a colorful character.

The government threw him out of Portugal because of his political satires. He lost an eye in north Africa and then was arrested for duelling after he returned to Lisbon. He escaped to Goa (India) where writing got him in trouble again, so he fled to Japan and China. In the mid-1500s, perhaps in the Camoes gardens, he wrote his masterpiece Os Lusiados, an epic poem about Vasco da Gama's journey to India. This very popular poem was published in 1572, but did not help Camoes much. He died in poverty in 1578. The museum is open 11am-5pm and closed Wednesday.

Next door is the **Camoes Grotto and Gardens**. Old, twisted, banyan trees with long hanging roots shade the entrance of this large, pleasant park. On the hill, between some boulders is a bust of Camoes from 1860 and a copy of his famous poem.

On the other side of the museum is the **Old Protestant Cemetery**, a walled cemetery with a small church. Macau was all Catholic. In the early years this was a problem, because Protestants (mainly British) were not allowed to be buried on Catholic soil. The Chinese didn't want the barbarian dead buried on their soil either, so Protestant funerals took place outside the city walls in secret. If the Chinese found out, funerals often turned into brawls. Sometimes they dug up the Protestant dead.

In the 1800s, the governor let the British East India Company buy some land and establish a cemetery. Some people moved their previously buried relations here. The oldest stone Linda found was from 1767. George Chinnery, the famous artist who lived in Macau and died in 1852, Dr. Robert Morrison a missionary who wrote the first English-Chinese dictionary and Lord Spencer Churchill, Winston's ancestor are buried here. Nearby is **St. Anthony Church**.

MACAU GRAND PRIX MUSEUM

Open 10am-6pm. Adults are $10. Kids under 18 are $5; under 11, $3. The **Museo de Grande Premio** *is in the basement of the Tourism Activities Centre, next to the Forum near the Kingsway Hotel. 798-4108.* This is a must for racing fans. The small, well-laid out museum features six motorcycles and 10 cars including a replica of the TR2, which won the first Grand Prix. There is also a video, a model of the circuit and a display on its history. Titles are in English, Portuguese and Chinese. The museum sells books about the Macau Grand Prix.

GUIA FORTRESS

Open 9am-5:30pm. It's best to take a taxi up the winding cobblestone road through a wild, subtropical park to the fort, and then walk down.

This was built in the 1630s. As you enter notice the metal mesh typhoon signals. Stop for a coffee at the information office. The fort is on Guia Hill, the highest point in Macau. It has the best view of the outer harbor and Taipa. This is also the site of the Guia Lighthouse. Built in 1865, it is the oldest lighthouse on the China coast, but is closed to visitors. The fortress has a small chapel from 1687. You walk over an anonymous grave as you enter.

LOU LIM IEOC GARDEN

Open 6am-9pm. Admission is $1 but over age 60 free. At Estrada de Adolfo Louriero and Rua da Esperaca, this is the most beautiful and authentic, traditional Chinese garden in Macau or Hong Kong. It contains all the elements, water, plants, buildings and rocks symbolizing mountains; a microcosm of China. A twisting bridge crosses a pond, cats sleep between the tiles on roofs and men air their birds in bamboo cages. Surprisingly, the colonial mansion set in the middle of the pond seems to blend in.

A wealthy Chinese merchant Lou Kau established the garden in the 1800s. His son Lou Lim Ieoc took it over in 1906, but the family lost its fortune and gradually sold the estate in the mid 1900s. The main building became a school in the 1960s. The government bought the site and renovated the neglected, overgrown garden and buildings. In 1974, a smaller version of the original garden opened .

MEMORIAL HOME OF SUN YAT-SEN

Open 10am-1pm, Saturday and Sunday 3-5pm, and closed Tuesday. Located at 1 Rua Ferreira do Amaral. This moorish-style building from 1918 is around the corner from the Lou Lim Ieoc Garden. Sun Yat-sen was a doctor in Macau between 1892 and 1894. Then he became a hero during the Chinese revolution of 1911 and the first president of the Chinese republic. Dr. Sun never lived in this house which now contains historical photographs and a Chinese Nationalist reading room. He built it for his first wife.

KUN IAM TEMPLE

On Avenida do Coronel Mesqita, the largest Buddhist temple complex in Macau is a fascinating maze of buildings. It was probably built between 1279 and 1308 and has an ancestral hall and lots of old paintings. An overgrown terraced garden is behind it with a few armchair-style graves. In 1844, the United States and China signed their first friendship/trade treaty here. You can sit at the granite table where Caleb Cushing and the Viceroy of Canton, Kiying signed it. The event is commemorated on a plaque, all in Chinese, on the wall of a tiny pavilion behind the table. In the main temple, a glass case contains 18 small statues of wisemen. The one with the big nose is supposed to be Marco Polo. **Kun Iam** (Kwan Yin) is the goddess of mercy.

JARDIN DE MONTANA RUSSA

This garden is located at the northern end of Estrada de Ferriera do Amaral, two blocks from the Kun Iam temple. The small, semi-wild tropical garden covers a small hill. A few of the trees have name tags. A nice outdoor patio restaurant is here.

RED MARKET

Located on Rua Do Padre Joao Climaco and Avenida do Ouvidor Arriaga towards the northern part of the mainland near the Chinese shipyard for junks. For a native market, there's **Hung Guy See**, a genuine red brick produce market where local people shop. Its official name is **Mercado Municipal Almirante Lacerda**. In addition to such local produce as pressed duck, fresh fish, flowers, and birds, in the neighborhood you might also find wreaths of flowers for the dead.

THE BARRIER GATE

The Chinese built the gate at the border of Macau and China in 1573. It is in the most northern part of Macau. **Sun Yat-sen Park**, built on reclaimed land, is to the west of the gate. It has a playground, garden, aviary and a green house.

THE ISLANDS - TAIPA AND COLOANE

We suggest you rent a car to explore Macau's islands. They are slower, more relaxed and less developed than the mainland. You would never know that they used to be full of pirates. A monument in Coloane Village commemorates the last battle between Coloane pirates and villagers in the early 1900s. When the people of Taipa gave up pirating, they turned to making firecrackers.

Macau is attached to Taipa by a bridge and Coloane is attached to Taipa. The Taipa-Macau bridge is very busy going to Macau in the morning and returning to Taipa in the evening. A new, second bridge was completed in 1994.

Developers have drastically altered the south side of Taipa in the last few years. Fortunately the north side with Taipa Village has been spared so far. It includes food street and one of the most beautiful areas in Macau; a cobblestone street lined with 1920s houses including the **Taipa House Museum**. The east side is the site of the 1995 international airport.

Construction on Coloane has been limited. Visit Coloane Park, Macau's only two beaches and a village where junks and fishing boats are still built.

TAIPA ISLAND

Taipa was actually two islands until the channel silted up. As you cross the bridge to Taipa look to your right. That tall black thing sticking out of the water near the mainland is the **Gate of Understanding**, a 40-meter high monument to Chinese-Portuguese friendship. It was finished in 1993, cost US$4.5 million and is made of concrete and panels of black Brazilian granite.

You will see first the **Hyatt Regency Hotel**. A taxi from the Lisboa costs about $25. As you leave the Hyatt, turn right and walk along the waterfront for eight minutes. You will come to the tiny, white **Kun Iam Temple**, below the **University of East Asia**. In the other direction up the road from the Hyatt is the **Pou Tai Un Temple**, *open 9am-6pm*. This colorful Buddhist temple complex is the largest on the islands and has a vegetarian restaurant. It serves oysters, because Buddhists believe oysters are the only animal without a brain. The menu is in English but not much is spoken. The main temple has a huge gold Buddha. There are also three smaller temples, an ancestral hall, a Thai-style four-faced Buddha shrine, a small garden and a pond.

On the south side of the island is **Taipa Village** and food street (Rua do Cunha), a small alley with lots of restaurants including the Galo and Mozambique. The village also has a few small temples and you can rent bikes in the main square. Head down to the waterfront to Avenida da Praia. Green and white, 1920s houses, former summer homes of wealthy Macanese line this beautiful, cobblestone street. The *praia* was on a beach, but that has been replaced by silt and grasses.

You should also visit the **Taipa House Museum**, *open 9:30am-1pm and 3pm-5:30pm; closed Monday*. Inside this charming building are a kitchen, living/dining room, two bedrooms and a drawing room, all with European and Chinese furniture from the early 1900s. The small, 100-year-old Lady of Carmel Church with its tiny, charming garden is on the hill behind. On the west side of the island is the Macau Jockey Club which has horse races. A Thai-style Four-Faced-Buddha Shrine is in front. The former Trotting Club bought it to increase business, but it didn't help. The east side of the island has the large **United Chinese Cemetery** and is the site of Macau's first international airport, to be completed in 1995.

COLOANE ISLAND

Coloane island is the least developed place in Macau. It has nature trails and Macau's only beaches. Coming from Taipa, turn right for

Coloane Park, *open 9am-5:30pm. Entrance fee $5.* It has ponds, botanical gardens, a walk-in aviary with about 200 species and a restaurant.

Follow the coastal road to pleasant **Coloane Village** across the Pearl River from China. Here is the small **Chapel of St. Francis Xavier** built in 1928. It houses the bones of Japanese martyrs killed in Nagasaki in the late 1500s and the right arm bone (humerus) of St. Francis. Known as the Apostle of the East, he died in 1552, close to Macau. Saint Francis was a famous and very successful Roman Catholic missionary in Asia. In front of the chapel is a monument to the pirate combatants of 1910. The defeat of Coloane's pirates is celebrated yearly on July 13th.

Walk along the waterfront to the small but interesting **Tam Kong Miu Temple**. Inside are about six whalebones, including one that has been exquisitely carved into a boat. From here head to **Cheoc Van Beach**, Macau's nicest. This small beach has white sand and silty, not dirty, water. There is also an outdoor pool, changing rooms, La Tore Italian restaurant and Pousada de Coloane, a small hotel and Portuguese restaurant.

Further on is **Hac Sa Beach**, Coloane's largest. It has dark sand and water, from the silt. **Hac Sa Sports and Recreation Complex**, *open 9am-9pm,* has an outdoor pool, tennis courts, roller skating, mini-golf and playground. On the other side of the parking lot is **Fernando's**, a good Macanese restaurant and a place that rents horses. The far end of the beach is dominated by the large **Westin Resort**.

26. ADDRESSES CHARTS, & TABLES

HONG KONG ADDRESSES

Hong Kong Hong Kong Tourist Association (HKTA)
Head Office: 35/F, Jardine House, 1 Connaught Place, Central. Tel. (852) 801-7111.

Information and Gift Centers
Star Ferry Concourse, Kowloon. *Open 8am-6pm (Weekdays); 9am-5pm (Weekends and public holidays);* **Shop 8**, *Basement, Jardine House, 1 Connaught Place, Central (building with portholes near Star Ferry). Open: 9am-6pm (Weekdays) and 9am-1pm (Saturdays).*

Telephone Information Service
Tel. 801-7177. 8am-6pm. (Weekdays); 9am-5pm, Saturday, Sunday and public holidays.

Facsimile Information Service
177-1128 (English). 24-hour Visitor Information. HK$2 per minute 8am-9pm. HK$1 per minute all other times.

HKTAs Around the Globe!
- **Australia HKTA**, *Level 5, 55 Harrington St., The Rocks, Sydney, N.S.W. 2000, Australia, tel. (02) 251-2855 or (008) 251-071*
- **Britain HKTA**, *5/F, 125 Pall Mall, London, SW1Y 5 EA, U.K. Tel. (071) 930-4775*
- **Canada HKTA**, *347 Bay St., Suite 909, Toronto, Ont., M5H 2R7. Tel.(416) 366-2389*
- **New Zealand HKTA**, *P.O.Box 2120, Auckland. Tel. (09) 521-3167.*
- **US HKTA**, *333 North Michigan Ave., Suite 2400, Chicago, Ill 60601-3966. Tel.(312)782-3872; 590 Fifth Ave., 5/F, New York, N.Y. 10036-4706. Tel.(212) 869-5008/9; 10940 Wilshire Boulevard, Suite 1220, Los Ange-*

les, CA 90024. Tel. (213) 208-4582; 360 Post St., Suite 404, San Francisco, CA 94108. Tel. (415) 781-4582

MACAU ADDRESSES

Macau Tourist Information Bureaus (MTIBs)Around the Globe!

• **Australia MTIB**, *449 Darling St., Balmain, Sydney, N.S.W. 2041. Tel:(02) 555 7548*
• **Canada MTIB**, *13 Mountalan Ave., Toronto, Ont., M4J 1H3. Tel/fax:(416) 466-6552; and Suite 157, 10551 Shellbridge Way, Richmond, B.C., V6X 2W9. Tel:(604) 231-9040. Fax:231-9031*
• **France – Portuguese National Tourist Office**, *7 Rue Scribe, 75009 Paris. Tel:742-55-57*
• **Germany – Portuguese National Tourist Office**, *Kaiderstr 66-IV, 6000 Frankfurt-Main. Tel:(69)234097. Fax:231433*
• **Japan MTIB**, *4/F, Toho Twin Tower Building, 5-2 Yurakucho 1-chrome, Chiyoda-ku, Tokyo 100. Tel:(03) 3501-5022.*
• **New Zealand MTIB**, *PO Box 42-165, Orakei, Auckland 5. Tel:64-9-5203317. Fax:5203327.*
• **Portugal – Macau Tourist Representative**, *Avenida 5 de Outubro, 115-5th floor, 1000 Lisbon. Tel:769964.*
• **Singapore MTIB**, *11-01A PIL Building, 140 Cecil St., 0106. Tel:2250022 Fax:(65) 2238585.*
• **Thailand MTIB**, *150/5 Sukhumvit 20, Bangkok, 10501. Tel/fax:(662) 258-1975.*
• **United Kingdom MTIB**, *6 Sherlock Mews, Paddington St., London, W1M 3RH. Tel:(071)224-3390. Fax:224-0601*
• **US: California MTIB**, *3133 Lake Hollywood Drive, P.O. Box 1860, Los Angeles, 90078. Tel:(213) 851-3402/(800) 331-7150. Fax:(213) 851-3684;* **Hawaii MTIB**, *999 Wilder Ave., Suite 1103, Honolulu, 96822. Tel:(808) 538-7613;* **Illinois MTIB**, *P.O. Box 350, Kenilworth, 60043-0350. Tel: (708) 251-6421. Fax:256-5601;* **New York MTIB**, *Suite 2R, 77 Seventh Ave., New York, 10011. Tel:(212) 206-6828. Fax: 924-0882*

CELSIUS-FAHRENHEIT CONVERSION TABLE

Centigrade (Celsius)		Fahrenheit
-40°		-40°
-20°		-4°
0°	Freezing Point	32°
10°		50°
20°		68°
30°		86°
40°		104°
50°		122°
60°		140°
70°		158°
80°		176°
90°		194°
100°	Boiling Point	212°

To convert Fahrenheit to Celsius subtract 32, multiply by 5, and divide by 9. To convert Celsius to Fahrenheit multiply by 9, divide by 5, and add 32.

WEIGHTS AND MEASURES

1 gong-jin (kilogram)	= 2.2 pounds	
1 jin or gun (catty)	= 1.33 pounds	= .604 kg
1 dan (picul)	= 100 catties	= 133 pounds or 60.47kg
1 mi (meter)	= 39.37 inches	
1 gong li (kilometer)	= .6 mile	= 1 km.
1 li (Chinese mile)	= .3106 mile	= 1/2 km.
1 mu	= .1647 acres	
1 hectare	= 2.471 acres	= 10,000sq. meters
100 hectares	= 247.1 acre	= 1 sq. km.
259 hectares	= 1 sq. mile	

MILE-KILOMETER CONVERSION TABLES

To convert kilometers to miles, multiply by 6 and divide by 10.

Miles	Kilometers	Kilometers	Miles
1	1.6093	1	.621
2	3.2186	2	1.242
3	4.8279	3	1.863
4	6.4372	4	2.484
5	8.0465	5	3.105
6	9.6558	6	3.726
7	11.2651	7	4.347
8	12.8744	8	4.968
9	14.4837	9	5.589
10	16.093	10	6.21
20	32.186	20	12.42
30	48.279	30	18.63
40	64.372	40	24.84
50	80.465	50	31.05
60	96.558	60	37.26
70	112.651	70	43.47
80	128.744	80	49.68
90	144.837	90	55.89
100	160.93	100	62.1
200	321.86	200	124.2
300	482.79	300	186.3
400	643.72	400	248.4
500	804.65	500	310.5
600	965.58	600	372.6
700	1126.51	700	434.7
800	1287.44	800	496.8
900	1448.37	900	558.9
1000	1609.3	1000	621

27♦ BIBLIOGRAPHY

The Hong Kong Tourist Association and the Macau Government Tourism Office supplied us with invaluable information and we highly recommend their publications, many of which are free. We also recommend and are grateful to the following:

Armentrout, Fred. *Images of Hong Kong*. Hong Kong: Hong Kong Publishing Co., 1982.

Augustin, Andreas. *The Peninsula*. Hong Kong Shanghai Hotels, 1992.

Burkhardt, V. R., *Chinese Creeds and Customs*. Hong Kong: South China Morning Post Ltd., 1982.

Bard, Dr. Solomon. *In Search of the Past: A Guide to the Antiquities of Hong Kong*. Hong Kong: Urban Council, 1988.

Birch, Alan and Martin Cole. *The Captive Years: The Occupation of Hong Kong 1941-45*. Hong Kong: Heinemann Asia 1982.

Bloomfield, Frena. *The Occult World of Hong Kong*. Hong Kong: Hong Kong Publishing Co., 1980.

Boothe, Martin. *The Jade Pavilion*. London: Arrow Books 1988.

Briggs, Tom & Colin Crisswell. *Hong Kong: The Vanishing City*. South China Morning Post Ltd., 1977; *The Vanishing City Vol. II*. 1978.

Coates, Austin. *A Macau Narrative*. Hong Kong: Heinemann Asia, 1978; *Myself A Mandarin*. Hong Kong: Oxford University Press, 1993; *Whampoa, Ships on the Shore*. Hong Kong: South China Morning Post Ltd., 1980.

Chamberlain, Jonathan. *Chinese Gods*. Malaysia: Pelanduk Publications, 1988.

Chao, G.H. *The Life and Times of Sir Kai Ho Kai*. Hong Kong: Chinese University Press, 1981.

Clavell, James. *Noble House*. New York: Delacorte Press, 1981. Taipan. New York: Dell Publishing, 1977.

Crisswell, Colin N. *The Taipans: Hong Kong's Merchant Princes*. Hong Kong: Oxford University Press, 1993.

Davies, Shann. *Macau Miscellany*. Macau: Derwent Communications Ltd., 1992.

Elegant, Robert S. *Dynasty*. New York: McGraw-Hill Inc. 1977.

Endacott, G. B. *A History of Hong Kong*. Hong Kong: Oxford University Press, 1979; *Hong Kong Eclipse*. Hong Kong: Oxford University Press, 1978.

Forrest, Ronald et al. *Selected Walks in Hong Kong*. Hong Kong: South China Morning Post Ltd., 1979.

Geddes, Philip. *In the Mouth of the Dragon*. London: Century Publishing Co., 1982.

Gillingham, Paul. *At The Peak: Hong Kong Between the Wars*. Hong Kong: MacMillan Publishers Ltd., 1983.

Guillen-Nunez, Cesar. *Macau*. Hong Kong: Oxford University Press, 1984.

Hayes, James. *The Rural Communities of Hong Kong*. Hong Kong: Oxford University Press, 1983.

Hill, Dennis & Karen Phillipps. *A Colour Guide to Hong Kong Animals*. Hong Kong: The Government Printer, 1981.

Hoe, Susanna. *The Private Life of Old Hong Kong: Western Women in the British Colony 1841-1941*. Hong Kong: Oxford University Press, 1992.

Lang, Graeme & Lars Ragvald. *The Rise of the Refugee God: Hong Kong's Wong Tai Sin*. Hong Kong: Oxford University Press, 1993.

Leventhal, Dennis A. *Sino-Judaic Studies: Whence and Whither*. Hong Kong: Hong Kong Jewish Chronicle, 1985.

Lilius, Aleko E. *I Sailed With Chinese Pirates*. Hong Kong: Oxford University Press, 1991.

Lindsay, Oliver. *The Lasting Honour: The Fall of Hong Kong 1941*. London: Sphere Books, 1980.

Malloy, Ruth Lor. *China Guide*. Washington D.C.: Open Road Publishing, 1994.

Morris, Jan. *Hong Kong*. New York: Random House, 1988; *Hong Kong: An Epilogue to an Empire*. London: Penguin Books 1990.

O'Neil, Hugh B. *Companion to Chinese History*. New York: Facts on File Publications, 1987.

Pullinger, Jackie. *Chasing the Dragon*. London: Hodder and Stoughton, 1993.

Rafferty, Kevin. *City on the Rocks: Hong Kong's Uncertain Future*. Penguin Books, 1990.

Romer, J.D. *Illustrated Guide to the Venemous Snakes of Hong Kong*. Hong Kong: Urban Council, 1977.

Savidge, Joyce. *This is Hong Kong: Temples*. Hong Kong: Government Publication, 1977.

Schepel, Kaarlo. *Magic Walks*. Hong Kong: Alternative Press, 1994; *Magic Walks (volume 2)*. 1992. Magic Walks (volume 3). 1991.

Shepherd, Bruce. *The Hong Kong Guide 1893*. Hong Kong: Oxford University Press, 1982.

Tang, Madeleine H., et al. *Historical Walks Hong Kong Island*. The Guidebook Co., 1988.

Universal Publications. *Hong Kong Guidebook*, 1993.

Urban Services Department. *Hong Kong Trees*. Hong Kong: Urban Council, 1972.

Viney, Clive and Karen Philipps. *A Colour Guide to Hong Kong Birds*. Hong Kong: The Government Printer, 1979.

Warner, John. *Fragrant Harbour: Early Photographs of Hong Kong*. Hong Kong: John Warner Publications, 1976.

Williams, Jeff. *Macao*. New York: Chelsea House Publishers, 1988.

Witt, Hugh, ed., *Hong Kong 1993: A Review of 1992*. Hong Kong: Government Information Services, 1993.

INDEX

FROM THE PUBLISHER

Our goal is to provide you with a guide book that is second to none. Please remember, however, that things do change: phone numbers, prices, addresses, quality of food served, value, etc. Should you come across any new information, we'd appreciate hearing from you. No item is too small for us, so if you have any recommendations or suggested changes, please write to the author care of Open Road.

The address is:

Ruth Lor Malloy & Linda Malloy
c/o Open Road Publishing
P.O. Box 11249
Cleveland Park Station
Washington, DC 20008

TRAVEL NOTES

TRAVEL NOTES

TRAVEL NOTES

TRAVEL NOTES

TRAVEL NOTES

TRAVEL NOTES

YOUR PASSPORT TO GREAT TRAVEL! FROM OPEN ROAD PUBLISHING

THE CLASSIC CENTRAL AMERICA GUIDES

COSTA RICA GUIDE by Paul Glassman, 5th Ed. Glassman's classic travel guide to Costa Rica remains the standard against which all others must be judged. Discover great accommodations, reliable restaurants, pristine beaches, and incredible diving, fishing, and other water sports. Revised and updated. **$14.95**

BELIZE GUIDE by Paul Glassman, 6th Ed. This guide has quickly become the book of choice for Belize travelers. Perhaps the finest spot for Caribbean scuba diving and sport fishing, Belize's picture-perfect palm trees, Mayan ruins, tropical forests, uncrowded beaches, and fantastic water sports have made it one of the most popular Caribbean travel destinations. Revised and updated. **$13.95**

HONDURAS & BAY ISLANDS GUIDE by J.P. Panet with Leah Hart and Paul Glassman, 2nd Ed. Open Road's superior series of Central America travel guides continues with the revised look at this beautiful land. **$13.95**

GUATEMALA GUIDE by Paul Glassman, 9th Ed. Glassman's treatment of colorful Guatemala remains the single best source in print. **$16.95**

OTHER TITLES OF INTEREST

AMERICA'S MOST CHARMING TOWNS & VILLAGES by Larry Brown. The book everyone's talking about! Larry Brown shows you the 200 most charming and quaint towns in America - all 50 states included. Great coverage of each town includes local sights, interesting historical notes, and up-to-date information on where to stay and eat. **$14.95**

CHINA GUIDE by Ruth Lor Malloy, 8th Ed. The classic guide to China, 704 pages long, written by the premier China travel specialist. Malloy brings you more destinations and more great ways to enjoy traveling to China than ever before. From the Silk Road to the Forbidden City and everything in between, you won't want to visit China without this indispensable guide. **$17.95**

SOUTHERN MEXICO & YUCATAN GUIDE by Eric Hamovitch. Complete coverage of beautiful southern Mexico and the Yucatan peninsula. Discover terrific beaches, majestic Mayan ruins, great water sports, and the latest on hotels, restaurants, activities, nightlife, sports and more! Available Fall 1994. **$14.95**

PLEASE USE ORDER FORM ON NEXT PAGE

ORDER FORM

Name and Address: _____

_____

_____

_____ Zip Code: _____

Quantity	Title	Price

Total Before Shipping _____

Shipping/Handling _____

TOTAL _____

Orders must include price of book <u>plus</u> shipping and handling. For shipping and handling, please add $3.00 for the first book, and $1.00 for each book thereafter.

Ask about our discounts for special order bulk purchases.

ORDER FROM: **OPEN ROAD PUBLISHING**
P.O. Box 11249, Cleveland Park Station, Washington, D.C. 20008